IMPORTS AND ECONOMIC GROWTH

INTERNATIONAL STUDIES IN ECONOMICS AND ECONOMETRICS*

Volume 10

1. Harder T: Introduction to Mathematical Models in Market and Opinion Research With Practical Applications, Computing Procedures, and Estimates of Computing Requirements. Translated from the German by P.H. Friedlander and E.H. Friedlander. 1969.

2. Heesterman ARG: Forecasting Models for National Economic Planning. 1972.

3. Heesterman ARG: Allocation Models and their Use in Economic Planning. 1971.

4. Durdağ M: Some Problems of Development Financing. A Case Study of the Turkish First Five-Year Plan, 1963-1967. 1973

5. Blin JM: Patterns and Configurations in Economic Science. A Study of Social Decision Processes. 1973.

6. Merkies AHQM: Selection of Models by Forecasting Intervals. Translated from the Dutch by M. van Holten-De Wolff. 1973.

7. Bos HC, Sanders M and Secchi C: Private Foreign Investment in Developing Countries. A Quantitative Study on the Evaluation of its Macro-Economic Impact. 1974.

8. Frisch R: Economic Planning Studies Selected and Introduced by Frank Long. Preface by Jan Tinbergen. 1976.

9. Gupta KL: Foreign Capital, Savings and Growth. An International Cross-section Study.

* The first nine volumes of this series were published by D. Reidel Publishing Company, Dordrecht/Boston/London.

Imports and Economic Growth

by

Cornelis Abraham van Bochove

1982

Martinus Nijhoff Publishers

The Hague/Boston/London

Distributors:

for the United States and Canada

Kluwer Boston, Inc.
190 Old Derby Street
Hingham, MA 02043
USA

for all other countries

Kluwer Academic Publishers Group
Distribution Center
P.O. Box 322
3300 AH Dordrecht
The Netherlands

Library of Congress Cataloging in Publication Data CIP

Bochove, Cornelis Abraham van.
Imports and economic growth.

(International studies in economics and econometrics ; v. 10)
Includes bibliographical references and indexes.
1. Commerce. 2. Economic development. I. Title.
HF1411.B625 1982 338.9 82-14028

ISBN 90-247-3052-x (this volume)
ISBN 90-247-2730-8(series)

PRINTED IN THE NETHERLANDS

To Hille Steendam

CONTENTS

TABLES

Table 15. (Continued)

Taxon	Author	Locale	Clay	Silt ('fine grained')	Sand ('coarse grained')	Gravel	Algal substrate
Cibicides refulgens	Pujos, 1972	Bay of Biscay			×		
Cibicides refulgens	Morishima, 1948b	Japanese bays			×		
Cibicides spp.	H. Schmidt, 1953	Bay of Naples					×
Cornuspira spp.	H. Schmidt, 1953	Bay of Naples					×
Cribroelphidium cuvillieri	Rosset-Moulinier, 1972	Breton Coast		×			
Discorbis spp.	H. Schmidt, 1953	Bay of Naples					×
Eggerella advena	Leslie, 1965	Hudson Bay			×		
Eggerella advena	Vilks, 1968	Gulf of St. Lawrence			×		
Eggerella scabra	Bouysee & Le Calvez, 1967	French Coast	×				
Eggerella scabra	Pujos, 1971	Bay of Biscay		×			
Elphidium crispum	Myers, 1943c	Plymouth, England			×		
Elphidium crispum	Atkinson, 1971	Cardigan Bay, Wales			×		
Elphidium gunteri	Shenton, 1957	Matagorda Bay, Texas		×			
Elphidium gunteri	Haake, 1962	North German Coast		×			
Elphidium incertum	Leslie, 1965	Hudson Bay	×	×			
Elphidium magellanicum	Atkinson, 1971	Cardigan Bay, Wales			×		×
Elphidium spp.	Giunta, 1955	Ligurian Sea			×		
Elphidium spp.	Phleger & Lankford, 1957	Texas lagoons		×			
Eponides repandus	Pujos, 1972	Bay of Biscay			×		
Eponides spp.	H. Schmidt, 1953	Bay of Naples					×

Table 15. Substrate preference of certain benthonic foraminifera; × – preference; A – avoidance

Taxon	Author	Locale	Clay	Silt ('fine grained')	Sand ('coarse grained')	Gravel	Algal substrate
Acervulina sp.	Pujos, 1972	Bay of Biscay			×		
Ammobaculites spp.	Bouysse & Le Calvez, 1967	French Coast	×				
Ammonia catesbyana	Pujos, 1972	Bay of Biscay		×			
Asterigerinita mamilla	Pujos, 1972	Bay of Biscay			×		
Bigenerina nodosaria	Bouysse & Le Calvez, 1967	French Coast	×	×			
Bolivina spp.	H. Schmidt, 1953	Bay of Naples		×			
Buccella planidorso	Rosset-Moulinier, 1972	Breton Coast	×				
Bulimina buchiana	Pujos, 1972	Bay of Biscay			×		
Bulimina marginata	Pujos, 1972	Bay of Biscay			×		
Bulimina spp.	H. Schmidt, 1953	Bay of Naples		×			
Bulimina spp.	Kustanowich, 1964	Milford Sound, New Zealand		×			
Buliminella elegantissima	Leslie, 1965	Hudson Bay	×				
Cassidulina norcrossi	Leslie, 1965	Hudson Bay	×	×			
Cassidulina spp.	Zalesny, 1959	Santa Monica Bay, California			×	×	
Cassidulina spp.	Kustanowich, 1964	Milford Sound, New Zealand			A	A	
Cibicides lobatulus	Sen Gupta, 1971	Newfoundland			×		
Cibicides lobatulus	Morishima, 1948b	Japanese bays			×		
Cibicides pseudoungerianus	Pujos, 1972	Bay of Biscay			×		

PREFACE

The research for this project was carried out while the author was at the staff of the Economics Faculty of Erasmus University Rotterdam. The core results were recorded in discussion papers 7821/G, 7901/G, 7910/G and 8002/G of the faculty's Institute for Economic Research. Working on the project I incurred considerable debts to some professors and fellow staff members of the faculty. Professor P.J. Verdoorn initiated this study by suggesting its subject and by encouraging me to turn my initially hesitantly held view of imports as 'indispensable' inputs into the cornerstone of the analysis; he also read the final manuscript. Professor H.C. Bos' enthusiastic encouragement greatly stimulated me in the arduous phase of the writing of the manuscript; his advise on style and emphasis considerably improved the presentation while his careful reading of the various versions of the manuscript eliminated many non sequiturs and some errors. I am deeply in debt to A.S.W. de Vries who scrutinized not only the manuscript but also the preliminary discussion papers; while sharing an office room with him for six years I had the benefit of many stimulating discussions and he equanimously put up with my moods when I was stuck at some point. I am also in debt to D.P. Broer for checking and improving the optimal control theorem in chapter 7; to Professor R. Harkema for inducing me to write sections 5.1 and 5.3, by pointing out the empirical vulnerability of the separability assumption and to L.E. van Dijk of the Economic-Geographic Institute for drawing the two figures. Finally, I am very grateful to Mrs. E.F.F. Jonker who expertly typed the manuscript and accepted the many revisions with amazing cheerfulness. Naturally, the blame for all remaining errors is mine alone.

Rotterdam, May 1982 Cornelis van Bochove

1. INTRODUCTION

The pure theory of international trade is afflicted with an archaic view of national economies and their interrelations. A national economy is conceived as an independent and basically self-sufficient unit. It can choose freely between producing in perfect autarky or obtaining a modest gain by specializing in some products and exporting these in exchange for other goods it previously made at home. All imported goods can be perfectly produced domestically and there are no adjustment costs involved in replacing imports by such domestic produce. Usually trade is thought to consist of finished goods, with intermediates and raw materials playing only a marginal role. The consequence of this prevailing view of a semi-autarkic state is that the long-run growth rate of national income is thought to be independent of trade: at best trade can only temporarily affect growth.

This conception may have been adequate in the eighteenth century, and possibly in the early nineteenth century. As Kuznets (1967, p.25) puts it: 'In a pre-industrial economy a large part of the national product is consumed within the producer's household, and the proportion of complicated products assembled from many fabricated parts is relatively small'. Consequently the role of trade in the production process is minor. This finds expression in a low proportion of trade to income: around 1700 circa 7% for England; circa 3% for the world as a whole in 1800 (Kuznets, 1967, pp. 96 and 7 respectively). Accordingly, when the classical theory of international trade emerged early in the nineteenth century, its view of trade may have been realistic.

The neoclassical and the modern theory, developed in the mid-twentieth century, use different production functions and demand specification but still have the same basic view of trade as the classical theory: trade is a luxury that can, at some cost, be dispensed with. However, extent and nature of international trade have changed considerably since the late eighteenth century. By 1913 the proportion of world trade to world income had risen to 33% 'and major channels of flow and interdependence were established in what was previously a congeries of relatively isolated economic societies' (Kuznets, 1967, p.7). Of course two world wars and the depression of the thirties lowered the proportion of trade to income but the growth of recent decades has raised it again to its 1913 level. Most of these sizeable imports must be considered as 'indispensable' in the sense that there are no perfect domestic substitutes for them or that sizeable adjustment costs permanently prevent the production of perfect substitutes. There are various reasons for this. First, a large part of the imports of primary products is based on specific factors that a country lacks. In chapter 3 we shall show that 70% of the primary product imports of the U.S.A., Germany, Japan and The Netherlands is generated by lack of such specific factors; this amounts to one third of these countries' total imports. Second, technological know-how plays a similar role as a specific factor: the general level of skills in a country determines what products it cannot produce at home but must import from abroad. In addition even technologically advanced countries usually lack specific know-how in individual products; this is caused, for example, by a failure to produce some product in the early stages of its development whereas catching up with the leaders was prevented by the latters' advantages due to economies of scale and learning by doing. A third reaso for 'indispensability' of imports is adjustment costs. Even if a country would eventually have a comparative advantage for a product it currently imports, it must pass through a period with high adjustment costs to make the product domestically; the discounted gain caused by the eventual comparative advantage may well be insufficient to offset these costs of adjustment.

Not only has trade grown tremendously and become 'indispensable', but its composition is also quite different from that envisaged by most of th pure theory. In 1974 the share of industrial inputs and fuels in total imports was roughly two-thirds, both in developed and less-developed countries. That of consumer goods, the central concern of the main body c trade theory, was only one-fifth for developed countries and an even more modest one-ninth for developing countries.

This state of things implies that the view of national economies as isolated production processes that trade some of their final outputs with one another, but could basically do without trade, is outdated. Countries cannot possibly hope to produce perfect domestic substitutes for all thei imports, whether final good, intermediate, or raw material. Products are frequently hauled several times back and forth across borders, in several stages of completion, before becoming a finished good somewhere. Moreover even imported finished goods require further processing: assembling, transportation and marketing (including distribution). Each economy is, at every level of its industries, inextricably linked up with other economies so that an almost indecomposable international production system has evolved.

In recent years there have been a number of contributions to the literature that explicitly consider trade in produced means of production. Some of these, following Oniki and Uzawa (1965), generalize the Heckscher-Ohlin-Samuelson framework and add capital accumulation if growth is to be analysed. Others, notably Steedman (1979a, b), utilize a neo-Ricardian approach: fixed coefficients under a steady-state assumption. However, all assume that perfect domestic substitutes exist for the imports and that resources can be shifted to the sectors producing import substitutes without any adjustment costs. This implies perfect homogeneity of capital and labour in addition to absence of non-traded specific factors, innovation, economies of scale, learning. Very little work has been done on the consequence of trade in produced means of production for which no perfect domestic substitutes exist, for growth and the long-run growth rate. This is a serious deficiency: if national economies are not self-contained production systems, but merely parts of an integrated international process, it hardly makes good sense to analyse the growth of such a part <u>as if</u> it were a complete system in itself. Thus the theory of economic growth, developed for closed economies, is unlikely to be applicable to most modern countries. Therefore the purpose of the present study is to analyse the economic growth of nations and groups of nations whose production process is inextricably interwoven with that of other nations. More concretely, <u>our aim is to investigate the consequences for economic growth of the large-scale trade in indispensable inputs that characterizes the modern world economy; in particular we concentrate on the rate of growth of national income</u>.

Section 1.1 of this introduction describes our approach; section 1.2 gives the plan of the book and summarizes our results.

1.1. Approach

We capture the two central characteristics of modern trade, viz. most imports' being 'indispensable' and the preponderance of intermediates in world trade, by considering *all* imports as an input in the national production function for which no perfect domestic substitutes exist. This approach provides a better approximation of modern trade than traditional theories; in addition it has two major practical advantages.

First, it allows for a *one*-sector analysis. This greatly simplifies the theoretical analysis of growth and avoids the complications of describing the *composition* of final demand and output. This has the advantage of highlighting the dependence of growth on aggregate trade without sidetracking the train of thoughts to subtle issues of sectoral shares and patterns of specialization. An added benefit is that the analysis now becomes sufficiently transparent to handle other interesting complications. Specifically, we consider Hicks-neutral technical progress and increasing returns.

The *second* practical advantage is that empirical implementation of the models obtained is fairly easy. The major problem in estimating a traditional trade model, in which imports are delivered directly to final demand and compete with perfect homemade substitutes, is to obtain a correspondence in the commodity breakdown of the statistics of trade, consumption and production. This is especially prohibitive at the most aggregate level, viz. the two-sector model, where exportables should be distinguished from importables in production and consumption statistics - a virtually impossible job. This problem is avoided if the fact is recognized that in general no perfect domestic substitutes for imports exist. If, in addition, all imports are treated as inputs, one has only a single production function to estimate instead of both demand equations for imports and domestic produce - derived from a community indifference curve - and a production function for the latter. Moreover, in the case of disaggregate analysis the differences between various categories of imports and outputs can be handled by allowing for additional inputs and several outputs in a joint production process.

Actually, there already are a number of empirical studies that treat all imports as a factor of production (cf. section 3.2). We shall not contribute to this body of empirical knowledge but instead make a start in developing the theoretical implications for economic growth. Nevertheless it is important to keep an eye on the possibilities for empirical implementation and practical applicability.

To treat imports as an 'indispensable' factor of production in growth models is not an entirely new approach. Several models for small countries implicitly or explicitly follow this line. However, all these models use restrictive assumptions on the shape of the production function, frequently that of complementarity and no technical progress, always that of constant returns to scale. We use more general neoclassical production functions admitting substitutability between labour, capital and imports. Wherever possible we avoid specifying the values of the elasticities of substitution a priori. Thus in our single-country analysis (chapter 4) we admit both near-perfect complementarity and near-perfect substitutability. This means we take a step toward bridging the gap between trade theory and development-planning theory. In the latter the two-gap theory is prominent. This theory relates to each level of output certain capital requirements and an amount of imports. Thus the model can be viewed as taking all imports as a factor of production, the production function being one of perfect complementarity. If a certain growth rate is desired two gaps may prevent it: a saving gap, arising from a shortage of capital, and a trade gap. In our model the production structure is less rigid and capital and imports may be substituted for one another yielding a trade-off between the two gaps and restoring the role of the price mechanism. Thus we heed the call of Díaz-Alejandro (1975, pp. 99/100) in his survey of trade policies and development: 'A promising development is the introduction of some non-zero substitution possibilities into planning models that generate two-gap situations [...]. This route seems to lead to convergence of neoclassical and structuralist models [...]. The suggested convergence is likely to be aided by fresh work on models in the neoclassical spirit, which directly embody possible effects of trade on growth'.(1)

When dealing with economic growth or, put differently, with the basic movement of an economy, some alternative approaches are possible. One may, as in Keynesian(2) models, specify (dynamic) relations between flow variables only. The advantage of this approach is that the dynamics of the system are fairly simple. However, this type of analysis fails to describe explicitly the capital accumulation that is the basic generator of growth; as a consequence the approach must also remain vague about the structure of production. Therefore we shall throughout treat capital accumulation explicitly and expressly specify the production function.

Some different methods to analyse accumulation are available. An increasingly popular one is the 'neo-Ricardian' approach that postulates that the system is in a 'long-period equilibrium', or 'steady state', where the growth rates of all variables are constant and mostly equal to one another. This approach has the advantage of achieving great analytical simplicity: there is no need to analyse the changes of the growth rates in the course of time. Hence there is no need to study non-linear differential equations and one can do with simple linear algebra and geometry. As a consequence it is possible to master the intricacies of heterogoneous capital and of capital accumulation and avoid the tricky issues that led to the 'Capital Debate' of the nineteen-sixties. But the neo-Ricardian approach also has some serious drawbacks.(3) First, it is not clear just what the underlying production process and consumer behaviour are. The long-period equilibrium is specified in terms of growth rates of some key variables and the relation between those variables is specified a priori. This means that one can never be sure what hidden assumptions have been introduced. This is particularly troublesome in our case as we start from an outspoken view of modern trade and aim to investigate its consequence for growth. The neo-Ricardian approach has a second, even more serious, drawback: it is not clear if, or how, a given economy will arive at the postulated steady state from a given initial point. Thus one runs the risk of spending a lot of pages to careful scrutiny of the properties of a steady-growth path that is unstable and towards which no actual economy tends.

The alternative to the neo-Ricardian approach is the traditional neo-classical analysis:(4) the production process, saving behaviour, etc., are fully specified at the outset and the analysis aims to determine the direction in which the system moves and to investigate whether or not it converges in the course of time to a steady-growth path or if convenient additional restrictions can achieve the latter. Clearly, this approach is analytically superior to the neo-Ricardian one since the stability of the long-period equilibrium does not have to be accepted on faith. The price to pay is more elaborate dynamics. This implies that not too many sectors or types of capital goods can be handled: with three capital goods matters already are quite involved even in closed-economy analysis; if one wishes as in our case, to concentrate on foreign trade treating capital as homogeneous is virtually mandatory. Thus one has to ignore some of the points made in the capital debate. Accepting this with regret we opt for the neoclassical approach in view of the more serious drawbacks of the neo-Ricardian one.

A further question is whether to analyse steady-growth paths at all. Why not be content with investigating the direction in which a system moves, measured by a few key variables such as the capital-labour ratio, the terms of trade and per capita income, without bothering with steady states? This question is particularly relevant if a system does not move naturally to a steady state but if restrictions must be designed specifically for this purpose. The great advantage of steady-growth analysis is that it allows for a quantitative assessment of the relation between the basic growth rate of income and the parameters that capture the structure of the economy and the conditions of foreign trade. Thus one can go beyond results like 'per capita income rises under such and such circumstances' and obtain conclusions like 'given reasonable parameter values an improvement of the structural growth rate of world trade by one percent raises the long-run growth rate of income by 1/3 of a percent'. Even more important, steady-growth analysis admits a richer set of policy conclusions: one can show how parameters that can be influenced by economic policy measures affect the long-term growth rate; thus one obtains a framework to discuss policy issues.

Of course the analysis of steady-growth paths presupposes that these are empirically relevant. Whether they are, depends on the degree of realism of the basic assumptions about production, trade and investment. But even if these are carefully selected and if they imply a stable steady-growth path, the latter is only of practical importance if the economy adjusts sufficiently fast towards it. For if it takes too long to get close to a steady-growth path after disturbances, of which wars which imply large-scale destruction of capital are the major ones, no actual economy approximates such a path. Some work has been done on the adjustment time in closed-economy models. In a neoclassical model with a linear homogeneous Cobb-Douglas production function, no technical progress, no depreciation, a constant growth rate of labour and a constant rate of saving, R. Sato (1963) shows the adjustment period to be quite long: after a displacement of the rate of saving by about one percent it takes a century before the economy has watered 90 percent of the resulting shift in the growth rate of income. This result seems disastrous for the relevance of steady growth. However, for two reasons the latter is more relevant than Sato's considerations would lead to believe. The first one was pointed out by K. Sato (1966). He argues that minor, but realistic, modifications of the growth model greatly reduce the adjustment period. In particular, explicit introduction of depreciation and embodied technical progress serve this purpose; the 100 year adjustment period is thus reduced to 25 à 37 years. In addition, it is not difficult to show that if the rate of saving is flexible, being above its normal value if the capital stock is too small and below if there is 'surplus capital', the adjustment period is again considerably shortened. Similarly, Morishima (1969, pp. 57/58) has shown that disaggregation of a one-sector model to a two-sector one reduces the adjustment period even more: from 100 to 5 years. None of these modifications alters the stability properties or the value of the steady-state growth rate in an essential way. Thus it is safe to say that highly stylized one-sector growth models are useful to derive and examine steady-growth paths and their stability conditions, but greatly exaggerate the adjustment periods concerned.

Analysis of steady-growth paths is relevant for a second reason. We are primarily interested in the rate of growth of income. If this rate is sufficiently close to its value on a steady-growth path, analysis of the latter provides a satisfactory approximation of reality. R. Sato (1963, p.18, note 2) already noted that even the impact of a considerable rise of the rate of saving is of only minor importance to the growth rate of income.[(5)] The same is true for other disturbances that cause the economy to diverge from its steady-growth path. Thus, if e.g. a war destroys a large amount of capital the rate of growth of capital rises sharply but this has only limited impact on income growth. The cause of this is the relatively low share of capital in total inputs (say 25% vs. 75% for labour where domestic factors are concerned). Therefore the rates of growth of labour, technology and foreign trade dominate that of capital in income's growth rate.

In summary, the growth rate of income on a steady-growth path provides, as long as the path is stable and the basic relations are selected carefully, a good approximation of the actual secular, or 'long-run', growth rate of income.

1.2. Plan of the book and results

We attempt to present the analysis in such a way that it is readable to a broader circle than just specialists in the field of trade and growth. Therefore we ban as much of the mathematics as possible to proofs of theorems and appendices; the theorems themselves are discussed in not overly technical language and much attention is given to their applications and policy implications. For the non-specialized reader we provide cursory surveys of the specialized subjects we deal with. To facilitate quick reading by hurried readers each chapter begins with a brief summary and an overview of the core results. The same hurried readers may skip chapters five and eight without loss of continuity. A list of main symbols is to be found at the end of the book.

This book starts with a survey of the literature on trade and growth, to show that trade does only affect the long-run growth rate if imports are 'indispensable'. We argue that most imports are indeed indispensable and, besides, should be treated as a factor of production. Next, the consequences of this view for the long-run growth of moderate-sized economies are analysed; in particular the importance of the growth rate of foreign demand is clearly brought out, along with a number of policy implications. The analysis is then extended to a two-region system; here the most outstanding result is the beneficial effect of growth of one region on the other one. Next, we carry this result somewhat further and show that transfers to the partner region may have beneficial effects on the home region if the capital-accumulation effects of transfers are accounted for. Finally, we discuss the implications of our view for the short-run stability of the goods market and the balance of trade.

This being the broad outline of the work, we may now give a more detailed summary of the chapters and the main results. Chapter two surveys the results the trade and growth literature obtains with respect to the long-run growth rate of open economies. The central conclusion drawn from this survey is that the growth rate converges to the natural rate, i.e. the growth rate of labour, and is independent of trade as long as there are perfect domestic substitutes for imports and their production can be expanded or contracted without adjustment costs. This independence result is valid under a broad range of alternative descriptions of the economy: various kinds of saving behaviour, free trade and tariffs, free transport and transport costs or non-traded goods, two sectors or more, different types of sectors (including intermediate goods sectors), homogeneous capital and heterogeneous or dated capital goods. However, if imports are 'indispensable', in the sense that there are no perfect domestic substitutes or that there are adjustment costs, the long-run growth rate does depend on international circumstances. This means that in the analysis of long-run growth the many refinements of the traditional trade models are not of primary interest; instead attention should be concentrated on the consequences of 'indispensability' of imports. The analysis can therefore be confined to highly aggregate models as long as they capture the 'indispensability' of modern trade.

Chapter three considers the arguments to treat all imports as 'indispensable' inputs in detail and it discusses the production function implied, introducing a number of convenient properties and definitions. Thus the production function employed is a neoclassical three-factor function in capital, labour and imports. For convenience we usually restrict the analysis to the case where the production function is separable between imports on the one hand and capital and labour on the other. This allows us to express many results in terms of the elasticity of substitution between imports and domestic factors, thus providing a handy measure of the degree of substitutability between imports and domestic produce or, put differently, of the degree of 'indispensability' of imports. However, the separability assumption is merely convenient, not essential: chapter five generalizes all qualitative results to non-separable cases.

Chapter four starts the analysis of economic growth with indispensable imported inputs in earnest. The chapter aims to describe the aggregate growth of individual countries. In the present world economy no country - with the possible exception of the U.S.A. - is large enough to influence the secular growth rate of the world economy. This means that the growth of foreign demand for a country's products is independent of the aggregate level of economic activity in that country. This is conveniently expressed by postulating that at constant prices foreign demand grows exponentially at a constant rate. On the other hand, each country exports many goods that cannot be readily substituted by the produce of other countries - because of short-term or long-term capacity shortages abroad, differences in quality (e.g. technology content) and styling, inertia of consumer habits and specific design (particularly in the case of intermediates) that can only be duplicated by other countries with a considerable time lag. Therefore almost no country is 'small' in the usual sense that its terms of trade are given as a consequence of an infinite elasticity of substitution in demand. Instead it is more reasonable to postulate a finite terms of trade elasticity of foreign demand; for convenience we take the latter to be constant. Import demand is determined by the marginal productivity rule and the balance of trade is in equilibrium. Labour input grows exponentially, saving is proportional and there is no depreciation; in contrast we do admit non-constant returns and Hicks-neutral technical progress.

We first consider the direction in which the capital-labour ratio evolves. The core result confirms and extends the conclusion of the survey of chapter two: because of the preponderance of 'indispensable' imported inputs in modern trade each economy's long-run growth rate depends on the conditions of foreign trade; this conclusion holds true for all finite values of the elasticity of substitution between imports and domestic factors. How depends the long-run growth rate on foreign trade? To answer this we develop a steady-growth theorem. This theorem expresses the long-run growth rate in terms of the rate of technical progress, the growth rate of the labour force, foreign demand's growth rate and terms of trade elasticity, the elasticity of substitution between imports and domestic factors and the import share. To achieve constancy of the latter two, and through this of the growth rate of income, we impose the restriction on the production function that this elasticity and share tend to constant values as the ratio of imports to domestic factors (on which they depend) becomes very small or very large.

With this expression for the long-run growth rate we are able to analyse the role of each parameter. To this end we compare the growth of trading economies with that of comparable 'autarkic' ones. The 'autarkic' growth rate is not equal to the natural rate, i.e. the growth rate of the labour force, since we admit non-constant returns and technical progress, both of which influence the 'autarkic' growth rate. The term 'autarkic' is put between quotes as in our view autarkic production is virtually impossible as imported inputs are 'indispensable'. Thus the 'autarkic' growth rate refers to the growth rate that closed-economy analysis and traditional trade and growth analysis mistakenly predict, rather than to the growth rate the economy would attain if it decided to refrain from trading.

We find that the long-run growth rate is positively related to that of foreign demand; if the latter exceeds the 'autarkic' growth rate, the growth rate of the trading economy is higher than closed-economy analysis predicts. But even if foreign demand is sluggish there may still be a 'gain', specifically if technical progress is rapid. This result means that measures that raise the growth rate of foreign demand are effective in promoting long-run growth. In particular industrial policies that increase the share of products of which demand grows rapidly with income and that increase the rate of technical progress raise the secular growth of income considerably more than traditional growth theory indicates. Another result is that the long-run growth rate is higher if the country produces goods for which foreign demand is inelastic than if its exports are elastic as long as foreign demand grows rapidly relative to 'autarkic' output; if foreign demand growth is sluggish the reverse is true. This implies that a country is best off producing raw materials in which it has a monopoly, or in which cartels are formed, if that country is incapable of achieving rapid technical progress and if the growth rate of the world economy is high. If the world economy grows slowly a country is better off producing highly competitive goods as long as it succeeds in attaining rapid productivity growth. A third conclusion is that the value of the import share is irrelevant to the sign of the difference between the open-economy growth rate and that of the 'autarkic' one; but the absolute value of the difference is amplified by a high share. Clearly this implies that import substitution policies are useful if the growth of the world economy is slow - provided of course that not every country follows this policy; if the world economy grows rapidly policies to stimulate exporting sectors will lead to export-led growth. A final result is that it is disadvantageous under any circumstances if domestic factors and imports are complements. Hence it is important that a country maintains flexibility of its production structure by not allowing any essential sector to vanish completely, but neither supporting uncompetitive industries to such an extent that innovative ones - necessary to maintain or achieve substitutability between domestic produce and technology-intensive imports - are hurt by the costs of the measures supporting the weak sectors.

In summary, in chapter four we find that each country's long-run growth rate depends to a considerable extent on the growth of the world economy and on the commodity composition of its imports and exports; much more so than traditional trade and growth theory indicates; policies that stimulate the right export sectors can be very effective in raising the long-run growth rate. Clearly our analysis provides a convenient framework in which to discuss industrial, trade and development policies, a framework which has been sorely lacking so far.

Chapter six carries the analysis from the individual-country level to a two-region analysis. Formally this system is the two-region extension of the model in chapter 4: the partner region's demand equation for imported inputs takes the place of the export-demand equation in the single-country analysis. This two-region system can both be considered as stepping stone to multi-country models and as a breakdown of the world economy in two blocs. For illustrative purposes we adopt the latter interpretation and denote both regions as 'north' and 'south', which in the numerical exercises stand for the developed and the less-developed market economies, respectively. With respect to the long-run growth rate of each region we once again find it to diverge from what closed-economy analysis would predict. Thus in the two-region system too, the recognition of the 'indispensability' of imports implies a dependence of secular growth on international conditions; in the standard two-region models of trade and growth theory where imports are dispensable, the long-run growth rate does not depend on trade.

To determine how the growth rate depends on trade we again develop a steady-growth theorem. The core result is that north-south trade has two basic effects on both hemispheres' long-run growth rate. First, it transmits growth from the region with the highest 'autarkic' growth rate to the other one, leaving the former worse and the latter better off than closed-economy analysis or traditional trade and growth models indicate. Second, trade generates growth in both regions as soon as both hemispheres' per capita 'autarkic' incomes grow. Thus both regions are better off than closed-economy analysis predicts if the two 'autarkic' growth rates do not differ too much and exceed their respective natural rates substantially. To determine the extent of the two effects we provide tentative estimates of the parameters of the system for the past quarter of a century. These indicate that the transmission of growth has consistently been from south to north, as the south's 'autarkic' growth rate exceeded that of the north. However, there also has consistently been generation of growth. Prior to 1973 the latter compensated the impact of the transmission of growth. After 1973 the north's 'autarkic' growth collapsed and in this period the generation of growth was insufficient to offset the south's 'loss' due to the transmission effect. This is not to say that the south could have improved its growth by limiting trade: this would have cost it all traditional gains from trade that are not explicitly described by us but simply assumed to be so large as to make the need for trade imperative. Instead our analysis shows that neglecting the necessity of north-south trade in the analysis of growth may yield a bias; in the sixties the south's expected growth rate would thus be biased downward, in the seventies upward. However, quantitatively the impact of north-south trade has been minor, due to the low share of the flows in both regions' total output. Our estimates therefore lead to the conclusion that in the past 25 years internal factors rather than trade relations have dominated both hemispheres' growth. This will, however, change in the future as the size of north-south trade increases as a consequence of growth of the south's income relative to the north's. In an illustrative scenario 1980-2050 we show that explicit recognition of north-south trade may have two major effects in this period. First, it slightly, and later on substantially, increases the expected growth of the south as a consequence of the generation effect that will increasingly dominate the negative transmission effect. Second, it raises the north's expected income growth - due again to the generation - and retards the catching up of the south's income with that of the north - due to transmission of growth from south to north. This scenario presupposes that the north succeeds in creating new technologies as the south learns to apply the older ones. If the north succeeds it will gain considerably from the development of the south.

A central result of chapter six is that rapid development of the south does not only improve the south's own lot, but also increases the north's long-run growth rate. This raises the question whether this mutually benificial process can be enhanced by direct policy measures; in particular: can north-south aid augment the north's own income? This question is tackled in chapter seven. The standard answer in the literature, particularly on the transfer problem, is negative: it is conceivable that the effects of aid bestow a 'secondary blessing' on the donor region, but not to such an extent that the cost of the aid are fully compensated. However, the standard literature, apart from neglecting the indispensable nature of modern trade, fails to analyse the issue in the context of growth. We show that the growth that aid induces in the south also increases the north's income. Particularly because of the small size of the south's capital stock compared to that of the north, this accumulation effect of aid may be substantial and conceivably large enough to offset completely the costs of aid, leaving the north with a net profit. Extending this result we demonstrate, for a simplified case, that if the north wishes to maximize its consumption in some planning period, it should give aid to the south in the early part of this period as long as the south's initial capital stock is small enough compared to that of the north. Of course only empirical evidence could indicate whether the south's capital stock is indeed 'small enough', but our analysis clearly shows that the net effect of aid on the north's income is much less negative than current trade literature indicates. Aid is less altruistic and more in the north's own interest than this theory would lead to believe.

The final chapter, eight, is not concerned with growth but instead brings out an important short-run implication of the preponderance of indispensable inputs in modern trade: its consequences for the stability of equilibrium on the product market and on the balance of trade. If imports differ from their optimal value, i.e. from the value minimizing factor cost or maximizing profits, entrepreneurs gradually adjust their actual imported inputs in the direction of the optimal value. However, we show that this process need not be stable under the standard stability condition of trade theory, the Marshall-Lerner condition. Specifically, if the adjustment of the terms of trade towards balance of trade equilibrium is faster than the quantity adjustment of imports, both the product market and the balance of trade equilibrium are unstable. A major policy implication of this is that flexible exchange rates may be undesirable: these speed up the adjustment of the terms of trade and this leads, paradoxically, to instability. If the economy is to be able to achieve efficiency in production, exchange rates must not change too rapidly and violently.

The present study is only a first exploration of the consequences of the large share of indispensable inputs in modern trade for economic growth. Much further research should be done. In the theoretical field multi-country analyses will be fruitfull; for completeness non-traded goods, public goods and the finished consumer and investment goods that after all still constitute some thirty percent of world trade should be more explicitly integrated in our framework. The consequences of the quantity adjustment implied by imported inputs must be investigated more thoroughly than we do in chapter eight, particularly in a comprehensive monetary framework. Empirical tests must be made of our results: the validity of steady-growth results needs evaluation and non-steady-growth models should be developed for prediction, planning and policy purposes.

Nevertheless the present study already uncovers a great deal of new insights by simply recognizing the preponderance of indispensable inputs and concentrating on this fact alone, disregarding refinements. In summary we may conclude that economic growth of modern nations is much more intricately linked up with other countries than traditional trade theory indicates and that, consequently, policies aimed at restructuring an economy to cope better with trade conditions are far more effective than standard theory implies.

2. THE LONG-RUN GROWTH RATE IN ALTERNATIVE THEORIES OF TRADE AND GROWTH: A SURVEY OF THE LITERATURE

There is a peculiar contrast between the standard 'Keynesian' multiplier model of trade and income, and the theory of trade and growth. In the multiplier approach imports and income are directly related to each other. As a consequence, the rate of growth of income is linked to the foreign growth rate.(1) Similar views appear to be reflected by the frequent complaints of developing countries of the consequences of the lack of trade opportunities for development, and by the widespread notion in small developed countries that sluggish growth of world trade causes a low domestic rate of growth. Yet in the dominant theory of trade and growth the long-run growth rate of open economies is independent of international circumstances and depends on the domestic rates of growth of the working force and the (Harrod neutral) rate of technical progress alone. Of course, one explanation could be that the multiplier theory and the export-propelled growth notion are only valid in the short run and with excess capital and labour. Another explanation, however, is that the long-run independence of the growth rate of trade is a consequence of specific assumptions about the structure of production and trade.

The latter is indeed the case. The independence depends crucially on two assumptions. First: imports can also be produced domestically even though possibly with a production function differing from the one abroad. Second: import substitution is possible without friction causing adjustment costs; this implies e.g. perfect homogeneity and mobility between sectors of capital and labour. With a single exception all models applying these assumptions to the home and foreign country generate the growth rate's independence of trade variables. This point has not been explicitly noted in the trade and growth literature, possibly because there is no comprehensive survey. Therefore we bring it out by surveying the literature in so far as it is relevant for the long-run growth rate; i.e. we do not consider the patterns of specialization, the level of income, etc., though some of the more interesting results are given in notes.

In section 2.1 we consider the basic neoclassical two-sector model with consumption and investment goods and proportional saving. The model is discussed in some detail in order to elucidate how the mechanism of convergence to the natural rate works and to show that the stability conditions are not too restrictive. Section 2.2 shows that the independence result of the basic neoclassical two-sector model remains valid under a broad range of extensions: alternative saving behaviour, introduction of transport costs and tariffs, more sectors or different ones (intermediate goods, mixed consumption-investment goods), dated capital goods. This means that, as long as one is primarily interested in the long-run aggregate growth rate, refinements at these points are of secondary interest only. Section 2.3 shows the single exception to the rule that the independence result holds as soon as the two assumptions are satisfied. This exception is the two- (or more-) sector model with complementarity in production and unlimited labour. As soon as labour is the scarce factor in the long run, the growth rate once more is the natural rate, with and without trade. This exception does not seem to be of great practical importance. The crucial role of the perfect substitutability of imports becomes clear in section 2.4 where the few models that do not incorporate it are discussed. Clearly, if imports are complementary - either as inputs in production or as final goods in consumption and investment - and cannot be produced at home, the growth rate may depend on the international circumstances determining their availability. However, even if imports are imperfect substitutes (e.g. for domestic factors) their availability enters the growth rate. This case is important. For, as will be noted in the next chapter, though often domestic production of imports may be technically possible, there usually are adjustment costs. These may even be so huge that they always exceed the discounted value of the gains from domestic production of imports. But also if they are less, they nevertheless make substitution, in general, imperfect. This is adequately described by admitting imperfect substitutability between imports and domestic factors or produce, precluding the possibility of domestic production of perfect substitutes. Section 2.5 briefly discusses the neo-Ricardian theory of trade and growth, that claims to be an alternative for the remainder of the literature. This theory introduces time-phased production and many goods. However, none of the conclusions with respect to the growth rate adds anything to the results described in previous sections. Moreover, the indiscriminate assumption of steady state made in neo-Ricardian analysis appears to be quite hazardous. Explicit description of production and explicit stability analysis are required to obtain reasonably reliable results.

Since we are interested in long-run growth rates, we only deal with models where accumulation and growth are treated explicitly. Thus e.g. Bhagwati's immizering growth (cf. e.g. Bhagwati, 1969) and Chichilnisky's (1981) recent analysis of immizerizing effects of growth abroad are not considered.

The main conclusion of this chapter is that, if complementarity of capital and labour is precluded, the basic choice that should be made when analysing trade and growth, is whether or not perfect domestic substitutes can be produced without adjustment costs. The next chapter argues that they usually cannot. Thereupon the model to describe the long-run growth rate should be as straightforward as possible, since there is no indication that all refinements with respect to the number of products, saving behaviour, time structure of production and capital have much importance. Most existing models where imports are indispensable treat all imports as a factor of production. This has not only the advantage of parsimony (no need to postulate a national utility function or indifference curve), but it also captures in a very direct way the effects of imports without perfect domestic substitutes on the growth rate, since these are basically caused by influencing the growth rate of scarce production factors. The next chapter argues that to treat imports as a factor of production is also the most adequate description of modern trade.

2.1. The two-sector neoclassical theory: the basic model

Formal mathematical theories of trade and growth have been rather late in developing. The two authoritative surveys of the mid-nineteen sixties, of trade theory (Chipman, 1965a, b, 1966) and growth theory (Hahn and Matthews, 1964) both omit the subject. This is not too surprising: to describe the growth of open economies, one needs both a theory of trade that is explicit about production and a theory of accumulation.(2) The formal mathematical theory of accumulation did not evolve until the nineteen-forties and fifties. The Heckscher-Ohlin-Samuelson model of trade was developed in the same period. The natural sequel was to link these theories, particularly by extending Uzawa's (1961-2, 1962-3) two-sector growth model to open economies. The basic model then obtained was introduced simultaneously by Oniki and Uzawa (1965) and Bardhan (1965a). We first discuss the model, next the results obtained for the small-country case and finally the two-country system.

The model

Consider two countries, 1 and 2, each producing two products, 1 and 2. We first describe country 1 only and hence omit a country index. The production functions are:

$$v^i = v^i(k^i, \ell^i). \qquad (i = 1,2) \tag{2.1}$$

Superscripts indicate products or sectors; v^i is output, k^i capital and ℓ^i labour. Capital and labour are perfectly homogeneous and perfectly mobile between sectors. The functions v^i are assumed to be twice continuously differentiable, linear homogeneous and to satisfy the Inada (1963) conditions:

$$\begin{aligned} &v^i_K(K, 1) > 0 \; ; \; v^i_{KK}(K, 1) < 0 \; ; \\ &v^i(0, 1) = 0 \; ; \; v^i(\infty, 1) = \infty \; ; \; v^i_K(0, 1) = \infty \; ; \; v^i_K(\infty, 1) = 0. \end{aligned} \tag{2.2}$$

Here $K = k/\ell$ denotes the capital-labour ratio; v^i_K is $v^i(K, 1)$'s derivative to K, v^i_{KK} the second-order derivative.

The neoclassical assumptions about factor rewards are:

$$p^k \geqslant p^i \frac{\partial v^i}{\partial k^i} \; ; \; p^\ell \geqslant p^i \frac{\partial v^i}{\partial \ell^i} \; . \tag{2.3}$$

Here p^k and p^ℓ are the renumerations of capital and labour. The equality signs hold as soon as the output concerned is positive. Equation (2.3) implies absence of adjustment costs.

Denote trade flows by x^i , defined positive if country 1 exports i, negative if it imports i. The balance of trade is in equilibrium:

$$x^1 + Px^2 = 0 \; ; \; P = p^2/p^1 \; , \tag{2.4}$$

where P is the terms of trade between goods 1 and 2. Capital and labour are fully employed and perfectly mobile between sectors:

$$\ell^1 + \ell^2 = \ell \; ; \; k^1 + k^2 = k \; . \tag{2.5}$$

Labour grows exponentially (dots indicate time derivatives):

$$\dot{\ell} = \lambda\ell \; . \tag{2.6}$$

For saving three alternative behavioural assumptions are considered in the literature, but here we consider proportional saving only:

$$s = \sigma y \; ; \; y = v^1 + Pv^2 \; , \tag{2.7}$$

where both saving, s, and income, y, are expressed in terms of good 1; the rate of saving, σ, is constant.

To describe capital accumulation, an assumption is used that greatly simplifies things: good 1 is a pure capital good and good 2 a pure comsumption good. This way the necessity of specifying a utility function next to the saving function is avoided. Capital accumulation is now determined by two equations:

$$\dot{k} = s - \delta k, \tag{2.8}$$

which states that net accumulation equals savings minus depreciation, δ being the rate of depreciation;

$$\dot{k} + \delta k = v^1 - x^1 \; ; \tag{2.9}$$

gross investment equals output less exports of the capital good.

This completes the description of the economy of country 1. All variables are now determined as functions of the terms of trade P, the capital-labour ratio $K = k/\ell$, and the labour force, ℓ. To see this, note that, for given terms of trade, equations (2.3) determine the allocation of capital and labour over sectors. As the latters' total stocks are fixed, the production functions (2.1) then yield the outputs. By (2.7) savings are given as a function of these outputs and the terms trade alone; thus (2.9) determines net trade in the capital good residually. Finally, trade of the consumption good is obtained from the balance of trade equation (2.4).

Because the production functions are linear homogeneous, per capita saving is a function of the capital-labour ratio and the terms of trade only. Accordingly (2.8) can be written as:

$$\dot{K} = S(K,P) - (\delta+\lambda)K, \qquad (2.10)$$

where $S = s/\ell$ is per capita saving. Clearly, (2.10) completely determine the motion of the system as soon as the time path of P is known.

The small-country case

To obtain the time path of the terms of trade a description of the second country is required. The simplest case is that the second country is large and country 1 small. Then the terms of trade are completely independent of country 1 variables and may be assumed constant. This small-country model was first considered by Inada (1968); geometric treatments are given by Johnson (1971a, b, 1972), Vanek (1971), Bertrand (1973), Deardorff (1974b) and Smallwood (1975).

From (2.10) it is immediately evident that if an equilibrium capital-labour ratio - that is, a ratio that remains constant over time - is to exist, it should satisfy:

$$\frac{S(K,P)}{K} = \delta + \lambda \,. \qquad (2.11)$$

Moreover, a sufficient condition for such a ratio, say K^*, to globally stable, is:

$$\dot{K} \lesseqgtr 0 \quad \text{if } K \gtreqless K^*, \qquad (2.12)$$

or equivalently:

$$\frac{S(K,P)}{K} \lessgtr \delta + \lambda \quad \text{if} \quad K \gtrless K^* . \qquad (2.13)$$

Clearly, a sufficient condition for both the existence of a unique K* satisfying (2.11) and for (2.13) is that the ratio of gross investment to capital, S/K = s/k, is a decreasing function of the capital-labour ratio K. For the open economy this is recognized by Inada (1968a, p. 327) and Deardorff (1974a, p. 85). The same condition is sufficient in the case of Uzawa's closed economy (Inada, 1968, appendix A).

There is, however, a difference in the implication of this condition in both cases. In the case of the closed economy the terms of trade between both sectors are not constant, but endogenously determined and eliminated. Then, to obtain a decreasing rate of gross investment to capital, additional restrictions must be made with respect to production functions and to saving behaviour.(3)

In the case of the small open economy no such additional assumptions are required. The model (2.1) - (2.9) already implies the gross investment condition; thus trade can be said to stabilize the system. This result is independent of the patterns of specialization on the way to equilibrium: the possibilities of complete specialization and of trade reversals do not alter the stability properties,(4) though they complicate the calculations somewhat. Thus under fairly general conditions the open neoclassical two-sector model of a small economy converges to a steady-state path where capital (and labour and income) grow at the natural rate. This is the same rate at which the economy would grow in autarky. Thus trade does not alter the long-run growth rate in this type of model.(5)

The two-country system

The pioneering papers on open neoclassical two-sector models did not use the small-country assumption to close the model, but instead explicitly described the foreign country symmetrically to the home country. That is, both countries have identical production functions (this is, however, not crucial and many authors drop the assumption), and proportional saving, though the rates of saving may be different. The standard assumption is that both countries have equal natural rates, but this assumption can also be relaxed.

In the two-country case (2.10) continues to hold, but the symmetric equation for the foreign country is added. The terms of trade are now endogenous and depend on both countries' capital-labour ratios. Accordingly we obtain a system of two equations:

$$\dot{K} = f(K, \bar{K}) \tag{2.14}$$

$$\dot{\bar{K}} = \bar{f}(\bar{K}, K) \tag{2.15}$$

Here bars indicate the foreign country. The shapes of these functions depend on the saving functions, the production functions and the patterr of specialization. A typical phase diagram is figure 2.1, taken from Oni and Uzawa (1965, p. 35).

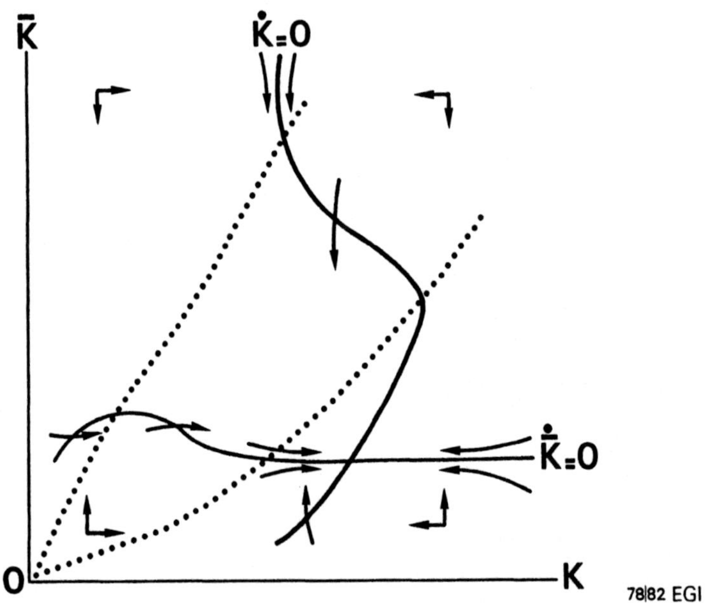

Figure 2.1. Example of a phase diagram of the neoclassical two-country, two-sector model.

In figure 2.1 the system moves towards the intersection of the $\dot{K} = 0$ and $\dot{\bar{K}} = 0$ curves, hence to a globally stable pair of constant capital-labour ratios. The dotted lines are the boundaries of the regions where one of the countries is specialized in investment goods (that is: outside the region between the curves). Thus the diagram is incomplete in that it does not show the regions where countries are completely specialized in the consumption good, but to obtain uniqueness and stability the latter is not necessary.

To establish uniqueness and stability of equilibrium, first the boundaries of the regions of (incomplete) specialization must be restricted such as to rule out multiple intersections. In figure 2.1, as in most of the literature, the underlying restriction is such that both boundaries are upward sloping. Next, when the boundaries are suitably restricted, the $\dot{K} = 0$ and $\dot{\bar{K}} = 0$ lines and the dynamic equations must satisfy appropriate conditions.

A sufficient condition to achieve all this is that the 'capital-intensity condition' is satisfied, viz. that consumption goods are more capital intensive than investment goods, for all values of the wage-rentals ratio.(6) This is true if both countries' natural rates are equal, cf. Oniki and Uzawa (1965), but also if they are unequal, cf. Kemp (1970).(7) If the capital-intensity condition is not satisfied, the equilibrium can still be unique and stable, though the literature does not contain explicit conditions for this case. But the results, to be indicated below, that are reported for other saving assumptions make it likely that with proportional saving stability holds too under more general conditions than just the capital-intensity one.

Conclusion

The conclusion of this discussion is that in a neoclassical world the long-run growth rate converges to the natural rate and is not altered by the opening up of trade. This result is quite generally valid for a small country and still correct in a two-country system, though then an additional restriction must be imposed. In the two-country system the result is not only true if both countries' natural rates are equal, but also, as might at first sight be surprising, when they differ.

2.2. Extensions and variations of the basic neoclassical model

In this section a number of extensions and variations of the neoclassical two-sector model of the previous section are discussed.[8]

Alternative saving behaviour

Instead of the proportional savings described in equation (2.7), one m also assume classical savings: a constant fraction of profits is saved a nothing out of wages:

$$s = \sigma' k p^k . \tag{2.16}$$

Of course (2.7) and (2.16) can be combined; in that case constant fractions are saved of both wages and profits, the latter having the higher propensity.

The model behaves in essentially the same way as under proportional saving. In the case of the small economy here too no additional stabilit conditions, beyond the basic assumptions of the model, have to be impose (Stiglitz, 1970; Deardorff, 1974a).[9]

In contrast, the capital-intensity condition, sufficient for stability of the two-country system with proportional savings, is not sufficient under classical saving. In this case oscillations around equilibrium ca occur, though local stability is ensured. To rule out the possibility o oscillations, it is sufficient to assume that the absolute value of the elasticity of substitution in the consumption-goods industry is higher than labour's value share in this industry.[10] Again this result is no only valid for equal natural rates (Stiglitz, 1970, pp. 479-487), but a for unequal ones (Khang, 1971).

If the capital-goods industry is capital intensive rather than labour intensive, a sufficient stability condition is that the elasticities of substitution in both industries exceed unity (condition stated by Bardh 1965; the correct dynamic analysis is given, in a lucid treatment, by Stiglitz, 1970).

Still another assumption about saving behaviour is rational saving: maximize discounted utility of consumption (per capita) over an infinit horizon. Once again the basic analysis remains unaffected. In the small·

country case stability is once more obtained without additional assumptions (Stiglitz, 1970). The two-country case has not been considered in the literature, probably because the saving behaviour of the trade partner must enter the optimizing process, and vice versa. But papers by Bardhan (1965b) and Ryder (1967) partially fill this gap. They follow the halfway solution of allowing the terms of trade to vary by introducing a foreign demand function, without explicitly considering accumulation abroad. Bardhan assumes the foreign offercurve to be completely static, whereas Ryder allows for growth, at a constant rate, of non-price foreign demand. As might be expected, the long-run growth rate is not affected by this modification.

Both sectors' goods can be consumed

So far, it was assumed that each good can be used for only one purpose. Instead, e.g. Atsumi (1971)(11) and Hanson (1971) admit consumption of capital goods. The latter refers to one sector, the pure consumption goods, as agriculture and to the other, mixed, one as manufacturing. Of course, as is implicit in Atsumi and clearly demonstrated by Hanson, the properties of the utility function - specifically the price elasticities of demand - now enter the stability conditions. But the long-run growth rate is the same as in the basic two-sector model.

Transport costs

There is a strange failure in the theory of international trade to treat transport in an analytically satisfactory manner. Essentially, transport is simply a good produced like all other goods, but serving as input for the part of other products that is traded internationally.(12) The intensity with which this input is used depends on the spatial dimensions of international trade and on the physical characteristics of the product concerned. However, it is not treated this way. The most explicit way in which transport costs are described is as a constant mark-up on prices. In the context of growth even this highly stylized approach is absent. But this treatment is almost equivalent to that of a constant ad valorem import duty; and the latter is considered in the neoclassical two-sector models, cf. Stiglitz (1970, section 6); Atsumi (1971, section 6); Negishi

(1972, pp. 174-177); Smith (1976, p. 275) and Bruce (1977). The modification does not, however, influence the long-run growth rate, nor, in any significant way, the stability properties of the model.

An alternative way to introduce transport costs, is to assume that one good is non-tradeable, transport costs being prohibitive. Findlay (1970) introduces a small-country model with two traded consumption goods and (non-traded capital good, all produced with neoclassical production functions. Saving is proportional. Implicitly he assumes incomplete specialization but this is only correct, as Deardorff (1974a) notes, unc specific conditions. The general case is discussed in a lucid and analytically powerful paper by Manning (1981) whose model differs slight from Findlay's: capital goods are produced by a fixed-coefficients proce and saving is rational. Aarrestad (1978) has presented a similar model where the accumulating factor is knowledge instead of physical capital.

Intermediate goods[13]

To the basic two-sector model a third sector can be added, producing a intermediate good that is an input for the other two sectors, having a zero lifetime. In that case, however, the pattern of trade and of production becomes indeterminate if all goods are traded, cf. Melvin (1969) and Batra and Casas (1973, p. 305/6). Therefore Kuo (1977) considers the case of one non-traded intermediate good; the input-output coefficients for this good are constant. Kuo concludes that there is a globally stable pair of capital-labour ratios of the two countries if th rate of saving from profits exceeds that from wages and if capital goods are labour intensive both in the gross and in the net sense. Here 'net' takes only capital and labour directly employed into account, 'gross' includes the factors incorporated in the intermediate good.

Corden (1971) considers precisely the opposite case. He introduces two intermediate goods and assumes only these are traded, whereas both consumption and investment goods do not cross borders. For the small-country case with fixed terms of trade, Corden demonstrates once again t stability of a constant capital-labour ratio; the same holds if foreign demand is imperfectly elastic.

In an elegant paper, Khang (1969) avoids the indeterminacy problem by considering two sectors only: an intermediate good and a second one tha can both be consumed and invested. Khang proves that, if there are no factor-intensity reversals and if saving is classical, the two-country system approaches a constant pair of capital-labour ratios in the long run. This is once again true both if the two countries' natural rates are equal and if they are not; production functions are identical internationally.

To conclude: the presence of traded or non-traded intermediate goods does not alter the equality of long-run growth rates with and without trade.

Dated capital goods: vintage models

In the models discussed so far, capital goods are identical, independent of the date they were produced. Instead one may assume that machines of a later vintage have a higher productivity. The models used in the trade literature usually are of the clay-clay type: no substitution between capital and labour before installation of the machines, nor *ex post*. The only way to substitute capital for labour is thus to vary the economic life of machines. The closed two-sector model of this kind is developed by Bardhan (1966b, 1970) and Gabisch (1975, section 3) opens it up to trade in consumption and new investment goods. It should not come as a surprise that the long-run growth rate is the same with and without trade: the rate of growth of labour plus that of labour productivity. The same is true of variations of the model. Petith (1972), for example, considers two consumption goods, produced by different machines with vintage technology; the machines are produced jointly, and are not traded - therefore a main feature of the model is that factor prices are not equalized. In Smith's (1974, 1976a, b) one-sector model, there is trade in used machines and new ones (that is: current output); *production functions are identical between countries*, or allowed to differ by a multiplicative constant at most (1974, p.272). Here too, the presence of trade does not modify the long-run growth rate.

A most illuminating exception to the equality of growth rates with and without trade has been discovered by Gabisch (1975, section 4), also cf. Smith (1976c). The exception is obtained by allowing trade in second-hand machines between countries *with differing rates of growth of productivity* of the home-produced machines. In the steady state the country with the slower productivity growth imports the obsolete machines of the foreign country. As a consequence it picks up the latter country's higher rate c productivity growth. Thus the long-run rate of growth is improved: with trade it equals the rate of population growth plus the foreign country's growth rate of productivity; without trade, population growth is only augmented by the lower domestic productivity growth. The mechanism of second-hand machines trade through which this is accomplished, is of course rather special and probably only relevant for some developing countries. But the basic point is well taken: because essentially import can not be produced domestically (namely machines with a high level of productivity), the growth rate is influenced by trade: technological progress is imported.

Relaxing balance of trade equilibrium

The models discussed so far assume balance of trade equilibrium. Instead, one may introduce money and allow for trade in a monetary asset cf. Ramanathan (1975), Roberts (1978) and Shieh and Takayama (1980). A more common approach was introduced by Kemp (1968, 1969, pp. 237-249). I allowed, in the context of the growing two-sector economy, for international investment, or trade in securities. If both securities an investment goods are traded, the pattern of trade and indebtedness beco indeterminate if all markets are perfect. Some authors therefore assume the capital good to be non-tradeable, e.g. Frenkel (1971), Fischer and Frenkel (1974a), Bazdarich (1978) who consider the small-country case, Fischer and Frenkel (1974b), the two-country model. Alternatively, Fisc and Frenkel (1972) admit a difference between the world's and the domes rate of return to physical capital, by admitting more or less efficient production at home than abroad. Somewhat similarly, Kapur (1981), thoug he does not discuss the indeterminacy problem explicitly, appears to av it by allowing the real interest rate on bonds to differ from the real rental on physical capital. Hori and Stein (1977) solve the indetermina problem by avoiding factor-price equalization, postulating complete specialization. Bade (1973) assumes labour to be immobile between sectc to achieve the same effect; nevertheless import substitution is still frictionless in this model because capital is perfectly mobile between sectors.

In all these cases the long-run rate of growth is the same as that in autarky. Thus the balance of trade equation is not essential in the determination of the long-run rate.

Conclusion

Having considered a host of modifications of the basic neoclassical two-sector model, we can still stand by the main conclusion of the preceding section. Trade does not alter the long-run growth rate as long as imports can be produced domestically and import substitution is frictionless.

2.3. Two-sector growth with complementarity in production

A central feature of the basic neoclassical two-sector model as discussed above is the possibility of capital-labour substitution in both sectors. Instead Gabisch (1977) postulates complementarity in production; thus production functions (2.1) are replaced by:

$$v^i = \phi_k^i k^i = \phi_\ell^i \ell^i, \tag{2.17}$$

where ϕ_k^i and ϕ_ℓ^i are constant output-input ratios. Gabisch assumes the presence of unlimited labour such that capital is the only scarce factor. This scarcity might of course be alleviated by international lending, that is, admitting balance of trade surplusses and deficits, in order to restore full employment of labour (cf. essay 16, part III of Steedman, 1979a). But the more interesting case arises when labour is unlimited. Saving is, as usual, proportional.

In the small-country case the terms of trade are once again given. Gabisch assumes that the country specializes according to comparative advantage. This means that specialization depends on whether the international terms of trade exceed or fall short of the autarkic terms, the latter being the slope of the transformation curve. Specifically, remembering that good 1 is the investment good, the country imports capital goods if:

$$P > \frac{\phi_k^1}{\phi_k^2}. \tag{2.18}$$

In autarky the growth rate is $\sigma\phi_k^1$, but with trade and under (2.18) the importing of capital goods causes a rise of the growth rate to $\sigma\phi_k^2P$; thu the (long-run) growth rate with trade exceeds the autarkic one. If, on th contrary, the reverse of (2.18) holds, the country imports consumption goods and the growth rate is unaffected by trade. In the two-country case a similar result is valid: both countries approach the long-run growth rate that the country specializing in investment goods would have in autarky.

In an early contribution, Tinbergen and Bos (1962, pp. 63-5) discuss a discrete-time three-sector model with two exported consumption goods and one imported investment good. All are produced with fixed coefficients assuming unlimited labour. Apart from the number of consumption goods, th model only differs from Gabisch's (1977), in that trade is not determine by comparative advantage. Instead exports of consumption goods are fixed and grow exogenously. Assuming the terms of trade fixed, imports are the determined by the balance of trade. Tinbergen and Bos do not explicitly consider the long-run growth rate, but if only one consumption good is retained, the rate is not difficult to determine. It equals the minimum Gabisch's rate for the case of investment-goods imports, $\sigma\phi_k^2P$, and the growth rate of exports in the long run, viz. if the export demand constraint is effective. In both cases the growth rate may either be higher or lower than the autarkic one, depending on whether (2.18) is satisfied and on the growth rate of foreign demand.

The explanation of these effects on the growth rate of countries importing capital goods, is that these countries import, as it were, a higher capital-output ratio for its aggregate (consumption plus investment) final demand. Therefore, in a sense, the rule that trade doe not alter the long-run growth rate as long as perfect domestic substitut can be produced without friction, is not violated. For this model is equivalent to one where the aggregate productivity of imported capital goods exceeds that of domestically produced ones; in that case imports a different from their domestically produced substitutes.

Of course the effect depends on capital being the scarce factor. If th labour restriction in (2.17) is effective the country cannot grow faste than its natural rate, with or without trade. In the neoclassical model the possibility of substitution between the two factors forces labour to be the scarce factor in the long run.

2.4. Growth with indispensable imports

Though the main body of the literature assumes that imports can be produced domestically, nevertheless a number of models exist where imports cannot be (perfectly) replaced by domestic produce. In principle such imports can either be consumption goods, or inputs. Much of the effects depends on the shape of the utility functions or the production functions. We first consider the case where imports are perfect complements and next the more recent extensions to substitution.

Complementarity of imports

If the imports are not produced at home, there is no need to use models with more than one production sector in each country. Hence output can be described by a single production function. For the case of complementarity the resulting model has been introduced by Johnson (1953, 1958) whose exposition we broadly follow, modifying it only in that prices are written explicitly. The production function is:

$$v = \min\{\ell\phi_\ell,\ k\phi_k,\ m^v\phi_m\}. \tag{2.19}$$

Here m^v is the amount of imported input; ϕ_ℓ, ϕ_k and ϕ_m are the constant output-input coefficients. The equalities $\ell\phi_\ell = k\phi_k = m^v\phi_m$ should hold to achieve full employment.

Saving is proportional to the value of output less that of imported inputs (though the trade balance might be included too):

$$sp = \sigma(vp - m^v\bar{p}), \tag{2.20}$$

Here s is real saving measured in terms of the country's ('country 1') output; p is the price of output, $\bar{p}$ that of imports.

Apart from imported inputs there are also imported consumption goods. If the demand side is described by complementarity too, this yields:

$$m^c\bar{p} = \gamma_m(vp - m^v\bar{p}), \tag{2.21}$$

where m^c is the amount of imported consumption goods; the marginal propensity to import, γ_m, is constant under the complementarity assumption. The imported consumption goods are taken to be identical witl imported inputs, but this assumption could be relaxed without difficulty

Instead of assuming strict equality of saving and investment, international lending or borrowing can be admitted. Thus the weaker restriction should be satisfied that the value of imports plus savings equals that of exports plus investment:

$$sp + (m^v + m^c)\bar{p} = \dot{k}p + \bar{m}p, \tag{2.22}$$

$\bar{m}$ being exports, assumed to be exogenous:

$$\bar{m} = \bar{m}^{ex}. \tag{2.23}$$

If capital is fully employed, this yields for the growth rate of capit- equal to that of output, income and imports:

$$\frac{\dot{k}}{k} = \phi_k\{\sigma(1 - \frac{1}{P\phi_m} - \frac{T}{v}\}. \tag{2.24}$$

$$T \equiv \frac{p\bar{m} - \bar{p}(m^v + m^c)}{pv} = \frac{\bar{m}}{v} - \frac{1}{P\phi_m} - \gamma_m(1 - \frac{1}{P\phi_m}). \tag{2.25}$$

Here T is the trade balance and P the terms of trade: $P = p/\bar{p}$.

In the closed economy (2.24) is replaced by $\dot{k}/k = \phi_k\sigma$, ϕ_k being the inverse of the capital-output ratio. Thus there are two ways in which th growth rate with trade can be different from that in autarky. First, the growth rate is increased if the value of imports exceeds that of exports ($T < 0$). The reason is clear: income and saving are raised, growth is in effect subsidized from abroad.

The second source of a difference in the growth rate is the imported inputs term, $-1/P\phi_m$. This term appears to lower the growth rate.(14) However, this result is deceptive, since in general the capital-output ratio with trade is not the same as the autarkic one. This is because imported inputs are substitutes for capital, since the capital outlays required to produce the imported inputs at home are made superfluous by trade. Thus ϕ_k is higher with trade than without, and the negative effect of $-1/P\phi_m$ on the growth rate is offset to some extent, the total effect of imported inputs being ambiguous. However, the effect of changes in the terms of trade is perfectly clear: if imported inputs become cheaper, income increases, and so does saving, improving the growth rate. This point is not made by Johnson, who sets all prices equal to unity. This procedure is valid as long as prices are constant and units of measurement properly selected. But if prices change it is not.

This model has been elaborated by a number of authors. Verdoorn (1956), Johnson (1958, pp. 139-149), and others, replace the assumption of constant terms of trade by a dependency of exports on the terms of trade. Verdoorn (1956) assumes the input coefficients to be non-linear; he is also the first to provide an application of the model, viz. long-term projections for the Netherlands. Brems (1956) assumes a fixed share of imports in investment but no trade in consumption goods. His two-country model exhibits a common rate of growth in the long run; under some assumptions, notably equality of both countries' overall capital-labour ratios, the common growth rate is close to the one the country with the highest rate of saving would sustain if it could do without imports.

Another modification is to admit different non-zero propensities to import for consumption and investment, cf. Chenery and Bruno (1962).

The model may be used for economic planning by setting a target rate of growth and calculating the corresponding aid and saving. This approach is easy to apply empirically and in the development literature referred to as the two-gap model; cf. Chenery and Bruno (1962), Chenery and Strout (1966) and also e.g. Voivodas (1973). Wasow (1978, 1979) concentrates on the capital imports, suppressing trade.

A very important extension is to describe labour more explicitly and allow for a variable capital-labour ratio. Itsumi and Morigushi (1978) assume a Cobb-Douglas production function and consider an imported complementary factor. Exports depend on export price and growth of world trade. The long-run behaviour depends on the difference between the growth rate of world demand(15) and the rate of labour growth. If the latter is smaller than the former, the long-run growth rate is the natural rate. In the opposite case of world demand growing slower than labour, the growth rate of capital converges to that of world demand if the difference is moderate; if world demand grows substantially slower than labour, per capita income even declines to zero.

The essential argument, both in Johnson's basic model and in the elaborations, is that the growth rate depends on international circumstances, both in the short and in the long run. If imports are a factor of production, output and growth are affected as soon as imports are somehow restricted - for example because exports and capital imports are insufficient or not profitable enough for the required imports. Similarly, if imports are essential in consumption and investment, a comparable mechanism exists.

Clearly this happens because imports cannot be produced at home. However, it remains to be seen whether these results are modified if imports, though still not produceable domestically, are nevertheless substitutes for domestic factors, instead of complements.

Substitutability of imports and domestic factors

Recently, two models, Findlay (1980) and Taylor (1981), have been presented that can be considered as two-region elaborations of Johnson's model, with some substitution possibilities added. They deal with 'north-south' trade and essentially describe the south by capital-labour complementarity with unlimited labour and a fixed real wage. The south produces a consumer good only and must import its capital goods from the north, the latter producing a mixed consumption-investment good. Thus in the south there is, in Johnsonian fashion, no substitutability of imports and domestic goods or factors while in the north imperfect substitutability of the domestic and imported consumption goods is admitted. The north is modelled quite differently by both authors. Findla describes it with a neoclassical model, implying that the natural rate is the crucial parameter for long-run issues, whereas Taylor postulates excess capital and labour caused by factor-price rigidities and thus obtains a Keynesian model where demand parameters, particularly those pertaining to the investment-saving balance, are crucial; in addition Taylor introduces 'oil imports from OPEC', but here he simply assumes proportionality of oil to the other factors and assumes that OPEC's incom equals its exports to the north and that it spends a fixed proportion of it on northern imports, so that autonomous developments in the OPEC regio are absent and hence cannot influence the north's long-run growth.

In spite of these differences in the way the north is modelled, both authors arrive at the same result with respect to long-run growth rates: both regions' long-run growth rates are equal and depend on conditions in the north alone. Thus in Findlay's model the long-run growth rate is the north's natural rate, in Taylor's model it depends on the north's demand conditions and oil-input requirements. This would seem to indicate that even imperfect substitutability of imports and domestic produce is sufficient to free the long-run growth rate from foreign influences. However, this conclusion appears to be unwarranted: both Taylor and Findlay model the south as an appendix of the north; the south's growth possibilities depend completely on its trade with the north and there are no autonomous developments in the south that can act as a break or accelerator on the north's growth. To analyse whether with imperfect substitutability of inputs the long-run growth rate depends on foreign conditions, one needs a model where these foreign conditions are not fully determined by domestic developments.

Khang (1968) develops a model where imports (envisaged as natural resources) are an input in a Cobb-Douglas production function, along with labour and capital. Thus, under constant returns, (2.19) takes the form:

$$v = m^{\xi_m} \ell^{\xi_\ell(1-\xi_m)} k^{(1-\xi_\ell)(1-\xi_m)}, \qquad (2.26)$$

where ξ_ℓ, ξ_m $(0 < \xi_\ell, \xi_m < 1)$ are constant; if factor prices and marginal productivity are equal, ξ_m is imports' factor share and ξ_ℓ labour's value share in the two domestic factors capital and labour. Khang takes exports to depend on the terms of trade, with a constant elasticity $\bar{\varepsilon}$ and on an <u>autonomously</u> growing term. Thus:

$$\bar{m} = \beta_0 P^{-\bar{\varepsilon}} \exp(\beta t), \qquad (\beta > 0, \bar{\varepsilon} < 0) \qquad (2.27)$$

β being constant. The model is closed by assuming equality of imports' marginal productivity to the terms of trade, exponential growth of labour, proportional saving and balance of trade equilibrium. Then the long-run growth rate of capital and output is easily obtained since no patterns of specialization need to be examined. It can be written as:

$$\lambda + \frac{\xi_m}{\xi_m - \xi_\ell(1 - \xi_m)\bar{\varepsilon}} (\beta - \lambda). \tag{2.28}$$

Clearly, notwithstanding the possibility of substitution, the long-run growth rate depends on international-trade variables. Specifically, the rate exceeds the natural rate, if and only if foreign-demand growth β exceeds the natural rate λ.

The importance of autonomous foreign-demand growth is caused by the dependence of imports on export demand. In the general case of growth with imported inputs that are imperfect substitutes (in a Cobb-Douglas function) for domestic factors, long-run growth depends on the growth rate that can be achieved for imported resources. This is made clear by Black (1970). He points out that even if such an input can be produced domestically, the growth rate can nevertheless be improved by trade if the possibility of trade causes a higher rate of growth of such a factor. This view is rather eclectic, as it does not become clear precisely how this higher rate of input growth is achieved. Khang's model gives one cause: autonomous shifting of the foreign offercurve, given a finite foreign elasticity of demand. One reason for the latter would be that the exports of Khang's country cannot be produced abroad and are not perfect substitutes for the trade-partners' own products and factors. If this is no longer the case, the long-run growth rate must once again be the natural rate.(16) This becomes clear from the treatment of Gale (1971, 1974) and Dei (1979). They analyse the case where imports are, for all countries, perfect substitutes for capital and output(17) ; the growth rate converges to the natural rate.

2.5. An alternative theory? The neo-Ricardian approach

A recently developed approach(18) is, by a number of its proponents (most notably Steedman, 1979a, b), claimed to be an alternative to the neoclassical two-sector growth and trade model. In its treatment of production and accumulation, this 'neo-Ricardian' approach follows the venerable tradition of Ricardo (1817), Marx (1885, pp. 446-465, 501-517; cf. Samuelson, 1974), Leontief (1941), Sraffa (1960) and also Von Neumann (1938). The main purpose of the approach is to emphasize that production is time-phased(19), or, put differently, that there are many capital good and intermediates.

To achieve this, the economy is usually described by a discrete-time, single-period input-output system.[20] The fundamental assumption is that of steady-state growth, or 'long-period equilibrium'. This amounts to constant growth rates of all inputs, outputs and intermediate flows. In addition, all these variables' growth rates are taken to be equal. Thus the input-output coefficients and the composition of final demand are constant over time; frequently only one consumption good is considered.

The growth rate

Formally, the model is an extension of Gabisch' fixed-coefficients model (cf. section 2.3), if the latter model is in steady growth. This means that, if labour is the restrictive primary factor, the system's growth rate is the natural rate, both with and without trade.[21] This is the situation assumed in most of the literature; frequently the natural rate itself is taken to be zero, so that the system does not grow at all.

If labour is unlimited, and if the same applies to all other primary factors, the growth rate depends on saving. Steedman (1979b, p.25) assumes classical saving. Then the growth rate of the system is $\sigma_k p^k$, with σ_k the propensity to save from profits, and p^k the rate of profits (or interest). Thus the growth rate depends on how the rate of profits is determined. This rate is related to the wage rate by the input-output coefficients - at least under competitive pricing, constant returns and a constant commodity composition of final demand; the two latter assumptions are implied by steady growth at constant and equal rates. This means that there are two possibilities for the determination of the profit rate.

First, the wage rate may be fixed (e.g. institutionally). Then, even if wages remain unaltered by the opening up of trade, the rate of profit, and hence the growth rate, is nevertheless affected because the effective input-output coefficients are altered in the same way as in Gabisch' simple model. (The generalized case is discussed by e.g. Steedman, 1979b, chapter 9, and in Parrinello's contribution to Steedman, 1979a).

Alternatively, the rate of profit itself may be determined exogenously (e.g. by a rate of intertemporal preference). Clearly, in that case the growth rate is unaffected by trade; accordingly this time the wage rate is altered in response to the change in effective input-output ratios.

. This sums up the neo-Ricardian results with respect to the growth rate. Qualitatively, these are the same as those obtained in the neoclassical two-sector models, or, where relevant, Gabisch' fixed-coefficients two-sector model. Thus the extension to time-phased production and heterogeneous capital does not alter anything essential. This result corresponds with Ethier's (1979) (also compare Metcalfe and Steedman, 1981, and Ethier, 1981) conclusions about the influence on the four main theorems of the HOS-model: these remain valid unless assumptions are made (e.g. non-traded goods, capital-intensity reversals) that also invalidate these theorems in the HOS-model.

The reason for these invariances is the use of the steady-state tool. Under the assumption of steady state, many production theories are equivalent. As a consequence, the main points of time-phased production and heterogeneous capital are swept under the carpet, being transitional phenomena. Interesting results are once again obtained if adjustment processes are studied, compare e.g. Samuelson (1975, 1978a, b), Krugman's (1981) recent analysis of uneven development caused by external economies in the industrial sector and the beautiful early paper of Bensusan-Butt (1954), that is unfortunately neglected in the recent literature. A related interesting topic is intertemporal gains from trade, cf. Smith (1979); here too the fact that production is time-phased is essential.

The steady-state method

Neither the many refinements of the two-sector neoclassical model as discussed in section 2.2, nor the neo-Ricardian introduction of time-phased production and heterogeneous capital, alter the results with respect to the long-run growth rate that were obtained in the simple two-sector neoclassical (and fixed-coefficient) models. Nevertheless it is conceivable that such refinements have some influence if imports can not be produced at home; moreover, they describe phenomena that are of interest in their own right. Thus it might still be a preferable research strategy to analyse aggregate growth as the outcome of a more detailed theory, instead of utilizing as highly aggregated a model as possible - provided the costs of disaggregation in terms of added analytical complexity are not prohibitive. The neo-Ricardian tool kit of steady state with equal growth rates for all variables offers precisely the means to obtain greater detail with simple analytical instruments. However, this is not achieved without sacrifice. Though ostensibly 'the emphasis is on the role of production and produced means of production' (Steedman, 1979b, p.9), the theory is not explicit at all about the technical properties of the production process underlying the constant input-output matrix that is implied by equal, constant, rates of growth of all flows. (The same of course applies to the utility function vis á vis the commodity composition of consumption.) How then might this constancy be achieved?

One possibility sometimes hinted at, is that the constant input-output system is generated by a neoclassical input-output system with continuous-substitution production functions. In the long run such a neoclassical system is then taken to converge to a steady state with constant coefficients.

However, results obtained for such a steady state are only meaningful if the steady state is actually stable. Recently a lot of research has been done on the stability of closed-economy, heterogeneous-capital neoclassical growth models. Stability can indeed be demonstrated in a number of cases, but the pertinent conditions are quite specific and by no means trivially satisfied. In the standard two-capital goods optimal growth model with an infinite horizon, perfect foresight and a unique steady state, this steady state can be totally unstable, the system giving rise to a closed orbit. This happens under fairly general conditions, specifically involving a not too small rate of discount. This result is due to Benhabib and Nishimura (1979, 1981, section 4) who provide an example with Cobb-Douglas technology. As such, this result need not be disastrous for steady-state centered analysis, because stability properties depend on the adjustment process specified. In the present case the perfect-foresight assumption is probably crucial. An indication to this effect is obtained from the model of Wan and Majundar (1980). They replace the assumption by that of optimizing agents who throughout take prices to remain constant. Their model is in discrete time, includes trade and has log-linear (Cobb-Douglas) utility and production functions. If there is no primary factor, their model converges with constant returns to a steady-growth path and with diminishing returns to a stationary state. However, if labour and non-traded capital goods are introduced - a case Steedman (1979b) frequently considers - a unique and stable steady state does not result, but instead a continuum of golden-age paths, <u>none</u> of which has relative stability. The conclusion must therefore be that, with neoclassical production functions, convergence to a constant input-output matrix is certainly not guaranteed and even somewhat doubtful in many cases.

Even if the stability problem is solved, there is still another problem: the steady-state constant input-output matrix that results from a neoclassical production model, however stable it may be, nevertheless changes as soon as relative prices are changed. This may happen if trade is opened up,(22) but also if, in an originally free-trade steady state, tariffs are imposed. Thus, when analysing these transitions, the original input-output matrix cannot be used, but it should be recomputed.

All this does not only apply to continuous-substitution production functions, but also, <u>mutatis mutandis</u>, to systems where substitution is discrete, with either an infinite or a finite number of feasible values for the input-output coefficients. Only if there is no choice of technology at all, and the matrix is constant because the coefficients remain fixed for purely technical reasons, the difficulties are avoided. It is, however, certainly for long-run purposes, hard to swallow this assumption as realistic. Moreover, even so the stability problem is only partly removed, as the constancy of the long-run growth rate should still be established.

Thus it is clear that results obtained by naive steady-state analysis - without explicit specification of the conditions of production and thorough analysis of stability conditions - must be distrusted.(23) The validity of their implications remains yet to be made plausible. The neo-Ricardian short-cut to results in the many goods, time-phased production systems, should be eyed with suspicion, since it simply replaces essential steps of the argument by hazardous assumptions.

Therefore, we shall analyse aggregate growth using the most straightforward <u>aggregate</u> model, making explicit the structure of production (and the saving and optimality behaviour); and we consider only the steady states of which the stability has been established first. It is clear from the previous section that, if imports can not be produced domestically, the treatment of all imports as factor of production provides for an elegant and convenient analysis of growth. In the next chapter we argue that this also is an adequate description of modern trade.

3. IMPORTS AS AN INDISPENSABLE FACTOR OF PRODUCTION

The long-run growth rate of open economies does not depend on international-trade variables as long as perfect domestic substitutes can be produced for imports; but if such perfect substitutes cannot be made, the growth rate does depend on international circumstances. This is the central conclusion of the preceding chapter. The first section of the present chapter gives a number of reasons why imports usually are indeed indispensable in this sense. Section 3.2 argues that it has to be preferred to treat aggregate imports as a factor of production instead of a finished consumption good, because the bulk of world trade is in intermediate goods, most socalled final goods still require further processing and the essence of the role of trade in modern economies is described more adequately this way than by traditional trade theories. Because the effects of disaggregation on the growth rate may be expected to be minor, as became evident in the preceding chapter, we use aggregate models, with all imports as a factor of production; section 3.3 considers the production function and a number of properties we shall use. Section 3.4 discusses the optimizing behaviour, section 3.5 defines an autarkic economy that 'corresponds' with the open one where imports are indispensable inputs.

3.1. Imperfect substitutability of imports

Prior to considering the causes of imperfect substitutability, or 'indispensability', of imports, the meaning of this concept should be clarified. The, implicit, perfect substitute assumption of traditional theory can be broken down in two components. First, it is assumed that a country is technically capable of producing a perfect substitute for every imported product. Here a product is a perfect substitute for another one if the elasticity of substitution between the two in the utility function or, in the case of intermediates, in the production function, is minus infinity. The second assumption is concerned with the conditions under which an economy actually produces a perfect substitute for imports. Suppose the country would have a comparative advantage in the product concerned once production is under way. Then traditional theory assumes that production actually occurs. Put differently, whether a country shifts its production to a perfect substitute of an importable, depends only on the relative cost of production after the shift.

We define an imported product as 'indispensable' if either of both above assumptions is violated. Thus an imported product is 'indispensable' not only if the country cannot produce its perfect substitute for technical reasons, but also if the country can produce the perfect substitute but does not do so even if it has some comparative advantage in this product.

Our basic argument is that aggregate imports must be viewed as 'indispensable' in the above sense because at any time the bulk of individual imported products is indispensable as a consequence of factors to be elaborated below. Thus a group of products cannot be produced domestically, now, or ever. Another group cannot be produced at a given time, though after some period production becomes possible; but then they have been replaced by other imported products that cannot be made at home at the time, so that the aggregate of both groups continues to be indispensable. Finally, there are many products that could be produced at home and for which the country has a long-run comparative advantage, but that continue to be acquired exclusively from abroad because of adjustment costs.

Indispensability of imports caused by specific non-traded factors

One obvious reason why a country can only to a limited extent produce an imported good domestically, or even not at all, is that the good requires a specific non-traded factor that the country does not possess in sufficient quantity and cannot produce either. Examples abound. Agricultural products require land with soil of suitable fertility and an appropriate climate. To produce ore one needs ore deposits and it is particularly hard to extract crude petroleum if no oil fields are available. Imports necessitated by lack of such specific factors bulk large in world trade. Unfortunately, no comprehensive data to show this are readily available. However, table 3.1 shows tentative data for the world's three largest importers and for the Netherlands.(1) The table shows for each of the five primary-products' SITC categories what part of imports is generated by lack of specific factors. To determine precisely which commodities to include, occasionally requires detailed analysis of the conditions of production of an individual commodity. This is avoided; instead table 3.1 includes all commodities where domestic production is less than 20% of imports. A single exception is made: US petroleum imports are included notwithstanding a sizeable domestic output; but clearly the imports are based on a specific factor of which the domestic stock is limited and insufficient. Details and sources of the table are provided in appendix 3.1.(2)

Table 3.1. Imports generated by lack of specific factors, as a percentage of total imports in each primary-product SITC category; USA, FR Germany, Japan, Netherlands; 1976.

	SITC class	USA	FR Germany	Japan	Netherlands	All four countries
0	Food & live animals	37	31	42	45	38
1	Beverages & tobacco	0	41	0	82	22
2	Crude materials excl. fuels	17	51	58	44	46
3	Mineral fuels, etc.	94	88	82	100	90
4	Animal, vegetable oils & fats	91	57	51	59	68
0-4	Primary products	70	61	68	73	68
0-9	All products	31	25	54	30	34

The table clearly brings out the importance of imports generated by lack of specific factors: two-thirds of the four countries' primary imports are of this type, the figure being roughly the same for each of the countries. This amounts to one-third of the countries' total imports, though here the figure for Japan is markedly higher: 54% of Japan's total imports is caused by lack of specific factors.(3)

The most important specific-factor based commodity is of course petroleum. However, in the other commodity groups, specific-factor based goods are important too. With some exaggeration, the conclusion is: <u>if primary products are imported, this happens because the country lacks</u>

specific factors necessary to produce them domestically.

It is almost superfluous to stress the importance to growth of trade in these products and of the circumstances under which this trade is conducted. Tsuru (1980, p.x) suggests, for example, that Japan has benefitted greatly from the low world price of oil in the sixties and fifties, this specifically because it did not have to protect relatively high cost domestic resources from the low import prices - because it had no domestic resources.

The role of innovation and technological improvements

One of the prime phenomena of modern economic growth is the continual appearance of new products. These new products are both final goods and intermediate goods (incidentally the latter implies that distinction of process innovation and product innovation of traded goods is rather difficult). It is now well established (cf. e.g. Hirsch, 1975) that skills are an important determinant of trade: products pass through the product cycle with 'new', 'growth' and 'mature' phases; specialization in such a phase is typically associated with the (relative) levels of skill of trading countries. Consequently, though the composition of imports changes in the course of time, they nevertheless have a certain relative skill intensity in common as long as the relative skills are constant. This situation amounts to the same thing as that of a specific, non-traded factor discussed above.

The argument is not limited to the general level of skills in a country. Once a country has specialized in a given set of products, product and process innovations generate specific technical knowledge and skill that in turn cause further innovations; this process impedes a catching up by other countries. The consequence is that trade patterns are to some extent caused by historical accidents instead of factor endowments or comparative advantage in the static sense. For example, the fact that Gerard Philips and his father established an electric-lamp factory in Eindhoven in 1891, is a better explanation of the 1975 Dutch value share of 27% in total OECD electric-lamp exports, than the factor endowments of the Netherlands.

Indispensability of imports caused by adjustment costs

If the output of one sector is to be expanded, either by using idle resources or by freeing resources through the contraction of another sector, this usually causes adjustment costs. These occur prior to the gains from the expansion of the sector concerned. Hence, for such an import substitution to be profitable, it is not enough if the welfare derived from the consumption after the operation exceeds that prior to it Instead, the gain should not only be positive, but the discounted gain must exceed the adjustment costs. Even if the eventual rise of consumptio is considerable and permanent, it may nevertheless be insufficient to offset adjustment costs, specifically if the discount rate is high. This argument, essentially boiling down to Samuelson's (1975), depends on two assumptions. First, that there is a non-zero rate of discount in the allocation of resources; second that, in contradistinction to the assumptions of both the trade and the trade and growth literature, adjustment is not costless and instantaneous.

A non-zero rate of discount is caused, first of all, by a positive rate of time preference: consuming now is preferred to consuming later. This i reflected in the rate of interest a company has to pay on funds to financ substitution. A second cause is uncertainty. It is not certain that expansion of one sector in favour of another will be profitable; moreover foreign competitors might lower their prices just after the switch has been made. Similarly, the fear of technical progress at home or abroad adds to the rate of discount.

Adjustment costs spring from a number of sources. First, in reality capital is not the perfectly malleable factor that trade theory usually postulates. Instead, if one sector's output is expanded, machines from another sector, or idle ones, have to be converted at some cost. If this is impossible, the old machines are left idle, are scrapped, or, at best, sold abroad at low prices - and new ones have to be installed. Even if capital is perfectly homogeneous and can be shifted instantly, there are still adjustment costs that can prevent an economy to shift its productio to the sectors where it has a long-run comparative advantage. This was recently shown by Manning (1981, p. 258): if an economy maximizes discounted utility when producing two traded consumer goods and one non-traded capital good, a shift of production from the capital-intensive to the other consumer good implies that there is temporarily 'too much' capital in the economy whereas with a shift in the other direction there is 'too little' for optimality; this implies a temporary loss of utility and Manning proves that the discounted long-run gain from the shift can be insufficient to offset the temporary loss.

Similarly, labour is not perfectly homogeneous. To acquire the right kind of labour demands training and takes time. Moreover, only after sufficient time has elapsed, learning by doing raises the level of efficiency sufficiently. This implies a loss of output in the meantime.

Economies of scale are a further, and frequently prohibitive, source of adjustment costs. Specifically in the initial phase, at low levels of output, high unit costs that decrease with output may be expected; this is true even if at higher output levels constant returns prevail.(4) One cause of this phenomenon is high initial investment costs that are only compensated by lowered marginal costs if output is sufficiently large. The consequence is a loss of output in the transition process.

Another source of adjustment costs is that to market the new output, a high initial marketing effort is required; particularly a distribution network has to be established.

The factors causing adjustment costs are likely to be intensified by two developments: technical progress and intra-industry specialization. The former implies increased specialization of labour and capital, since more skills are required from labour and often more specific machinery. Similarly intra-industry specialization increases the division of labour: if a single production process of one final good is split up into two distinct processes, one producing an intermediate good, the other the final good, the gains of the operation are precisely caused by this increased specialization. Consequently, both factors raise dependence on international trade and make substitution more difficult.

Conclusion

Other, minor, phenomena may prevent import replacement. For example, political considerations may play a role: a country may consider an industry vital for national security. Another example is external economies.[5]

All phenomena combined impede the production of perfect domestic substitutes for imports - even if production functions are identical internationally and exhibit constant returns to scale above some level of output. Precise quantitative assessment of the empirical importance of al these factors is impossible, but they clearly affect, one way or another, almost all trade. Consequently, in modern trade, imperfect substitutabibity of imports is the rule rather than the exception; hence for growt purposes Heckscher-Olin type models are inapplicable.

These arguments apply to a country's imports from the rest of the world As opposed to this, the rest of the world, being larger, has more possibilities to substitute for its imports from the country concerned. Nevertheless, usually countries' products are fairly specific and only a limited number of competitors are capable of producing close substitutes; moreover, expansion in these countries is not costless, sometimes only possible to a limited extent or not at all (as with agricultural products), and not always desired; basically the same reasoning given above applies, if to a lesser degree. For the aggregate of its imports, one may expect that the 'rest of the world' substitutes somewhat easier than individual countries, but still imperfectly. This view is borne out by the 'Tinbergen two', that is, for example, found for the elasticity of substitution on the world market for Dutch exports (cf. e.g. Hasselman, Post and Van den Beld, 1977, p. 88). For a 'small' country such as The Netherlands traditional trade theory instead assumes given relative price and an infinite elasticity of foreign demand.

3.2. Imports as an input

The lion's share of international trade is in intermediate products. Traditionally, a large part of total trade was in primary products, most of which serve as intermediate inputs. Table 3.2 shows the share in total world trade of primary products, and fuels in particular. Sources of the table are described in appendix 3.1.

Table 3.2. Share of primary products and fuels in world trade, 1881-1979.

Year	Value share in world trade, % Total primary products (SITC 0-4)	Fuels (SITC 3)
1881	64.4	(2.2)
1900	65.6	n.a.
1913	64.1	4.8
1929	61.9	6.3
1937	63.8	7.5
1953	50.3	10.1
1972	34.5	10.2
1979	38.3	20.3

The table clearly brings out how important this type of trade still is. As is well known, the share has been declining (for total primary products) from roughly two-thirds up to the second world war, to one-third immediately before the oil crisis of 1973. Subsequently the share has risen again, because of the sharp increase of the value of oil. Fuels (oil and coal) are of course the most important primary product. Their share shows a long-term trend from an insignificant 2% a century ago, to an impressive one-fifth now.(6)

In spite of the decline of the share of primary products, trade in inputs dominates world trade as a consequence of the importance of trade in manufactured intermediate goods. This is evident from a quick glance at trade statistics and has been confirmed recently by the systematic evidence provided by UNIDO (1979), summarized in table 3.3.

The table utilizes two alternative classifications: by end-use and by processing stage. The first shows that more than two-thirds of total imports of both developing and developed countries is either industrial input, or fuel. The latter category (21.5% for developed countries and 15.5 for developing) is largely intermediate too.(7) Only 20% of developed countries' imports and 12% of that of developing countries consists of consumption goods, though the latter are the main concern of trade theory. Significantly, the present share of fuels in world trade (cf. table 3.2)

Table 3.3. Distribution of imports over categories of end-use; and of exports over processing stages; developed market economies and developing countries, 1974.

	Imports by end-use Percent of total		Exports by processing stage Percent of total, fuels excluded		
	Developed Market Ec.'s	Develop-ing countries		Developed Market Ec.'s	Develop ing countri
Consumer goods	19.6	11.8	1. Raw materials	11.8	35.3
			2. Processed raw materials	6.7	7.8
Capital goods	11.4	17.2	3. Semi-processed product	9.0	12.6
			4. First transform-ation or raw finished product	13.0	8.3
Industrial inputs, fuels and lubricants	67.7	69.9	5. Second transform-ation or simple finished product	9.7	9.9
			6. Complex finished product	49.9	26.1

Source: UNIDO, 1979, pp. 166; 192.

exceeds that of consumer goods. A similar picture emerges if the breakdow of exports by processing stage is considered: only one-half of the developed countries' exports and a mere one-quarter of that of developing countries is in the final, complex finished products class. Of this category a part is still used for intermediate purposes, though of course part of the less processed products might be delivered to final demand.

The conclusion is clear: trade in intermediate inputs is the bulk of world trade, finished capital and consumption goods are of much less importance. This dominance of intermediates makes it more natural to consider aggregate imports as a factor of production than as a final good. This does not mean that the relevance of such a treatment is restricted to intermediate goods. As noted by Burgess (1974a, p. 104) even final goods usually require further processing, viz. transport and marketing, i.a. distribution. Thus to some extent they too have the character of intermediates.

These facts impose a new basic view of open economies. To get the picture as clear as possible, suppose that a country wants to consume a number of commodities in fixed proportions. Then the traditional view is that a number of them are not produced at home at all, but imported in their finished state. Of a second group, a part is produced from domestic labour and capital (or land) alone and the remainder imported as a finished good. A third group is similarly produced and a part is exported. Instead, consideration of empirical data like those just quoted, leads to the view that such a country imports virtually all commodities in different stages of completion and, to obtain final goods, adds the required amounts of domestic factors. In the same way, it may be expected that almost all commodities are exported, also in different stages of production. By varying the import content (processing stages) of individual final products, substitution between imports and domestic factors is possible and imports are determined so as to maximize the level of consumption.

In this argument, substitutability of imports and domestic factors depends on the assumption that for each individual product substitution of imports is possible. Above, we argued that such substitution is almost never perfect, but this does not mean that none at all is possible. Frequently the same, or almost the same, product is imported simultaneously in different stages of processing (simultaneous imports of crude oil and refined products, etc.). Changing the share of each stage then provides for substitutability of imports, even if the composition of final demand is constant. Note that this argument is analogous to the wellknown Houthakker (1955/6)-Levhari (1968)-Sato (1975) distribution-function approach to the derivation of aggregate production functions.[8] Apart from this, the possibility of substitution between aggregate imports and domestic factors does not depend exclusively on the substitutability of imports of individual products. Instead, substitutability of aggregate imports is achieved by varying the product composition of final demand.

As a consequence, the most natural way to describe aggregate imports i as an input in a national production function, allowing for substitution between domestic factors and imports.(9) Whether this yields a reasonabl stable function, is essentially an empirical question. Fortunately, empirical evidence is now becoming available. Burgess (1974a) directly estimates a production function along these lines for the US; the dual cost functions are estimated by Burgess (1974b) for the US, by Kohli (1978) for Canada and by Kreijger (1980) for The Netherlands. Results ar encouraging: good fits and low standard errors for the coefficients of t translog production and costs functions employed; the (Allen) elasticiti of substitution between imports and domestic factors differ significantl from zero and frequently exceed unity. A lot more research needs to be done,(10) specifically on the stability of the functions if the sample periods are altered and if inputs and outputs are disaggregated into several commodity classes. But these initial results clearly indicate th imports behave sufficiently regular to validate the imports as an indispensable input approach.

3.3. The production function

This section discusses the assumptions on the production function that will be employed in subsequent chapters. After a discussion of some general properties of the production function we introduce a separabilit assumption that makes it possible to capture in a very direct way the degree of substitutability between imports and domestic factors, or the indispensability of imports, as emphasized above. Finally, in order to b able to derive steady-growth theorems, we introduce conditions on the behaviour of the production function at extreme input ratios; these conditions differ from Inada's well-known ones, not only in that our approach admits elasticities of substitution differing from unity, in contrast to Inada's conditions, but also in that with our conditions models where the long-run factor ratios do not tend to constant values b keep on changing indefinitely can be handled, i.e. by deriving explicit expressions for their asymptotic growth rates; Inada's conditions are on useful for steady-growth analysis if the capital-labour ratio tends to a constant value.

The assumptions introduced in this section are briefly repeated at the points in subsequent chapters where they are used; we just refer back to the present section for their justification and for details. Thus the reader mainly interested in the subjects of subsequent chapters, may consider skipping the present section. The same applies to the remaining sections of this chapter.

Properties of the production function

Throughout this volume we use the neoclassical production function:

$$v = v(\ell, k, m)\exp(\nu t). \tag{3.1}$$

Here v is output, ℓ labour input, k capital input, m imports, t time and ν the rate of technical progress. Throughout this volume a number of assumptions are made.

First, we assume v to be twice continuously differentiable with strictly positive first-order derivatives.

Next we assume output v to be perfectly homogeneous. Instead, one might replace the left-hand side of (3.1) by a function of consumer-goods output, capital-goods output and exports, the latter being mostly intermediate goods. Then, in the long run, divergent price movements of these three outputs may be caused by conditions of international demand and by saving behaviour. These, in turn, might conceivably affect the path of accumulation and income that is our prime concern. In the present study, however, we abstract from this refinement and concentrate directly on aggregate output and income. This has the advantage of simplicity: a one-sector model is obtained. Thus we can construct relatively easily a reference path and analyse its properties. Consequences of refinements are then, in further research, conveniently analysed as divergences from this reference path. Moreover, the latter may well be an adequate representation of what happens in more complicated cases, provided conditions are not too extreme.

We admit Hicks-neutral technical progress. This captures better than the more usual Harrod-neutral labour-augmenting variety the essential feature of technical progress as a prime source of growth quite distinct from factor accumulation. Anyway, our analysis takes Harrodian progress into account as well since we assume a positive rate of labour growth.

Note that we assume that capital and labour are homogeneous over time. Therefore such factors as improved education and knowledge can only ente the production function through the technical-progress term. In empirica studies we should correct for this accumulation of human capital and improvement of physical capital, as e.g. Jorgenson and Griliches (1967) do. But in growth models the exogenous growth term is acceptable; in so far as technical progress is produced it is produced mostly by labour; thus the labour input in the production function may be interpreted as total labour force employed, less the part engaged in producing technica progress. The advantage of this, rather crude, device is that it permits us to avoid the explicit analysis of still another endogenous factor. Fo suggestive work towards a more explicit analysis of technological innovation, cf. Hill and Utterback (1979).

Another assumption maintained throughout is that v is a homogeneous function. But, unlike the usual literature, we do not assume linear homogeneity. Instead we admit both increasing and decreasing returns. Thus, by Euler's rule:

$$\rho v = \ell v_{\ell} + k v_{k} + m v_{m}, \tag{3.2}$$

where $\rho > 0$ represents the rate of returns to scale and v_{ℓ} the first derivative of v to ℓ. One reason to diverge from the constant-returns assumption is that empirical studies frequently point towards increasing returns. For some references at the macro level, cf. e.g. Kennedy and Thirlwall (1973, pp. 130-131); convincing micro evidence is e.g. given f a typical small developing country (Malaysia) by Hoffmann and Weber (1976). Furthermore, the desirability of allowing for increasing returns exists in particular in the presence of international trade, because modern trade is characterized by intra-industry specialization. One of t major causes of such specialization is the economies of scale that can only be exploited by specializing in very specific varieties of final goods or intermediates.(11) Empirical evidence to this effect is found b Finger and De Rosa (1979). To cope with this, Ethier (1979b) suggests to have the rate of returns to scale depend on the size of the world market rather than that of domestic output; the larger an industry is globally, the more intra-industry specialization becomes possible. Instead, we achieve the same by assuming increasing returns to domestic factors and imports combined: an expansion of the three factors implies both increased domestic division of labour and specialization of capital, and international intra-industry specialization.

Of course sometimes a country may face decreasing returns too: if agriculture is substantial, and no fertile unused land idle, or if mines are approaching exhaustion and new ones must be made operational, etc. Therefore, we shall not restrict the analysis to $\rho > 1$, but admit decreasing returns as well.

Separability

Intuitively speaking, the degree of indispensability of imports should be expressed in the elasticity of substitution between imports and domestic factors. However, the latter is not always defined. Rather there are separate elasticities of substitution between each of the domestic factors and imports. Nevertheless for some wellknown specific functions the elasticity of substitution between imports and the domestic factors combined, E, does exist. This is true for the three-factor Cobb-Douglas where E = -1, equal to the elasticity of substitution between the two domestic factors capital and labour, H. It is also true for the three-factor CES function, where E and H are equal and constant but may differ from minus unity. Similarly, E exists and differs from H in the case of Sato's (1967) two-level CES, essentially given by:

$$v = [\{\ell^{\alpha} + k^{\alpha}\}^{\frac{\theta}{\alpha}} + m^{\theta}]^{\frac{\rho}{\theta}} \quad . \; (\theta, \alpha < 1; \; \rho > 0)$$

Here H is given by $-1/(1-\alpha)$, while E can be obtained by defining

$$z = \{\ell^{\alpha} + k^{\alpha}\}^{\frac{1}{\alpha}} ,$$

so that

$$v = \{z^{\theta} + m^{\theta}\}^{\frac{\rho}{\theta}} .$$

The function z is a linear-homogeneous CES function of labour and capita and can be denoted as 'domestic factors'. Then E is simply the elasticit of substitution between z and m, with $E = -1/(1-\theta)$ since v is a CES function (homogeneous of degree ρ) in z and m.

The reason why E can be defined in the above case is that the original function can be 'separated' in a function in $z(\ell,k)$ and m. In general, this is possible if v is separable in the Sono (1945)-Leontief (1947a,b) sense in ℓ and k on the one hand and m on the other. The definition of this concept is that the marginal rate of substitution between ℓ and k i independent of m:

$$\frac{\partial(v_{\ell}/v_k)}{\partial m} = 0. \qquad (3.3)$$

Given this assumption the production function can be 'separated' and written as:

$$v = v'(z(\ell, k), m)\exp(\nu t). \qquad (3.4)$$

This equation says that there is at least one function $z(\ell, k)$ of ℓ and alone, such that total output is a function of z and m. Actually there i a whole class of them; but it can be narrowed down. In the two-level CES case, z was linear homogeneous in ℓ and k, with v homogeneous of degree ρ in z and m. In theorem 3.1 we state that there always is a z th is linear homogeneous in ℓ and k, such that v is homogeneous of degree ρ in z and m. This z is unique up to a scalar multiplier. Thus if e.g., $z(1, 1) = 1$, we have defined a unique linear homogeneous domestic input function.

Theorem 3.1: In (3.4) there is at least one z (ℓ, k) that is linear homogeneous in ℓ and k, with v' homogeneous of degree ρ in z and m; moreover, z is unique up to a scalar multiplier and may be selected so a to have $z(1, 1) = 1$.

Proof: The proof is very simple; for $\rho = 1$, Solow (1955-6, p. 103) prov the first part of the theorem. Thus (dropping the technical progress term):

$$v = [\{v(\ell, k, m)\}^{1/\rho}]^{\rho} = [v''(\ell, k, m)]^{\rho} = [v'''(z, m)]^{\rho}. \quad (3.5)$$

Since the function v" here defined is linear homogeneous, the last equality in (3.5) follows from Solow's result if z is taken linear homogeneous. By defining $v' = [v''']^{\rho}$ we therefore demonstrated the first part of theorem 3.1. Now, by Euler's rule:

$$\rho v = mv_m + zv_z. \quad (3.6)$$

Suppose there are two z's, z_1 and z_2, satisfying (3.5). Then, from (3.6): $z_1 v_{z_1} = z_2 v_{z_2}$, $v_\ell = v_{z_1} z_{1_\ell}$ and similarly for k. Hence:

$$\frac{z_{1_\ell}}{z_{2_\ell}} = \frac{z_{1_k}}{z_{2_k}} = \frac{z_1}{z_2}, \text{ thus } \frac{\partial z_1/z_2}{\partial \ell} = \frac{\partial z_1/z_2}{\partial k} = 0. \quad (3.7)$$

Accordingly all z's are linear functions (with zero intercepts) of one another. Since all linear functions of some z also satisfy (3.5), z is not only unique up to a multiplicative scalar, but may also be selected so as to have z(1, 1) = 1.

Q.E.D.

The separability assumption makes possible a much more lucid and elegant analysis. However, empirically it is not justified. It is rather easy to test the assumption, since it is equivalent to equality of the Allen-Uzawa partial elasticities of substitution labour-imports and capital-imports (cf. e.g. Blackorby, Primont and Russel, 1978, chapter 7). Burgess (1974a, b) and Kreijger (1980) find, for the US and The Netherlands, respectively, significant differences between the two elasticities. Nevertheless we retain the assumption for the same reason we do not distinguish between consumption-, investment- and export-goods: to obtain a clearer insight in the aggregate rate of growth, from which refinements would distract. However, in section 5.1 we show that, at least for the case of our individual-country analysis (chapter 4), relaxing the separability assumption does not make any difference to the main results. Thus, though for estimation purposes separability should not be assumed if biases are to be avoided, for theoretical work the assumption can be conveniently retained.

Share and elasticity functions

Much of our analysis will be carried out in terms of share functions a elasticities, instead of first- and second-order derivatives of the production function, because the former are more appealing intuitively, spite of Samuelson's (1947, p. 125) famous derogatory remarks on them; moreover, it turns out that the analysis is in many instances facilitate by this approach.

Define, for the separable production function:

$$q_m = \frac{1}{\rho}\frac{mv_m}{v} \; ; \; 1 - q_m = \frac{1}{\rho}\frac{zv_z}{v} \; ; \; 0 < q_m < 1. \qquad (3.8)$$

$$q_\ell = \frac{\ell z_\ell}{z} \; ; \; 1 - q_\ell = \frac{kz_k}{z} \; ; \; 0 < q_1 < 1. \qquad (3.9)$$

In (3.8) and (3.9) the second equalities follow from the homogeneity of and z; the restrictions on q_m and q_ℓ are caused by the positivity of the first-order derivatives of v. Under optimizing conditions discussed in t next subsection, the functions q_m and q_ℓ represent imports' value share factor costs and labour's value share in domestic factors. Thus e.g. capital's share in the total value of inputs is $(1 - q_\ell)(1 - q_m)$.

Convenient expressions for second-order derivatives can be obtained in terms of the two direct Hicks-elasticities of substitution; formally, th partial elasticity of capital-labour substitution is defined by:

$$H = \frac{d \ln \ell/k}{d \ln v_\ell/v_k} = \frac{d \ln \ell/k}{d \ln z_\ell/z_k} \text{ (m constant, v constant)}, \qquad (3.10)$$

and the elasticity of imports-domestic factors substitution by:

$$E = \frac{d \ln m/z}{d \ln v_m/v_z} \quad \text{(v constant)}. \qquad (3.11)$$

In appendix 3.2 we show that all first-order derivatives can be expresse in v, ℓ, k, m and the two share functions and that the second-order derivatives can similarly be expressed in these variables, functions and the two elasticities of substitution. Nevertheless, one other function of a second-order derivative is of interest:

$$e = \frac{v_m}{m v_{mm}} , \tag{3.12}$$

under optimizing conditions the elasticity of import demand with respect to the terms of trade. From appendix (3.1) we obtain for the relation between e and E:

$$e = \frac{E}{1 + q_m\{E(\rho-1)-1\}} \ ; \ E = (1-q_m) \frac{e}{1 - q_m e(\rho-1)} \ . \tag{3.13}$$

If there are constant returns, this boils down to the familiar equation $E = e(1 - q_m)$; then e and E always have the same sign. However, if there are increasing or decreasing returns, this need not be the case. This is important, because, as shown in subsection 3.4, one type of optimizing behaviour yields the restriction that e should be negative, whereas another type requires negativity of E. Negativity of e is obtained by the conditions shown in (3.14).

$$e < 0 \quad \begin{cases} \text{if } E < 0, \text{ provided } E > -\dfrac{1 - q_m}{q_m(\rho-1)} \text{ if } \rho > 1 \\ \text{and if } E > -\dfrac{1 - q_m}{q_m(\rho-1)} > 0 \text{ if } \rho < 1. \end{cases} \tag{3.14}$$

Clearly, if the elasticity of substitution is positive and sufficiently large, negativity of e is still obtained if there are decreasing returns. On the other hand, even if E is negative, e need not be negative; under increasing returns a value of the import share too close to unity is a spoil-sport. To clarify the relation between e and E intuitively, consider table 3.4. This table shows, for $q_m = \frac{1}{2}$, the values of e as a function of E for decreasing returns ($\rho = .8$), constant returns and increasing returns ($\rho = 1.2$).

The table clearly shows the divergence from the constant-returns case, and the popping-up of 'wrong' signs of e, that is: signs of e differing from that of E, at the two extremes (decreasing returns and high positive values of E; increasing returns and high negative values of E).

Table 3.4. e as a function of E and ρ; $q_m = \frac{1}{2}$.

		ρ .8	1.0	1.2
	∞	-10.0	∞	10.0
	10	-20.0	20.0	6.7
	5	$\mp\infty$	10.0	5.0
	1	2.5	2.0	1.7
E	0	0	0	0
	- 1	- 1.7	- 2.0	-2.5
	- 5	- 5.0	-10.0	$\mp\infty$
	-10	- 6.7	-20.0	5.0
	$-\infty$	-10.0	$-\infty$	10.0

In table 3.3, the value E = -1 corresponds to a Cobb-Douglas function with m and z as arguments. In that case q_m is a constant and

$$e = \frac{-1}{1 - \rho q_m} \; ; \; q_m = \frac{1 + e}{\rho e} \; . \tag{3.15}$$

If the function v is of the two-level CES type, E is constant, and so i H.

The share and elasticity functions have an important property. The import share, q_m, the elasticity of substitution imports-domestic facto E, and the import-demand elasticity, e, are functions of the ratio of domestic factors to imports, Z = z/m, only; similarly q_ℓ and H are functions of the capital-labour ratio, K = k/ℓ, only. This property is convenient because it implies for example that, once the time path of K determined, that of q_ℓ is also known - without any information about imports being necessary. The property is easily proved.

Theorem 3.2: Define Z = z/m and K = k/ℓ. Then e, E and q_m are functions Z alone, and H, q_ℓ of K alone.

Proof: Define:

$$A(K) = z(1, k/\ell) \quad V(Z) = v(1, z/m). \tag{3.16}$$

Then, using the homogeneity properties of z and v, we have:

$$v = m^{\rho} V \exp(\nu t); \; v_z = m^{\rho-1} V_Z \exp(\nu t);$$

$$v_m = m^{\rho-1}(\rho V - Z V_Z)\exp(\nu t). \tag{3.17}$$

$$\ell = \ell A; \; z_k = A_k; \; z_\ell = A - KA_K. \tag{3.18}$$

Accordingly q_m and v_m/v_z can be written as:

$$q_m = 1 - \frac{ZV_Z}{\rho V} \; ; \; \frac{v_m}{v_z} = \rho \frac{V}{V_Z} - Z. \tag{3.19}$$

Thus, in view of definition (3.16) both q_m and v_m/v_z are functions of Z only. Since E is defined by $d \ln Z/d \ln(v_z/v_m)$ it too is a function of Z alone. By (3.13) e is a function of E and q_m, thus e too depends on Z alone. Proof for H, q_ℓ is analogous.

Q.E.D.

To avoid confusion we note that the statement that H is a function of K alone does not imply that a change in K always results in a change in H. If dH(K)/dK is zero, H is constant, as in the case of CES functions. What the theorem says is that if the elasticity of substitution varies (as e.g. in case of the production function given in appendix 3.3), it varies with K alone, not with both K and either ℓ or k.

The production function at extreme factor ratios

To obtain conclusive results in one-sector growth models, some information is required about the behaviour of the production function at extreme values of the capital-labour ratio. Usually the Inada (1963) conditions (2.2) are imposed. These state that per capita output is zero if per capita capital is zero, and infinite if the latter is infinite; if per capita capital is zero, the marginal increase in output due to a rise in per capita capital is infinite, and it is zero if the capital-labour ratio is infinite. Though these assumptions appear to be perfectly reasonable at first glance, they nevertheless have two disadvantages.

First, in general CES functions do not satisfy them. If the elasticity of substitution is smaller than minus one, $v(0, 1) = 0$ is violated; if it exceeds minus unity $v_K(0, 1) = \infty$ is violated. Only if the elasticity of substitution is minus unity, the Cobb-Douglas case, Inada's conditions ar satisfied. This has led him (1968b) to suggest that the conditions imply that the elasticity goes to minus one as the capital-labour ratio goes to zero, but he has not succeeded in proving or disproving this. The limitation of Inada's condition is not innocuous. At one extreme, gathering and hunting societies[(12)] achieve non-zero output per capita without capital (implying an elasticity of substitution below minus unity). At the other extreme, in post-industrial societies the increased demand for outputs for which the possibilities of capital-labour substitution are limited (a number of services such as medicare, arts, education, science, social and psychological training), possibly combined with saturation in the demand for output of high-substitution sectors, depresses the aggregate substitution possibilities. Moreover, increasing scarcity of natural resources and destructive cumulative effects of pollution may well imply that, with labour forces constant, much of the capital accumulation in the industrial sector goes into maintaining outp (conventionally measured) at the same level, though with less pollution and a decreased volume of resource inputs. This would imply that, as per capita capital grows, per capita output reaches a maximum - whereas Inada's conditions imply that it would become infinite. Rostow (1976; 1978, p. 653) argues that, though important, these phenomena will not prevent a rise in per capita income - not even of its traditional components. Nevertheless it is desirable to use a production function th can handle them if only because there are economists (e.g. Daly, 1977) w believe that maximum output is almost upon us.

The second disadvantage of Inada's conditions is somewhat less obvious but for our purpose even more prohibitive. In the closed one-sector mode of economic growth, under constant returns and with no (Hicks-neutral) technical progress, Inada's conditions guarantee existence and neat convergence to a unique constant capital-labour ratio (growth at the natural rate). But this is no longer true under increasing returns and technical progress; then labour is no longer the sole prime mover of growth and the long-run growth rate depends on the interplay of the basic sources of growth. The interplay of labour and technical progress depends on the properties of the production process. Consequently, the characteristics of the production function enter the long-run growth rate; the capital-labour ratio does not tend to a constant value, but increases steadily. Under these circumstances Inada's conditions are insufficiently informative. They only determine total per capita output and marginal productivity but not e.g. the competitive shares of factors and the elasticities of substitution at these values.(13) To determine the way the prime sources of growth combine in the long-run growth rate, precisely these shares and elasticities should be known. In our case this deficiency is even more serious, because, apart from non-constant returns and technical progress, we also have to deal with imported inputs. This alone implies that Inada's conditions cannot be used.

As noted above, the previous authors that followed the approach of treating imports as an indispensable input, solve the problem by considering specific production functions. Johnson (1953), Verdoorn (1956), Chenery and Bruno (1962) use functions with complementarity; Khang (1968) and Bardhan (1970) Cobb-Douglas functions; and Itsumi and Morigushi (1978) assume complementarity of imports and domestic factors, the latter being a Cobb-Douglas function of labour and capital.

We admit all non-zero, finite values of the two elasticities of substitution and do not restrict them to be constant throughout. Instead, to replace Inada's conditions, we assume only that the elasticities and shares become constant at infinite input ratios. Thus if $K \to 0$, q_ℓ and H attain constant values and if $Z \to 0$ the same applies to E, e, q_m. Actually a somewhat weaker and more attractive set of assumptions is possible, viz. that just the elasticities move to finite, non-zero values and are monotone for extreme values of the factor ratios. This already implies that the shares have limits. The limits of the shares are zero or one if the limits of the elasticities of substitution are not equal to minus one; if the latter are minus one, the shares have intermediate values. We now state these ideas somewhat more formally in theorem 3.3.

Theorem 3.3:

(1) $\lim q_m$ $(Z \to \infty)$ exists if $\lim E(Z \to \infty)$ exists, provided E is monotone

for high Z.

(2) Lim q_m $(Z \to \infty)$ exists if lim $e(Z \to \infty)$ exists, provided e is monoton for high Z.

(3) Lim $E(Z \to \infty)$ exists if lim $e(Z \to \infty)$ exists, provided e is monotone for high Z and $\lim\{e(\rho-1) - 1\} < 0$ (strictly).

(4) For $Z \to 0$, (1), (2) and (3) also hold true, mutatis mutandis.

(5) Lim $q_\ell(K \to \infty)$ exists if lim $(K \to \infty)$ exists, provided H is monotone for high K.

(6) Mutatis mutandis, (5) also holds true for $K \to 0$.

(7) Let E be non-zero and finite for all Z. Also let q_m be non-zero and unequal to one as long as Z is non-zero and finite. Let the assumptions of (1) and (4), or those of (2), (3) and (4) be satisfied. Then q_m may have any limit on (0,1) if lim E = -1 $(Z \to \infty$ or $Z \to 0)$; if lim E ≠ -1 the limits of q_m are zero or one, indicated in table 3.5.

(8) Mutatis mutandis (7) also holds true for H, q_ℓ, K.

Table 3.5. Limits of share functions.

		$\lim_{Z\to\infty} q_m$	$\lim_{Z\to 0} q_m$
$\lim_{Z\to\infty} E$	> -1		1
	< -1		0
$\lim_{Z\to 0} E$	> -1		0
	< -1		1

Remark: It is convenient to have a short-hand notation for the limits of the functions. Accordingly define:

$E_0 = \lim E(Z \to 0);$

$\varepsilon_0 = \lim e(Z \to 0);$

$\xi_{m0} = \lim q_m(Z \to 0);$

$H_0 = \lim H(K \to 0);$

$$\zeta_{\ell 0} = \lim q_{\ell}(K \to 0),$$

and similar definitions for $Z \to \infty$ and $K \to \infty$.

Proof:

(1), (5) Differentiate the definitions of q_m and q_ℓ with respect to Z and K, respectively. This yields the analogon of Solow's (1959, p. 629) equation for the elasticity of labour's share with respect to the capital-labour ratio in the closed neoclassical model.

$$\frac{dq_m}{dZ} = - \frac{q_m(1-q_m)}{Z} \left(\frac{1+E}{E}\right). \tag{3.20}$$

$$\frac{dq_\ell}{dK} = - \frac{q_\ell(1-q_\ell)}{K} \left(\frac{1+H}{H}\right). \tag{3.21}$$

Consider (3.20). Let $Z \to \infty$. Since E is monotone for high Z, there exists a Z' with E either above minus one, or below it, for all $Z > Z'$ possibly converging towards minus one, but never oscillating about it). Hence by (3.20) q_m is monotone too. As q_m is bounded by zero and one, the limit exists. Proof for q_ℓ is similar.

(2) Equation (3.20) may be transformed, using (3.13):

$$\frac{dq_m}{dZ} = - \{1 + \frac{1}{e} - \rho q_m\} \frac{q_m}{Z} \equiv - G \frac{q_m}{Z} . \tag{3.22}$$

Let $Z \to \infty$. Above some Z' the function 1/e of Z (cf. theorem 3.2) is monotone, since e is so by assumption. Suppose 1/e is increasing. Let $G < 0$ at some point. Then $dq_m/dZ > 0$, hence $-q_m$ decreases. Thus the increase of 1/e pushes G upward but the decrease of $-\rho q_m$ downward. Accordingly, either G remains negative for all $Z > Z'$, implying that q_m is monotone and the limit exists, or G becomes zero at some value of Z. In the latter case q_m can remain constant, namely if e is constant, and q_m attains the limit $q_m = \frac{1+e}{\rho e}$. If q_m does not remain constant, G becomes positive at, say, Z". Then q_m decreases as Z increases, hence $-\rho q_m$ increases and (as $\frac{1}{e}$ is nondecreasing) G remains positive for all $Z > Z''$. Hence q_m is monotone and as it is bounded the limit exists. Proof for the case where 1/e is decreasing is similar.

(3) The condition $e(\rho - 1) - 1 < 0$ implies that the denominator of the right-hand side of the second equality in (3.13) cannot be zero. Hence, since $\lim e(Z \to \infty)$ and $\lim q_m(Z \to \infty)$ exists, so doe $\lim E(Z \to \infty)$.

(4) (6) Proof is completely similar to that of (1), (2), (3), (5).

(7) By (1)-(4) the limits exist; the Cobb-Douglas satisfies the assumptions and can generate any value for q_m on (0,1). Note the the statement does not say that $q_m = 0$ or 1 is impossible.

Of the other statements we prove that $\lim E < -1$ $(Z \to \infty)$ implies $\lim q_m = 0$ $(Z \to \infty)$. Suppose not. Then q_m converges to some limit $\neq 0$. Thus a Z' exists with $q_m(Z') \neq 0$ and $E < -1$ fo $Z > Z'$ (note that this holds true whether or not E is monotone, since $\lim E \neq -1$). Thus, from (3.20):

$$\int_{q_m(Z')}^{\lim q_m} \frac{dq_m}{q_m(1-q_m)} = \int_{Z'}^{\infty} \frac{1+E}{E}\frac{dZ}{Z} < \int_{Z'}^{\infty} \alpha \frac{dZ}{Z} . \tag{3.23}$$

Here α is some strictly negative finite (as $E \neq -\infty$) constant, either equal to $\lim(1+E)/E$ (if E increases) or to $\{1 + E(Z')\}/E(Z')$ if E decreases. Evaluating the integrals we must have:

$$\ln(\lim q_m) - \ln(1 - \lim q_m) - \ln q_m(Z') + \ln\{1 - q_m(Z')\} < \alpha(\ln \infty - \ln Z'). \tag{3.24}$$

The right-hand side of (3.24) is minus infinity, as α is negative; the left-hand side is finite, as by assumption $\lim q_m \neq 0$. Hence a contradiction is obtained and we must have $\lim q_m(Z \to \infty) = 0$. The remainder of (7) and (8) is proved similarly.

Q.E.D.

In the next chapter we shall show that the long-run growth rate of an individual open economy can be expressed in the growth rates of labour, foreign demand, technology and in the limiting values of elasticities anc shares as Z, $K \to 0, \infty$. The latter exist under the assumptions of theorem 3.3. These are not very restrictive. They only exclude perfect substitutability, perfect complementarity and oscillatory behaviour of the elasticities of substitution at extreme factor ratios; none of these possibilities are particularly interesting or realistic.

Our conditions cover a wide range of functions. First, of course, they include the Cobb-Douglas and other CES-type functions; in that alone they are more useful than Inada's (1963) conditions, particularly if the latters' (1968b) hunch is correct that his conditions imply a unit asymptote of the elasticity of substitution. Consequently, our conditions are capable of handling both models for 'gathering and hunting societies', post-industrial 'limits to growth' economies and all cases in between.

In addition to being quite general, our conditions are very practical in the analysis of growth because they provide explicit expressions for the elasticities and shares at extreme factor ratios, while admitting fluctuations in between. Thus the elasticities of substitution may have unit asymptotes - implying that all factors retain non-zero value shares - combined with variable, non-unit elasticities in the intermediate range. Appendix 3.3 provides an example of such a function, the 'Transitional Function'. Its elasticity of substitution is minus unity at a zero-valued capital-labour ratio, next either increases or decreases to some value as K increases and subsequently again converges to minus unity. As a consequence, the factor shares display a transition between two values as the capital-labour ratio grows.

The conditions of theorem 3.3 are sufficient to obtain steady-growth theorems in the analysis of individual countries, both if separability is assumed (chapter 4) and, with some minor modification, if separability is dropped (section 5.2). However, when a full-fledged two-region system is analysed (chapter 6) further restrictions are required, just as in the HOS two-sector growth models Inada's conditions must be supplemented in the two-country case.

3.4. Import demand

In determining the demand for inputs, there are two distinct questions. The first one takes for granted the existence of a macro production function with homogeneous inputs and outputs and some kind of aggregate optimal behaviour. Then the question is, what the input demand functions are under the various kinds of optimal behaviour that are conceivable. The second question is, how such a macro production function and the optimal behaviour can come about in a world where only micro production functions and decision makers, equipped with heterogeneous capital, have tangible existence.

In the case of constant returns to scale the answer to the first question is particularly simple. One may assume that prices of factors and output are given, and either maximize profits, or maximize output subject to a nonnegativity constraint on profits. Alternatively, factor prices and the volume of output may be given and factor costs minimized. All this yields the same equality of input-output terms of trade to marginal productivity. Moreover, if factor prices and a Marshallian demand curve are given, profit maximization still, implicitly, yields the same 'factor demand' (cf. Samuelson, 1978d).

The aggregation problem is more complicated, but various solutions have been found for the constant-returns case. The simplest one, though involving the most stringent conditions, is the Solow (1964) - Fisher approach (for a summary, cf. Fisher, 1969). In this approach micro production functions should be almost identical.(14) We could without difficulty generalize this type of analysis to include imported inputs, a long as these are perfectly homogeneous. The alternative way to achieve exact aggregation, the efficiency distribution approach (Houthakker, 1955/6, Levhari, 1968, Sato, 1975), imposes less stringent conditions on the macro functions, but instead requires that the distribution of output over firms (i.e. over efficiency characteristics) satisfies regularity conditions. A third, and perhaps the most promising, approach, is to require that aggregation is only approximately valid. Fisher (1971) and Fisher, Solow and Kearl (1977) show by simulation experiments that, thoug micro functions of Cobb-Douglas and CES type, respectively, do not satisf the conditions for exact aggregation, nevertheless a stable macro production function can be established under fairly general circumstances with wages equal to the macro marginal productivity of labour.

If non-constant returns prevail, things get more complicated. We mainly consider the first type of question: the shape of the input demand functions. The generalization of the three approaches to aggregation to the case of non-constant returns would probably require another book. Therefore we do not attempt this, but give only some elementary examples, using Marshall's representative-firm device: all firms have identical production functions and endowments.

Profit maximization with non-constant returns

First consider the case that profits are maximized, given factor prices and an expected price of output. The maximizer considers the supply of imports to be perfectly elastic, but recognizes maximum levels for capital and labour. Denote expected profits by w^e and the expected price of output by p^e; maximum levels of ℓ and k are ℓ_{max} and k_{max}. The problem is:

$$\text{maximize } w^e = p^e v - \ell p_\ell - k p_k - m p_m, \qquad (3.24)$$
$$\text{subject to } \ell \leq \ell_{max} \ ; \ k \leq k_{max} \ .$$

The cases of increasing and decreasing returns yield different results. First consider that of decreasing returns, $\rho < 1$. Then either capital and labour attain their maximum levels, a case considered below, or an interior profit maximum exists. The first-order conditions are:

$$v_a = p_a/p^e \quad (a = \ell, k, m). \qquad (3.25)$$

Expected profits thus are, using Euler's rule:

$$w^e = p^e(1 - \rho)v \ . \qquad (3.26)$$

Clearly expected profits are positive. Accordingly, if the true price were to equal the expected one ($p = p^e$), there is a positive profit. This is the notorious 'adding-up problem', debated at the beginning of the century, cf. Hicks (1932, pp. 233-239). What happens to the surplus?

One assumption would be that it goes to the owners of capital. Let P, P_ℓ, P_k denote the actual terms of trade between output and imports, output and labour, and output and capital, respectively; thus these terms of trade are after redistribution of the surplus and show the quantity of output one unit of input actually receives. Then we have, if all profits go to capital owners:

$$P_k^{-1} = v_k + \frac{v}{k}(1 - \rho);$$
$$P_\ell^{-1} = v_\ell \ ; \ P^{-1} = v_m. \qquad (3.27)$$

We prefer, however, another assumption that corresponds somewhat closer to conditions of perfect competition: the neutral case obtained by redistribution of the surplus according to the expected cost shares:

$$P_a^{-1} = v_a/\rho \quad (a = \ell, k); \ P^{-1} = v_m/\rho. \qquad (3.28)$$

One way to derive this condition from micro behaviour, is to take into account that production takes time. If all firms have identical production functions and periods and expect the same price, they all make their production decisions the same period of time before the output becomes available. If factors are paid in money terms, the money stock is held constant and money is used for transactions only (no (dis)savings), competitive pressure lowers the money price of output in the interval while production takes place, up to the point where profits are zero.(15) This implies that in an economy with decreasing returns there may be a deflationary tendency.(16)

This argument still poses a few conundrums, notably how expectations of the factor owners should be worked out. However, (3.28) can also be derived under other assumptions about production behaviour than straightforward profit maximization, as will be shown below.

The case where capital and labour attain their maximum levels does not pose any basically new problems: expected profits are simply somewhat lower than without maximum levels. Clearly, though, there is no natural way to obtain (3.28). One way to get rid of the surplus problem would be to assume that the surplus fully goes to the two scarce factors, labour and capital. In that case the import demand equation would be $P^{-1} = v_m$. This would, for example, be the result if firms are forced to supplement wages and capital renumeration in order to assure future availability of these scarce factors.

Next consider the case of <u>increasing returns</u>, $\rho > 1$. If there would be no factor constraints, output and profits are expanded to infinity. Thus at least one of the domestic factors is used at its maximum level; full employment of the other factor can always be achieved by assuming its factor price to be sufficiently low. Then maximization of expected profits yields for imports: $v_m = p_m/p^e$. The expected profits are positive if the maximum levels of capital and labour are not too low. The most natural assumption about the distribution of profits then again is that it goes to the two scarce factors. Accordingly profit maximization under increasing returns yields for the import-demand equation:

$$p^{-1} = v_m. \qquad (3.29)$$

This equation is compatible with a competitive output market, notwithstanding the presence of increasing returns: let labour and capital not only be fixed, but also immobile between firms, with identical production functions and equal endowments for all firms; then (3.29) is immediately obtained. Of course, this is unrealistic in the long run, specifically where the immobility of factors between firms is concerned. But it takes more time to shift capital and labour about than to contract or expand imports. Accordingly, a temporary equilibrium exists, without immediate emergence of a monopoly. In the long run, though, monopolistic tendencies must exist, but are counteracted by innovation. Actually, situations with many small companies immediately after a major innovation and monopoly or olichopoly afterwards, are not uncommon.

Cost minimization with output constraint

Frequently firms do not maximize expected profits, given an expected price of output, but instead first determine the quantity of output the market can bear at some price level and next proceed to produce that output against minimal costs (cf. e.g. Brems, 1959). Thus we obtain the problem:

$$\text{Minimize } \ell p_\ell + kp_k + mp_m, \text{ subject to } v = v^*. \qquad (3.30)$$

Here v* is planned output. This yields the first-order conditions:

$$v_a = p_a/L \quad a = \ell, k, m. \qquad (3.31)$$

Here L is the Lagrange multiplier. Let all firms have identical productio functions and the same planned outputs. Then competitive pressures only allow them to realize these planned outputs at zero profits, implying:

$$p = \frac{\ell p_\ell + kp_k + mp_m}{v} . \qquad (3.32)$$

Hence the Lagrange multiplier is given by $L = \rho p$. Therefore from (3.31) w obtain, in a quite natural way, the factor-demand equations (3.28).

The foregoing shows that with non-constant returns, the factor-demand equation is not unambiguously determined, but depends crucially on the choice of the way of distributing profits and that of the optimization rule. The most natural import-demand equation is the one given in (3.28). Therefore we shall use this equation in subsequent chapters. Nevertheless an element of arbitrariness remains. Therefore we consider on occasion th consequences of using (3.29) instead. Fortunately, for the analysis of growth, the difference between the two is unimportant.

Second-order conditions

Under unconstrained profit maximization, v should be concave, implying decreasing returns and negative elasticities of substitution. If capital and labour are fixed, a sufficient second-order condition is $v_{mm} < 0$, implying negativity of the terms of trade elasticity of import demand. If however, costs are minimized subject to an output constraint, quasi-concavity of v is sufficient:

$$\begin{vmatrix} 0 & v_\ell & v_k \\ v_\ell & v_{\ell\ell} & v_{\ell k} \\ v_k & v_{\ell k} & v_{kk} \end{vmatrix} > 0; \quad \begin{vmatrix} 0 & v_\ell & v_k & v_m \\ v_\ell & v_{\ell\ell} & v_{\ell k} & v_{\ell m} \\ v_k & v_{\ell k} & v_{kk} & v_{km} \\ v_m & v_{\ell m} & v_{km} & v_{mm} \end{vmatrix} < 0. \qquad (3.33)$$

These last two principle minors of the bordered Hessian can be written as respectively (using the appendix formulas):

$$\frac{-\rho^3 v^3 (1-q_m)^3 q_\ell (1-q_\ell)}{\ell^2 k^2 H} \; ; \; \frac{-\rho^4 v^4 q_m q_\ell (1-q_m)^2}{\ell^2 k^2 m^2 EH} \, . \tag{3.34}$$

Clearly, the sign conditions in (3.33) are met as soon as both elasticities of substitution are negative:

$$E, H < 0. \tag{3.35}$$

In the preceeding section we noted that this is not a sufficient condition for negativity of the import-demand elasticity: even if (3.35) holds, e can be positive, viz. under increasing returns. Thus output-constrained cost minimization yields, as should be the case, less restrictive second-order conditions than profit maximization. Below, we shall only assume (3.35).

3.5. Defining a corresponding autarkic economy

Modern trade is indispensable to national production. Therefore autarkic production is almost impossible. If, for whatever reason, an economy might nevertheless wish to produce in autarky, a change in production techniques is involved. The smooth opening up of a non-trading economy to trade is a very imaginary thing. This implies that there is no ready definition of an autarkic economy corresponding to the one described by equation (3.1). Clearly, the theory of trade presented here is not designed to demonstrate gains from trade, but simply assumes that the losses from no trade are too massive to admit autarky. Nevertheless it is convenient to define an 'autarkic economy' that is technologically as similar to the trading one as possible, but achieves all the advantages the latter derives from trade, without any trade. The differences between this illusory closed economy and the open one show the effects of international developments on national growth that are caused precisely by the impossibility of open economies to do without trade and that are neglected by closed-economy theory and traditional trade and growth theory alike.

Every definition is to some extent arbitrary. The most useful one is the one corresponding as closely as possible to the open economy. If the open-economy production function is not separable between imports and domestic factors, the only parameters that can be preserved are the rates of returns to scale and technical progress. In the more convenient case of separability a more elegant definition is possible:

$$v_{au} = \{z(\ell, k)\}^{\rho}\exp(\nu t), \tag{3.36}$$

where v_{au} is autarkic output and z is the domestic factor function defined in (3.4). Proceeding this way not only ρ and ν are preserved, but also labour's (q_ℓ) and capital's share, and the elasticity of substitution between capital and labour.

One way to derive a function such as (3.36), would be to proceed as if the economy were also capable of producing the imports domestically; then (3.36) would be the net result of a two-sector model with inter-industry flows. In this line of thought one could, like Samuelson (1965) and Chacoliades (1978, pp. 229-233), derive 'sweeping theorems', stating that if e.g. the gross functions are homogeneous and concave, so are the net functions. However, in our case the whole argument centers on the impossibility of producing the imports domestically; the function (3.36) is a purely imaginary construct designed to obtain a reference path. If in reality a country would have to produce its imports domestically, this would mean that export- and domestic goods-sectors have to be contracted to such an extent that none of the characteristics of the production function (3.1) needs to be valid any more.

Appendix 3.1. Tables 3.1 and 3.2, methods and sources

Table 3.1.

Sources of the trade statistics are: UNO, Commodity Trade Statistics (1976); UNO, Yearbook of International Trade Statistics (1976); FAO, Trade Yearbook, vol. 32 (1978). Production data are taken from: UNO, Yearbook of Industrial Statistics, vol. II (1976); FAO, Production Yearbook, vol. 32 (1978).

Most trade flows are analysed at the 3- and 4-digit SITC (rev. 1) level; occasionally 2-digit flows are comparable with production statistics and in some cases 5-digit data were used to achieve this.

The trade flows included are:

(i) Those in crude products of which domestic production is less than 20% of imports.

(ii) Simple transformations of the crude products of the previous category.

Thus, if e.g. soybean production is less than 20% of imports of soybeans (SITC 221.4), not only this flow is included, but also imports of soybean cake and meal (SITC 081.31) and of soya bean oil (SITC 421.2). Similarly, if production of iron ores and concentrates (SITC 281) is less than 20% of imports, the imports of iron and steel scrap (SITC 282) are also included. In addition petroleum imports of the US are included.

The commodities included under the above rule are (SITC, rev. 1 classification between brackets):

All four countries: coffee (071), cocoa (072), vanilla (075.21), natural rubber (231.1), jute (264), vegetable fibres excl. cotton & jute (265), petroleum and products (33).

Germany, Japan and Netherlands: maize (044), raisins (051.6), nuts, edible (051.7), dates (051.96), vegetable oil residues (081.3), oil seeds, nuts and kernels (221), cotton (263), wool, grease and degreased (268.1,2), natural calcium, phosphates, etc. (271.3), iron ore and concentrates (281), iron and steel scrap (282), fixed vegetable oils and fats (42).
Germany and Netherlands: rice, paddy (042), oranges, tangerines,

clementines (051.1), lemons, grapefruit, etc. (051.2), bananas (051.3), tea (074.1), pepper & pimento (075.1), tobacco (12), sulphur (274), non-ferrous metal ores & concentrates (283), non-ferrous metal scrap (284).
USA: bananas (051.3), coconuts (051.71), tea (074.1), sesame seed (222.5) rape & mustard seed (222.6), palm nuts & kernels (223.3), silk (261), bauxite (283.3), tin ores & concentrates (283.6), manganese ore (283.7), chromium ore & concentrates (283.91), aluminium scrap (284.04), magnesium scrap (284.05), tin scrap (281.09), olive oil (421.5), rape & colza & mustard oil (421.7), palm oil (422.2), coconuts, copra oil (422.3), palm kernel oil (422.4), castor oil (422.5).
Germany: tomatoes (054.4), onions (ex.054.5), silk (261).
Japan: horsemeat (011.5), wheat & flour (041), barley (043), rye (045.1), oats (045.2), cereals NES (045.9), lemons and limes (051.21), bovine & equine hides, raw (211.1), sheepskins with and without wool (211.6, 7), goat and kid skins, raw (211.4), natural abrasives, NES (277), copper ores & concentrates (283.1), nickel ores & concentrates (283.2), bauxite (283.3), manganese ore (283.7), copper waste & scrap (284.02), nickel waste & scrap (294.04), aluminium scrap (284.4).

Table 3.6. Value of domestic production of table 3.1 commodities, as a percentage of imports.

	USA	FR Germany	Japan	Netherlands	Four countries combined
0	.06	2.8	2.3	.6	1.5
1	-	0	-	0	0
2	5.8	1.1	1.4	0	1.6
3	-	3.8	.2	1.7	1.6*
4	0	0	0	0	0
0-4	1.3*	3.0	.7	1.3	1.5

* Excluding petroleum and products, USA.

Netherlands: horsemeat (011.5), cereals, NES (045.0), leguminous vegetables, dry (054.2), grapes (051.5), natural honey (061.6), wine, vermouth and similar (112.1), natural abrasives NES (277), coal, coke & briquettes (32).

For most of these commodities domestic production is far less than 20% of imports. Table 3.6 shows the actual percentage for each one-digit SITC-classes; domestic production is evaluated at import unit-values; the data show the percentage domestic production constitutes of the imports included in the above list, not of total imports in each SITC class.

Table 3.2

For the share of total primary products, sources are as follows. 1881, 1900: Lewis (1952), whose data are based on Hilgerdt's revision of his League of Nations work (Hilgerdt, 1945). For 1913, 1929, 1937: Yates (1959, pp. 222-223). For the overlapping years the correspondence between Lewis' and Yates' figures is quite good. For 1953, 1972, 1979: various issues of the UNO Monthly Bulletin of Statistics. All data refer to exports and are FOB.

From 1913 onward, the shares of fuel have been taken from the same sources as the primary totals. The estimate for 1881 is obtained from Mulhall (1909, p. 130). Mulhall shows two relevant tables: for 1880 the tonnage of sea-borne merchandise, i.a. that of coal and petroleum. A second table shows, for the same categories, total tonnage and total value of sea-borne merchandise in the 27-year period ending in 1887. From the latter table unit-values have been calculated and applied to the tonnage for 1880 to obtain an estimate for the 1880 value share.

Appendix 3.2. Derivatives and Allen partial elasticities of substitution of a separable function

This appendix gives expressions for the first- and second-order derivatives and for the Allen partial elasticities of substitution of the three-factor separable function in terms of the rate of returns to scale, the two share functions and the two Hicks elasticities of substitution defined in the text.

From (3.8) we obtain for the first-order derivatives:

$$v_m = q_m \frac{\rho v}{m} . \tag{3.37}$$

$$v_\ell = v_z z_\ell = q_\ell(1 - q_m) \frac{\rho v}{\ell} . \tag{3.38}$$

$$v_k = (1 - q_\ell)(1 - q_m) \frac{\rho v}{k} . \tag{3.39}$$

Definition (3.11) of E can be restated as (cf. e.g. Krelle, 1969, p. 108)

$$E = \frac{mv_m + zv_z}{v_m} . \frac{v_m v_z}{v_{mm}v_z^2 + v_{zz}v_m^2 - 2v_m v_z v_{mz}} . \tag{3.40}$$

Using the homogeneity condition (3.6) we obtain:

$$\rho\text{-}1 = \frac{zv_{mz} + mv_{mm}}{v_m} = \frac{mv_{mz} + zv_{zz}}{v_z} . \tag{3.41}$$

With (3.41), and using definition (3.12) of e, we obtain (3.13). Also using the similar equations in ℓ, k and H, we obtain for the second-order derivatives:

$$v_{mm} = \frac{\rho q_m v}{m^2} . \frac{1+q_m\{E(\rho-1)\}}{E} . \tag{3.42}$$

$$v_{\ell\ell} = \frac{\rho q_\ell(1-q_m)v}{\ell^2} [\frac{1-q_\ell}{H} + q_\ell\{(1-q_m)(\rho-1) + \frac{q_m}{E}\}]. \tag{3.43}$$

$$v_{m\ell} = \frac{\rho q_m q_\ell(1-q_m)v\{E(\rho-1)-1\}}{m\ell E} . \tag{3.44}$$

$$v_{k\ell} = \frac{\rho q_\ell(1-q_m)(1-q_\ell)v}{k\ell}\left[-\frac{1}{H} + (1-q_m)(\rho-1) + \frac{q_m}{E}\right] . \qquad (3.45)$$

Equations for v_{kk} and v_{km} are symmetrical to $v_{\ell\ell}$ and v_{km}: replace the ℓ's by k's and q_ℓ by $(1-q_\ell)$, and vice versa.

In general the Allen partial elasticity of substitution (cf. Allen, 1938, p. 508) between factors x and y, AL_{xy}, is defined by:

$$AL_{xy} = \frac{\sum_{h=\ell,k,m} hv_h}{xy} \frac{F_{xy}}{F} , \qquad (3.46)$$

where F is the determinant of the bordered Hessian as given in the right-hand side of (3.33), while F_{xy} is the cofactor of v_{xy}; thus F_{mm} is the determinant in the extreme left-hand side of (3.33).

Since we only use the Allen-elasticities in the case where constant returns is assumed (cf. section 5.2), we derive their formulas for this case too. Applying the assumption of linear homogeneity to (3.46), we obtain:

$$AL_{xy} = \frac{v}{xy} \frac{F_{xy}}{F}. \qquad (3.47)$$

Using (3.34), we obtain for the Allen-elasticities if the assumption of separability is imposed:

$$AL_{\ell\ell} = \frac{1}{1-q_m} \{q_m E + \frac{H}{q_\ell(1-q_m)}\}. \qquad (3.48)$$

$$AL_{kk} = \frac{1}{1-q_m} \{q_m E + \frac{H}{(1-q_\ell)(1-q_m)}\}. \qquad (3.49)$$

$$AL_{mm} = \frac{1-q_m}{q_m} E. \qquad (3.50)$$

$$AL_{k\ell} = -E + \frac{1}{1-q_m} (E-H). \qquad (3.51)$$

$$AL_{m\ell} = AL_{km} = - E. \qquad (3.52)$$

Appendix 3.3. The Transitional Production Function

This appendix provides an example of a production function that non-trivially satisfies the conditions of theorem 3.3. It has a variable elasticity of substitution that converges to minus unity both at a zero-valued capital-labour ratio and at an infinite ratio. The competitive value share of labour monotonically moves from one value differing from zero and unity at a zero capital-labour ratio to another non-zero, non-unity value at an infinite ratio. Hence the label 'Transitional Producti(Function' is appropriate.

The function is a CES-weighted average (i.e. a weighted harmonic mean) of two Cobb-Douglas functions; for the domestic factor function:

$$z = [\{\ell^{\psi}\ell^{1-\psi}\}^{\theta} + \{\ell^{\phi}k^{1-\phi}\}^{\theta}]^{1/\theta}. \qquad (0 < \phi < \psi < 1) \qquad (3.53)$$

It is easily verified that this function has strictly positive first-orde derivatives and is linear homogeneous in ℓ and k. As shown below, it is strictly quasi-concave provided

$$\theta < \{\frac{\psi - \phi}{\sqrt{\phi(1-\psi)} + \sqrt{\psi(1-\phi)}}\}^2. \qquad (3.54)$$

Labour's competive value share, defined in (3.9) is given by:

$$q_{\ell} = \frac{\psi K^{\psi\theta} + \phi K^{\phi\theta}}{K^{\psi\theta} + K^{\phi\theta}}. \qquad (3.55)$$

Table 3.7. The labour share of the Transitional Production Function at extreme capital-labour ratios.

	θ	
	>0	<0
$\lim_{K\to 0} q_{\ell}$	ϕ	ψ
$\lim_{K\to\infty} q_{\ell}$	ψ	ϕ

As K moves from zero to infinity, q_ℓ moves from ψ to ϕ or vice versa, depending on whether θ is positive or negative; the precise correspondence is shown in table 3.7. For intermediate values of K, q_ℓ takes a value between ϕ and ψ. If, e.g., K = 1, the labour share equals the arithmetic mean of ϕ and ψ.

The elasticity of substitution is given by:

$$H = [-1 + \frac{\theta(\psi-\phi)^2}{\psi(1-\psi)K^{\theta(\psi-\phi)} + \phi(1-\phi)K^{\theta(\phi-\psi)} + \psi(1-\phi) + \phi(1-\psi)}]^{-1}. \quad (3.56)$$

If θ is positive, H is seen to be negative for all values of K as long as (3.54) holds. In that case H is smaller than minus unity and has a minimum value at

$$K = (\frac{\psi(1-\psi)}{\phi(1-\phi)})^{\frac{1}{2\theta(\phi-\psi)}}, \quad (3.57)$$

the minimum of H being:

$$H_{min} = [-1 + \frac{\theta(\psi-\phi)^2}{\{\sqrt{\phi(1-\psi)} + \sqrt{\psi(1-\phi)}\}^2}]^{-1}. \quad (3.58)$$

Thus if θ equals the right-hand side of (3.54), the minimum of H is minus infinity.

If θ is negative, H has a value between minus one and zero, its maximum being attained at value of K given by (3.57) and the value of the maximum being the right-hand side of (3.58).

It is easily verified that the limits of H for $K\to 0$ and $K\to\infty$ are both minus unity. Thus the elasticity of substitution starts at minus unity as K ranges from zero to infinity, monotonically increases to a maximum or decreases to a minimum and then monotonically approaches minus unity again. Clearly this fully corresponds with the conditions imposed in theorem 3.3. Put briefly, the function (3.53) represents a transition of one Cobb-Douglas function to another via an intermediate Variable Elasticity of Substitution stage.

Of course the function v(z,m) can be written completely analogously to (3.53) and does not have to be spelled out explicitly.

It should be noted that one can also obtain a function that represents a transition of one CES function to another, by replacing the two Cobb-Douglas functions in (3.53) with two CES functions. The resulting functio displays a constant, non unit-valued elasticity of substitution at the extremes and a variable elasticity in between.

4. ECONOMIC GROWTH IN ECONOMIES OF MODERATE SIZE: THE CASE OF FREE TRADE AND SEPARABILITY OF IMPORTS AND DOMESTIC FACTORS

In this chapter we investigate the consequences for the economic growth of individual countries of the two central features of modern international trade emphasized in the preceding chapter: the bulk of trade is in intermediates, and imports are indispensable. The first section explains the basic relations and assumptions. These have been selected so as to be applicable to most modern economies: the country they describe is neither very 'large' in the sense that it is capable of influencing the growth rate of world trade, nor so 'small' that it faces given terms of trade. Hence the term 'economy of moderate size' is adopted.

Our prime purpose is the analysis of the rate of growth of income. The literature has found it convenient to investigate the latter by concentrating on the capital-labour ratio. Section 4.2 considers the conditions under which this ratio evolves to a constant value and those under which it eventually becomes infinite or zero; particular attention is paid to the influence of international circumstances. We find that the capital-labour ratio can converge to a constant value in accidental cases only; in general, capital grows either faster or slower than labour. Then the question is, at precisely which rate it grows. This question is tackled in section 4.3. Here we provide a steady-growth theorem that expresses the long-run growth rate of the capital-labour ratio and of per capita income in the basic parameters that summarize the conditions of foreign trade and the structure of production. We take non-constant returns and disembodied technical progress into account. Section 4.4 analyses the long-run growth rate. We do not only consider how the growth rate depends on each of the parameters of our system, but also discuss extensively the difference between the open-economy growth rate and the one that is obtained for a hypothetical corresponding closed economy. The purpose of the latter is to assess to which extent closed-economy growth theory - that is, the main body of growth theory - remains valid for open economies trading in indispensable imports. We find that international circumstances crucially affect the growth rate; the latter usually differs significantly from the rate stipulated by closed-economy analysis. Moreover, in open economies domestic parameters sometimes influence the growth rate in a different way than closed-economy analysis predicts; th is true for e.g. the growth rate of the labour force, labour's share in domestic factors, the rate of technical progress. Consequently, results based on theorizing about closed economies provide at the very best an unreliable first approximation of reality. The consequences of large-sca trade in intermediates without perfect domestic substitutes are too important to ignore.

This result differs, of course, from that based on Heckscher-Ohlin-Samuelson open growth models, where the maintained hypothesis is that perfect domestic substitutes exist for imports. In our case, the growth rate is indeed once again invariant to trade as soon as imports and domestic factors are perfect substitutes, provided there are constant or decreasing returns: in the case of increasing returns the long-run growt rate is altered by trade, even if imports and domestic factors are perfe substitutes. This point is missed in the literature surveyed in chapter because constant returns is another maintained hypothesis throughout.

The present chapter describes in a pocket-sized aggregate theory the essence of the way modern trade links economic growth to circumstances abroad. This provides a good framework in which to discuss the effects o industrial, trade and development policies on growth; such a framework h been sorely lacking so far. Section 4.5 demonstrates how these policies can be discussed using our framework. To this end it first considers the practical interpretation of the parameters relating to trade and the way economic policy can influence them; as a specific example of a policy issue, we show how the framework can be employed to clarify the conditio under which import substitution and export-propelled growth policies are advisable.

4.1. Basic relations and assumptions

As explained *in extenso* in section 3.3, we introduce what we have identified as two central features of modern trade very concisely. Thus all imports, m, are described as a factor of production in the aggregate production function, along with domestic factors labour, ℓ, and capital

$$v = v(z(\ell,k),\ m)\exp(\nu t). \qquad (\nu > 0) \qquad (4.1)$$

Here v denotes output, idealized as a perfectly homogeneous commodity. We allow for Hicks-neutral technical progress at a rate ν; time is denoted by t. In (4.1) the production function is taken to be separable in imports and domestic factors. This allows for a more elegant and straightforward analysis, but, as will be shown in chapter 5, the essential results of the present chapter can also be obtained if the separability assumption is relaxed. As usual, marginal productivities v_a ($a = \ell, k, m$) are strictly positive and v is strictly quasi-concave. Moreove, v is homogeneous of degree $\rho > 0$ in ℓ, k, m; thus we refrain from adopting the customary constant returns to scale, but admit increasing and decreasing returns as well. The function $z(\ell, k)$ is linear homogeneous, implying (cf. theorem 3.1) that v is homogeneous of degree ρ in z and m.

Since no perfect domestic substitutes are produced for imports, import demand depends on input decisions in the framework of the production function (4.1) alone. It is given by the neoclassical equality of marginal productivity to the relative factor price, corrected in the present case by the rate of returns to scale, ρ:

$$v_m = \rho P^{-1}, \qquad (4.2)$$

where P denotes the country's terms of trade, $P = p/\bar{p}$, the ratio of the price of output and exports to the import price.

Under non-constant returns, alternative assumptions about optimizing behaviour yield different import-demand functions that are identical only for constant returns. The alternative to (4.2) is $v_m = P^{-1}$, as shown in section 3.4. The consequences of using this alternative equation are shown to be minor, in section 5.2.

Since chapter 2 has made clear that with indispensable imports the long-run growth rate may depend on international circumstances, we have to provide a description of the latter. Following Khang (1968) and Itsumi and Morigushi (1978), we summarize them in two parameters: the finite terms of trade elasticity of export demand, $\bar{\varepsilon}$, and the exogenous growth rate of foreign demand at constant terms of trade, β.

The introduction of a finite terms of trade elasticity of export demand implies that we do not employ the convenient 'small-country' assumption of a major part of trade theory, i.e. that the terms of trade are exclusively determined by conditions abroad and hence exogenous to the exporting country. Allowing for a finite elasticity is necessary in view of the fact, noted in the last part of section 3.1, that the 'rest of the world usually cannot, at least not immediately, provide perfect substitutes fo the goods imported from any individual country. The terms of trade elasticity is taken to be constant, thus providing the simplest possible characterization of the nature of the country's exports.

With the possible exception of the United States, no single country is so large that its aggregate rate of growth - transmitted abroad by forei trade - significantly influences foreign accumulation. This is expressed by assuming that the growth of foreign demand that is not caused by term of trade changes is exogenous; this (non-price) growth rate of foreign demand is taken constant for convenience. Of course this rate can be influenced by the country, e.g. by altering the commodity composition of its exports. But its value is taken to be independent of the aggregate endogenous variables we deal with.

The country described this way is neither 'small' nor 'large'; we adop Ryder's (1967) term in referring to this type of economy as of 'moderate size'. For practical purposes this term covers virtually all modern economies, the only exceptions being small countries highly specialized a single primary good in which it does not have a monopoly, and, as note above, on the other end of the scale possibly the United States.

Exports are now given by:(1)

$$\bar{m} = \bar{m}_0 P^{\bar{\varepsilon}} \exp(\beta t), \qquad (\bar{\varepsilon} < 0) \tag{4.3}$$

where $\bar{m}_0$ denotes exports $\bar{m}$ at $t = 0$ and $P = 1$.

The description of trade flows is completed by requiring balanced trad

$$\bar{m} = P^{-1} m. \tag{4.4}$$

Equations (4.1)-(4.4) give the terms of trade, exports, imports and outp as functions of labour, capital and time, provided a solution exists. In theorem 4.1 we shall establish that a unique solution exists if either o two sets of conditions is satisfied. The first of these is:

$$e,\ 1/e < -\Delta. \tag{4.5}$$

$$1 + e + \bar{\varepsilon} < -\Delta, \tag{4.6}$$

Δ being some (small) positive constant. Condition (4.5) states that the terms of trade elasticity of import demand, e, (cf. 3.12) is strictly negative and bounded; the former corresponds to v being concave.

The second condition (4.6) is usually referred to as the 'Marshall-Lerner' condition, though this label is rather inappropriate, cf. Chipman (1978, p. 67). Its conventional role is to secure stability of the equilibria of the balance of trade and of demand and supply on the product market. The stability of these equilibria in the presence of imported inputs will be discussed in chapter 8.

Conditions (4.5) and (4.6) are formulated in terms corresponding closely to trade theory. Alternative conditions are linked to production theory, being expressed in terms of the direct Hicks elasticity of substitution between imports and domestic factors, E, (cf. 3.11) and the rate of returns to scale, ρ:

$$E,\ 1/E < -\Delta. \tag{4.7}$$

$$B \equiv 1 + E + \bar{\varepsilon} < -\Delta. \tag{4.8}$$

$$\gamma \equiv \bar{\varepsilon}(\rho-1) + \rho > 0. \tag{4.9}$$

Here (4.7) states strict negativity and boundedness of E; the former is already implied by the strict quasi-concavity of v and only repeated for symmetry. Clearly $E < 0$ is weaker than $e < 0$, the condition given by (4.5). The Marshall-Lerner condition (4.6) is replaced by (4.8) and (4.9). Here (4.8) is stronger than the Marshall-Lerner condition, unless there are substantial decreasing returns; (4.9) precludes an extremely high rate of increasing returns combined with very elastic foreign demand: the latter combination would lead to an infinite expansion of production. Conditions (4.8) and (4.9) taken together imply[2] the Marshall-Lerner condition, provided both $E < 0$ and $e < 0$; but the reverse is not true. Thus neither of the two sets of conditions taken as a whole is just a subset of the other, though there is substantial overlap; only if $\rho = 1$ are both sets equivalent.

Theorem 4.1: If either (4.5) and (4.6), or (4.7), (4.8) and (4.9) are satisfied for all values of ℓ, k, m and t, the system (4.1) - (4.4) has a unique solution, with finite non-zero trade flows.

Proof: First let $\bar{\varepsilon} \neq -1$. Obtain from (4.4) an expression for P. Substitute this into (4.2) and (4.3). Elimination of $\bar{m}$ from the result yields:

$$mv_m^{1+\bar{\varepsilon}} = \rho^{1+\bar{\varepsilon}}\bar{m}_0 \exp(\beta t). \tag{4.10}$$

The right-hand side of (4.10) does not depend on m; the left-hand side a continuous function of m; moreover:

$$\frac{d \ln\{mv_m^{1+\bar{\varepsilon}}\}}{d \ln m} = \frac{1 + e + \bar{\varepsilon}}{e} = \frac{(1-q_m)B + Eq_m\gamma}{E}. \tag{4.11}$$

The second equality in (4.11) is obtained using (3.13); q_m, being imports' value share in total inputs, is positive and smaller than unit Thus assumptions (4.5), (4.6), and (4.7) - (4.9) imply that the right-hand side expressions in (4.11) are strictly positive and bounded from above. Therefore, integrating (4.11) over the boundaries, (4.10) takes all values from zero to infinity as m ranges from zero to infinity, onc and only once. Thus the right-hand side of (4.10) is equal to the left-hand side for precisely one finite, non-zero, value of m. The solutions for the other endogenous variables, $\bar{m}$, P and v, are easily seen to foll suit.

If $\bar{\varepsilon} = -1$, substitution of $P^{-1} = \bar{m}/m$ into (4.3) yields $m = \bar{m}_0\exp(\beta t)$ Then P follows from (4.2) and there always is a positive, unique value of $\bar{m}$ that closes the balance of trade.

Q.E.D.

To complete our picture of the average modern economy, the dynamics mu be specified, specifically the growth of the labour force and the accumulation of capital. We abstract from feedbacks of income on population growth and from business-cycle swings about the long-term trend, but instead consider the impact of a given, constant, rate of growth, λ, of the labour force actually employed:

$$\dot{\ell} = \lambda\ell. \qquad (\lambda > 0) \tag{4.12}$$

Saving is treated as proportional to income, since more refined functions do not alter anything essential, at least not in the neoclassical two-sector model of section 2.2. Income is defined by:

$$y = v - mP^{-1}, \qquad (4.13)$$

that is, as output minus imports, the latter valued in units of output. Since our purpose is the analysis of long-run growth, not of the business cycle, equality of saving and investment is taken for granted; capital does not depreciate, since this usually does not affect the growth rate in any interesting way. Using the balance of trade equation (4.4), equal to the balance of payments, saving of a constant proportion σ of income accordingly implies:

$$\dot{k} = \sigma(v - \bar{m}), \qquad (4.14)$$

which says that a proportion σ of the output not shipped abroad is invested.

4.2. Direction of the evolution of the capital-labour ratio.

In the present section we rigorously show that in the case of indispensable imports, international circumstances affect the long-run growth rate. This has already been shown, implicitly of explicitly, for some specific production functions. Thus Johnson (1953) postulates complementarity of all three factors of production, Khang (1968) uses a Cobb-Douglas function and Itsumi and Morigushi (1978) consider the intermediate case of complementarity between imports and a Cobb-Douglas function of labour and capital. We proceed to generalize and extend these approaches by using the general production function, admitting all degrees of substitution between the three production factors, barring of course the polar cases of perfect substitutability and perfect complementarity. We first show that the dependence of the long-run growth rate on the conditions of trade does indeed hold true for the general case. This implies that, generally, the capital-labour ratio is not constant in the long run, but becomes either infinite or zero eventually. Therefore we add sufficient conditions for the capital-labour ratio to increase to infinity and to decline to zero. Finally, we consider a case where the behaviour the capital-labour ratio is of even greater interest than usually: zero labour growth and no technical progress. Theories of closed economies predict that this causes stagnation of growth, but we show that trading economies can avoid this fate.

At this point, the preoccupation with the capital-labour ratio that we share with most of the growth literature requires some explanation. We a primarily interested in the rate of growth of income, or per capita income. But these growth rates depend on that of the capital-labour rati Their relation is particularly straightforward in the case of proportion saving considered here. Then per capita income is given by:

$$\frac{y}{\ell} = \frac{1}{\sigma}(\dot{K} + \lambda K), \qquad (4.15)$$

where $K \equiv k/\ell$ is the capital-labour ratio. Clearly, if the capital-labo ratio is constant ($\dot{K} = 0$), so is per capita income. Moreover, suppose th capital-labour ratio strictly increases monotonically ($\dot{K} > 0$). Then, fro (4.15): $d(y/\ell)/dt = \frac{1}{\sigma}(d\dot{K}/dt + \lambda\dot{K})$. Since $\dot{K}$ is strictly positive for all values of t, $d\dot{K}/dt$ can only temporarily be negative. Hence per capita income must rise in the long run. Similarly, if the capital-labour ratio declines to zero, so does per capita income. Finally, if the capital-labour ratio grows at a constant rate ($d\dot{K}/dt = 0$), per capita income gro at the same rate. In short: <u>in the long run, the evolution of the capita labour ratio is an adequate indicator for that of per capita income</u>.

<u>Non-constancy of the capital-labour ratio under steady growth of capital</u>

In the closed-economy neoclassical growth model, the capital-labour ratio associated with steady growth of capital is constant if there are constant returns ($\rho = 1$) and no Hicks-neutral technical progress ($\nu = 0$) Theorem 4.2 establishes that this statement does not hold true in genera if imported inputs without perfect domestic substitutes are taken into account.

<u>Theorem 4.2</u>: Let Inada's conditions (2.2) be satisfied. Then, even unde constant returns and without technical progress, steady growth of capita at the natural rate is only possible in the specific case that foreign

demand also happens to grow at the natural rate.

Proof: Define $Z \equiv z/m$ as the ratio of domestic inputs to imports. In addition, define $A(K) \equiv z(1, K)$, per capita domestic inputs, and, similarly, $V(Z) = v(1, Z)$. Using (3.17) and (3.18) some elementary arithmetic reduces the model (4.1)-(4.4), (4.12), (4.14) to:

$$\dot{K} = \sigma A V_Z - \lambda K. \tag{4.16}$$

$$Z = A(V - ZV_Z)^{1+\bar{\varepsilon}} \exp\{(\lambda - \beta)t\}. \tag{4.17}$$

Here V_Z is V's derivative to Z. Equations (4.16) and (4.17) are the straightforward generalization of Solow's (1956) fundamental dynamic equation for the closed-economy neoclassical growth model. Our system is collapsed to Solow's equation by setting $v = z$, hence $V = A$, and $v_m = 0$. Accordingly (cf. 3.17) $V = Z\,V_Z$. Inserted into (4.16) this yields Solow's equation $\dot{K} = \sigma A - \lambda K$.

In (4.6) A is an increasing function of K alone. Thus if K is to be constant, A is constant and V_Z has to be constant at a finite non-zero value as well, equaling $\lambda K/\sigma A$. Now, V_Z is a function of Z alone. Under Inada's conditions V_{ZZ} is strictly negative. Hence V_Z is only constant if Z is constant, implying that constancy of K requires constancy of Z. Thus the right-hand side of (4.17) should be constant. In this expression the term: $A(V - ZV_Z)^{1+\bar{\varepsilon}}$ is indeed a constant if K and Z are constant, but the term: $\{(\lambda - \beta)t\}$ can only be constant if $\beta = \lambda$. Consequently steady growth of capital at the natural rate is not possible unless $\beta = \lambda$.

Q.E.D.

Remark: Note that theorem 4.2 requires that the Inada-conditions are satisfied. If the latter are violated, V_Z can become constant for large and small values of Z, implying the possibility of steady growth at the natural rate.

Long-run growth of the capital-labour ratio

Theorem 4.2 just states that the capital-labour ratio can only be constant if foreign demand happens to grow at the domestic natural rate.

But what are the conditions under which the ratio increases and decrease with time? Theorem 4.3 below develops a set of two conditions for this ratio to increase monotonically. This set is not necessary: in appendix 4.1 the ratio is shown to increase in other cases as well. Nevertheless, the conditions given here are of interest, since they are likely to be satisfied for many countries and may accordingly be regarded as a description of the normal situation. The first condition of theorem 4.3 is:

$$\lambda(\rho - 1) + \nu > 0. \qquad (4.18)$$

This technical-progress condition is only violated if both decreasing returns prevail and technical progress is absent or almost absent. Empirical evidence (e.g. that referred to in section 3.3) indicates that this is unlikely to be the case for most countries, certainly where manufactured output is concerned, but usually for total output as well. The only exceptions are possibly poor non-industrial countries, these probably having a low rate of technical progress, a high rate of labour growth, and decreasing returns (since their output is mainly agricultural).

The second condition of theorem 4.3 states that trade circumstances ar reasonably favourable:

$$\beta - \lambda - (1 + \bar{\varepsilon})\{\lambda(\rho - 1) + \nu\} > 0. \qquad (4.19)$$

Given (4.18) this second condition is satisfied if the rate of growth oi foreign demand, β, exceeds the rate of labour growth, λ, and the terms ‹ trade elasticity of foreign demand, $\bar{\varepsilon}$, has an absolute value in excess ‹ unity. These conditions may be expected to be satisfied for most countries. For the world as a whole, the long-run (say: over the past century) growth rate of the volume of exports was 3 to 3.5%, that of gr‹ world product appears to have been in the order of magnitude of 2.5 to : Both could be used as indicators for the value of β, and both substantially exceed the 1% growth rate of world population. Consequenly, : the average country the growth rate of foreign demand must exceed that ‹ labour. Similarly, $\bar{\varepsilon}$ usually exceeds unity significantly in absolute value, its value centering around the 'Tinbergen two'. Hence (4.19) is satisfied for most countries. Of course this does not mean that all countries are necessarily covered by the condition. Here again, likely exceptions are poor, primary goods exporting countries. These usually have a high rate of expansion of population, and, specifically in periods of global depression, their foreign demand grows sluggishly. Thus $\beta - \lambda$ is negative and this need not be compensated by the second term in (4.19). But with this exception, (4.18) and (4.19) are nonrestrictive conditions.

Apart from the technical-progress condition (4.18) and the condition of favourable international circumstances (4.19), some regularity of production is required to obtain definite results: one of the two sets of conditions that have been shown, in theorem 4.1, to imply existence and uniqueness of temporary equilibrium, must hold. To both of these sets an additional restriction must be attached. In the case of the first set, (4.5) & (4.6):

$$e(\rho - 1) - 1 < 0, \qquad (4.20)$$

which states that strong decreasing returns should not be combined with extremely elastic import demand. In the case of the second set, (4.7) - (4.9), the additional restriction is:

$$E(\rho - 1) - 1 < 0, \qquad (4.21)$$

which prohibits the combination of strong decreasing returns and very high substitutability of imports and domestic factors.

In short, both sets of regularity conditions (4.5), (4.6), (4.20), and (4.7), (4.8), (4.9), (4.21), are met as long as there are no extreme increasing or decreasing returns and imported inputs are neither almost perfect complements, nor almost perfect substitutes to domestic factors. The latter is not a serious restriction, because these polar cases have been adequately analysed in the literature, as noted above; it is the intermediate range that needs filling up.

Theorem 4.3 establishes that, under the normal conditions (4.18) and (4.19) and given regularity of the production function, the capital-labour ratio increases in the long run.

Theorem 4.3: Let (4.18), (4.19) and either (4.5), (4.6), (4.20), or (4.7) (4.8), (4.9) and (4.21) be satisfied. Then, after a finite period of time the rate of growth of capital, g, permanently exceeds that of labour, λ, implying that the capital-labour ratio grows to infinity.

Proof: We first develop a convenient expression for the growth rate of capital, $g = \dot{k}/k$, and its time derivative, $\dot{g}$. From (4.4), (4.2):

$$\bar{m} = \frac{mv_m}{\rho} . \tag{4.22}$$

Substitute (4.22) in (4.14); using definition (3.8) of q_m this yields:

$$g = \sigma \frac{v}{k} (1 - q_m). \tag{4.23}$$

Differentiate g to time:

$$\frac{\dot{g}}{g} = \frac{\dot{v}}{v} - g - \frac{\dot{q}_m}{1-q_m} . \qquad (g \neq 0,\ q_m \neq 1) \tag{4.24}$$

From (4.1), again using (4.8), we obtain:

$$\frac{\dot{v}}{v} = \rho q_m \frac{\dot{m}}{m} + \rho(1-q_m) \frac{\dot{z}}{z} + \nu, \tag{4.25}$$

and, using (3.9):

$$\frac{\dot{z}}{z} = q_\ell \lambda + (1-q_\ell)g. \tag{4.26}$$

Differentiating q_m to time yields:

$$\frac{\dot{q}_m}{q_m} = \frac{\dot{m}}{m} - \frac{\dot{v}}{v} + \frac{zv_{zm}}{v_z}\frac{\dot{z}}{z} + \frac{mv_{mm}}{v_m}\frac{\dot{m}}{m} + \nu. \tag{4.27}$$

Insert (4.25) into (4.27) and replace v_{zm}, v_{mm} by expressions in e, usi (3.12), (3.41), and (3.8):

$$\frac{\dot{q}_m}{q_m} = \left\{\frac{1+e-\rho e q_m}{e}\right\}\left\{\frac{\dot{m}}{m} - \frac{\dot{z}}{z}\right\}. \tag{4.28}$$

Similarly we obtain, differentiating (4.10) to time:

$$\frac{\dot{m}}{m} = \frac{1}{1+e+\bar{\varepsilon}}\left[e\beta - e(1+\bar{\varepsilon})\nu - \{e(\rho-1) - 1\}(1+\bar{\varepsilon})\frac{\dot{z}}{z}\right]. \tag{4.29}$$

Finally, substitute (4.28) and (4.25) in (4.24) and replace $\dot{m}/m$ by (4.29) and $\dot{z}/z$ by (4.26), to obtain:

$$\frac{\dot{g}}{g} = C + MD, \tag{4.30}$$

$$C \equiv \lambda(\rho-1) + \nu + (\rho q_\ell - \rho + 1)(\lambda - g); \tag{4.31}$$

$$D \equiv \beta - \lambda - (1+\bar{\varepsilon})\{\lambda(\rho-1) + \nu\} + \gamma(1-q_\ell)(\lambda-g); \tag{4.32}$$

$$M \equiv \frac{q_m\{e(\rho-1) - 1\}}{(1-q_m)(1+e+\bar{\varepsilon})} = \frac{q_m\{E(\rho-1) - 1\}}{(1-q_m)B + q_m E\gamma}. \tag{4.33}$$

Here γ and B are defined in (4.9) and (4.8). The second equality of (4.33) is obtained by using (3.13).

Some elementary results are collected in lemma 4.1.

Lemma 4.1:

(i) (4.6) and (4.20) together imply $M > 0$; (4.7), (4.8), (4.9) and (4.21) together also imply $M > 0$.

(ii) (4.19) implies $D > 0$ if $g \leq \lambda$.

(iii) (4.18) implies $C > 0$ if $g \leq \lambda$.

Proof of lemma 4.1: Statement (i) is immediately obvious. The same is true of (ii) if $\gamma > 0$, an assumption implied by the second alternative set of assumptions of theorem 4.3, specifically (4.9), but not by the first set, (4.5), (4.6), (4.20). However, if $\gamma < 0$, the minimum value of (4.32) in q_ℓ and g is obtained for $q_\ell = 0$, $g = 0$. Then D can be written as (using the definition of γ): $D = \beta - (1+\bar{\varepsilon})\nu$. Now, $\gamma = \rho(\bar{\varepsilon}+1) - \bar{\varepsilon}$. since $\bar{\varepsilon} < 0$, therefore γ can only be negative if $\bar{\varepsilon} + 1 < 0$. In that case though, $\beta - (1+\bar{\varepsilon})\nu$ is positive and statement (ii) is valid once more. To obtain (iii), note that as $\lambda(\rho-1) + \nu > 0$, expression C can only be negative if $\rho q_\ell - \rho + 1 < 0$. But $C = \rho q_\ell \lambda + \nu - (\rho q_\ell - \rho + 1)g$, which is positive as soon as $\rho q_\ell - \rho + 1 < 0$.

Theorem 4.3 is now easily proved. If $g \leq \lambda$, (4.30) and the three statements of lemma 4.1 imply $\dot{g}/g > 0$. Thus g increases until it exceeds λ. The latter happens at a finite value of time, because $\dot{g}/g$ is bounded from below by a positive constant (viz. its value at $g=\lambda$). Once exceeds λ, it clearly never drops below this value.

Q.E.D.

Long-run decline of the capital-labour ratio

It is interesting whether the capital-labour ratio declines if the normal situation with respect to technical progress and the conditions of foreign trade does not prevail: as indicated above this case may be relevant for poor,non-industrial countries. If only one of the two normalcy conditions (4.18) and (4.19) is violated, the ratio can go both ways and additional restrictions must be imposed on the production function to obtain clearcut results; the case is analysed in appendix 4.1 If both normalcy conditions are violated, the capital-labour ratio indeed declines in the long run, approaching zero. This is established by theore 4.4. It is not surprising, because in this case all sources of per capita growth are absent: almost no technical progress, decreasing returns, no foreign-demand growth, inelasticity of foreign demand.

Theorem 4.4: Let

$$\lambda(\rho-1) + \nu < 0, \tag{4.34}$$

and

$$\beta - \lambda - (1+\bar{\varepsilon})\{\lambda(\rho-1) + \nu\} < 0. \tag{4.35}$$

In addition let either (4.5), (4.6), (4.20), or (4.7), (4.8), (4.9) and (4.21) be satisfied. Then, after a finite period of time, the capital-labour ratio monotonically declines to zero.

Proof: We first supplement lemma 4.1 by some similar results.

Lemma 4.2:

(i) (4.34) implies $C < 0$ if $g > \lambda$.

(ii) (4.35) implies $D < 0$ if $g > \lambda$.

Proof of lemma 4.2: Statement (i) is seen by noting that condition (4.34) implies $\rho < 1$; (ii) follows because (4.35) implies $\gamma > 0$, as is easily seen.

Lemma 4.2, (4.30) and statement (i) of lemma 4.1 imply $\dot{g}/g < 0$ as long as $g > \lambda$. Hence g declines to a value below λ, and, once below λ, never increases to λ again.

Q.E.D.

Trade and national limits to growth

There is one interesting special case where the influence of trade on the capital-labour ratio is particularly important. This is the case of limits to growth. These are imposed by stagnating expansion of population, for example due to high income levels, and by the necessity to devote an ever increasing part of capital to the substitution of scarce natural resources and to the reduction of pollution. This process is sometimes thought to prevent further growth in income, the latter measured traditionally, i.e. excluding resources saved and pollution prevented. In our model this situation amounts to a decline of the marginal productivity of capital to zero, at a finite value of output, as capital grows, combined with zero labour growth. Thus then(3) the production function is characterized by an elasticity of capital-labour substitution, H, with an absolute value below unity.

One way out of this trap is of course technical progress of the labour-augmenting or Hicks-neutral types. We are, however, primarily interested in the possibilities of foreign trade to alleviate the problem for individual countries and groups of countries. With regard to raw materials, a pattern of trade has long been established where industrialized countries exchange manufactures for the raw materials they have increasingly come to lack: Europe, though only in the twentieth century (cf. Landes, 1980), and Japan are prime examples. By importing inputs and substituting these for domestic labour and capital, these countries have been able to forestall secular stagnation. Recently, a similar pattern of specialization may be shaping up - though hard evidence is still scarce - with respect to pollution-intensive products. High-income countries reveal preferences biased (and increasingly so with further increases in income) to unpolluted environment and low levels of noise; put differently, in these countries the production factor 'pollution tolerance' is becoming scarce relative to other factors such a skills. On the other hand, in poor countries pollution tolerance is still much higher. As a consequence, high-income countries will probably specialize in clean products, intensive in e.g. skills, whereas pollution intensive production is relocated to countries with low income levels. Once again this means that further income growth in the rich countries is made possible through substitution of domestic factors by imports.(4)

Thus it should be expected that, with zero population growth, no technical progress and limited substitutability of capital and labour, growth of open economies is nevertheless still possible, provided foreign demand grows and substitution of imported inputs for domestic factors is sufficiently easy - more precisely: the elasticity of substitution betwee imports and domestic factors, E, exceeds unity in absolute value. Theorem 4.5 establishes that this is indeed the case.

Theorem 4.5: Let the regularity conditions (4.7), (4.8), (4.9) and (4.21 be satisfied. Let there be no growth of labour and no technical progress ($\lambda = \nu = 0$). Finally let the elasticity of capital-labour substitution, H, be smaller than unity in absolute value.

Then the long-run growth rate of capital is zero if there is no trade. If there is trade and if foreign demand growth, β, is strictly positive, the economy grows at a strictly positive rate if the elasticity of substitution between imports and domestic factors, E, has an absolute value in excess of unity. But if its absolute value falls short of unity, the growth rate declines to zero.

Proof: With $\lambda = \nu = 0$, equation (4.30) for the rate of change of g boils down to:

$$\frac{\dot{g}}{g} = -(\rho q_\ell - \rho + 1)g, \tag{4.36}$$

if there is no trade; and to

$$\frac{\dot{g}}{g} = -(\rho q_\ell - \rho + 1)g + M\{\beta - \gamma(1-q_\ell)g\}, \tag{4.37}$$

if there is trade. The no-trade equation can be derived by considering the simple neoclassical growth model of the economy defined in section 3.5; a shortcut is to put imports' value share to zero, implying $M = 0$, in equation (4.37). We now first demonstrate:

Lemma 4.3: After some finite period, $\rho q_\ell - \rho + 1$ is positive, and remains so, both for closed and open economies; for open economies the same applies to $\beta - \gamma(\nu - q_\ell)g$.

Proof of lemma 4.3: From table 3.5 and its derivation we find that, since $-1 < H < 0$, the labour share q_ℓ increases monotonically if the capital-labour ratio increases.

As g cannot be negative and $\lambda = 0$, the capital-labour ratio is non-decreasing. Hence $\rho q_\ell - \rho + 1$ is non-decreasing. Suppose this term is negative in the initial position; this is only possible under increasing returns, i.e. $\rho > 1$. Then $-(\rho q_\ell - \rho + 1)g$ is strictly positive. Accordingly, in the closed-economy case g increases until $\rho q_\ell - \rho + 1$ is positive, and remains so, as the latter function is nondecreasing. Similarly, g can only decrease if $M\{\beta - \gamma(1-q_\ell)g\}$ is negative in the open-economy case. The latter is, since M is positive (statement (i) of lemma 4.1), only possible if g is sufficiently large. Therefore (cf. 4.37) g can not decline to zero as long as $\rho q_\ell - \rho + 1$ remains negative. Hence the capital-labour increases until $\rho q_\ell - \rho + 1$ attains a positive value; the function does not become negative again as it is nondecreasing.

The long-run positivity of $\beta - \gamma(1-q_\ell)g$ now follows easily. As long as the function is negative, $\dot{g}/g$ is certainly negative. Thus g decreases until $\beta - \gamma(1-q_\ell)g$ is positive and remains so. This completes the proof of lemma 4.3.

Using lemma 4.3, the closed-economy growth rate is immediately seen to converge to zero, using equation (4.36). To prove the open-economy part of the theorem, consider the change in the ratio of domestic factors to imports, Z, as derived from (4.29):

$$\frac{\dot{Z}}{Z} = \frac{-E}{(1-q_m)B + q_m E\gamma} \{\beta - \gamma(1-q_\ell)g\}. \tag{4.38}$$

The premultiplier in (4.38) is negative. Hence lemma 4.3 implies that Z decreases monotonically after some finite initial period. Accordingly (cf. table 3.5 and its derivation) q_m converges to zero if $E > -1$ and to unity if $E < -1$. In the former case M approaches zero, (4.37) approaches the closed-economy equation (4.36) and g declines to zero. If $E < -1$, with q_m converging to unity, (4.37) approaches:

$$\frac{\dot{g}}{g} = -(\rho q_\ell - \rho + 1)g + \frac{E(\rho-1) - 1}{E\gamma}\{\beta - \gamma(1-q_\ell)g\}. \qquad (4.39)$$

The second term in the right-hand side of (4.39) is always positive, the first one negative, but since $\rho q_\ell - \rho + 1$ is bounded above by unity, if g declines $-(\rho q_\ell - \rho + 1)g$ must always become smaller in absolute value than the second, positive, term in (4.38); hence a decline of g is halted before g reaches zero. Accordingly g remains positive indefinitely.

Q.E.D.

Remark 1: Since g remains strictly positive if $E < -1$, the function q_ℓ converges to unity. As a consequence, if the production function is a two-level CES, with E constant, the growth rate converges to a steady rate, its value being $\beta\{E(\rho-1) - 1\}/E\gamma$. Under constant returns this boils down to $-\beta/E$, since $\gamma = 1$ if $\rho = 1$. Hence in this case the growth rate settles down to a constant fraction of the growth rate of foreign demand.

Remark 2: Theorem 4.5 is established for only one of the two sets of regularity conditions employed in theorems (4.3) and (4.4), viz (4.7), (4.8), (4.9) and (4.21). It is not established for the alternative set, (4.5), (4.6) and (4.20). The reason for this is that if q_m converges to unity, as it does under the relevant conditions of the theorem, e converges to $1/(\rho-1)$ (cf. 3.13). Hence $e(\rho-1) - 1 = 0$, which violates (4.20). Then M becomes indeterminate, if formulated in terms of e, since both the denominator and the numerator approach zero. Of course the value to which M actually moves is $\{E(\rho-1) - 1\}/E\gamma$, but to achieve positivity of this term, the other set of regularity conditions, (4.7) - (4.21) is required.

The convergence of the no-trade growth rate to zero does not depend crucially on the limited substitutability of capital and labour. Under constant returns, the convergence occurs for all values of the elasticity of capital-labour substitution; this case simply corresponds to Solow's (1956) theorem. Under decreasing returns the same is true and only under increasing returns long-run growth is possible, viz. if the absolute value of the elasticity of substitution is equal to or greater than unity - provided capital's share is (initially) large enough.(5)

However, the reason for the convergence is radically different if the elasticity of substitution's absolute value falls short of unity, than if it equals or exceeds this value. In the former case, under constant returns the elasticity of output with respect to capital declines to zero as the capital-labour ratio increases. Thus here even capital imports and capital-augmenting technical progress cannot raise output in the long run. If, however, the elasticity of substitution equals unity, the elasticity of output with respect to capital equals a constant value in the (0,1) interval. This is still insufficient to sustain growth if the only source of investment is current output, but if there are either capital imports, growing at a constant rate, or capital-augmenting technical progress, steady growth at a positive rate is achieved; the same is true if the elasticity of substitution exceeds unity in absolute value: then the elasticity of output with respect to capital tends to unity if the capital-labour ratio grows. In both of the two latter cases, the cause of stagnating growth is not that capital growth does not expand output in the long run, but rather capital scarcity; if the latter is alleviated by e.g. capital imports, growth continues.

As in the case of limited substitutability of capital and labour, trade can also raise the long-run growth rate to a non-zero value if the absolute value of the capital-labour elasticity of substitution exceeds unity. First, as in the limited-substitutability case of theorem 4.5, an absolute value of the elasticity of substitution between imports and domestic factors, E, in excess of unity does the trick. But in addition, under increasing returns steady growth is even possible if the absolute value of E falls short of unity, viz. if the import share is initially 'large enough'.(6)

4.3. A steady-growth theorem

The preceding section established that the long-run growth rate of capital and income usually differs from the natural rate. Particularly, theorem 4.3 demonstrates that capital's growth, under normal conditions, exceeds the natural rate. This, however, does not clarify precisely how the growth rate depends on the parameters of the system: foreign-demand growth, the terms of trade elasticity of foreign demand, the natural rate, technical progress and the rate of returns to scale. To make it possible to clarify this dependence, the present section develops a steady-growth theorem, providing conditions that imply convergence of the growth rate to a constant value, and an explicit expression for this long-run growth rate in terms of the parameters of the system. To obtain a constant growth rate the weighting scheme of the parameters should become constant in the course of time. This weighting scheme depends on the characteristics of the production function. As a consequence, to achieve a constant scheme, some additional postulates regarding the production function are required. These have been discussed *in extenso* in section 3.3. Here we state them only briefly.

Theorem 3.2 establishes that the terms of trade elasticity of import demand, e, the elasticity of substitution between imports and domestic factors, E, and imports' value share in total imputs, q_m, are functions of the ratio of domestic factors to imports, Z, alone. Similarly, the elasticity of capital-labour substitution, H, and labour's value share in domestic factors, q_ℓ, are functions of the capital-labour ratio, K, alone. We simply postulate that the elasticity and share functions have limits as their arguments approach zero or infinity. The long-run growth rate can then be shown to be a function of these limiting values of the elasticity and share functions. The Cobb-Douglas and two-level CES functions are examples satisfying these postulates. Appendix 3.3 provides a non-trivial example, the 'Transitional Production Function'; it represents a transition of one Cobb-Douglas function at a zero capital-labour ratio to another one at an infinite ratio. Thus the elasticity of substitution is unity at the extremes and non-unity in between, with the factor shares gradually developing from one value to another.

Briefly, we postulate:

The limits of e, E and q_m as $Z \to 0$ and as $Z \to \infty$ exist. (4.40)

The limits of H and q_ℓ as $K \to 0$ and as $K \to \infty$ exist. (4.41)

The limits are denoted by replacing the variable concerned by a close greek substitute and adding the subscript 0 or ∞ to indicate the value of the relevant factor ratio. Thus:

$$\xi_{\ell 0} = \lim q_\ell \ (K \to 0);$$

$$\xi_{m0} = \lim q_m \ (Z \to 0);$$

$$\varepsilon_0 = \lim e \ (Z \to 0); \qquad (4.42)$$

$$E_0 = \lim E \ (Z \to 0);$$

$$H_0 = \lim H \ (K \to 0);$$

and similarly for $Z \to \infty$ and $K \to \infty$. Theorem 3.3 establishes that, as long as the limiting values of the elasticities of substitution differ from unity, the limiting values of the value shares are either zero or unity; the precise correspondence is shown in table 3.5.

We can now give a brief intuitive account of how (4.40) and (4.41) serve to establish a stable steady-growth rate.

The most convenient way to analyse the long-run behaviour of the capital-labour ratio, is to consider the derivative of the growth rate of capital first; this can be written as:

$$\frac{\dot{g}}{g} = L\left(\frac{N}{L} - g\right). \qquad (L > 0,\ N > 0) \qquad (4.43)$$

Here L and N are functions, given below in (4.48) and (4.49), of the parameters β, $\bar{\varepsilon}$, λ, ν, ρ and of the functions $q_\ell(K)$, $q_m(Z)$, and e(Z) or E(Z). This implies that L and N are not constant as long as q_ℓ, q_m, and e or E are not constant. However, if L and N <u>would</u> be constants, it is immediately seen that N/L is the globally stable steady-growth rate: in that case (4.43) represents a Hôtelling curve and g follows a logistic, approaching the 'saturation level' N/L monotonically, either from below or from above, depending on g's initial value. The purpose of postulates (4.40) and (4.41) is to ensure that L and N converge to constant values in the course of time, with (4.43) approaching a Hôtelling curve. This purpose is achieved by these two postulates, because Z and K become either zero or infinite in the long run - the latter has already been demonstrated for two cases in theorems 4.3 and 4.4. Hence q_ℓ, q_m, e and E are drawn to their postulated limits and L and N to constant values.

This result is formally stated in theorem 4.6, for the case where the 'normal conditions' of reasonably favourable trade conditions and some technical progress prevail; the theorem can be extended to all other admissable values of the parameters as well, as is done in appendix 4.1. The economic implications of the theorem are discussed in section 4.4, the interpretation of the parameters and the implied policy conclusions in section 4.5.

We define:

$$\mu_i = \lim_{Z \to i} M. \qquad (i = 0, \infty) \tag{4.44}$$

$$\theta_{au} = \rho\xi_{\ell\infty} - \rho + 1. \tag{4.45}$$

$$\theta_i = \rho\xi_{\ell\infty} - \rho + 1 + (1 - \xi_{\ell\infty})\gamma\mu_i. \qquad (i = 0, \infty) \tag{4.46}$$

Theorem 4.6: Let the assumptions of theorem 4.3 be satisfied, that is: (4.18), (4.19), and either (4.5), (4.6) and (4.20), or (4.7), (4.8), (4.9) and (4.21). In addition, let (4.40) and (4.41) hold. Finally, let $\theta_\infty > 0$.

Then the growth rate g of capital converges to a constant value χ from any initial position, where χ is given by:

$$\chi = \frac{\nu + \rho\xi_{\ell\infty}\lambda}{\theta_{au}} + \frac{\mu_i}{\theta_i}\left[\beta - \frac{\bar{\varepsilon}\xi_{\ell\infty}\{\lambda(\rho-1) + \nu\}}{\theta_{au}} - \frac{\nu + \rho\xi_{\ell\infty}\lambda}{\theta_{au}}\right], \tag{4.47}$$

where i = 0 if both θ_{au} and the term between square brackets are strictly positive, and i = ∞ for all other values of θ_{au} and the bracketed term.

Remark 1: The formulation of the theorem already makes clear that the capital-labour ratio, K, is infinite in the long run (this is theorem 4.3), that eventually the ratio of imports to domestic factors, Z, is zero if θ_{au} and the bracketed term in (4.47) are positive and that Z is infinite otherwise.

Remark 2: The theorem has not been given in terms of the capital-labour ratio, as is common practice in the literature and as we did in the preceding section, but instead in terms of the growth rate of capital. The reason is, as indicated above, that in our system the capital-labour ratio does not become constant; instead the growth rate of capital is the more convenient variable to consider, as it still does tend to a constant value. Therefore we do not use the term 'steady state', associated with constancy of the capital-labour ratio, but prefer 'steady growth'. Of course the growth rate of the ratio is immediately obtained by subtracting the natural rate λ from the rate of growth of capital.

Remark 3: In theorem 4.6 the only condition not previously introduced is $\theta_\infty > 0$. It is only violated(7) if both $\theta_{au} < 0$ and $E_\infty < -1$. Then the growth rate explodes. The condition is discussed further in section 4.4.

Proof of theorem 4.6: It is easily seen that equation (4.30) for $\dot{g}/g$ can be written in the form given by (4.43), with:

$$L = \rho q_\ell - \rho + 1 + (1 - q_\ell)\gamma M, \tag{4.48}$$

and

$$N = M\beta + \{1 - (1+\bar{\varepsilon})M\}\nu + (\rho - \gamma M)q_\ell\lambda. \tag{4.49}$$

We first prove that, if L and N approach constant values L* and N* as time advances, g converges to N*/L*.

Lemma 4.4: Let $N \to N^*$ and $L \to L^*$, as $t \to \infty$, with N* and L* finite and constant. Then g converges globally to N*/L* if and only if N*, L* > 0.

Proof of lemma 4.4: Since N and L have limits for $t \to \infty$, they also have a supremum and infimum for $t > t_1$, t_1 being sufficiently large. Denote these by $\sup_{t>t_1} N$, etc. If N* and L* are positive, t_1 can be selected so large as to have $\inf_{t>t_1} N$ and $\inf_{t>t_1} L$ positive. From (4.43) we obtain:

$$\inf_{t>t_1} N - g \sup_{t>t_1} L < \dot{g}/g < \sup_{t>t_1} N - g \inf_{t>t_1} L. \tag{4.50}$$

Thus, for $t > t_1$:

$$\dot{g}/g > 0 \text{ if } g < \inf_{t>t_1} N/\sup_{t>t_1} L, \text{ and } \dot{g}/g < 0 \text{ if } g > \sup_{t>t_1} N/\inf_{t>t_1} L. \tag{4.51}$$

Selecting $t_2 > t_1$ sufficiently large, we obtain:

$$\inf_{t>t_1} N/\sup_{t>t_1} L < g(t_3) < \sup_{t>t_1} N/\inf_{t>t_1} L, \quad t_3 > t_2 > t_1. \tag{4.52}$$

From (4.52) the sufficient part of the lemma follows by taking limits as $t_1 \to \infty$. The necessary part is straightforward; the only other position admitting equilibrium (at a positive value of g) is $N^* < 0$, $L^* < 0$, but then the equilibrium is unstable: $\dot{g} > 0$ if $g > N^*/L^*$, $\dot{g} < 0$ if $g < N^*/L^*$. If $N^* < 0$, $L^* > 0$ the growth rate drops to zero, if $N^* > 0$, $L^* < 0$ it explodes.

A preliminary result to be used below is:

Lemma 4.5:
If $D < 0$ for all $t > t_1$, for some t_1, we have: $Z \to \infty$ as $t \to \infty$.
If $D > 0$ for all $t > t_1$, for some t_1, we have: $Z \to 0$ as $t \to \infty$.

Proof of lemma 4.5: From (4.29):

$$\frac{\dot{Z}}{Z} = \frac{-e}{1 + e + \bar{\varepsilon}} D = \frac{-E}{(1-q_m)B + q_m E\gamma} D. \tag{4.53}$$

Both premultipliers in (4.53) are strictly negative, by (4.5) and (4.6), and by (4.7), (4.8) and (4.9), respectively. Thus the lemma follows trivially.

We are now ready to show that N and L approach constant values. From theorem 4.3 we know that K increases monotonically to infinity, after some initial period. Consequently q_ℓ and H converge to their limits $\xi_{\ell\infty}$ and H_∞. Similarly $\rho q_\ell - \rho + 1$ converges to θ_{au}. Finally, g permanently exceeds λ after some point.

Suppose $\theta_{au} < 0$, implying $\xi_{\ell\infty} \neq 1$; then because $\theta_\infty > 0$, γ is positive even if (4.9) is not assumed. Then $\rho q_\ell - \rho + 1$ is strictly negative if t is sufficiently large. Hence $C > 0$, since $\lambda(\rho-1) + \nu > 0$ by (4.19). Accordingly (4.30) implies that g must continue to increase unless D is negative, M being positive. However, if g becomes large, D must necessarily become negative: for large t we have $q_\ell \neq 1$ since $\xi_{\ell\infty} \neq 1$, implying that in (4.32) the multiplier of γ is strictly negative, γ being positive. Once D is strongly negative the increase of g is halted, but g cannot decrease to such an extent that D becomes positive again because prior to that $\dot{g}$ once again becomes positive. Hence after some time D is strictly negative forever, and lemma 4.5 implies $Z \to \infty$; consequently $e \to \varepsilon_\infty$, $q_m \to \xi_{m\infty}$, $E \to E_\infty$, and N and L become constants. As is easily seen, N* is positive due to (4.19); $L^* = \theta_\infty$ is positive by assumption. Hence lemma 4.4 implies theorem 4.6 for $\theta_{au} < 0$, as follows by writing lim N/L ($K \to \infty$, $Z \to \infty$) in the form (4.47).

Now let $\theta_{au} = 0$, again implying $\gamma > 0$ even if (4.9) is not assumed. Then, if t is large enough, $\rho q_\ell - \rho + 1$ is close to θ_{au}, and we either have $C > 0$, and the same situation as above, or g becomes very large, implying $D < 0$ and (lemma 4.5) once more $Z \to \infty$.

Finally let $\theta_{au} > 0$ (implying $L^* > 0$). Denote by $C^*(g)$ and $D^*(g)$ the functions C and D at $q_\ell = \xi_{\ell\infty}$. Since $C^*(g)$ is linear and strictly decreasing in g, there is some $g_1 > \lambda$ with $C^*(g_1) = 0$, because $C^*(g=\lambda) > 0$. Suppose $D(g_1) > 0$. If γ is positive, D is a decreasing function of g. Thus, taking t large enough for q_ℓ to be sufficiently close to $\xi_{\ell\infty}$, we have C strictly negative at all values of g for which $D \leq 0$. Hence $\dot{g}/g < 0$ for all these values of g. As a consequence g must decline until D is positive permanently, and $Z \to 0$. If γ is negative, D is negative too since $g > \lambda$, implying again $Z \to 0$. Next, suppose $D(g_1) < 0$, immediately implying $\gamma > 0$. Then, once q_ℓ is close enough to $\xi_{\ell\infty}$, we obtain $C > 0$ and $D < 0$ forever, hence $Z \to \infty$. Lastly, suppose $D(g_1) = 0$ (hence $\gamma > 0$). Then g_1 is seen to be the globally stable equilibrium, using the same technique as in the proof of lemma 4.4. In this case Z takes on some intermediate value, but the latter is irrelevant to the value of the growth rate, as q_m, e and E are easily seen to drop out of the growth rate. Collecting results, and noting that $D(g_1) > 0$ corresponds to positivity of the bracketed term in (4.47), the statements of theorem 4.6 are established.

Q.E.D.

4.4. The influence of international circumstances and technology on the long-run national growth rate

Any country's long-run growth rate of capital, income, output and exports, as given by theorem 4.6, depends on international circumstances and technology in a fairly complicated way. In this section we first discuss the influence of each of the basic determinants of growth on the growth rate.

A second question is to what extent currently prevailing thought with regard to the growth rate-based on closed-economy analysis - should be modified in view of the preponderance of industrial inputs without perfect domestic substitutes in modern trade. To determine the answer to this question, we compare the growth rate with the one that would prevail in a comparable closed economy. The definition of the closed economy corresponding to the open one considered here has been given in section 3.5. It should be stressed that this closed economy is not a description of how the open economy discussed above would look should it decide to turn autarkic: given our central thesis that imports are 'indispensable', such a transition to autarky is impossible. Rather, the closed economy serves as a reference point, chosen in such a way that the mistakes are brought out that are made when analysing growth under the assumption that trade is irrelevant. Thus differences in income or growth rates between the open economy and the closed one are not 'gains' or 'losses' from trade in the usual sense (though for briefness and convenience we do use these terms), but just the errors caused by disregarding trade and the nature of trade in the theories of the growth of modern economies. For this purpose, the most useful definition of the hypothetical closed economy is the one preserving as many characteristics of the actual, open, one as possible. Thus, the closed economy is defined to have the same rates of returns to scale, ρ, technical progress, ν, and labour growth, λ, as the open one; similarly, the long-run value share of labour in domestic factors, $\xi_{\ell\infty}$, is the same in both economies. Then the 'autarkic' long-run growth rate, χ_{au}, is:(8)

$$\chi_{au} = \frac{\nu + \rho\xi_{\ell\infty}\lambda}{\theta_{au}} . \qquad (4.54)$$

A necessary condition for existence and stability of χ_{au} is positivity of denominator, θ_{au}; or (c.f. 4.46) alternatively:

$$\rho < \frac{1}{1 - \xi_{\ell\infty}} \leftrightarrow \theta_{au} > 0. \qquad (4.55)$$

Thus the rate of returns to scale should not exceed the inverse of capital's long-run share in domestic factors. Accordingly increasing returns are admitted as long as labour's share at an infinite capital-labour ratio is not vanishingly small. As noted in remark 3 on theorem 4.6, $\theta_{au} > 0$ is sufficient to ensure $\theta_\infty > 0$. The latter plays a role in the open economy similar to $\theta_\infty > 0$ in the closed economy. However, $\theta_{au} > 0$ is not necessary for $\theta_\infty > 0$; as long as $E_\infty > -1$ the latter is still satisfied even if $\theta_{au} < 0$. Accordingly open economies converge to a steady-growth path even in cases where comparable closed ones are thought not to do so. In this sense trade can be said to have a stabilizing effect on growth. In the HOS-type two-sector growth models surveyed in chapter 2 a similar result holds true: in the case of closed-economy growth conditions have to be imposed that are not necessary for small open economies. Throughout the remainder of this chapter we take θ_{au} to be positive, unless explicitly indicated otherwise.

The expression for the growth rate in (4.47) is written in such a form that the relation between the open-economy growth rate and the 'autarkic' one is immediately seen:

$$\chi = \chi_{au} + \frac{\mu_1}{\theta_1} [\beta - \frac{\bar{\varepsilon}\xi_{\ell\infty}\{\lambda(\rho-1) + \nu\}}{\theta_{au}} - \chi_{au}]. \qquad (4.56)$$

Here the growth rate is decomposed in two terms: the 'autarkic' growth rate, and a 'gains' term. The latter in turn consists firstly of a multiplier, μ_1/θ_1, depending on the parameters of the production function and the terms of trade elasticity of foreign demand; this multiplier is non-negative, implying that the sign of the 'gains' term is that of its second component, the bracketed term. For briefness we denote the latter as the 'sign indicator'. It depends not only on the parameters of the production function and the terms of trade elasticity of foreign demand, but also on the growth rates of foreign demand, technology and labour. The sign indicator is, however, independent of the import share and the elasticity of substitution between imports and domestic factors.

The most convenient interpretation of the sign indicator is that it gives the potential divergence between the open-economy growth rate and the one of the hypothetical closed economy, or, inaccurately but briefly, the 'potential gain'. The multiplier determines to what extent the divergence between foreign and domestic developments actually influences the growth rate.

With aid of (4.56) we now discuss the influence of each of the parameters separately. The reader who wishes to avoid 'dull reading of close reasoning' may prefer to skip the discussion proper, and read just the summary conclusions at the end of the section. However, to make things attractive for the less hurried reader, a number of numerical illustrations are provided. These serve both to underscore the points made algebraically with representative numerical examples, and to give an impression of the orders of magnitude involved. The examples are usually variations around a central position.

Table 4.1. Numerical illustration of the long-run growth rate: the central position.

β (%)	$\bar{\varepsilon}$	λ (%)	ρ	ν (%)	H_∞	$\xi_{\ell\infty}$ (%)	E_i	ξ_{mi} (%)	χ_{au} (%)	$\chi-\chi_{au}$ (%)	χ (%)
3.0	-2.0	1.0	1.1	1.0	-1.0	75.0	-1.0	20.0	2.52	0.45	2.97

The latter is shown in table 4.1. The parameter values in the central position may be considered as the long-run values for the average industrial and transitional economy (the latter in Chenery and Syrquin's (1975) sense of having partially completed the structural changes associated with a rise of per capita income from very low levels to the level achieved by industrial countries). Thus the value of β, 3%, corresponds approximately to the growth rate of world trade over the past century. The terms of trade elasticity of foreign demand, $\bar{\varepsilon}$, is chosen minus two, the celebrated 'Tinbergen two'. Labour expands at a 1% rate that exceeds the current rate of growth of the populations of the advanced market economies, but is substantially lower than the natural rate of transitional countries. There is one percent of technical progress and moderate increasing returns ($\rho = 1.1$); though reliable estimation of both parameters, and specifically discrimination between ρ and ν, is still fairly difficult, the values 1% and 1.1 are an average of many estimates, maybe even a bit on the low side. The long-run elasticity of substitution, H_∞, is taken to be unity, since this permits us to assign an intermediate value (i.c. 75%) to labour's value share in domestic factors; whereas with $H_\infty \neq -1$, the value share takes a polar long-run value, either unity (if $H_\infty > -1$) or zero (if $H_\infty < -1$). For the same reason the long-run elasticity of substitution between imports and domestic factors, E_i, is assigned a unit value. Here the value of the subscript i, with i = lim z/m ($t \to \infty$) is given by theorem 4.6. As long as $\theta_{au} > 0$, we simply have $i = 0$ if the sign indicator is positive, and $i = \infty$ if the indicator is negative. The long-run import share is assigned a 20% value. This corresponds to a 25% import share in GDP, which is, approximately, the normal value for a country with a per capita income of $ 1000 (1964 prices) and a 15 million population (c.f. Chenery an Syrquin, 1975, p. 39).

These parameter values generate a moderate 3% growth rate for the open economy; this can be decomposed in a 2½% 'autarkic' growth rate and a modest half percent 'gain'.

Foreign-demand growth

As soon as a stable steady-growth rate in autarky exists ($\theta_{au} > 0$) and (4.18) is satisfied (i.c. $\lambda(\rho-1) + \nu > 0$), the second term of the sign indicator is non-negative. Thus there is a potential 'gain from trade' if the growth rate of foreign demand, β, exceeds the 'autarkic' rate χ_{au}. But clearly this is not a necessary condition: even if $\beta < \chi_{au}$, there still is a 'gain' if technology growth is rapid, provided labour's share $\xi_{\ell\infty}$ is non-zero.

The influence of variations in β is illustrated numerically in table 4.2. All parameters have the values shown in table 4.1.

Table 4.2. Impact of variations in foreign-demand growth.

Rate of growth of foreign demand, β (%)	Rate of growth of income, χ (%)
1.0	2.64
3.0	2.97
4.0	3.13
8.0	3.79

The growth rate of foreign demand is increased from 1% to 8%. The former is the growth rate of world trade in the period 1913-1939, the 8% rate corresponds to the growth of world trade in the two decades preceding 1973. It is clear that such a difference can have considerable impact on the growth rate of income, viz. 1.15 % in table 4.2. Since 1973 the grow rate of world trade has halved: in table 4.2 this causes a decline of th growth of income with 2/3 of a percent.

Table 4.2 does not show the 'autarkic' growth rate, as this is, of course, invariant with respect to changes in β. However, it should be noted that even with the sluggish growth of foreign demand at 1 %, the growth rate of the trading economy still exceeds the 'autarkic' rate of 2.52 % displayed in table 4.1.

The terms of trade elasticity of foreign demand

The role of the terms of trade elasticity of foreign demand, $\bar{\varepsilon}$, is mor ambiguous than that of foreign demand growth. This is because in (4.56), $\bar{\varepsilon}$ occurs not only in the sign indicator, that determines whether potentially there is a 'gain' or a 'loss', but also in the multiplier th fixes the extent to which this potential 'gain' or 'loss' actually influences the open-economy growth rate. In the sign indicator, $\bar{\varepsilon}$ enters in the term:

$$-\bar{\varepsilon}\xi_{\ell\infty} \frac{\nu + \lambda(\rho-1)}{\theta_{au}} . \tag{4.57}$$

Due to (4.18), i.e. $\lambda(\rho-1) + \nu > 0$, the sign of (4.57) is that of θ_{au}. Thus, whenever a stable 'autarkic' growth rate exists ($\theta_{au} > 0$), the sign indicator is the higher, the more elastic foreign demand is. Accordingly, in these circumstances elasticity of foreign demand is favourable to the occurence of 'gains from trade'. This is not difficult to understand intuitively. For the combination of technical progress and increasing returns that generates (4.18), in principle allows a country to expand production; a high elasticity of foreign demand makes it possible to market the expanding output, enabling the country to grow faster than a hypothetical non-trading economy. Of course this effect is not present if $\theta_{au} < 0$, since then the 'autarkic' growth rate explodes.

The effect of variations in $\bar{\varepsilon}$ on the multiplier of the 'gains term' in (4.56) is analysed in appendix 4.2. It depends on the value of the rate of returns to scale, ρ, imports' share, ξ_{mi}, and labour's share, $\xi_{\ell\infty}$.

For most values of these parameters, the multiplier increases if the absolute value of $\bar{\varepsilon}$ decreases. Only if a high rate of returns to scale is combined with a high value the import share, ξ_{mi}, or of capital's share, $1-\xi_{\ell\infty}$, is the multiplier raised by an increase in $\bar{\varepsilon}$.

Where does this leave us regarding the overall effect of a change in $\bar{\varepsilon}$ on the growth rate? First consider the case of increasing returns combined with a 'sizeable' import share, implying a multiplier varying directly with the absolute value of the elasticity of foreign demand. Since the sign indicator also varies directly with the latter, an increase in the latter raises the growth rate in this case if there are 'gains' to begin with. Hence - at least as long as labour's share is non-zero - a very high absolute value of $\bar{\varepsilon}$ is favourable for the growth rate, since this causes both the existence of a 'gain' and a high value for the multiplier of the 'gains' term.

Whenever the import share is small, and the more so if there are constant or decreasing returns, the multiplier decreases if the absolute value of $\bar{\varepsilon}$ increases. Thus if there is a 'loss' from trade, a marginal increase in $\bar{\varepsilon}$'s absolute value not only lowers the absolute value of the negative sign indicator, implying a tendency to diminish the 'loss', but also diminishes the impact of the 'loss' on the growth rate. However, if the absolute value of $\bar{\varepsilon}$ increases so much that the sign indicator turns positive, further increases raise the growth rate through the indicator but lower it through the multiplier, the total effect being indeterminate. This case can be clarified by considering the special case of constant returns combined with a unit-valued elasticity of substitution between imports and domestic factors. Then the sign of the derivative of the growth rate with respect to $\bar{\varepsilon}$ is given by:

$$\frac{\partial \chi}{\partial \bar{\varepsilon}} \lesseqgtr 0 \text{ according to } \xi_{\ell\infty}(1-\xi_{mi})(\beta-\chi_{au}) - \xi_{mi}\nu \lesseqgtr 0. \qquad (4.58)$$

Clearly, a high elasticity of foreign demand is advantageous if (non-price) foreign-demand growth is slow relative to the domestic sources of growth and particularly relative to technical progress. Moreover, the higher the import share is, the more important the role of technical progress in (4.58); thus for a country trading intensively, a high elasticity of foreign demand is particularly advantageous if technical

Table 4.3. Impact of variations of the terms of trade elasticity of foreign demand.

T.o.t. elasticity of foreign demand, $\bar{\varepsilon}$	Foreign-demand growth, β (%)	Import share, ξ_{mi} (%)	Open-economy growth, χ (%)
-0.5	3.0	20.0	2.98
-2.0	3.0	20.0	2.97
-10.0	3.0	20.0	2.97
-0.5	3.0	30.0	3.13
-2.0	3.0	30.0	3.23
-10.0	3.0	30.0	3.28
-0.5	8.0	20.0	5.18
-2.0	8.0	20.0	3.79
-10.0	8.0	20.0	3.16

progress is rapid. On the other hand, if the country's import share is not too large and foreign demand grows rapidly, the country is better off producing inelastic goods than elastic ones.

Table 4.3 illustrates the impact of changes in $\bar{\varepsilon}$ numerically. Once again all parameters not shown here have the value indicated in table 4.1. The first three lines show that as $\bar{\varepsilon}$ decreases from a value as high as -.5 to a low -10.0, the growth rate declines marginally. If the import share is not 20% but 30% this movement is reversed. The last three lines show that, with a higher value of β, the decrease of the growth rate caused by an increase of $|\bar{\varepsilon}|$ is much more pronounced; specifically with inelastic foreign demand the 'gain' is considerable: 5.18 - 2.52 = 2.66%.

The rate of growth of labour, labour's share in domestic factors and the elasticity of capital-labour substitution

Closed-economy growth theory holds a high rate of labour growth, λ, to be favourable to the long-run growth rate. This is correct for the open-economy rate too, but less so than closed-economy analysis predicts. This is easily seen: the derivative of the 'gains term' in (4.56) is negative as long as $\gamma > 0$ (condition 4.9). Intuitively this result is not difficult to understand: an economy with a high natural rate becomes, *ceteris paribus*, large relative to one with a low natural rate. Consequently, the 'gain', if it exists at all, is of minor importance; if there is a 'loss', it is the higher, the higher the natural rate is, because the bottleneck of essential, but scarce, foreign supplies is felt increasingly.

Table 4.4. Impact of variations of the natural rate.

Labour growth, λ (%)	Foreign-demand growth, β (%)	'Autarkic' growth, χ_{au} (%)	'Gain', $\chi-\chi_{au}$ (%)	Open-economy growth, χ (%)
0.0	3.0	1.38	0.61	1.99
1.0	3.0	2.52	0.45	2.97
2.0	3.0	3.66	0.30	3.96
1.0	1.0	2.52	0.12	2.64
2.0	1.0	3.66	-0.03	2.63
3.0	1.0	4.79	-0.18	2.61

Table 4.4 provides a numerical illustration. The first three lines sh the regular case of a 'gain from trade': as the natural rate increases from 0 to 3%, the 'gain' is halved. Interestingly, as a consequence per capita income of the open economy remains constant, instead of increasi as in closed-economy theory (given increasing returns). The last three lines of the table provide an example of a 'loss'. This could have been achieved by raising λ to unrealistically high values; instead β is lowe to 1%. Then with a natural rate of 1% there still is a slight 'gain', b at λ = 3% this 'gain' is converted to a 'loss'.

The impact of variations in labour's share in domestic factors, $\xi_{\ell\infty}$, ambiguous. It is easily seen that the 'autarkic' growth rate declines w a rise in this share, provided (4.18), $\nu + \lambda(\rho-1) > 0$, holds. With an increase in $\xi_{\ell\infty}$, the sign indicator increases if (4.18) holds. But, as shown in appendix 4.2, the multiplier is a decreasing function of $\xi_{\ell\infty}$ · except, of course, if it is zero because imports' share is zero. Hence total effect of a rise in $\xi_{\ell\infty}$ on both the 'gains term' and the growth r of the open economy itself is ambiguous. However, some numerical analys (not reported here) shows that reasonable parameter values yield a decrease of the 'gain'. The major exception is the case of very inelast foreign demand. The regular case is illustrated in table 4.5.
As $\xi_{\ell\infty}$ increases from 60 to 90 both the 'autarkic' growth rate and the 'gain' decline somewhat.

Table 4.5. Impact of variations in labour's share in domestic factors.

Labour's share in domestic factors, $\xi_{\ell\infty}$ (%)	'Autarkic' growth, χ_{au} (%)	'Gain', $\chi-\chi_{au}$ (%)	Open-economy growth, χ (%)
60.0	2.96	0.49	3.45
75.0	2.52	0.45	2.97
90.0	2.24	0.41	2.65

The elasticity of capital-labour substitution, H_∞, does not enter the growth rate directly, but only influences it by co-determining the valu of the labour share: under the normal conditions of our steady-growth theorem, labour's steady-growth share is zero if $H_\infty > -1$ and intermedia values are possible if $H_\infty = -1$. Consequently, the results of the preceding paragraph imply that the 'autarkic' growth rate is highest if $H < -1$, and lowest if substitution is difficult. The same should ordinarily apply to the 'gain from trade'.

Technical progress and the rate of returns to scale

The 'autarkic' growth rate is influenced positively by the rate of technical progress, ν, provided θ_{au} is positive. The multiplier of ν in the sign indicator of the open-economy growth rate is:

$$-\frac{(1+\bar{\varepsilon}\xi_{\ell\infty})}{\theta_{au}}. \tag{4.59}$$

Since the 'gains' multiplier is invariant with respect to ν, an increase of the latter raises the 'gain' as soon as $\bar{\varepsilon}\xi_{\ell\infty} < -1$, once again provided $\theta_{au} > 0$. Thus foreign demand should be elastic and labour's share not too small. This condition is certainly satisfied for industrial countries and probably for poorer countries as well, the only possible exception being monopolistic primary-goods exporters.

Numerically, an illustration is given in table 4.6. The first lines show the case where $\bar{\varepsilon}\xi_{\ell\infty} < -1$ is satisfied: the 'gain' increases as ν increases from 0% to 2%. The last three lines show an example where the condition is

Table 4.6. Impact of variations in the rate of technical progress.

Technical progress, ν (%)	Terms of trade elasticity of foreign demand, $\bar{\varepsilon}$	'Autarkic' growth, χ_{au} (%)	'Gain', $\chi-\chi_{au}$ (%)	Open-economy growth, χ (%)
0.0	-2.0	1.14	0.34	1.48
1.0	-2.0	2.52	0.45	2.97
2.0	-2.0	3.90	0.57	4.46
0.0	-0.5	1.14	0.84	1.98
1.0	-0.5	2.52	0.46	2.98
2.0	-0.5	3.90	0.08	3.98

violated: here the 'gain' diminishes.

The 'autarkic' growth rate is easily seen to be an increasing functio of the rate of returns to scale, ρ.

Appendix 4.2 demonstrates that the same applies to the gains multipli The derivative of the sign indicator with respect to ρ is:

$$-(1 + \bar{\varepsilon}\xi_{\ell\infty}) \frac{(1 - \xi_{\ell\infty})\nu}{\theta^2_{au}} . \qquad (4.60)$$

Once again, the condition for this expression to be positive is $\bar{\varepsilon}\xi_{\ell\infty} < -1$. If this condition is satisfied, there are two possibilities for the effect of an increase in ρ on the 'gain'. First, if at a value of ρ there is at least some 'gain', raising ρ increases both the sign indicator and the multiplier. Consequently, the gain is unambiguously increased. Since the 'autarkic rate' increases too, the open-economy growth rate is unambiguously increased. However, if there is 'loss' fro trade, an increase in ρ draws the (negative) sign indicator a bit close to zero, causing a tendency to diminish the 'loss'; but the multiplier increased implying a tendency to blow up the 'loss'. The full influence of ρ is therefore ambiguous in this case. Table 4.7 provides the numeri illustration. In the first three lines there is a 'gain', which is seen

Table 4.7. Impact of variations in the rate of returns to scale.

Rate of returns to scale, ρ	Foreign demand growth, β (%)	Rate of growth of labour, λ (%)	'Autarkic' growth, χ_{au} (%)	'Gain' or 'loss' from trade, $\chi - \chi_{au}$ (%)	Open econ grow (%
0.9	3.0	1.0	2.16	0.32	2.
1.0	3.0	1.0	2.52	0.45	2.
1.1	3.0	1.0	2.71	0.54	3.
0.9	0.0	3.0	3.90	-0.31	3.
1.0	0.0	3.0	4.79	-0.35	4.
1.1	0.0	3.0	5.29	-0.35	4.

increase with ρ; the last three lines display a 'loss', created by raising λ and lowering β. Here the decrease of the multiplier dominates the decrease of the absolute value of the sign indicator, causing a slight increase of the 'loss' as ρ increases.

Imports' share and the elasticity of substitution between imports and domestic factors

The share of imports in total inputs, ξ_{mi}, occurs only in the multiplier of the 'gains' term. Appendix 4.2 shows this multiplier to be an increasing function of the share, provided $\theta_{au} > 0$. Consequently, the value of the import share does not determine whether there is a 'gain' or a 'loss', but the impact of the 'gain' or 'loss' on the growth rate is proportional to the import share. Thus in the normal case of 'gains from trade', the 'gain' is the more substantial the more intimately a country is linked up with other economies. Table 4.8 shows that variations in imports' share may influence the growth rate substantially. The first four lines show that even with a modest growth of foreign demand, 3%, the 'gain' still becomes a substantial 1% if the import share is 40%. If foreign demand grows rapidly, at 8%, increasing the import share from 10% to 40% greatly raises the growth rate.

Table 4.8. Impact of variations in the import share.

Share of imports, ξ_{mi} (%)	Foreign-demand growth, β (%)	Open economy growth χ (%)
10.0	3.0	2.73
20.0	3.0	2.97
30.0	3.0	3.23
40.0	3.0	3.50
10.0	8.0	3.13
20.0	8.0	3.79
30.0	8.0	4.51
40.0	8.0	5.29

Like the import share, the elasticity of substitution between imports and domestic factors, E, enters the growth rate only through the multiplier.

Here it occurs both directly and indirectly, viz. by influencing the import share. If $E_i = -1$, the import share may have any value; but with $E_i \neq -1$, the import share is either zero, or infinite. Its precise val depends on whether E_i exceeds or falls short of minus unity and on the value of i. As noted above, the value of i depends on the sign indicato Thus the precise value of the import share is displayed in table 4.9, where $\theta_{au} > 0$ is assumed; to obtain table 4.9, compare table 3.5.

Table 4.9. Steady-growth import share with non-unit valued elasticity o substitution between imports and domestic factors.

	Import share	
	Potential 'gain from trade'	Potential 'loss from trade'
	$i = 0$	$i = \infty$
$E_i < -1$	100.0	0.0
$E_i > -1$	0.0	100.0

Table 4.7 clearly shows that the influence of the value of E depends on the sign indicator, that is on whether a potential 'gain' or 'loss' exists. Consequently, in tracing the influence of E on the growth rate, the cases of 'losses' and 'gains' must be treated separately.

Appendix 4.2 derives that, if there is a 'loss', the multiplier is an increasing function of E; hence the 'loss' is blown up most if imports a near-perfect complements of domestic factors. Consequently, if the conditions of trade are unfavourable, this depresses the growth rate mo the more complementary imports and domestic factors are.

If there is a 'gain', the multiplier is lowest if $E > -1$; in that case the import share, and hence the multiplier, is zero. If $E < -1$, the situation is less clearcut. First consider the case $E = -1$. Then the import-share, ξ_m, may have any value, including unity; the multiplier is an increasing function of ξ_m. Now let $E < -1$. Then $\xi_m = 1$; in addition, the multiplier is an increasing function of E. Consequently the highest value of the multiplier is attained at $E = -1$, $\xi_m = 1$. Since the value

$\xi_m = 1$ is reached in a natural way only if $E < -1$, a value of the elasticity of substitution between imports and domestic factors slightly below minus unity, maximizes the growth rate if the conditions of trade are favourable.

Table 4.10. The impact of variations in the substitutability of imports and domestic factors under unfavourable conditions of trade.

Elasticity of substitution, E_∞	Import share, $\xi_{m\infty}$ (%)	Foreign-demand growth, β (%)	Labour growth, λ (%)	Open-economy growth*, χ (%)
0.0	100.0	1.0	3.0	0.00
-0.5	100.0	1.0	3.0	2.73
-1.0	100.0	1.0	3.0	3.44
-1.0	50.0	1.0	3.0	4.28
-1.0	20.0	1.0	3.0	4.61
<-1.0	0.0	1.0	3.0	4.79

*) The 'autarkic' growth rate, χ_{au}, has a value of 4.79% throughout.

Table 4.10 provides a numerical example for the case of 'losses' from trade. The decrease of the 'loss' as E decreases is clearly brought out. Table 4.11 provides an illustration of the case where a 'gain' is present: here all parameters once more have the values of the central position displayed in table 4.1. The gain increases substantially as E decreases from zero to minus unity and as ξ_m too is raised from zero to unity. From $E = -1$ onward, further decreases of E slowly diminish the gain, until only 0.41% remains at $E = -\infty$.

That any 'gain' at all is retained if imports and domestic factors are perfect substitutes is surprising: the central result of our survey of chapter 2 was that trade does <u>not</u> alter the long-run growth rate in this case. Actually, the 'gains' multiplier is given by (c.f. appendix 4.2):

$$\frac{\rho - 1}{\gamma \xi_{\ell\infty}} \,. \tag{4.61}$$

Table 4.11. The impact of variations in the substitutability of import and domestic factors under favourable conditions of trade.

Elasticity of substitution, E_0	Import share, ξ_{m0} (%)	Open-economy growth, χ (%)
>-1.0	0.0	2.52
-1.0	20.0	2.97
-1.0	90.0	5.38
-1.0	100.0	5.89
-1.1	100.0	5.68
-2.0	100.0	4.62
-10.0	100.0	3.31
$-\infty$	100.0	2.93

Clearly, this is reduced to zero only if $\rho = 1$: constant returns. If, however, there are increasing returns, trade raises the growth rate, e' though there are perfect domestic substitutes for imports.(9) Thus we l discovered a second major reason for the invariance of the long-run gr rate to trade as found in the standard literature: the neglect of economies of scale.

Summary of conclusions

1. The long-run growth rate χ of an open economy's income is an increas function of the growth rate of foreign demand, β. If the latter exc the country's 'autarkic' rate, χ_{au} - that is, the growth rate close economy theory predicts for the country - the open-economy growth rate χ also exceeds χ_{au} . But even if foreign demand is sluggish, tl still may be such a 'gain', particularly if technology growth is ra
2. Though the influence of the terms of trade elasticity of foreign demand, $\bar{\varepsilon}$, is fairly complicated, a good rule of thumb is that a country is better off producing inelastic goods if foreign-demand growth is rapid relative to 'autarkic growth', and should prefer elastic goods if foreign-demand growth is relatively slow.
3. The growth rate of an open economy is increased less by a rise of tl

natural rate than closed-economy analysis predicts.

4. The growth rate of an open economy is increased more by a rise of the rate of technical progress than closed-economy analysis predicts - provided foreign demand is fairly elastic and labour's share in domestic factors, ξ_ℓ, not too small (specifically: $\bar{\varepsilon}\xi_\ell < -1$).
5. The growth rate of an open economy is increased more by a rise of the rate of returns to scale than closed-economy analysis predicts - provided there is at least some 'gain from trade'. If, however, there is a 'loss from trade' the impact of a rise in the rate of returns to scale is ambiguous.

   The mere existence, in the case of a 'potential gain',(10) of increasing returns implies that the open-economy growth rate exceeds the one predicted by closed-economy theory, even in the case where imports and domestic factors are perfect substitutes.
6. The value of the import share is irrelevant to the question whether the open-economy growth rate exceeds the one predicted by closed-economy theory. But the absolute value of the difference between the two is an increasing function of the import share. Consequently, if trade conditions are favourable, a country's growth rate benefits more, the more open the economy is; but under unfavourable conditions of trade the more open economies suffer most.
7. It is disadvantageous under any circumstances if a country's imported inputs and its domestic factors are complements, i.e. if the elasticity of substitution between the two, E, has a value between minus unity and zero. If trade conditions are favourable, the optimum value of E is slightly below minus unity; under unfavourable trade conditions the rule is: the closer substitutes imports and domestic factors are, the better.(11)

4.5. Practical interpretation and policy implications

The preceding section discussed the influence of each of the paramete of our system on the long-run growth rate. We showed a number of these affect the growth rate substantially. This raises the question of the practical relevance of this growth rate. We have calculated it as the long-run, or steady-growth, rate of growth of capital and income. In chapter one we argued that the steady-growth rate of income is practica relevant, both because the adjustment of the growth rate of capital to long-run value is much faster than one-sector growth models would seem imply at first glance and because the growth rate of income is usually fairly close to its 'long-run' rate even if that of capital differs significantly from it. Consequently, provided capital stocks do not dif to an extreme degree from their steady-growth values as a consequence o e.g. major wars, the steady-growth rate represents a good approximation the actual, average, growth rate of income in a period where the underlying parameters (i.e. those describing foreign demand, the natura rate and the asymptotic production function parameters) are roughly constant. Therefore, the question becomes relevant how these parameters particularly those to which the growth rate of income is most sensitive are determined and how economic policy can influence them. Clearly, parameters that can be influenced by economic policy can be used as instruments in e.g. development programs. We discuss specifically the parameters relating to foreign trade, i.e. the growth rate of foreign demand, the terms of trade elasticity of foreign demand and the import share.

Using the parameters as policy variables, our model is well suited to deal with issues in trade, development and growth policy. As an example we conclude the chapter by considering the choice between import substitution and export-led growth as development and growth strategies

The rate of growth of foreign demand

The rate of growth of foreign demand, β, has been shown to be one of key parameters. Its determinants are conveniently broken down into:

(i) The rate of growth of world trade.

(ii) Divergences from the latter due to the geographical direction of exports.

(iii) Divergences due to exports' commodity composition.

(iv) Other divergences.

The growth rate of world trade has displayed long swings. As Lewis (1980) notes, it has gone down from an unprecedented 8% in the two decades preceding 1973, to about one-half of that value since. Lewis explores in a suggestive, but informal, discussion the consequences for developing countries. We may bring our model to bear on the question. Clearly, a lower growth rate of world trade implies that the average country's growth rate of foreign demand is lowered; this may cause a substantial downward shift of the growth rate of both developing and developed countries, as our exercises of the preceding section show. In addition, it is likely that lowering just our parameter β underestimates the true impact of a decline in world-trade growth. This is because rapid growth of world trade may well be a stimulus for technical progress: it is accompanied by increased specialization with the implied advantages of scale, by rapid technology transfers and by the innovations that are caused by fast growth as such. If this is correct, our technical progress parameter ν is positively correlated with β, instead of being independent of it. For example, let ν be directly proportional to β, with a 2% value of ν being associated with β = 8% and ν = 1% with β = 4%. Then the growth rate of our standard economy of section 4.4 is 5.3% if β = 8% - remarkably close to the average less-developed country's growth rate in the sixties -, but when world-trade growth is halved to the 4% level, the growth rate drops to 3.1%. Clearly, here trade serves as Nurkse's (1961) 'Engine of growth' rather than as Kravis' (1970) 'Handmaiden of growth'.

The growth rate of world demand depends, of course, on the growth rates of the individual economies of the world system. But our analysis emphasizes that the latter, in turn, depend on the growth rate of world trade itself. Obtaining greater knowledge of the working of this mechanism requires a lot of further research: analysis of multi-country systems (our two-region model of chapter 6 is a modest step in this direction), and, particularly, endogenization of technical progress. However, this system determining the structural growth rates of world trade and technology may well possess multiple equilibria; an indication to this effect (though i: a case of minor importance) is found in the two-region analysis of chapt 6. Existence of multiple equilibria may provide an explanation of the occurrence of long swings in world-trade growth. If there are multiple equilibria, the system can be kicked from a high growth rate to a low on and vice versa, by 'system shocks' (Maddison's (1980) phrase) or by appropriate policy measures. Thus OPEC's oil-price rises of 1973 and 197 may well have provided the downward kick causing the halving of world-trade's growth. To reverse this, the system should be given an upward kick, e.g. by simultaneous Keynesian demand stimulation in many industri countries, preferably combined with temporarily lowered energy prices.(1 Obviously this type of policy is beyond the scope of individual countrie requiring concerted action of many countries. Cooperation through the various international agencies currently existing may go some way toward achieving this. But it is unlikely to be enough. Shocks are bound to occ again, and probably more frequently as a number of natural resources becomes scarce and industrialization spreads rapidly over the southern hemisphere. The impact of these shocks increases (c.f. conclusion 6 of section 4) as trade becomes more intensive due to technical progress and increased specialization. To prevent or counter these shocks internation agencies with mere coordinating powers are insufficient; rather, the optimal arrangement would be something close to a planetary authority wi sufficient powers to enforce a global economic policy.(13) As long as th remains utopian, recurrence of long swings, transmitted to all countries by world trade through the mechanism discussed in the present chapter, m well be inevitable.

The rate of growth of non-price foreign demand may diverge from the growth rate of world trade due to the geographical direction of exports. If these are concentrated on countries whose growth exceeds or falls sho of the world average, β differs from the growth rate of world trade. In consequence, export promotion used to achieve a sizeable market share in rapidly growing economies, is a good way for individual countries to rai β, even if the rate of growth of world trade goes down; naturally this policy can only be followed succesfully by a limited number of countries

The main cause of divergence between β and the growth rate of world trade is a diverging commodity-composition of exports: the <u>average</u> growt rate of demand for a country's output is raised by increasing the share products of which demand grows relatively rapidly. Thus economic policy should aim at stimulating production of products with high income elasticities of demand and of the inputs and capital goods used in their production; similarly, of raw materials, intermediates and capital goods used with increasing intensity. Naturally, investments should be stimulated only in those products for which the country has, or can acquire, some degree of comparative advantage. The latter can be generated by the presence of specific factors, or the abundance of intensively used ones.(14) Policies aimed at government-induced industrial restructuring to achieve rapid growth of exports and technology, have long been and still are very successfully practised by a number of countries, notably Japan, Korea, Taiwan, etc. Since 1975, for example, the Japanese government has channelled hundreds of millions of dollars in micro-processor technology, the explicit purpose being to establish a new industry to serve as the hard core of future export expansion (c.f. e.g. Orme, 1979, chapter 1). In the U.S. and Europe proposals for similar policies are made with increasing frequency.(15) Our analysis confirms that such policies accelerate the structural growth of an economy very considerably.

Of the remaining divergences between β and the growth rate of world trade, the most important one probably is that caused by diverging price movements of competitors. These are not necessarily reflected in the terms of trade. The latter are only an adequate representation of the relative price determining foreign demand for its products if the shares of all countries in all markets are equal to their shares in the market of our 'economy of moderate size'. But systematic share divergences are reflected in the 'non-price' growth rate of foreign demand. These divergences are the higher, the closer substitutes competitors' products are and the more growth rates of unit costs differ. The latter implies that high domestic rates of technical progress and of returns to scale (e.g. caused by specialization) raise the 'non-price' growth rate of foreign demand, β.

Thus the positive association between β and ν described above works both ways: policies raising the progress of technology are likely to increase foreign demand as well.

The terms of trade elasticity of foreign demand

The terms of trade elasticity of foreign demand, $\bar{\varepsilon}$, is an average of the elasticities of the individual products in the country's export basket. The demand elasticities of the latter can be broken down (c.f. e.g. Verdoorn, 1952, p.74; 1960, p.320; Armington, 1969; Van Bochove and De Vries, 1977, pp.191, 192) in the elasticity of total demand for the product concerned and a component expressing the possibilities to substitute between alternative producers. Then the absolute value of $\bar{\varepsilon}$ for some individual commodity is high if the world market for the product is large and if there are close substitutes.

Combined with conclusion 2 of section 4.4, the above interpretation of $\bar{\varepsilon}$ implies that a country should specialize in highly competitive products for which large markets exist if its 'autarkic growth' is rapid relative to foreign-demand growth. The latter is the case if technical progress is more rapid at home than abroad, but also if labour grows relatively rapidly. Then the growth of foreign demand is insufficient to absorb the exports that must pay for rapidly growing imports. Exports can only be expanded sufficiently by lowering prices; this has its greatest effect if exports compete with close foreign substitutes and thus have a large market to expand into.

On the other hand, if non-price foreign-demand growth is rapid relative to domestic expansion, a country is well off specializing in not too competitive goods, specifically in goods for which monopolies and cartels are feasible (compare OPEC). Clearly this implies that exporting raw materials and other primary products was the best way to achieve growth for poor countries in the fifties and sixties, but this is not so anymore competitive manufactures should now be their best bet. Another implicatio is that less-developed countries that have used the primary-exports proceeds in the past two decades to establish industries producing exportable manufactures, should be able to maintain a reasonable growth rate through the present decade; but countries that have failed to do so will experience a much greater loss in their growth rate due to the globa slow growth.

Import substitution and export-led growth

A central policy issue in development economics has been the usefulness of import substitution *vis à vis* export-led growth policies. The former aims at development of sectors for which the country currently depends on imports, the latter at export-oriented sectors. So far, the definite results on the conditions for both policies to be succesful in promoting long-run growth have been meagre. As Krueger (1980) writes: 'There are few useful theorems about the effects of alternative trade policies on growth'. Our approach is helpful in clarifying the essential factors on which the issue hinges.

The growth rate has been shown to be favourably affected by a high share of imports if the conditions of foreign trade are favourable: e.g. if foreign demand grows rapidly, or if technical progress is reasonably fast. In this situation a country should not try to restrict its imports, but rather intensify trade to take maximum advantage of the favourable conditions. If, however, foreign demand is sluggish and domestic technical progress not too fast, import substitution, i.e. lowering the import share, is a good way to minimize loss; the latter provided not too many countries follow the same policy: then foreign demand would be even more depressed.

Export-led growth corresponds to raising the growth rate of foreign demand in our model. We have shown this to be unambiguously favourable to the growth rate. Thus, in principle, there may be situations in which a combination of export stimulation and import substitution is the optimal approach: specifically if demand for the countries' traditional exports is sluggish. However, it should be noted that import substitution always is a defensive policy: it just limits the loss due to unfavourable conditions of trade; instead, export promotion improves these conditions. Consequently, really rapid development can only be export-led.

Restructuring the economy can do only so much in achieving a better growth rate of foreign demand: the foreign-trade regimes of trade partners may well obstruct attempts to achieve export-led growth. In the fifties and sixties with rapid world-trade growth and trade liberalization, export-led growth was doubtless superior to import substitution. But now that trade is depressed and north-south trade appears to be subject to increasing protectionist tendencies, developing countries that are not already on a path of rapid industrialization are probably better off with import substitution, to minimize the negative effects of the deterioration of the foreign-trade climate. As Diaz-Alejandro (1980, p.299) puts it 'An industrialized world riddled with unpredictable tariffs and import quotas could turn export drives into disasters.'

One set of policies is beneficial under all circumstances: those achieving increased flexibility of the economy. We showed (c.f. conclusion 7 of section 4.4) that easy, but not perfect, substitutability of imports and domestic factors is both instrumental in maximizing the growth rate in a favourable international setting and in minimizing the impact of difficult circumstances. Therefore a country should attempt to achieve an industrial structure that can, in bad times, produce most essential goods; but that is also capable, in periods of global expansion, of producing the export goods best suited to achieve rapid intensifying of trade. No country or fairly integrated group of countries like the EEC, should allow essential sectors to vanish completely,[16] but neither should they, when uncompetitive, be supported to such an extent that no resources and growth possibilities remain for innovative industries.

Appendix 4.1. Steady growth under unfavourable conditions of trade and stagnating technical progress

The present appendix generalizes the steady-growth theorem 4.6 to the cases where (4.18) or (4.19) fail to hold.

Theorem 4.7: Let all assumptions of theorem 4.6 hold, save (4.18) and (4.19). Let instead (4.34) and (4.35) be satisfied; and let lim N ($K \to 0$, $Z \to i$) be positive for $i = 0, \infty$. Assume θ_i $(i = 0, \infty) > 0$ in addition, where θ_i is defined as in (4.46), but with $\xi_{\ell\infty}$ replaced by $\xi_{\ell 0}$. Then the growth rate g of capital converges to a constant value χ from any initial position, with χ given by (4.47), except that $\xi_{\ell\infty}$ is replaced by $\xi_{\ell 0}$ (both in (4.47) and in definition (4.45) of θ_{au}). The subscript i in (4.47) is ∞ if the term between square brackets in the latter equation is negative and $i = 0$ if the bracketed term is positive.

Proof: Theorem 4.4 has already established that the capital-labour ratio declines monotonically to zero. Hence $q_\ell \to \xi_{\ell 0}$ as $t \to \infty$. The functions C and D become functions of g only; denote these by C*(g) and D*(g). Since $\rho < 1$ as a consequence of (4.34), C* is strictly decreasing in g. As C* $(g = 0)$ is easily seen to be positive, there is a value g_1 of g, $0 \leq g_1 < \lambda$, with $C^*(g_1) = 0$; moreover $C^* > 0$ if $g < g_1$ and $C^* < 0$ if $g > g_1$.

Suppose $D^*(g_1) > 0$. This implies, in view of (4.35), that D*(g) is strictly decreasing in g. Consequently $D^*(g) > 0$ for $g \leq g_1$. As D* is continuous in g, D*(g) is still positive if g slightly exceeds g_1. If t_1 is selected sufficiently large, $D(g, q_\ell)$ is close to D*(g) and hence also positive for all $t > t_1$ as long as $g < g_1 + \alpha$, with α some positive constant.

Since $C^* < 0$ if $g > g_1$, there always is a t_2 such that $C(g, q_\ell) < 0$ for all $t > t_2$ and for all $g > g_2$, with $g_1 \leq g_2 + \alpha$. Consequently, for all $t > \max[t_1, t_2]$, C is negative; D may be negative, but if it is, $\dot{g} < 0$ (c.f. 4.30) and g declines until D becomes positive at some value of g exceeding g_2. Such a value exists since D is positive for all $g < g_1 + \alpha$. Clearly g can never rise again to such an extent that D becomes negative, as $\dot{g}$ drops to zero first. Accordingly, after some time $\dot{Z}$ is positive forever and Z moves to zero. Hence (lemma 4.4) the growth rate converges to the constant value given by theorem 4.7, noting that $D^*(g_1) > 0$ is equivalent to positivity of the bracketed term of the growth rate expression (4.47).

Next suppose $D^*(g_1) < 0$. Then, by similar reasoning as above, Z moves to infinity (to verify this, note that $\gamma > 0$ if $\rho < 1$).

If $D^*(g_1) = 0$, g_1 is the globally stable equilibrium, as is seen by sandwiching g between the relevant infinum/supremum ratios à la (4.52).

Q.E.D.

Theorem 4.8: Let all the assumptions of theorem 4.6 hold true, but with (4.19) replaced by (4.35) and let lim N ($K \to i$, $Z \to \infty$) be positive for $i = 0, \infty$. In addition to $\theta_\infty > 0$, with θ_∞ defined as in (4.46), also assume that $\theta_\infty > 0$ if in (4.46) $\xi_{\ell\infty}$ is replaced by $\xi_{\ell 0}$.

Define:

$$\zeta_\infty = \nu + \lambda(\rho-1) + \mu_\infty\{\beta - (1+\bar{\varepsilon})\nu - \gamma\lambda\}. \tag{4.62}$$

Then the growth rate converges globally to a constant value given by (4.47), with $i = \infty$. If $\zeta_\infty > 0$ the subscript of ξ_ℓ is ∞; if $\zeta_\infty < 0$ the subscript is 0. If $\zeta_\infty = 0$ the growth rate converges to the natural rate.

Proof: Write

$$\dot{g}/g = N - \lambda L - L(\lambda-g), \tag{4.63}$$

where it is noted that $\zeta_\infty = \lim(N - \lambda L)$ as $Z \to \infty$. Clearly, if $g > \lambda$, $\dot{Z} > 0$ (c.f. 4.53). If $g < \lambda$ and $D > 0$, $\dot{g}/g > 0$ since $\min(C) = \nu > 0$ if $\rho q_\ell - \rho + 1 < 0$. Then g increases until eventually $D < 0$ and g never decreases again to such an extent that D reaches zero again.
Hence $Z \to \infty$. Accordingly $N - \lambda L$ converges to ζ_∞.

Suppose $\zeta_\infty > 0$. Let t be sufficiently large, such that $N - \lambda L$ is close to ζ_∞, and $N - \lambda L > 0$. If $g = \lambda$, $\dot{g}/g > 0$. Hence, once $g > \lambda$, it remains so. Let $g < \lambda$. If $L > 0$ for all values of q_ℓ, g increases to λ and above Thus the value of L is crucial. It depends on the value of $\rho - \gamma M$, as $L = 1 - (1-q_\ell)(\rho - \gamma M)$.

If $\rho - \gamma\mu_\infty$ (= $\lim(\rho - \gamma M)$, $Z \to \infty$) ≤ 0, there always exists a t_1 such that $\rho - \gamma M < 0$ for $t > t_1$. Then L is a non-increasing function of q_ℓ; accordingly it has its minimum at $q_\ell = 1$; there its value is unity. Thus for $t > t_1$, L is positive and g increases to λ and above.

If $\rho - \gamma\mu_\infty > 0$, the minimum of $\lim L$ ($Z \to \infty$) in q_ℓ is $1 - \rho - \gamma\mu_\infty$. If this minimum is strictly positive, so is lim L and L too, for high t. Hence g once more increases until it exceeds λ. If, on the other hand, $1 - \rho - \gamma\mu_\infty \leq 0$, the minimum of $\dot{g}/g$ in g is attained at $g = 0$. This minimum value is $\beta M + \nu\{1 - M(1+\bar{\varepsilon})\}$. From $\rho - \gamma\mu_\infty > 0$ we obtain: $\rho\{1 - \mu_\infty(1+\bar{\varepsilon})\} + \mu_\infty\bar{\varepsilon} > 0$, hence $1 - \mu_\infty(1+\bar{\varepsilon}) > 0$. Thus, for large t, $1 - M(1+\bar{\varepsilon})$ is positive and the minimum of $\dot{g}/g$ for $g < \lambda$ is positive too. Accordingly $g > \lambda$ forever after some initial period. By lemma 4.4 the growth rate therefore converges to the value stated by theorem 4.8.

Now suppose $\zeta_\infty < 0$. Select t large, such that $N - \lambda L < 0$. If $g = \lambda$, then $\dot{g}/g < 0$, hence once $g < \lambda$, it remains so. Now, let $g > \lambda$. If $L > 0$, $\dot{g}/g < 0$. The only possibility for L <u>not</u> to be positive at large values of t is $\rho - \gamma\mu_\infty \geq 0$. Since ζ_∞ can be written as $\nu\{1 - \mu_\infty(1+\bar{\varepsilon})\} + \mu_\infty\beta + \lambda\{\rho - 1 - \gamma\mu_\infty\}$, the conditions $\rho - \gamma\mu_\infty > 0$ (which implies, as noted above, $1 - \mu_\infty(1+\bar{\varepsilon}) > 0$) and $\zeta_\infty < 0$, can only be combined if $\rho - 1 - \gamma\mu_\infty < 0$. But L can be written as $1 - \rho + \gamma M + q_\ell(\rho - \gamma M)$, which can, at large t, only be negative if $\rho - 1 - \gamma\mu_\infty > 0$ as long as $\rho - \gamma\mu_\infty > 0$. Accordingly $\zeta_\infty < 0$ implies $L > 0$ for large t. Hence g decreases to a value below λ and proof of the theorem for the case $\zeta_\infty < 0$ is complete.

Finally suppose $\zeta_\infty = 0$. Write $\zeta_\infty = \nu + \{1 - \mu_\infty(1+\bar{\varepsilon})\} + \beta\mu_\infty + \lambda\{\rho - 1 - \gamma\mu_\infty\}$. Suppose $\rho - 1 - \gamma\mu_\infty \geq 0$. Then, <u>a fortiori</u>, $\rho - \gamma\mu_\infty > 0$, hence $1 - \mu_\infty(1+\bar{\varepsilon}) > 0$, thus $\zeta_\infty > 0$, a contradiction, unless $\beta = \lambda = \nu = 0$, which is trivial. Accordingly $\zeta_\infty = 0$ implies $\rho - 1 - \gamma\mu_\infty < 0$. Hence $\lim L(t \to \infty) > 0$ and, for large t, $L > 0$. Thus $g = \lambda$ is the globally stable equilibrium.

Q.E.D.

<u>Theorem 4.9</u>: Let all the assumptions of theorem 4.6 hold, but with (4.18) replaced by (4.34); in addition assume $\theta_0 > 0$, where θ_0 is defined as in

(4.46), but with $\xi_{\ell\infty}$ replaced by $\xi_{\ell 0}$. Define ζ_0 analogously to ζ_∞ in (4.62). Then the growth rate converges globally to the constant value given by (4.47), with $i = 0$; here the subscript of ξ_ℓ is zero if $\zeta_0 < 0$ and ∞ (as in 4.47) if $\zeta_0 > 0$.

Proof: If $g < \lambda$, $D > 0$ since $\gamma > 0$ because $\rho < 1$ is implied by (4.34). If $g > \lambda$, $C < 0$. If $D < 0$, therefore, g decreases until $D > 0$. Hence for all t larger than some t_1, $D > 0$ and $Z \to 0$. The remainder of the proof easily follows along the lines of theorem 4.9, if it is noted that $\rho < 1$ implies $L > 0$.

Q.E.D.

Theorem 4.10: Let the assumptions of theorem 4.6 hold, save (4.18) and (4.19). In addition assume $\theta_i > 0$ $(i = 0,\infty)$, both with $\xi_{\ell\infty}$ and with the latter replaced by $\xi_{\ell 0}$. Then, if either (4.64) or (4.65), or both, hold:

$$\lambda(\rho-1) + \nu = 0, \tag{4.64}$$

$$\beta - \lambda - (1-\bar{\varepsilon})\{\lambda(\rho-1) + \nu\} = 0, \tag{4.65}$$

the growth rate g converges globally to a constant value provided neither (4.66), nor (4.67), nor (4.68) holds true:

$$\nu = 0,\ \rho = 1,\ \beta > \lambda,\ H_\infty < -1,\ E_0 > -1. \tag{4.66}$$

$$\nu = 0,\ \rho = 1,\ \beta < \lambda,\ H_0 > -1,\ E_\infty < -1. \tag{4.67}$$

$$\nu = 0,\ \lambda = 0,\ \rho\xi_{\ell\infty} - \rho + 1 \leq 0,\ E_0 > -1. \tag{4.68}$$

If (4.65) and (4.34) hold, the value of the growth rate is:

$$\frac{\lambda(\rho-1) + \nu}{1 - (1-\xi_{\ell j})(\rho-\gamma\mu_i)}, \tag{4.69}$$

with $j = 0$ and $i = 0$. If (4.65) and (4.18) hold, the growth rate is given by (4.69), with $j = \infty$ and $i = \infty$.

If (4.64) holds, but $\nu, \lambda \neq 0$ (implying $\rho < 1$) and in addition (4.35) holds true, the growth rate's value is (4.47), with ξ_ℓ subscripted by 0 and with $i = \infty$, as long as $E_\infty > -1$ and it is the natural rate if $E_\infty < -1$.

If (4.64) holds with ν, $\lambda \neq 0$ and if in addition (4.19) holds, the growth rate is given by (4.46), with $i = 0$, as long as $E_0 \leq -1$ and by the natural rate if $E_0 > -1$.

If both (4.64) and (4.65) hold, but ν, $\lambda \neq 0$, the long-run growth rate is the natural rate.

If $\nu = 0$ and $\lambda = 0$ and $\rho\xi_{\ell\infty} - \rho + 1 < 0$, the growth rate is

$$\frac{\beta\mu_0}{1 - (1-\xi_{\ell\infty})(\rho-\gamma\mu_0)}, \tag{4.70}$$

provided $E_0 \leq -1$. If $\nu = 0$ and $\lambda = 0$ and $\rho\xi_{\ell\infty} - \rho + 1 = 0$, the growth rate is β, provided $E_0 \leq -1$.

If $\nu = 0$ and $\lambda = 0$ and $\rho\xi_{\ell\infty} - \rho + 1 > 0$, the growth rate equals the natural rate if $E_0 > -1$ and (4.70) with μ_∞ instead of μ_0 if $E_0 \leq -1$.

If $\nu = 0$ and $\rho = 1$ and $\beta < \lambda$, the growth rate equals the natural rate if $E_\infty \leq -1$ <u>and</u> $H_0 \leq -1$; it equals

$$\frac{\beta\mu_\infty + (1-\mu_\infty)\lambda\xi_{\ell 0}}{1 - (1-\xi_{\ell 0})(1-\mu_\infty)}, \tag{4.71}$$

provided $E_\infty \geq -1$.

If $\nu = 0$ and $\rho = 1$ and $\beta = \lambda$, the growth rate equals β and λ, as long as (4.66) and (4.67) are not violated.

Finally, if $\nu = 0$ and $\rho = 1$ and $\beta > \lambda$, the growth rate equals the natural rate if $E_0 > -1$ <u>and</u> $H_\infty \geq -1$, and if $E_0 \leq -1$ <u>and</u> $H_\infty < -1$. It equals (4.71) with μ_∞ raplaced by μ_0 and ξ_{ℓ_0} by $\xi_{\ell\infty}$ if $E_0 \leq -1$ and $H_\infty \geq -1$.

<u>Proof</u>: First consider $\lambda(\rho-1) + \nu = 0$. In the case excluded by (4.68) the differential equation is:

$$\frac{\dot{g}}{g} = -(\rho q_\ell - \rho + 1)g + M\{\beta - (1-q_\ell)\gamma g\}. \tag{4.72}$$

Suppose $\rho q_\ell - \rho + 1 > 0$ initially. If g is small $\beta - (1-q_\ell)\gamma g$ is positive and hence (c.f. 4.53) Z decreases. Then, as $E_0 > -1$, M tends to converge to $\mu_0 = 0$, with g moving to zero as long as $\rho\gamma_\ell - \rho + 1$ is still positive; if g is close to zero, the capital-labour ratio ceases to increase, implying that $\rho q_\ell - \rho + 1$ is no longer drawn to the negative value associated with an infinite ratio by (4.68). Thus the growth rate, if g is small to begin with, may get stuck at $g = 0$. However, if g is large originally, Z increases, M retains a positive value, and g will converge to a positive value. Hence there are two locally stable equilibria, which is why the theorem excludes the case.

If $\rho = 1$, $\dot{g}/g$ boils down to:

$$\frac{\dot{g}}{g} = q_\ell(\lambda-g) + M\{\beta - \lambda + (1-q_\ell)(\lambda-g)\}. \qquad (4.73)$$

From this equation it is easily seen that once again two locally stable equilibria may exist if (4.66) or (4.67) are satisfied and that the other statements of the theorem hold true if not.

The final possibility with $\lambda(\rho-1) + \nu = 0$ is $\rho < 1$. Then $\rho q_\ell - \rho + 1 > 0$, and the relevant statements of the theorem are easily proved. The cases where (4.65) hold are also simple and proof is omitted.

Appendix 4.2. Parameter variations and the steady-growth rate

The present appendix derives algebraically the impact of parameter variations on the steady-growth rate given by (4.56).

Terms of trade elasticity of foreign demand

Differentiation of the 'multiplier' in (4.56) to $\bar{\varepsilon}$ yields:

$$\frac{-\mu_i}{\theta_i^2(1+\varepsilon_i+\bar{\varepsilon})}\left[\theta_{au} + \mu_i(\rho-1)(1+\varepsilon_i+\bar{\varepsilon})(1-\xi_{\ell\infty})\right]. \qquad (4.74)$$

We consider only the case $\theta_{au} > 0$, implying $\theta_i > 0$, leaving the case $\theta_{au} < 0$ to the reader.

First consider the case where the Marshall-Lerner condition is satisfied: $1 + \varepsilon_i + \bar{\varepsilon} < 0$. If the regularity conditions are formulated in terms of ε, Marshall-Lerner is satisfied by assumption (4.6). If the alternative formulation is adopted, the additional restriction $1 + \xi_{mi}\{(\rho-1) - 1\} > 0$ is sufficient to ensure Marshall-Lerner. Violatioı of this condition implies positivity of ε_i, and is obtained under high increasing returns combined with a sizeable import share. Now, as long as $1 + \varepsilon_i + \bar{\varepsilon} < 0$, $\rho < 1$ immediately implies positivity of (4.74). The same is true if there are some increasing returns, combined with a not too higl value of $\mu_i(1 + \varepsilon_i + \bar{\varepsilon})$. The latter term can be written as $\xi_{mi}\{\varepsilon_i(\rho-1) - 1\}/(1-\xi_{mi})$, which is small for low values of ξ_{mi} and moderate increasing returns.

If $1 + \varepsilon_i + \bar{\varepsilon} > 0$, (4.74) is negative, since μ_i is positive, and $1 + \varepsilon_i + \bar{\varepsilon} > 0$ implies $\rho > 1$.

Briefly: (4.74) is positive under constant, decreasing and moderate increasing returns combined with a low import share. It is negative if high increasing returns prevail in combination with a sizeable import share.

If $\rho = 1$ and $E = -1$, (4.74) boils down to:

$$\frac{\xi_{mi}\xi_{\ell\infty}(1-\xi_{mi})}{\{\bar{\varepsilon}\xi_{\ell\infty}(1-\xi_{mi}) - \xi_{mi}\}^2} \,. \tag{4.75}$$

Thus:

$$\frac{\partial \chi}{\partial \bar{\varepsilon}} = \frac{\xi_{mi}\{\xi_{\ell\infty}(1-\xi_{mi})(\beta-\lambda) - \nu\}}{\{\bar{\varepsilon}\xi_{\ell\infty}(1-\xi_{mi}) - \xi_{mi}\}^2} \tag{4.76}$$

Condition (4.58) easily follows.

<u>Labour's share in domestic factors</u>

The derivative of the multiplier $\frac{\mu_i}{\theta_i}$ to $\xi_{\ell\infty}$ is:

$$-\frac{\mu_i}{\theta_i^2} \cdot \frac{\rho B_i + \xi_{mi}\bar{\varepsilon}\{E_i(\rho-1) - 1\}}{(1-\xi_{mi})B_i + \xi_{mi}E_i\gamma} \,. \tag{4.77}$$

Since μ_i is positive and the denominator of (4.77) negative as long as (4.8) and (4.9) are satisfied, the sign of (4.77) is that of the numerator. The latter can be written as

$$\rho\bar{\varepsilon}(1-\xi_{mi}) \tag{4.78}$$

if $E_i = -1$; (4.78) is negative. If $E_i \neq -1$, ξ_{mi} is either zero (implying a zero multiplier) or unity. In the latter case the numerator of (4.77) is:

$$(1 + E_i)\{\bar{\varepsilon}(\rho-1) + \rho\}, \qquad (4.79)$$

which is negative if $E_i < -1$, and positive if $E_i > -1$.

The combination $E_i > -1$ and $\xi_{mi} = 1$ can, by table 3.5, occur only if $Z\to\infty$; theorem 4.6 states that this happens only if there is a 'loss' - assuming $\theta_{au} > 0$. Thus if there is a 'gain', the multiplier is either zero, viz. if $E_0 > -1$, or a decreasing function of $\xi_{\ell\infty}$. Proof for the formulation of the regularity conditions in terms of e is left to the reader.

Rate of returns to scale

The derivative of the multiplier μ_i/θ_i to ρ is:

$$\frac{\xi_{mi} B_i \{E_i \xi_{\ell\infty} - 1 + \xi_{\ell\infty}}{\{(1-\xi_{mi})B_i + \xi_{mi} E_i \gamma\}^2} \cdot \qquad (4.80)$$

If $B < 0$, (4.80) is positive. This is true by assumption if the regularity conditions are cast in terms of E. But if they are written in terms of e, we have $1 + \varepsilon_i + \bar{\varepsilon} < 0$ and then $E_i - \varepsilon_i < 0$ is a sufficient condition for $B = 1 + \bar{\varepsilon} + E < 0$. We may write:

$$E_i - \varepsilon_i = -\frac{\varepsilon_i \xi_{mi} \{\varepsilon_i(\rho-1) - 1\}}{\xi_{mi} \varepsilon_i(\rho-1) - 1} \cdot \qquad (4.81)$$

This is negative if the regularity conditions are given in terms of e.

Import share

The role of the import share is only relevant if $E_i = -1$, since for $E_i \neq -1$, the share is either zero or unity. The derivative of the multiplier μ_i/θ_i with respect to ξ_{mi} is, for $E_i = -1$:

$$-\frac{\bar{\varepsilon}\mu_i^2 \theta_{au}}{\rho\xi_{mi}^2 \theta_i^2}, \qquad (4.82)$$

which is positive provided $\theta_{au} > 0$. Thus, given $E = -1$, the value of the multiplier is maximal at $\xi_{mi} = 1$. Then its value is:

$$\frac{\mu_i}{\theta_i} = \frac{\rho}{\gamma} \, (E_i = -1;\ \xi_{mi} = 1). \tag{4.83}$$

Elasticity of substitution between imports and domestic factors

The relation between the multiplier and E_i depends on the value of ξ_{mi}. If $\xi_{mi} = 0$, the multiplier is zero, irrespective of the value of E_i. If $\xi_{mi} = 1$, we have:

$$\frac{\mu_i}{\theta_i} = \frac{E_i(\rho-1) - 1}{\gamma\{E_i \xi_{\ell\infty} + \xi_{\ell\infty} - 1\}} \cdot (\xi_{mi} = 1) \tag{4.84}$$

From (4.84), (4.61) easily follows. The derivative of (4.84) to E_i is:

$$\frac{\theta_{au}}{\gamma\{E_i \xi_{\ell\infty} + \xi_{\ell\infty} - 1\}^2} \cdot \tag{4.85}$$

This is positive as long as θ_{au}, $\gamma > 0$. Thus, given $\xi_{mi} = 1$, the value of the multiplier is a decreasing function of the absolute value of E_i.

If $i = 0$, $E_i > -1$ implies $\xi_{mi} = 0$, and $E_i < -1$ implies $\xi_{mi} = 1$. This is the case obtained if there is a 'gain'. Thus in this case the multiplier is highest if $E_i = -1$, $\xi_{mi} = 1$. If there is a 'loss', $i = \infty$ and the multiplier is maximal at $E = 0$: then $\xi_{mi} = 1$.

5. ECONOMIES OF MODERATE SIZE: CONSEQUENCES OF TARIFFS AND NON-SEPARABILITY OF IMPORTS AND DOMESTIC FACTORS

The present chapter extends the theory developed in the preceding one in two directions: the consequences of dropping the assumption of domestic factors-imports separability are considered; and instead of postulating free trade, tariffs on imports are allowed for.

Section 5.1 shows that dropping the assumption of imports-domestic factors separability does not affect the results of chapter 4: provided some minor modifications of the conditions are made, all theorems continue to hold. Thus the long-run growth rate is not altered if non-separability is assumed at intermediate factor ratios. In the latter case the rate still converges to the same long-run value obtained under separability, as long as our earlier assumptions on the behaviour of the production function at extreme factor ratios are properly modified.

Section 5.2, once more employing the separability assumption, introduces import duties at home and abroad. We first consider the effect of tariff changes on income in the short run, i.e. with capital and labour constant. This yields the standard optimum-tariff formula, though in our case it is modified to compensate for the rate of returns to scale. Next, retaliation is brought into the picture by the simple assumption that the foreign import duty always equals that of the home country. Naturally, the optimal duty is much lower with retaliation than without.

Next, we consider the consequences of a constant duty for the long-run development of the economy. All theorems of chapter 4 are shown to remain valid, given some minor adjustments of their conditions. Thus the development of the capital-labour ratio is not affected; neither is the long-run growth rate: its value is independent of the duty. Of course the level of income is not independent of the duty: we show the original impact of alternative tariff policies to be amplified in the long run, at least for Cobb-Douglas technology. In addition to this effect on the level of income, duties do influence the long-run growth rate if they are not constant but change. We do not analyse the possibility of long swings in duties explicitly, but no doubt such oscillations cause long-run cyclical behaviour of growth and trade.

In chapter 3 we noted that, with non-constant returns, there are two alternative specifications for the import-demand equation: one based on adjusting inputs so as to minimize factor cost at each given level of output, the other on maximizing profits with given stocks of labour and capital. In chapter 4 we used just the first of these two specifications. In the last part of section 5.2 we investigate the consequences of employing the alternative equation. We show that though the optimum-tariff formulas are slightly modified, all the other results obtained with the cost-minimizing function remain valid with the profit-maximization assumption; particularly the long-run theorems of chapter 4 and the value of the long-run growth rate are impervious to altering the import-demand equation.

Finally, section 5.3 combines both extensions and analyses the impact of duties if the production function is not separable. Once more all results neatly generalize.

In short, the present chapter shows that our results on the long-run growth of modern economies are robust in the sense of not depending crucially on either the postulate of free trade, or the assumption of separability. The reader willing to accept this conclusion without going into the details, may skip the remainder of the chapter without loss of continuity, since we again postulate free trade and separability in subsequent chapters: because qualitatively similar results are obtained both with and without these assumptions, the simplest case is preferable for theoretical work.

5.1. Non-separability of imports and domestic factors

In chapter 4 separability of imports and domestic factors has been assumed. This assumption is made for analytical convenience and simplicity of presentation. However, there is some empirical evidence contradicting the hypothesis. First, there are, as noted in section 3.3, some direct tests for the U.S. and The Netherlands, cf. Burgess (1974a,b), and Kreyger (1980). They test the equality of the Allen-Uzawa partial elasticities of substitution that is implied by separability.(1) Second, there is much recent empirical evidence (for an overview, cf. Berndt and Wood, 1979) that capital and energy broadly are complements, at least for some definitions of 'complement', cf. Berndt and Wood (1979) and Solow (1979).

If this is correct, the separability assumption is violated for countries with a high share of energy in imports, as soon as labour and energy are substitutes.

In view of these empirical considerations, it should be demonstrated that the results obtained for the case of domestic factors - imports separability do not depend crucially on this assumption, but carry over to more general cases. The present section is devoted to this job. We restrict the analysis to the case of constant returns, to obtain a simpler presentation, but it is not difficult to generalize the results to non-constant returns.

We first formulate the model, next discuss the long-run development of the capital-labour ratio, establish a steady-growth theorem and finally discuss the interpretation of the assumptions made to obtain the theorem.

Formulation of the model without separability assumption

The production function (4.1) must, without separability assumption, be written in the more general form:

$$v = v(\ell, k, m)\exp(\nu t), \qquad (5.1)$$

with v, according to the assumption of constant returns, homogeneous of degree one and strictly quasi-concave. Import demand is given by

$$v_m = P^{-1}. \qquad (5.2)$$

The export-demand equation is not altered:

$$\bar{m} = \bar{m}_0 P^{-\bar{\varepsilon}}\exp(\beta t), \qquad (5.3)$$

nor is the balance of trade restriction:

$$\bar{m} = P^{-1}m. \qquad (5.4)$$

There is no need to modify either the definition of the import share, q_1 (c.f. 3.8), nor that of the terms of trade elasticity of import demand, e Since there are constant returns, concavity of v implies

$$e < 0. \tag{5.5}$$

As in the case of separability, c.f. theorem 4.1, the Marshall-Lerner condition

$$1 + e + \bar{\varepsilon} < 0, \tag{5.6}$$

and (5.5) together imply existence of a unique solution to the model (5.1) - (5.4). In chapter 4 this was also achieved with conditions formulated in terms of E, the elasticity of substitution between imports and domestic factors. But without separability, no domestic factor function is defined; *eo ipso*, E is not defined.

Theorem 5.1: Let (5.6) be satisfied for all ℓ, k, m. Then the system (5.1) - (5.4) has a unique solution.

Proof: The proof is identical to that in the case of separability.

The dynamics of the model given in section 4.1 are not modified here. However, the role of the share of labour in domestic factors, q_ℓ, changes because without separability q_ℓ depends not only on the capital-labour ratio but on imports as well. Here it is more convenient to work with labour's share in total factor imports, q'_ℓ.

$$q'_\ell = \frac{\ell v_\ell}{v}, \quad (0 < q'_\ell < 1) \tag{5.7}$$

The capital-labour ratio in the long run

In chapter 4 a number of theorems has been established on the long-run development of the capital-labour ratio under separability: theorems 4.2 - 4.5. These theorems can be extended to the general case where no separability is assumed.

Generalization of theorem 4.2 can be omitted: this theorem states that the growth rate does not in general converge to the natural rate, even without technical progress and under constant returns. Clearly, to show lack of convergence in a special case is enough to prove the absence of a general law.

Theorem 4.3 states that the capital-labour ratio rises in the long run under normal conditions. The same is true without separability assumptio provided capital and imports are weak substitutes, i.e. the capital-imports cross-derivative of the production function is positive:

$$v_{km} > 0. \qquad (5.8)$$

This condition is not implied by quasi-concavity of v. However, separability cum quasi-concavity implies (5.8); hence in chapter 4 the condition is redundant.

In addition to (5.8) we impose the same normalcy conditions employed i the case of separability (c.f. 4.18 and 4.19). Under constant returns th collapse to:

$$\nu > 0, \qquad (5.9)$$
$$\beta - \lambda - (1+\bar{\varepsilon})\nu > 0.$$

We now state:

Theorem 5.2: Assume (5.6), (5.8), (5.9), but do not assume separability. Then the growth rate, g, of capital exceeds that of labour, λ, permanent after an initial period.

Proof: Differentiating (5.1) and using (5.7) we obtain:

$$\frac{\dot{v}}{v} = q_\ell'\lambda + q_m\frac{\dot{m}}{m} + (1 - q_\ell' - q_m)g + \nu. \qquad (5.10)$$

Differentiation of (5.2) yields:

$$\frac{\dot{P}}{P} = \frac{1}{e}\left(\frac{\dot{m}}{m} - \lambda\right) + \frac{kv_{km}}{v_m}(g-\lambda) + \nu \qquad \left(= \frac{\dot{v}_m}{v_m}\right), \qquad (5.11)$$

where the right-hand side is obtained by substituting e for v_m/mv_{mm} and substituting:

$$\frac{kv_{km}}{v_m} + \frac{1}{e} = -\frac{\ell v_{\ell m}}{v_m}, \qquad (5.12)$$

this equation being due to linear homogeneity of v. Differentiation of (5.3) and (5.4) yields:

$$\frac{\dot{\bar{m}}}{\bar{m}} = -\bar{\varepsilon}\frac{\dot{P}}{P} + \beta. \tag{5.13}$$

$$\frac{\dot{\bar{m}}}{\bar{m}} = \frac{\dot{P}}{P} + \frac{\dot{m}}{m}. \tag{5.14}$$

As in chapter 4 we have:

$$g = \sigma\frac{v}{k}(1 - q_m), \tag{5.15}$$

and:

$$\frac{\dot{g}}{g} = \frac{\dot{v}}{v} - g - \frac{\dot{q}_m}{q_m}\cdot\frac{q_m}{1-q_m}, \tag{5.16}$$

with

$$\frac{\dot{q}_m}{q_m} = \frac{\dot{m}}{m} - \frac{\dot{v}}{v} + \frac{\dot{v}_m}{v_m}. \tag{5.17}$$

From (5.10) - (5.17) the growth rate's derivative with respect to time can be written as:

$$\frac{\dot{g}}{g} = \nu - \frac{q_\ell'}{1-q_m}(g-\lambda) - \frac{q_m}{(1+e+\bar{\varepsilon})(1-q_m)}\{\beta-(1+\bar{\varepsilon})\nu - \lambda + e\frac{kv_{km}}{v_m}(g-\lambda)\}. \tag{5.18}$$

Assumptions(5.6) and (5.8), along with $e < 0$, imply that the multipliers of $g - \lambda$ in (5.15) are negative or zero. Assumption (5.9) implies that the other terms (the intercept) are strictly positive. Consequently $\dot{g}/g$ is positive for $g < \lambda$. Hence after some initial period g exceeds λ forever.

Q.E.D.

Theorem 4.4 establishes for the separability case that the capital-labour ratio falls in the long run if the two normalcy conditions (4.18) and (4.19) are violated. The same is true if no separability is assumed; this is established by theorem 5.3.

Theorem 5.3: Assume (5.6) and (5.7) to hold and let:

$$\nu < 0, \tag{5.19}$$

$$\beta - \lambda - (1+\bar{\varepsilon})\nu < 0, \tag{5.20}$$

but do not assume separability. Then the capital-labour ratio declines monotonically to zero after a finite initial period.

Proof: It is easily seen, using (5.18), that the assumptions of the theorem imply negativity of $\dot{g}/g$ for $g > \lambda$. Hence g declines until it is smaller than λ, and remains so.

Q.E.D.

Theorem 4.5 states that in the absence of technical progress and labour growth, long-run growth at a positive rate still remains possible as long as foreign demand grows and the elasticity of substitution between import and domestic factors, E, exceeds unity in absolute value. This theorem generalizes to the non-separable case, but the elasticity of substitution condition must be replaced because this elasticity is not defined without separability. Instead we assume:

$$e(1-q_m) < -1, \tag{5.21}$$

and

$$\frac{kv_{km}}{v_m} - 1 + q_\ell' + q_m > 0. \tag{5.22}$$

Under separability, both conditions boil down to $E < -1$ (as is seen using (3.8), (3.9), (3.13) and the formulae of appendix 3.2). The latter condition is imposed in theorem 4.5 to prevent the import share q_m from vanishing. Without separability assumption, the time derivative of this share is:

$$\frac{\dot{q}_m}{q_m} = \left(\frac{e(1-q_m) + 1}{e}\right)\left(\frac{\dot{m}}{m} - \lambda\right) + \left(\frac{kv_{km}}{v_m} - 1 + q_\ell' + q_m\right)(g-\lambda). \tag{5.23}$$

Clearly (5.21) and (5.22) imply that q_m does not vanish as long as the capital-labour ratio and per capita imports rise. The former is true by theorem 5.2; to achieve the latter without separability assumption one additional restriction must be imposed: elasticity of foreign demand, i.e.

$$\bar{\varepsilon} < -1 \tag{5.24}$$

Given this condition, the crucial part of theorem 4.5 neatly generalizes to the non-separable case.(2)

Theorem 5.4: Assume (5.6), (5.8), (5.24) and (5.21), (5.22) to hold; in addition let $\beta > 0$ and $\nu = \lambda = 0$; but do not assume imports-domestic factors separability. Then there is a positive long-run growth rate of capital.

Proof: With $\lambda = \nu = 0$, (5.18) collapses to:

$$\frac{\dot{g}}{g} = -\frac{q'_\ell}{1-q_m} g - \frac{q_m}{(1+e+\bar{\varepsilon})(1-q_m)} \{\beta + e \frac{kv_{km}}{v_m} g\}. \tag{5.25}$$

The rate of growth of imports is:

$$\frac{\dot{m}}{m} = \frac{e}{1+e+\bar{\varepsilon}} \{\beta - (1+\bar{\varepsilon}) \frac{kv_{km}}{v_m} g\}. \tag{5.26}$$

Since $g > 0$, (5.24) and (5.7) imply non-negativity of $\dot{m}/m$. As $\lambda = 0$, this implies non-negativity of $\dot{q}_m$ (c.f. 5.23), since $e < 0$ and given (5.21) and (5.22). Hence q_m is always strictly positive. Consequently, in (5.25) β has a strictly positive multiplier and g cannot decline to zero, as $\dot{g}/g = 0$ at some $g > 0$.

Q.E.D.

A steady-growth theorem

The steady-growth theorem for the separable case, theorem 4.6, is founded on the extreme factor ratio conditions (4.40) and (4.41): these are sufficient to render the factor shares and the terms of trade elasticity of import demand constant in the long run. The conditions cannot be generalized unmodified to the non-separable case, because the conditions presuppose each of the relevant shares and elasticities to be functions of a single factor ratio only; but without separability this is not true and all shares and elasticities are functions of two factor ratios. In particular, theorem 5.7 establishes that q'_ℓ, q_m, e, and kv_{km}/v_m can all be written as functions of the capital-labour ratio and of per capita imports.

<u>Theorem 5.5</u>: The functions q'_ℓ, q_m, e and $\frac{kv_{km}}{v_m}$ are functions of $K = k/\ell$ and m/ℓ only.

<u>Proof</u>: Define $V = v/\ell$. Hence $V = v(1, K, \frac{m}{\ell})\exp(\nu t)$ is a function of K and m/ℓ alone. As is easily seen we have:

$$v_m = V_{m/\ell}, \tag{5.27}$$

$$v_{mm} = \frac{1}{\ell} V_{\frac{m}{\ell}\frac{m}{\ell}}, \tag{5.28}$$

$$v_k = V_K, \tag{5.29}$$

$$v_{km} = V_{K\frac{m}{\ell}} \cdot \frac{1}{\ell} \tag{5.30}$$

where $V_{m/\ell}$ is V's derivative to m/ℓ and $V_{\frac{m}{\ell}\frac{m}{\ell}}$ the derivative of $V_{m/\ell}$ to m/ℓ. Using (5.27) - (5.30), and the definitions of $q_m \left(= \frac{mv_m}{v}\right)$, $q'_k \left(= \frac{kv_k}{v}\right)$, $e\left(= \frac{v_m}{mv_{mm}}\right)$, we obtain:

$$q_m = \frac{\frac{m}{\ell} V_{m/\ell}}{V}, \tag{5.31}$$

$$q'_k = \frac{KV_K}{V}, \tag{5.32}$$

$$e = \frac{V_{m/\ell}}{\frac{m}{\ell} V_{\frac{m}{\ell}\frac{m}{\ell}}}, \tag{5.33}$$

$$\frac{kv_{km}}{v_m} = \frac{KV_{K\frac{m}{\ell}}}{V_{m/\ell}} \,. \tag{5.34}$$

Thus the functions in the left-hand sides of (5.31) - (5.34) depend on K and m/ℓ only. Since $q'_\ell = 1 - q_m - q'_k$, the same applies to q'_ℓ.

Q.E.D.

In view of theorem 5.5, we can replace the extreme factor ratio conditions of the separable case, (4.40) and (4.41), by the condition that the relevant shares and elasticities become constant if both K and m/ℓ become zero or infinite:

If both K is zero or infinite and $\frac{m}{\ell}$ is zero or infinite, q_m, q'_ℓ, kv_{km}/v_m and e attain constant finite values. (5.35)

Theorem 5.6 states that with condition (5.35) once more a stable steady-growth rate is obtained.

Theorem 5.6: Let (5.6), (5.7), (5.9), (5.24) and (5.35) hold. Then the growth rate g of capital converges globally to a constant value χ, given by:

$$\chi = \frac{\nu - \lambda\xi_\ell}{\xi_\ell} + \frac{\mu}{\xi_\ell - \mu\varepsilon\eta}\left[\beta - \bar{\varepsilon}\nu - \frac{\nu - \lambda\xi_\ell}{\xi_\ell} + \nu(1-\xi_\ell+\varepsilon\eta)\right]. \tag{5.36}$$

Here:

$$\xi_\ell = \lim_{\substack{K\to\infty \\ \frac{m}{\ell}\to\infty}} \frac{q'_\ell}{1-q_m} \,; \tag{5.37}$$

$$\mu = \lim_{\substack{K\to\infty \\ \frac{m}{\ell}\to\infty}} \frac{-q_m}{(1+e+\bar{\varepsilon})(1-q_m)} \,; \tag{5.38}$$

$$\varepsilon = \lim_{\substack{K\to\infty \\ \frac{m}{\ell}\to\infty}} e \,; \tag{5.39}$$

$$\eta = \lim_{\substack{K\to\infty \\ \frac{m}{\ell}\to\infty}} \frac{kv_{km}}{v_m} \tag{5.40}$$

Proof: By theorem 5.2 we have $K\to\infty$. From (5.10) - (5.17) we obtain for $\dot{m}/m - \lambda$:

$$\frac{\dot{m}}{m} - \lambda = \frac{e}{1+e+\bar{\varepsilon}} \{\beta - (1+\bar{\varepsilon})\nu - \lambda - (1+\bar{\varepsilon}) \frac{kv_{km}}{v_m} (g-\lambda)\}. \tag{5.41}$$

As $g > \lambda$ after some initial period, $\bar{\varepsilon} < -1$, $\beta - (1+\bar{\varepsilon})\nu - \lambda > 0$, $v_{km} > 0$ and $e/(1+e+\bar{\varepsilon}) > 0$, we have $\frac{\dot{m}}{m} - \lambda > 0$ after some initial perio Thus $m/\ell\to\infty$. Hence the functions in the right-hand side of (5.37) - (5.3 converge to their limits. The remainder of the theorem is proved in exactly the same way as lemma 4.4.

Q.E.D.

Interpretation of the steady-growth theorem

Two points regarding the steady-growth theorem 5.6 require a closer look: the value of the steady-growth rate and the extreme factor ratio condition.

At first sight the long-run growth rate given by theorem 5.6 differs from the one in the case of separability (4.47). However, theorem 5.7 establishes that the constancy of the import share in the long run impli equivalence of both growth rates.

Theorem 5.9: The growth rate (5.36), obtained under the conditions of theorem 5.8, has the same value as (4.47) with $\rho = 1$.

Proof: The long-run value of q_m is constant. Thus it is either zero, o non-zero. If it is zero, we have (c.f. 5.38) $\mu = 0$. Hence in that case (5.36) boils down to $(\nu - \lambda\xi_\ell)/\xi_\ell$, which is precisely the value of (4. with $\xi_m = 0$ and $\rho = 1$.

If the long-run value of q_m, ξ_m, is non-zero, we have $\dot{q}_m = 0$. Condition (5.35) states that q_m achieves its constant value if K and m/ℓ become infinite, irrespective of the value of the ratio of K to m/ℓ.

By (5.23) this implies $\{e(1-q_m) + 1\}/e \to 0$, and $\frac{kv_{km}}{v_m} - 1 + q'_\ell + q_m \to 0$ as $K \to \infty$ and $m/\ell \to \infty$. Thus in the long run we have:

$$\frac{kv_{km}}{v_m} = 1 - \xi'_\ell - \xi_m = (1-\xi_m)(1-\xi_\ell). \tag{5.42}$$

$$e = \frac{1}{1-\xi_m} . \tag{5.43}$$

Introduction of (5.42) and (5.43) in the growth rate (5.36) yields precisely (4.47), with $\rho = 1$.

Q.E.D.

Theorem 5.7 establishes that, with extreme factor ratio condition (5.35) imposed, the long-run growth obtained under separability of imports and domestic factors can also be obtained without this condition. Condition (5.35), however, has two drawbacks.

First, it is not a proper generalization of the corresponding conditions in the separable case: if separability is imposed in addition to (5.35), condition (4.40) is not implied; to achieve the latter an additional restriction on k/m would be required. Consequently, (5.35) is weaker than the extreme factor ratio conditions of chapter 4, and there is a price to pay for this: theorem 5.6 is valid only if foreign demand is elastic, whereas theorem 4.6 holds for inelastic foreign demand as well.

A second disadvantage of (5.35) is, that it is slightly arbitrary. For the functions q'_ℓ, q_m, e and kv_{km}/v_m may also be written as functions of k/ℓ and m/k, instead of k/ℓ and m/ℓ as in (5.35). Therefore one might assume (5.35) with m/k replacing m/ℓ. However, in that case theorem 5.6 does not follow. The reason for this is that the evolution of the imports-capital ratio is much more subtle than that of the capital-labour and imports-labour ratios.

In spite of these drawbacks, (5.35) is attractive: it covers non-separability at intermediate values of the capital-labour ratio and per capita imports, but also separability at the extremes. To show that (5.35) is compatible with non-separability of imports and domestic factors, we give two examples of classes of functions satisfying (5.35). Both are simply special cases of the two alternative cases of separability that are possible with a three-factor production function: separability of labour from imports and capital and separability of capital from labour and imports.

In both cases, however, one additional restriction is made: part of the function is Cobb-Douglas. In the former case the function of imports and capital has the Cobb-Douglas property, in the latter the master function is restricted in this way. By imposing conditions analogous to (4.40) and (4.41) on the remainder of the production function, condition (5.35) is seen to be satisfied.

Theorem 5.8: Consider two classes of functions. First the class where:

(i) v is separable in ℓ and w(m, k)

(ii) w(m, k) is Cobb-Douglas

(iii) lim $E_{\ell w}$, lim q'_ℓ as $w/\ell \to 0$ and as $w/\ell \to \infty$ exist.

Here v' is the 'separated' function; $H_{\ell m}$ is the direct Hicks elasticity of substitution between labour and imports, and q'_m is the value share of imports in labour and imports.

Both classes of functions satisfy (5.35).

Proof: We prove the theorem for the first class only: proof for the second class follows easily.

Let $k/\ell \to \infty$ and $m/\ell \to \infty$. Then $w/\ell \to \infty$. Hence by (iii) $E_{\ell w}$ and q'_ℓ approach their limiting values. Since the shares of capital and imports are constant by assumption (ii), so are the shares of all three factors in total inputs. For e and kv_{km}/v_m we obtain, using relations analogous to those in appendix 3.2:

$$e = \frac{-E_{\ell w}}{E_{\ell w}(1-\xi'_m) - \xi'_m q'_\ell} ; \tag{5.44}$$

$$\frac{kv_{km}}{v_m} = \frac{E_{\ell w}}{(1-\xi'_m)(E_{\ell w} + q'_\ell)} . \tag{5.45}$$

Here ξ'_m is imports' constant share in reproducible factors. From (5.44) and (5.45) e and kv_{km}/v_m are immediately seen to be constant for extreme values of k/ℓ and m/ℓ, since the right-hand sides depend on $E_{\ell w}$ and q'_ℓ alone and these two functions are constant at extreme factor ratios.

Q.E.D.

It remains to show that the two classes of functions of theorem 5.11 do not have the property of imports-domestic factors separability. The most illuminating way to show this, is to calculate the difference between the two Allen partial elasticities of substitution between imports and domestic factors, for this difference is zero if the latter two are separable. Appendix 3.2 provides the required formulas, table 5.1 gives the difference between the two. As the table shows, this difference may range from minus infinity to infinity, specifically for class 2 functions. Consequently, theorems (5.6) - (5.8) together prove that the steady-growth rate of chapter 4 can also be obtained without separability of imports and domestic factors.

Table 5.1. Differences between the Allen partial elasticities of substitution capital-imports and labour-imports, for three classes of functions.

Separability case	Further restrictions	Elasticity difference	Range of difference
$z(k,\ell)$, m (Chapter 4)		0	0
$w(k,m)$, ℓ ('class 1',theorem 5.8)	w Cobb-Douglas $E_{w\ell} < -1$	$\frac{E_{\ell w}+1}{1-q_\ell'}$	$(-\infty, 0)$
$u(\ell,m)$, k ('class 2',theorem 5.8)	$v(u,k)$ Cobb-Douglas	$\frac{H_{\ell m}+1}{1-q_m-q_\ell'}$	$(-\infty, \infty)$

5.2. Effects of import duties

This section considers the effects of import duties at home and abroad on the income of the economies of moderate size discussed in chapter 4. We first analyse the consequences for the short run; our main departure from the standard literature is to admit increasing and decreasing returns.

Next we consider the impact of duties on the long-run growth rate. In th present section we once again employ the assumption of separability of imports and domestic factors.

Short-run consequences of tariffs: optimum duties

We alter the model of chapter 4 in two ways: by introducing a foreign import duty in the export-demand equation and a duty in the country's import-demand equation.

Apart from the introduction of a duty, the import-demand equation employed in chapter 4 is not altered. Thus:

$$v_m = \rho P^{-1}(1+\tau), \qquad (5.46)$$

where τ is the ad valorem duty. An implication of (5.46) is, that the function q_m that plays an important role in chapter 4, no longer represents the value share of imports (or, more precisely, the ratio of the value of imports to that of output). Instead we now have:

$$q_m = (1 + \tau) \frac{mP^{-1}}{v}. \qquad (5.47)$$

Thus here q_m represents the share of imports plus the duty proceeds. In chapters 3 and 4, the only restriction imposed on q_m is $0 < q_m < 1$. In view of (5.47) the additional restriction

$$q_m < 1 + \tau, \qquad (5.48)$$

is required in order to ensure that the costs of imports do not exceed t value of output. Condition (5.48) is always satisfied if there is a positive duty; but if there is an import subsidy (equivalent to an expoı subsidy), (5.48) requires that q_m should not be too close to unity.

The export-demand equation is:

$$\bar{m} = \bar{m}_0 P^{-\bar{\varepsilon}}(1 + \bar{\tau})^{\bar{\varepsilon}} \exp(\beta t). \qquad (5.49)$$

Here $\bar{\tau}$ is the foreign import duty. There is no need to introduce an exp(tax or subsidy as well, because Lerner's (1936) symmetry holds: an impoı duty is equivalent to an export tax of the same percentage, as long as trade is balanced.

It is easily seen that an equilibrium of the balance of trade, with export equation (5.49) and import-demand equation (5.46), exists under the same conditions imposed in the free-trade case of chapter 4 (theorem 4.1).

The effect of the duties on income is obtained by totally differentiating the system and solving, in much the same way as was done in the proof of theorem 4.3. This yields:

$$\frac{dy}{y} = \frac{eq_m}{(1+\tau-q_m)(1+e+\bar{\varepsilon})} \{\gamma+\tau\rho(1+\bar{\varepsilon})\}\frac{d\tau}{1+\tau} + \frac{\bar{\varepsilon}q_m\{e\rho\tau+e(\rho-1)-1\}}{(1+\tau-q_m)(1+e+\bar{\varepsilon})} \frac{d\bar{\tau}}{1+\bar{\tau}} . \qquad (5.50)$$

Alternatively, this may be written in terms of E:

$$\frac{dy}{y} = \frac{Eq_m}{(1+\tau-q_m)\{(1-q_m)B+q_mE\gamma\}} \{\gamma+\tau\rho(1+\bar{\varepsilon})\} \frac{d\tau}{1+\tau}$$

$$+ \frac{\bar{\varepsilon}q_m[E\rho\tau + (1-q_m)\{E(\rho-1) - 1\}]}{(1+\tau-q_m)\{(1-q_m)B+q_mE\gamma\}} \frac{d\bar{\tau}}{1+\bar{\tau}} . \qquad (5.51)$$

As long as (5.48) holds, the standard regularity conditions of chapter 4 (i.e. (4.5), (4.6) and (4.7), (4.8), (4.9), respectively) imply positivity of the first part of the multipliers of $d\tau$ in (5.50) and (5.51). Hence the effect of changes in the duty on income depends on the sign of $\gamma + \tau\rho(1+\bar{\varepsilon})$, which equals $\rho(1+\bar{\varepsilon})(1+\tau)-\bar{\varepsilon}$. As usual, if foreign demand is inelastic ($-1 < \bar{\varepsilon} < 0$), any increase in the duty raises income; but with elastic foreign demand ($\bar{\varepsilon} < -1$) there is a finite optimum duty, given by:

$$1 + \tau_{opt} = \frac{\bar{\varepsilon}}{\rho(1+\bar{\varepsilon})} . \qquad (5.52)$$

This optimum-tariff formula dates back, for constant returns, to Bickerdyke (1907). A modern exposition in a HOS-type model is given by Chipman (1972) and Takayama (1974). Incidentally, Chipman prefers the term 'exploitative' to 'optimal', because the latter might suggest maximization of world welfare, whereas (5.52) only gives 'a simple formula for the optimum tax [...] if it is desired to exploit the foreigner' (Lerner, 1944, p. 382), or, in another context, a 'beggar my neighbour' remedy (Robinson, 1937).

In (5.52) the traditional formula is corrected for the rate of returns to scale. With increasing returns, the optimum duty is somewhat lower, with decreasing returns a bit higher than in the ordinary case of consta returns.

The major argument against protection is that it invites retaliation. show the consequences of the latter, one may specify various reaction patterns, in the tradition of Scitovsky (1941-2), Johnson (1953-4), Kuga (1973). But we avoid this by considering just the simplest possible pattern: instant retaliation with a duty of precisely the same value, i. $\tau = \bar{\tau}$, $d\tau = d\bar{\tau}$. In this case an increase in the duty always raises inc if $\bar{\varepsilon} > -\frac{1}{2}$ and not, as without retaliation, as soon as $\bar{\varepsilon} > -1$. If $\bar{\varepsilon} < -\frac{1}{2}$, there once again is a finite optimum duty:

$$1 + \tau'_{opt} = \frac{\bar{\varepsilon}(1+2e)}{\rho e(1+2\bar{\varepsilon})} = \frac{\bar{\varepsilon}[(1+E)(1-q_m) + E(1+\rho q_m)]}{\rho E(1+2\bar{\varepsilon})} . \tag{5.53}$$

As shown in appendix 5.1, τ'_{opt} is always lower than τ_{opt}: the possibili of retaliation lowers the duty.

If constant returns to scale prevail, the optimum duty is normally negative, specifically as soon as $\bar{\varepsilon} < e$. This condition says that it i easier for the rest of the world to replace its imports from an individ country than it is for that individual country to produce its imports a home. Thus normally, keeping Lerner's symmetry in mind, export subsidie are advantageous and import duties harmful. The only exception to this rule are monopolistic exporters of raw materials. Here e may fall short of $\bar{\varepsilon}$, implying that (positive) import duties are beneficial.

Increasing returns lower the optimal duty with retaliation, as they d without retaliation. If e.g. import elasticities at home and abroad are assigned equal values, i.e. $e = \bar{\varepsilon}$, the ad-valorem optimum duty plus uni equals the inverse of the rate of returns to scale.

Independence of the long-run growth rate of import duties

If constant, the foreign duty has no influence on the development of capital-labour ratio or the growth rate. It just shifts the foreign de curve once and for all and has only a temporary effect on the growth r This is immediately seen from (5.49): adding $(1+\bar{\tau})^{\bar{\varepsilon}}$ is equivalent to raising $\bar{m}_0$, and the latter parameter plays no role in long-run developments. If, in contrast, the foreign duty changes at a constant rate, the non-price growth rate of foreign demand is altered; instead of β it then is:

$$\beta' = \beta + \left(\frac{\dot{\tau}}{1+\bar{\tau}}\right)^{\bar{\varepsilon}} . \qquad (5.54)$$

The beneficial effects of a high rate of growth of non-price foreign demand have been discussed *in extenso* in chapter 4. Equation (5.54) makes clear that a gradual, sustained liberalization of world trade must have a similar positive effect on the basic growth rates of trading countries. Thus the gradual trade liberalization of the 35 years following world war II must have contributed substantially to the growth rate of most countries. Similarly, if the present trend towards more protectionism continues, the global depression of growth rates will be enhanced. Usually duties are lowered in the upward leg of long swings (of income's growth rate) and raised in the downswing. Our results of the preceding chapter combined with (5.54) confirm that this cyclical behaviour of tariff authorities intensifies the long cycles. *Clearly, an important step towards stabilizing long-term growth rates of trade and income, would be a globally implemented policy of high duties in periods of expansion and lower ones in depressions.*

Of course, in the 'long run' the growth rate of duties cannot be positive or negative, but must either be zero, or display oscillations. Hence in our long-run analysis we simply consider the case of constant duties; these may either be thought of as long-run averages or as describing just one leg of the long cycle in a growth model covering only that part of the cycle.

The long-run growth rate is not only independent of a constant *foreign* duty but also of a constant *domestic* one. This is established in theorem 5.1. Thus the growth rate given by (4.47), and extensively discussed in the last sections of chapter 4, is valid both for economies ridden by constant tariffs and for those with free-trade regimes. Of course the duty enters the conditions for convergence, but even this is of marginal importance only: just the regularity conditions (4.20) and (4.21) must be modified in a minor way. With free trade these conditions are:

$$e(\rho-1) < 0. \qquad (4.20)$$

$$E(\rho-1) < 0. \qquad (4.21)$$

These conditions are now replaced by:

$$e\rho\tau + e(\rho-1) - 1 < 0. \qquad (5.55)$$

$$E\rho\tau + (1-q_m)\{E(\rho-1) - 1\} < 0. \qquad (5.56)$$

Both inequalities are already implied by (4.20) and (4.21) respectively i $\tau > 0$, i.e. if there is an import tax; only if there is an import (or export) subsidy are (5.55) and (5.56) a bit more restrictive than (4.20) and (4.21).

Theorem 5.9: Let (5.48) hold true. Then theorems 4.2 through 4.6 are als valid if there are constant import duties at home and abroad, with the single modification that (4.20) and (4.21) are replaced by (5.48) and (5.49), respectively.

Proof: The duty enters the basic model of chapter 4 only in the import-demand equation. Income equation (4.13) is not affected, since income i still given as output less payments abroad for imports. Some calculatio now shows the duty to enter the fundamental growth equations, (4.30) - (4.33) in the free-trade case, in the function M alone:

$$M = \frac{q_m}{1+\tau-q_m} \frac{\{e\rho\tau+e(\rho-1)-1\}}{1+e+\bar{\varepsilon}} = \frac{q_m}{1+\tau-q_m} \frac{E\rho\tau+(1-q_m)\{E(\rho-1)-1\}}{(1-q_m)B + q_m E\gamma} . \qquad (5.57)$$

With respect to M's value, strict positivity at finite non-zero Z and K is the only restriction required to obtain theorems 4.2 through 4.5 an the part of theorem 4.6 establishing the existence of a stable growth rate. In the free-trade case of chapter 4, M is rendered positive by t regularity conditions; in the present case (5.48), (5.55) and (5.56) d the job. It remains to show that the duty does not occur in the steady growth rate. The only parameter through which it enters the rate at fi sight, is $\mu_1 \equiv \lim M(Z\to i,\ i = 0, \infty)$. Now, on the steady-growth path either of three equalities holds: $E = -1$, $\xi_{mi} = 0$, or $\xi_{mi} = 1$. The value of μ_i for these three cases is:

$$\mu_i = 0. \qquad (\xi_{mi} = 0)$$

$$\mu_i = \frac{-\rho\xi_{mi}}{\bar{\varepsilon}(1-\xi_{mi}) - \gamma\xi_{mi}}. \qquad (E = -1) \qquad (5.58)$$

$$\mu_i = \frac{\rho}{\gamma}. \qquad (\xi_{mi} = 1)$$

In all three cases the duty drops out, which completes the proof.

Effects of duties on the level of income

Apparently the role of a constant duty in long-run growth is similar to that of the rate of saving: it has only a temporary effect on the growth rate and does not influence its long-run value. However, like the rate of saving, the duty does affect the level of income in the long run. It is not possible to achieve any general quantitative results on the value of this income effect in the long run. But for the specific case of a Cobb-Douglas production function interesting results are obtained. The production function then is:

$$v = v_0[\{\ell^{\xi_\ell} k^{1-\xi_\ell}\}^{1-\xi_m} m^{\xi_m}]^\rho \exp(\nu t). \qquad (5.59)$$

Now suppose the country contemplates at time $t = 0$ the advantages of imposing an optimum duty; let the country assume absence of retaliation and impose the optimum no-retaliation duty τ_{opt}. However, let the no-retaliation assumption be incorrect: the rest of the world also imposes the same duty, $\bar{\tau} = \tau_{opt}$. We assume that, once the retaliationary measures have been triggered abroad, it is not possible to liberalize trade again: in practice trade liberalization takes a lot of time. What then is the ratio of the income thus obtained to that which would have prevailed had the retaliation been anticipated and the optimum duty been selected accordingly ($\tau = \bar{\tau} = \tau'_{opt}$)? Appendix 5.1 provides the basic derivations. At time $t = 0$, the ratio of both incomes, $\frac{y}{y'}$ $(t = 0)$, is:

$$\frac{y}{y'}(t=0) \equiv \frac{y(\tau=\bar{\tau}=\tau_{opt})}{y(\tau=\bar{\tau}=\tau'_{opt})}(t=0) = \frac{1+\tau_{opt}-\xi_m}{1+\tau'_{opt}-\xi_m}\left(\frac{1+\tau_{opt}}{1+\tau'_{opt}}\right)^{\frac{-\bar{\varepsilon}(1+\rho\xi_m)}{\bar{\varepsilon}(1-\rho\xi_m)-\rho\xi_m}} . \qquad (5.60)$$

On the steady-growth path this difference evolves to:

$$\frac{y}{y'}(t\to\infty) = \left[\frac{y}{y'}(t=0)\right]^{\frac{\bar{\varepsilon}(1-\xi_m) - \gamma\xi_m}{\bar{\varepsilon}(1-\xi_m)-\gamma\xi_m-\bar{\varepsilon}\rho(1-\xi_m)(1-\xi_\ell)}} . \qquad (5.61)$$

The denominator of the exponent and its numerator have the same sign, as long as labour's share in domestic factors, ξ_ℓ, is not too small. Moreover, the denominator is smaller in absolute value than the numeratoı Thus, normally, an initial difference in income is amplified on the steady-growth path.

Table 5.2 presents a numerical illustration of the optimum duties and their impact on incomes. The values of ξ_ℓ, $\bar{\varepsilon}$, i.e. 0.75 and -2.0, respectively, are those used in the standard example of chapter 4.

Table 5.2. Short- and long-run income effect of alternative tariff constellations.

Rate of returns to scale ρ	Import share ξ_m(%)	Optimum duty without retaliation τ_{opt}(%)	Optimum duty with retaliation τ'_{opt}(%)	Ratio of income with foreign domestic duties at τ_{opt} to th with both duties at τ'_{opt} y/y'(%) Initially(t=0)	Eventually (t
1.1	10	81.8	-32.7	93.3	91.1
1.1	20	81.8	-26.1	87.4	83.6
1.1	30	81.8	-19.4	82.1	74.4
0.9	10	122.2	-19.3	94.5	93.0
0.9	20	122.2	-12.6	89.5	87.0
0.9	30	122.2	- 5.9	84.9	81.9

The table shows that the loss of income due to the miscalculation of the foreign tariff reaction increases as a function of the rate of returns tc scale and the import share; the increase of the initial loss on the steady-growth path is brought out clearly.

Consequences of an alternative specification of import demand

In section 3.4 we found that, with non-constant returns to scale, there are two alternative import-demand equations, one based on cost minimization at each given level of output, the other one on profit maximization given the stocks of capital and labour. In chapter 4 and in the preceding part of the present section, we employed the first of these two specifications. But since there is no strong presumption in favour of either, the consequences of employing the alternative one should be explored too. We devote the last part of the present section to that job, because it turns out that the only interesting change caused by this modification of the import-demand specification is a change in the optimum-tariff formulae.

With profit maximization the import-demand equation, accounting for an import duty, is:

$$v_m = P^{-1}(1+\tau). \qquad (5.62)$$

We shall briefly demonstrate that use of (5.62) instead of (5.46) does not alter any long-run results, such as the value of the steady-growth rate, or the independence of the latter of duties. Only the interpretation of the 'share function', q_m, and the optimum-tariff formulae are modified. The share function (5.47) is to be replaced by:

$$q_m = \frac{1+\tau}{\rho}\,\frac{mP^{-1}}{v}. \qquad (5.63)$$

Thus q_m is no longer the value share of imports plus duty proceeds, but is interpreted to be the latter, corrected for the rate of returns to scale. Accordingly, condition (5.48) is to be replaced by:

$$q_m < \frac{1+\tau}{\rho}. \qquad (5.64)$$

Equation (5.50) now becomes:

$$\frac{dy}{y} = \frac{e\rho q_m\{1+\tau(1+\bar{\varepsilon})\}}{(1+\tau-\rho q_m)(1+e+\bar{\varepsilon})}\frac{d\tau}{1+\tau} + \frac{\bar{\varepsilon}\rho q_m(e\tau-1)}{(1+\tau-\rho q_m)(1+e+\bar{\varepsilon})}\frac{d\bar{\tau}}{1+\bar{\tau}}\,. \tag{5.65}$$

This yields as optimum duty without retaliation:

$$1 + \tau_{opt} = \frac{\bar{\varepsilon}}{1+\bar{\varepsilon}}\,, \tag{5.66}$$

which is precisely the traditional formula. Thus here no correction for the rate of returns to scale is necessary. Why this difference with (5.52)? The effect of an optimum duty is to redetermine imports such as t maximize income, instead of e.g. profits as the import-demand equation does. Therefore, with different import-demand equations, different duties are required to push imports to the income-maximizing level.

From (5.65) the optimum duty with retaliation is easily calculated as:

$$1 + \tau'_{opt} = \frac{\bar{\varepsilon}(1+2e)}{e(1+2\bar{\varepsilon})}\,, \tag{5.67}$$

which is once again similar to (5.53), but lacks the latter's correction for the rate of returns to scale.

Theorem 5.10 establishes that once again the long-run theorems of chapter 4 remain valid; the steady-growth rate is not altered. But, as above, the convergence conditions must be slightly modified. Here all conditions of chapter 4 are retained, but two new, though innocuous, ones are added:

$$e\tau - 1 < 0. \tag{5.68}$$

$$E\tau - 1 < 0. \tag{5.69}$$

The first one is added to the set (4.5), (4.6); these require negativity of e. Hence (5.68) is always satisfied if there is an import tax; it is not very restrictive if there is an export subsidy. Since $E < 0$ is assume throughout, the consequences of (5.69) are similar to those of (5.68).

<u>Theorem 5.10</u>: Let the import-demand equation be (5.62). Let (5.64) hold true. Then theorems 4.2 and 4.6 hold true, with the modification that (5.68) is added to the regularity conditions if these are cast in terms c e, and (5.69) if they are given in terms of E.

Proof: Some calculations show that the fundamental growth equation of the basic model of chapter 4 is, once again, only affected through the M function. Here the latter is given by:

$$M = \frac{\rho q_m(e\tau-1)}{(1+\tau-\rho q_m)(1+e+\bar{\varepsilon})} = \frac{\rho q_m[E\tau-1-q_m\{E(\rho-1) - 1\}]}{(1+\tau-\rho q_m)\{(1-q_m)B + q_m E\gamma\}} . \qquad (5.70)$$

The positivity required of M to establish theorems 4.2 - 4.6 is achieved due to the regularity conditions and (5.64), (5.68), (5.69). Consequently theorems 4.2 - 4.5 are valid here; the long-run growth rate is once again stable. On the steady-growth path we again have either $E_i = -1$ or $\xi_{mi} = 0$ or $\xi_{mi} = 1$. As is easily seen from (5.70) all three possibilities yield the same values for μ_i as given by (5.58). Thus the long-run growth rate is not affected.

Q.E.D.

5.3. Non-separability and import duties

We have shown that neither the introduction of tariffs, nor of non-separability alters the conclusions drawn in chapter 4 for a free-trade economy of moderate size with imports-domestic factors separability. It remains to show that the combination of the two extensions is equally innocuous.

The part of section 5.2 dealing with optimum tariffs does not employ separability. Thus we need only consider the long-run analysis. As in the case of non-separability with free trade, we restrict the discussion to the case of constant returns and consider only an import duty. Thus the import-demand equation now is:

$$v_m = P^{-1}(1+\tau). \qquad (5.71)$$

If a duty is present, we must, as in the separable case of section 5.2, impose the condition:

$$q_m < 1 + \tau \qquad (5.48)$$

The presence of a duty necessitates the imposition of two additional restrictions. The first of these is

$$e\tau - 1 < 0. \tag{5.68}$$

This condition is, given constant returns, equivalent to (5.55). Apart from (5.68) we need a second restriction to handle the non-separability of the production function. This may either be a further restriction of the production function,

$$v_{\ell m} > 0, \tag{5.72}$$

or a restriction on the duty:

$$1 + \tau(1+\bar{\varepsilon}) > 0. \tag{5.73}$$

The first restriction, (5.72), requires labour and imports to be weak substitutes; under separability it is always satisfied. In view of (5.48), restriction (5.73) is always satisfied for inelastic foreign demand; it requires the duty to be lower than the no-retaliation optimum duty (c.f. 5.52) if foreign demand is elastic. Clearly, for practical purposes it is quite reasonable to assume that at least one of these two conditions holds.

We now obtain:

Theorem 5.11: Let (5.48), (5.68) and either (5.72) or (5.73) hold true. Then theorems 5.1 through 5.4 are also valid if there is a constant ad valorem duty.

Proof: Proof for theorem 5.1 is completely similar to that in the free trade case. To obtain the proofs for theorems 5.2 - 5.4, consider the growth equation replacing (5.18):

$$\frac{\dot{g}}{g} = \nu - q'_{\ell}(g-\lambda) + \frac{q_m(e\tau-1)}{(1+e+\bar{\varepsilon})(1+\tau-q_m)} \Big[\beta - (1+\bar{\varepsilon})\nu-\lambda - \frac{1}{e\tau-1}$$

$$\Big\{\frac{kv_{km}}{v_m} e\{1+\tau(1+\bar{\varepsilon})\} + (1+e+\bar{\varepsilon})(\tau+q'_{\ell})\Big\}(g-\lambda)\Big]. \tag{5.74}$$

Theorems 5.2 through 5.4 can easily be extended to the tariff-ridden case as soon as both the multiplier of the term beween square brackets in (5.74) is positive and the premultiplier of g-λ in the bracketed term negative. The former is immediately seen to be positive, due to (5.68), (5.48) and (5.6). The multiplier of g-λ is negative for all values of q'_ℓ if:

$$\tau\{(1+e+\bar{\varepsilon})\left(1+e\frac{kv_{km}}{v_m}\right) - e\bar{\varepsilon}\frac{kv_{km}}{v_m}\} + e\frac{kv_{km}}{v_m} < 0. \qquad (5.75)$$

Condition (5.75) is seen to be satisfied if either (5.73) holds, or:

$$1 + e\frac{kv_{km}}{v_m} > 0. \qquad (5.76)$$

The latter condition is equivalent to (5.72), since linear homogeneity of v implies:

$$\frac{1}{e} + \frac{kv_{km}}{v_m} = -\frac{\ell v_{\ell m}}{v_m}. \qquad (5.77)$$

Q.E.D.

It can be proved quite generally that the duty drops out of any steady-growth rate with the property that the shares of imports and labour in total factor input, and the elasticities e and kv_{km}/v_m have constant values depending on technical conditions alone. This is the straightforward generalization of the invariance result for the separable case established in theorem 5.9.

Hence:

<u>Theorem 5.12</u>: Let there be a steady-growth rate with the property that q_m, q'_ℓ, e, kv_{km}/v_m are constant and have values determined by technical conditions alone. Then the steady-growth rate is independent of the value of a constant import duty.

<u>Proof</u>: The derivative of q_m is given by:

$$\frac{\dot{q}_m}{q_m} = \frac{1}{1+e+\bar{\varepsilon}}\left[\{\beta - (1+\bar{\varepsilon})\nu - \lambda\}\{1 + e(1-q_m)\}\right.$$

$$+ \frac{kv_{km}}{v_m} e\{q_m - \bar{\varepsilon}(1-q_m)\} - (1-q_\ell'-q_m)(g-\lambda)\Big]. \tag{5.78}$$

Since, by assumption, q_m is constant on the steady growth path, either $q_m = 0$, or the right-hand side of (5.78) is zero. In the former case we have, from (5.74):

$$\frac{\dot{g}}{g} = \nu - q_\ell'(g-\lambda), \tag{5.79}$$

implying a steady-growth rate $\chi = \lambda + \nu/q_\ell'$, which is independent of τ. If $q_m \neq 0$, the right hand side of (5.78) should be zero. Since the latter does not contain the duty explicitly, the value of g that renders it zero can only depend on τ through the elasticities and shares. But the latter are constant and depend on technical conditions alone, not on the duty. Hence χ is independent of τ.

Q.E.D.

Clearly, if the extreme factor ratio condition (5.35) holds, the shares and elasticities depend on technical conditions alone, not on the duty. Hence theorem 5.12 implies that the long-run growth rate obtained in the non-separable case of section 5.1 is impervious to the introduction of a constant duty.

<u>In short: neither the introduction of duties, nor the dropping of the separability assumption, nor the combination of the two invalidates any of the results of chapter 4.</u>

Appendix 5.1. Optimum duties and steady growth of Cobb-Douglas economies

This appendix first shows that τ_{opt}, the optimum duty without retaliation, always exceeds that with retaliation, τ'_{opt}. Next the short- and long-run income equations for Cobb-Douglas economies are derived.

Relation between τ_{opt} and τ'_{opt}

The no-retaliation optimum duty, τ_{opt}, is infinite if $\bar{\varepsilon} > -1$; the retaliation optimum duty, τ'_{opt}, has a finite value as long as $\bar{\varepsilon} < -\frac{1}{2}$. Thus, as long as $-1 < \bar{\varepsilon} < -\frac{1}{2}$, τ'_{opt} is exceeded by τ_{opt}; if $\bar{\varepsilon} > -\frac{1}{2}$ both are infinite. If $\bar{\varepsilon} < -1$ we have:

$$\tau'-\tau = \frac{-\bar{\varepsilon}(1+e+\bar{\varepsilon})}{\rho(1+\bar{\varepsilon})e(1+\bar{\varepsilon})} = \frac{-\bar{\varepsilon}\{(1-q_m)B+q_m E\gamma\}}{\rho E(1+\bar{\varepsilon})E(1+2\bar{\varepsilon})} . \tag{5.80}$$

Both right-hand side expressions are positive, under regularity conditions (4.5), (4.6) and (4.7) - (4.9), respectively.

Income of Cobb-Douglas economies

Given production function (5.59), the model can be solved analytically without difficulty, yielding for y:

$$y = xk^{\delta_1}\exp(\delta_2 t), \tag{5.81}$$

where

$$x = \left(1 - \frac{\xi_m}{1+\tau}\right)\left(\frac{\xi_m}{1+\tau}\right)^{\frac{1+\bar{\varepsilon}}{\bar{\varepsilon}}\rho\xi_m}(1+\bar{\tau})^{-\rho\xi_m \frac{\bar{\varepsilon}}{\bar{\varepsilon}(1-\rho\xi_m)-\rho\xi_m}} . \tag{5.82}$$

$$\delta_1 = \frac{\bar{\varepsilon}\rho\xi_m}{\bar{\varepsilon}(1-\rho\xi_m)-\rho\xi_m} , \tag{5.83}$$

$$\delta_2 = \frac{\bar{\varepsilon}\{\lambda(1-\xi_\ell)(1-\xi_m)\rho + \lambda + \frac{\beta}{\bar{\varepsilon}}\rho\xi_m\}}{\bar{\varepsilon}(1-\rho\xi_m) - \rho\xi_m} . \tag{5.84}$$

From(5.82), (5.60) easily follows.

Using (5.82), the fundamental dynamic equation of the model is:

$$\dot{k} = \sigma\, y = \sigma\, x k^{\delta_1} \exp \delta_2 t. \tag{5.85}$$

Thus we obtain:

$$\int_{k_0}^{k_{t_1}} k^{-\delta_1}\, dk = \int_0^{t_1} \sigma\, x \exp(\delta_2 t) dt. \tag{5.86}$$

Solving yields:

$$k_t = \{\sigma\, x \delta_2 (1 - \delta_1)(\exp\,(\delta_2 t_1) - 1) + k_0^{1-\delta_2}\}^{\frac{1}{1-\delta_2}}\,. \tag{5.87}$$

Hence income is given by:

$$y_{t_1} = x \exp(\delta_2 t) \{x \delta_1 (1-\delta_2)(\exp(\delta_2 t) - 1) + k_0^{1-\delta_2}\}^{\frac{\delta_2}{1-\delta_2}}\,. \tag{5.88}$$

This implies:

$$\frac{y'_{t_1}}{y_{t_1}} = \frac{x'}{x} \left\{\frac{x' \gamma_1 (1-\delta_2)(\exp(\delta_2 t)-1) + k_0^{1-\delta_2}}{x \gamma_1 (1-\delta_2)(\exp(\delta_2 t)-1) + k_0^{1-\delta_2}}\right\}^{\frac{\delta_2}{1-\delta_2}}\,. \tag{5.89}$$

Thus, since δ_2 is easily seen to be positive, we obtain:

$$\lim_{t_1 \to \infty} \frac{y'_{t_1}}{y_{t_1}} = \frac{x'}{x}^{\frac{1}{1-\delta_2}}\,, \tag{5.90}$$

from which (5.61) easily follows, using (5.81).

6. TRANSMISSION AND GENERATION OF GROWTH BY NORTH-SOUTH TRADE

In the two preceding chapters we discussed the growth of individual open economies. The growth of the rest of the world was not analysed explicitly; instead its demand for the country's exports was taken to grow at a given rate. In the present chapter we move one step ahead by discussing a two-region model that analyses accumulation and growth in both regions explicitly. This type of model serves two purposes. First, it is a stepping stone on the way to the construction of multi-region models. Second, it gives a summary description of the growth of two regions whose bilateral trade is large compared to their trade with third regions. The system of the developed market economies, 'north', and the less-developed ones, 'south', may serve as a good example. This example has the advantage that it provides illustrative figures for the key parameters that can be used in numerical examples; it also makes it easy to show how some policy questions and issues in the field of trade and development can be discussed in the type of framework developed by us. Moreover, it is quite appropriate to describe north-south trade as trade in indispensable inputs. The north's imports from the south still consist mainly of raw materials, inputs in the north's production process for which it usually does not possess perfect substitutes. In return the north exports mostly industrial goods; part of these are intermediates and the finished goods also need further handling in the south. The south lacks the technologies and skills required to produce the goods it imports from the north. Even if the south develops, north-south trade will still retain the character of trade in indispensable inputs, just as is presently the case with trade among industrial countries because of the large proportion of intermediates.

The two-region model and the conditions for the existence of a trade equilibrium are presented in the first section; as in chapter 4, we again employ the separability assumption since this has been shown (section 5.1) to be of limited consequence, at least in the single-country case. Section two discusses the direction into which both hemispheres' capital-labour ratios evolve. In the HOS-type trade and growth models discussed in chapter 2, these ratios converge to a constant value, implying that the long-run growth rate of the economy equals the natural rate (even if both regions' natural rates differ) and is hence independent of the presence of trade. In chapters 4 and 5 we showed that this is no longer true in the single-country case if imports are indispensable. Here we demonstrate that the same applies to a two-region system. Thus, even if technical progress is absent and constant returns prevail in both regions, steady growth at each region's natural rate is only possible if both regions' natural rates are equal. We also provide conditions for both regions' capital-labour ratios to increase in the long run, that is, for rising per capita incomes. These conditions are always satisfied if technical progress is fast in both regions; if it is slow - as may be the case when natural resources become scarce and a lot of innovations are required to substitute for them, without yielding a higher final output - the capital-labour ratios still rise in the long run.

Section three provides a steady-growth theorem, expressing the two hemispheres' long-run growth rates in terms of both regions' natural rates, their rates of technical progress and returns to scale and some production function parameters (import shares and shares of labour in regional factors, capital and labour). Conditions for the global stability of these growth rates are given.

In the single-country case, the only additional assumptions about the production functions required to obtain steady growth concerned the behaviour of factor shares and elasticities of substitution at extreme values of the ratios of the inputs. In that case however, foreign demand behaved quite nicely, its growth rate being independent of the accumulation in the economy considered. But here both regions' rates of accumulation depend on each other. This has a destabilizing effect on the growth path and opens the possibility of oscillations. If one wants to preclude this possibility, the production functions must be restricted at intermediate values of the imports-domestic factors ratios too. We employ the simplest restriction possible, by postulating Cobb-Douglas functions for both hemispheres. This yields stable growth rates well-suited for quantitative assessment of the impact of both regions' growth on each other. Section four analyses these growth rates and illustrates them numerically, using plausible values for the core parameters. As in the single-country analysis of chapter 4, we compare the growth rates with those that would be expected if north-south trade could be dispensed with. It turns out that north-south trade plays two roles. It transmits growth from the region that has the highest 'autarkic growth rate' - a composite of that region's natural rate and its rate of technical progress - to the other region. This imples a tendency for the region with the fastest growth to grow slower than closed-economy analysis would indicate and for the other one to grow faster. But in addition north-south trade generates additional growth in both hemispheres compared wo what closed-economy analysis predicts, as long as both regions' per capita 'autarkic growth rates' are fairly high-irrespective of their relative value. As should be expected these effects of north and south on each other are the higher, the higher the share of imports from the other hemisphere in the economy. Since that share is much higher for the south than for the north (ca. 13% vs 4% in the mid-seventies) the south is likely to be influenced more by developments in the north than vice versa.

In order to demonstrate how our two-region model can serve to analyse practical issues, the final section discusses the implications of the analysis for two core issues in north-south relations. The first is, whether the south would develop faster if it did not depend on north-south trade to obtain vital goods.We tackle this question by providing some 'guesstimates' of the parameters of the system for the past quarter of this century. The results indicate that until 1973 both regions' growth rates were higher than closed-economy analysis implies; because of the high 'autarkic' growth prevailing in both regions the growth-generation effect dominated the transmission. Because of the south's high import share, this hemisphere benefited more than the north; thus in this period the income gap was closed more, or widened less, than one would expect on the basis of closed-economy models. After 1973 growth in the north stagnated whereas in the south it retained a high value; in consequence some net growth was transmitted from south to north, though quantitatively the effect was of minor importance. The second central question in north-south relations is whether industrialization and development of the south will damage the north's growth rate. We tackle this question with an impressionistic scenario of the impact of development on the system in the next couple of decades. This scenario indicates that the north stands to gain very considerably from the south's development, provided it manages to develop new leading sectors and technologies to provide it with products to exchange for growing (industrial) imports from the south. The scenario also shows that the south's per capita growth can be substantially higher if north-south trade is taken into account than if it is neglected and closed-economy theory is applied.

6.1. Equilibrium trade

We formalize 'north-south' trade by describing both regions' production process with a production function similar to the one employed in chapter 4 to describe individual economies. Thus the production functions are twice continuously differentiable, have strictly positive first-order derivatives, are homogeneous of degree ρ and $\bar{\rho}$, respectively, quasi-concave, separable in imports and regional factors capital and labour and display Hicks-neutral technical progress.

$$v = v(z(\ell,k),m)\ \exp(\nu t). \tag{6.1}$$

$$\bar{v} = \bar{v}(\bar{z}(\bar{\ell},\bar{k}),\bar{m})\ \exp(\bar{\nu} t). \tag{6.2}$$

Symbols without bars denote variables relating to the north, barred ones relate to the south. The notation is the same as that of preceding chapters, v denoting output, z a linear homogeneous function of the two regional factors, labour, ℓ, and capital, k; m denotes imports and ν the rate of technical progress.

The production functions (6.1) and (6.2) are not simply the aggregate of the individual-country functions of chapter 4, because in (6.1) and (6.2) the imports m and $\bar{m}$ exclude internal trade of each region. As a consequence the value shares of imports are lower here than for the individual countries considered earlier. Thus the north's imports from the south are (for 1976-1977) 4% of the north's total output, whereas the south's imports from the north are 13% of the south's output.(1) The two regions' import-demand equations are:

$$v_m = \rho P^{-1}; \tag{6.3}$$

$$\bar{v}_{\bar{m}} = \bar{\rho} P; \tag{6.4}$$

These are supplemented by a condition of balanced trade:

$$\bar{m} = P^{-1}m. \qquad (6.5)$$

Here $P^{-1} = \bar{p}/p$ is the ratio of the south's export price to that of the north.

In principle the system (6.1) - (6.5) yields both countries' output, the two trade flows and the terms of trade as functions of the two capital stocks and labour forces. Precondition is of course existence and preferably uniqueness of a solution. To achieve this, two sets of conditions are sufficient. The first of these is formulated in terms of the import-demand elasticities:

$$e,\ 1/e < -\Delta; \qquad (6.6)$$

$$\bar{e},\ 1/\bar{e} < -\Delta; \qquad (6.7)$$

$$1 + e + \bar{e} < -\Delta, \qquad (6.8)$$

where Δ is a small positive constant and $e = v_m/mv_{mm}$ the terms of trade elasticity of import demand. Theorem 6.1 shows that conditions (6.6) - (6.8) are sufficient to establish the existence of a unique solution. These conditions are the straightforward generalization of conditions (4.5) and (4.6) in the single-country case: the 'Marshall-Lerner' condition is combined with negativity and boundedness of both countries' import-demand elasticities.

Theorem 6.1: If (6.6), (6.7) and (6.8) are satisfied for all values of ℓ, $\bar{\ell}$, k, $\bar{k}$, m, $\bar{m}$ and t, the system (6.1) - (6.5) has a unique solution with non-zero and finite values for both trade flows.

Proof: If trade is on the north's offercurve, we have:

$$\bar{m} = \frac{mv_m}{\rho}, \qquad (6.9)$$

which is obtained by substituting (6.5) into (6.3). Since mv_m is finite and non-zero for all finite non-zero m, there is a finite non-zero $\bar{m}$ satisfying (6.9). Similarly, there is an m, such that trade is on the south's offercurve:

$$m = \frac{\bar{\bar{m}}v_{\bar{m}}}{\bar{\rho}} , \qquad (6.10)$$

which is obtained from (6.4). Substituting (6.9) into (6.10) we find, writing the arguments of the v_m functions explicitly:

$$v_m(m) \cdot \bar{v}_{\bar{m}}\left(\frac{mv_m(m)}{\rho}\right) = \rho\bar{\rho} , \qquad (6.11)$$

where bracketed terms are the arguments of the functions before the brackets. Equation (6.11) is a function in m only; we have to show the existence of an unique, positive, finite m satisfying (6.11). Differentiating (6.9) with respect to m yields:

$$\frac{d \ln \bar{m}}{d \ln m} = \frac{1 + e}{e} . \qquad (6.12)$$

Accordingly we obtain for the derivative of the left-hand side of (6.11)

$$\frac{d \ln v_m \bar{v}_{\bar{m}}}{d \ln m} = \frac{1 + e + \bar{e}}{e\bar{e}} . \qquad (6.13)$$

Since v is twice continuously differentiable and v_m non-zero, e is continuous. Clearly (6.6) - (6.8) imply that both the numerator and the denominator of (6.13) are nowhere infinite or zero and, furthermore, tha the right-hand side is negative. Therefore as m ranges from near-zero to near-infinity, $v_m \bar{v}_{\bar{m}}$ moves from infinity to zero and attains the value $\rho\bar{\rho}$ along the way, once and only once.

Q.E.D.

<u>Remark</u>: Equations (6.9) and (6.10), obtained by confronting the two countries' import-demand equations with the balanced-trade relation, are relations between the two trade flows only; they closely resemble Marshall's offercurves, though there is some difference, to be discussed in chapter 8. For a two-region offercurve equilibrium Marshall (1879, proposition VIII) already established uniqueness and existence in the 'normal case', e, $\bar{e} < -1$. Thus our theorem is similar to Marshall's proposition. However, the latter is essentially a special case of the competitive equilibrium theorem with all goods gross substitutes, as established by Arrow, Block and Hurwicz (1959); on this, compare Chipman

(1965, pp. 725-727).

Conditions (6.6)-(6.8) are given in terms of the import-demand elasticities. In our long-run analysis below, theorem (6.1) will suffice. Nevertheless it is interesting to formulate, as in the case of the analysis of moderate-sized economies, a second set of conditions in terms of the elasticities of substitution between imports and regional factors, E and $\bar{E}$:

$$E,\ 1/E < -\Delta, \tag{6.14}$$

$$\bar{E},\ 1/\bar{E} < -\Delta, \tag{6.15}$$

$$1 + E + \bar{E} < -\Delta, \tag{6.16}$$

$$\bar{E}(\rho - 1) + \rho > \Delta, \tag{6.17}$$

$$E(\bar{\rho} - 1) + \bar{\rho} > \Delta, \tag{6.18}$$

$$\rho\ \bar{\rho} \leq 1. \tag{6.19}$$

The first five conditions, (6.14) - (6.18), are similar to those imposed on individual economies in chapter 4, with the single alteration that the elasticity of substitution between imports and regional factors replaces the terms of trade elasticity of foreign demand. Condition (6.19), however, is a novelty. It restricts the average rate of returns to scale to decreasing, or at most constant, returns. Without this condition multiple equilibria are possible. However this strong condition also generates a powerful result; existence and uniqueness regardless of the values the import shares may take.

Theorem 6.2: If (6.14) - (6.19) are satisfied for all values of ℓ, $\bar{\ell}$, k, $\bar{k}$, m, $\bar{m}$ and t, the system (6.1) - (6.5) has a unique solution with non-zero and finite values for both trade flows.

Proof: Using (3.13), the right-hand side of (6.10) is written as:

$$\frac{1}{E\bar{E}}\Big[-q_m\bar{q}_{\bar{m}}\ E\bar{E}(1 - \rho\bar{\rho}) + (1 - \bar{q}_{\bar{m}})(1 - q_m)(1 + E + \bar{E})$$

$$+ q_m(1 - \bar{q}_{\bar{m}})E\{\bar{E}(\rho - 1) + \rho\} + \bar{q}_{\bar{m}}(1 - q_m)\bar{E}\{E(\bar{\rho} - 1) + \bar{\rho}\}\Big]. \tag{6.20}$$

Here q_m is defined as in preceding chapters: $q_m = \frac{mv_m}{\rho v}$, $0 \leq q_m \leq 1$.

It is immediately seen that under the conditions of the present theorems all terms between brackets are non-positive and that at least one of the four terms is strictly negative. The remainder of the proof is similar t that of theorem (6.1).

6.2. Direction of the evolution of the capital-labour ratios

As in the individual-country case considered in chapters 4 and 5, we first analyse the direction of the two hemispheres' capital-labour ratios the next section develops a steady-growth analysis.

As before, we only consider exponential growth of labour and proportional saving, yielding equations analogous to (4.12) and (4.14), respectively:

$$\dot{\ell} = \lambda\ell, \qquad (\lambda > 0) \tag{6.21}$$

$$\dot{k} = \sigma(v - \bar{m}). \qquad (0 < \sigma < 1) \tag{6.22}$$

Here λ is the growth rate of the north's labour force, σ its rate of saving. For the south symmetric equations hold.

Non-constancy of the capital-labour ratios under steady growth of both regions' capital stocks

In the traditional Heckscher-Ohlin-Samuelson growth models in which al] imports have perfect domestic substitutes and where adjustment costs are absent, the long-run growth rate is independent of trade: in the small-country case it equals the country's natural rate, in the two-country system each country's growth rate converges to its own natural rate. Thi is no longer true if imports are 'indispensable'. In chapter 4, theorem 4.2, we show that the independence of the growth rate of trade breaks do in the case of individual countries 'of moderate size'. In the present section theorem 6.3 establishes that the same is true for a two-region system: if Inada's conditions are satisfied, neither of the two regions can grow at its natural rate, unless the two rates are equal. This is tr even under constant returns and without technical progress. This confirm that the central result of our survey in chapter 2, viz. that the long-r growth rate of economies with 'indispensable' imports differs from that of comparable closed economies, is also valid for a world trade system where both regions' growth rates are determined endogenously.

Theorem 6.3: Let both regions' production functions satisfy the Inada-conditions (2.2). Then, even under constant returns and without technical progress in both regions, steady growth of each region's capital stock at the region's own natural rate, is only possible if both regions' natural rates are equal.

Proof: Using the notation introduced in theorems 3.2 and 4.2, we may write $\dot{K}$ using (6.22) as:

$$\dot{K} = \sigma A V_Z - \lambda K. \qquad (6.23)$$

For Z we obtain:

$$Z = \frac{A}{\bar{A}} \bar{Z}(V - ZV_Z)\exp(\lambda - \bar{\lambda})t. \qquad (6.24)$$

Equations for $\dot{\bar{K}}$ and $\bar{Z}$ are symmetrical. Since A and $\bar{A}$ are functions of K and $\bar{K}$, respectively, (6.24) shows that constancy of K and $\bar{K}$ implies constancy of V_Z and $\bar{V}_{\bar{Z}}$ at a non-zero finite value. As noted in the proof of theorem 4.2, the latter is only possible if Z and $\bar{Z}$, respectively, are constant - as long as Inada's condition is satisfied. It is clear from (6.24) that constancy of Z and $\bar{Z}$, given constancy of K and $\bar{K}$, is only possible if $\lambda = \bar{\lambda}$.

Q.E.D.

Growth of the capital-labour ratios

Theorem 4.3 established that under normal conditions of technology and trade an individual country's capital-labour ratio grows in the long run. Theorem 6.4 states that this result can be extended to both hemispheres' capital-labour ratios: under normal conditions the ratios in both regions of the world system increase.

As in the individual-country analysis, the first normal condition is a technical-progress condition:

$$\lambda(\rho - 1) + v > 0, \qquad (6.25)$$

and similarly for the south.

There is little doubt about the presence of long-run technical progress in both north and south. Hence (6.25) is normally satisfied: only a combination of very fast expansion of labour and strongly decreasing returns can cause (6.25) to be violated as long as technology progresses.

In the analysis of individual countries, a second condition, (4.19), stated that trade circumstances are reasonably favourable. Here this condition regarding the north's export conditions is:

$$b - \lambda - (1 + \bar{e})\{\lambda(\rho - 1) + \nu\} > 0. \qquad (6.26)$$

Here b is the non-price growth rate of the south's demand for the north's exports. Unlike its analogon β in the single-country case, b is not exogenous and constant, but depends on the south's rate of capital accumulation. The precise relation is obtained by differentiating(2) the south's import-demand equation (6.4):

$$\frac{\dot{\bar{m}}}{\bar{m}} = b - \bar{e}\,\frac{\dot{P}}{P}, \qquad (6.27)$$

$$b \equiv -\bar{e}\bar{\nu} - \{\bar{e}(\bar{\rho} - 1) - 1\}\{\bar{q}_{\ell}\bar{\lambda} + (1 - \bar{q}_{\ell})\bar{g}\}, \qquad (6.28)$$

Where $\bar{q}_{\ell}$ is the share of labour in the south's local factors (cf. 3.9), and $\bar{g}$ the growth rate of its capital stock.

Assuming that the south's production function satisfies a regularity condition similar to (4.20):

$$\bar{e}(\bar{\rho} - 1) - 1 < 0, \qquad (6.29)$$

we obtain from (6.28) that condition (6.26) is only satisfied for all values of the south's rate of accumulation if it is satisfied at $\bar{g} = 0$; thus (6.26) is replaced by:

$$-\bar{e}\bar{\nu} - \{\bar{e}(\bar{\rho} - 1) - 1\}\bar{q}_{\ell}\bar{\lambda} - \lambda - (1 + \bar{e})\{\lambda(\rho - 1) + \nu\} > 0. \qquad (6.30)$$

Condition (6.30) is more restrictive than the favourable-trade condition in the single-country analysis. To see this, compare the two in the case of constant returns in both regions; the single-country condition (4.19) reduces to:

$$\beta - \lambda - (1 + \bar{\varepsilon})\nu > 0, \tag{6.31}$$

whereas (6.30) yields:

$$-\bar{e}\bar{\nu} + \bar{q}_{\bar{\ell}}\bar{\lambda} - \lambda - (1 + \bar{e})\nu > 0. \tag{6.32}$$

Condition (6.32) is less likely to be satisfied than (6.31) for two reasons. First, the absolute value of the terms of trade elasticity of the south's demand for the north's exports, $\bar{e}$, is likely to be lower than that of the export demand of a single country, $\bar{\varepsilon}$: in the latter case the rest of the world has more possibilities to replace its imports from a single country than the south has to substitute for the north's products. Second, the term that replaces β in (6.32), viz. $-\bar{e}\bar{\nu} + \bar{q}_{\bar{\ell}}\lambda$, is likely to be lower than β. This both because $\bar{\varepsilon} < \bar{e}$, implying that the influence of technical progress in the south on demand for northern exports is relatively small, and because the south's rate of growth of capital has been dropped in (6.30) and (6.32). The latter is done in order to obtain results that are valid regardless the initial values of the two regions' growth rates. Nevertheless, (6.30) is satisfied if technical progress in both regions is not too low compared to labour growth and both regions' import-demand elasticities are not too small in absolute sense. Besides, we will show below that even if (6.30) is violated, the two regions' capital-labour ratios nevertheless increase in the long run, provided the growth rates of the two capital stocks are sufficiently high initially.

Theorem 6.4: Let (6.6), (6.7), (6.8), (6.25), (6.29), (6.30) and the symmetrical conditions for the other hemisphere hold. Then both regions' capital-labour ratios monotonically increase after an initial period.

Proof: Substituting (6.9) in (6.22) and defining q_m as in (3.8), with $\bar{q}_{\bar{m}}$ symmetrically, we obtain:

$$g = \sigma \frac{v}{k} (1 - q_m), \tag{6.33}$$

where g is the north's rate of accumulation. Differentiate (6.33) to time and use (4.25) and (4.28):

$$\frac{\dot{g}}{g} = \rho \frac{\dot{z}}{z} + \nu - g - \frac{q_m\{e(\rho-1) - 1\}}{e(1-q_m)} \left(\frac{\dot{m}}{m} - \frac{\dot{z}}{z}\right). \tag{6.34}$$

From (6.9) we find:

$$\frac{\dot{\bar{m}}}{\bar{m}} = \frac{\dot{m}}{m} + \frac{\dot{v}_m}{v_m} = \frac{\dot{q}_m}{q_m} + \frac{\dot{v}}{v} , \tag{6.35}$$

where the second equality follows by differentiating $q_m = \frac{mv_m}{m}$.
Insert (4.25) and (4.28) into (6.35):

$$\frac{\dot{\bar{m}}}{\bar{m}} = \rho \frac{\dot{z}}{z} + \nu + \frac{1+e}{e} \left(\frac{\dot{m}}{m} - \frac{\dot{z}}{z}\right). \tag{6.36}$$

Solving $\dot{\bar{m}}/\bar{m}$ and $\dot{m}/m$ from (6.36) and the symmetrical equation for $\dot{m}/m$ yields for $\dot{Z}/Z = \dot{z}/z - \dot{m}/m$:

$$\frac{\dot{Z}}{Z} = \frac{-e}{1 + e + \bar{e}} D; \tag{6.37}$$

with D defined analogously to (4.32), b replacing β:

$$D \equiv b - \lambda - (1 + \bar{e})\{\lambda(\rho - 1) + \nu\} + \gamma(1 - q_\ell)(\lambda - g), \tag{6.38}$$

b being defined in (6.28) and γ (not constant in the present case) by (4.9); $\bar{D}$ is defined symmetrically.
Inserting (6.37) in (6.34) yields:

$$\frac{\dot{g}}{g} = C + MD, \tag{6.39}$$

where C and M are defined similar to (4.31) and (4.33):

$$C \equiv \lambda(\rho - 1) + \nu + (\rho q_\ell - \rho + 1)(\lambda - g); \tag{6.40}$$

$$M \equiv \frac{q_m\{e(\rho - 1) - 1\}}{(1 - q_m)(1 + e + \bar{e})} . \tag{6.41}$$

Now proof of theorem 6.4 is simple. By lemma 4.1, M is non-negative. Similarly, $g < \lambda$ implies both $D > 0$ and $C > 0$, as is seen in the same way as in the proof of statements (ii) and (iii) of lemma 4.1 - replacing (4.19) by (6.26) since the latter is implied by (6.30). Clearly, therefore, both $\dot{g}/g > 0$ if $g < \lambda$ and $\dot{\bar{g}}/\bar{g} > 0$ if $\bar{g} < \bar{\lambda}$; hence both g and $\bar{g}$ increase until they exceed λ and $\bar{\lambda}$, respectively.

Q.E.D.

The favourable-trade conditions imposed by (6.30) to obtain rising capital-labour ratios, are, as we noted above, more restrictive than those imposed in the individual-country analysis. However, they may be relaxed to some extent, by requiring (6.26) to hold, not for $\bar{g} = 0$ (and hence for all $\bar{g} > 0$), but only for $\bar{g} = \bar{\chi}^*$, $0 < \bar{\chi}^* < \lambda$:

$$b(\bar{\chi}^*) - \lambda - (1 + \bar{e})\{\lambda(\rho - 1) + v\} > 0, \qquad (6.42)$$

where $b(\bar{\chi}^*)$ is the value of b at $\bar{g} = \bar{\chi}^*$. Clearly, under regularity condition (6.29), (6.42) implies that (6.26) is satisfied for all $\bar{g} > \bar{\chi}^*$, since b is an increasing function of $\bar{g}$.

Theorem 6.5 establishes that, under (6.42) and its southern equivalent, the capital-labour ratios increase in the long run, provided the growth rates of the two regions' capital stocks are originally high enough:

$$g(t = 0) > \chi^*; \qquad (6.43)$$
$$\bar{g}(t = 0) > \bar{\chi}^*.$$

Thus we impose less restrictive conditions on the parameters of the system than in theorem 6.4, but the price to pay for this is a restriction of the growth rates' initial values.

If the growth rates' initial values do not satisfy (6.43), decline of the capital-labour ratios cannot be precluded.(3) This confirms our argument of section 4.5, where we discussed the possibility that a multi-country system has more than one growth equilibrium implying that shocks or policy measures may put the system from a slower growth- to a more rapid growth-equilibrium. Here the possibility cannot be precluded that the system can follow two distinct paths, one of declining per capita output in both regions, the other of expansion. System shocks or powerfu policy impulses (e.g. temporary forced saving and investment) may shift the system from one path to another, both downward and upward. However, the present two-region analysis this possibility is not of great practic significance, since it requires fairly high values of both regions' impo shares whereas currently these are still quite low.

We now state:

Theorem 6.5: Let (6.6) - (6.8), (6.25), (6.29), (6.42), (6.43) and the symmetrical conditions for the other hemisphere hold true. Then both regions' capital-labour ratios monotonically increase after an initial period.

Proof: It is seen analogously to the proofs of statements ii and iii of lemma 4.1, that $C > 0$ if $g < \lambda$ and $\bar{g} > \bar{\chi}^*$; similarly $D > 0$ if $g < \lambda$ and $\bar{g} > \bar{\chi}^*$. Mutatis mutandis the same applies to $\bar{C}$ and $\bar{D}$. Consequently $g < \lambda$ implies $\dot{g}/g > 0$ as long as $g > \chi^*$. Clearly, provided $g > \chi^*$ and $\bar{g} > \bar{\chi}^*$ initially, neither rate of accumulation can decrease below χ^* and $\bar{\chi}^*$, respectively - since $\chi^* < \lambda$ and $\bar{\chi}^* < \bar{\lambda}$. Hence g and $\bar{g}$ must increase until they exceed the corresponding natural rate.

Q.E.D.

In the individual-country case, we supplemented the theorem on long-ru growth of the capital-labour ratio by one providing conditions for long-run decline of this ratio. One of these conditions was that of technical stagnation: $\nu + \lambda(\rho - 1) < 0$. For some individual countries this combination of slow technical progress with decreasing returns is not impossible; but it is extremely unlikely that such conditions are ever obtained in both the entire northern and the entire southern hemisphere over any significant period of time. Therefore we do not investigate thi possibility of declining capital-labour ratios for the two-region world but instead turn to the derivation and interpretation of a steady-growth theorem.

6.3. A steady-growth theorem

In deriving a steady-growth theorem for individual countries in chapte

4, we introduced some additional properties of the production function: constancy of the shares of capital and labour in domestic factors at extreme values of the capital-labour ratio, K; and constancy of imports' share and of the elasticity of import demand at extreme values of the ratio of domestic factors to imports, Z. Both K and Z can unambiguously be shown to move to zero or infinity in the long run of the individual country. Hence the extreme factor ratio conditions imply constancy of the share and elasticity concerned in the long run; consequently the long-run growth rate of the system can be expressed in the limiting values of the shares and elasticities.

In the present two-region system, the direction in which K and $\bar{K}$ evolve can (cf. theorems 6.4 and 6.5) once again be determined unambiguously. But this is not true with respect to Z and $\bar{Z}$. For the direction of change of Z depends on the partner regions' elasticity of import demand and on the non-price growth of its demand for imports; in the two-region world these are not given (i.e. independent of the home region's aggregate trade), as they are for individual countries, but depend on the partners' factor ratio and through this ratio on the home region's own ratio as well. Therefore, oscillatory behaviour of Z and $\bar{Z}$ is not a priori impossible. To preclude this, some additional restriction on the terms of trade elasticities of the two regions and on their import shares are required. In particular, both should not change too rapidly if the domestic factors - imports ratios Z and $\bar{Z}$ on which they depend, change. Assuming changes in the two elasticities of substitution between imports and domestic factors to be slow, the import shares and the terms of trade elasticities are seen to change slowly as functions of Z if the import shares are small. For practical purposes this condition is not restrictive in view of the current low values of these shares. Alternatively, changes in shares and elasticities are seen to be slow if the elasticities of substitution are close to minus unity. For this reason and for computational convenience we limit our analysis to the simple case of unit-valued elasticities of substitution, implying constant import shares and import demand elasticities. Thus we assume v and $\bar{v}$ to be Cobb-Douglas functions.[(4)]

Perhaps it should be noted that the possibility of oscillatory behaviour of Z and $\bar{Z}$ is not directly related to that of multiple growth paths raised above in connection with theorem 6.5: here we were concerned with the capital-labour ratios, K and $\bar{K}$, and the possibility that these might follow different paths depending on initial conditions. However, both possibilities are precluded by the same conditions of either small impor shares or unit-valued elasticities of substitution.

The need to add additional restrictions in the two-region system finds it parallel in the HOS two-sector growth models surveyed in chapter 2: i these models a small country converges to its steady-growth path without any restrictions on the production functions beyond the Inada-conditions but in the two-country case stability is only obtained if further restrictions are made, such as the 'capital-intensity condition'.

A unit-valued elasticity of substitution between the north's imports a its local factors is at first glance too high for the present north-sout system, since the north's imports from the south consist mainly of low-substitutability goods such as raw materials, fuels and food. However, t south increasingly exports manufactures to the north (in 1980 as much as 37% for the non-OPEC south, though only 1% for OPEC), which raises substitutability. In addition, the north as a whole, being a vast region has more possibilities to substitute its imports from the south with northern produce than individual northern countries have to replace thei imports from the south with domestic products. But the most important factor that raises the elasticity of substitution between the north's imports from the south and its own factors is that, as Tinbergen (1949) already demonstrated, long-term elasticities of substitution in foreign trade are much higher than short-term ones. In the analysis of growth th should be accounted for. One way to achieve this, would be to describe t dynamic structure of the technological process of substitution more explicitly, allowing it to take several years instead of assuming it to instantaneous as we do. However, the former approach is quite cumbersome Therefore we incorporate the long-term substitution simply in our instantaneous elasticity, implying that the latter should be higher than the elasticity of substitution as it may be measured from annual fluctuations. This approach is valid for steady-growth purposes, since both approaches are equivalent on a steady-growth path. The implication for empirical purposes is that annual data cannot be used as such, but only averages over some period (in section 6.5 we employ five- to ten-ye averages). In view of these arguments, the Cobb-Douglas model may be expected to yield a reasonable first approximation of the structural development of the north-south system.

To obtain a stable, unique steady-growth rate in the case of two Cobb-Douglas economies, the two regions' basic growth rates, of labour and technology, do not have to be restricted in any way beyond the non-negativity condition. The production functions must satisfy only a single regularity condition:

$$\rho\xi_m + \rho(1 - \xi_m)(1 - \xi_\ell) < 1, \tag{6.44}$$

and symmetrically for the south; ξ_m denotes imports' constant value share in total inputs and ξ_ℓ labour's constant share in domestic factors. Thus $\rho\xi_m$ is the elasticity of output with respect to imports (m's exponent in the production function) and $\rho(1 - \xi_m)(1 - \xi_\ell)$ that of output with respect to capital. Condition (6.44) simply states that there are decreasing returns to just the two factors capital and imports; only with respect to all three factors constant or increasing returns are admitted.

We now state:

Theorem 6.6: Let both regions' production functions be Cobb-Douglas and let (6.44) and its equivalent for the south hold. Then the growth rates g and $\bar{g}$ of the north's and south's capital stocks and incomes converge to constant positive values χ and $\bar{\chi}$, given by:

$$\chi = \frac{1}{\phi}[\{\nu + \lambda\rho(1 - \xi_m)\xi_\ell\}\{1 - \bar{\rho}(1 - \bar{\xi}_{\bar{m}})(1 - \bar{\xi}_{\bar{\ell}})\} + \rho\xi_m \{\bar{\nu} + \bar{\lambda}\bar{\rho}(1 - \bar{\xi}_{\bar{m}})\bar{\xi}_{\bar{\ell}}\}], \tag{6.45}$$

and symmetrically for the south; here

$$\phi = \{1 - \rho(1 - \xi_m)(1 - \xi_\ell)\}\{1 - \bar{\rho}(1 - \bar{\xi}_{\bar{m}})(1 - \bar{\xi}_{\bar{\ell}})\} - \rho\bar{\rho}\xi_m\bar{\xi}_{\bar{m}}. \tag{6.46}$$

Proof: Recall that with v Cobb-Douglas, e is (cf. 3.15) given by:

$$e = \frac{-1}{1 - \rho\xi_m}. \tag{6.47}$$

Clearly (6.44) implies $\rho\xi_m < 1$; hence e, and $\bar{e}$, are negative;

$$1 + e + \bar{e} = \frac{\rho\bar{\rho}\xi_m\bar{\xi}_{\bar{m}} - 1}{(1 - \rho\xi_m)(1 - \bar{\xi}_{\bar{m}})}, \tag{6.48}$$

which is negative too. Thus, by theorem 6.1, the two-region system has a unique solution with non-zero and finite values for both trade flows at all values of the capital stocks.

We may now write the north's growth rate (6.39) as:

$$\frac{\dot{g}}{g} = \alpha_1 + \alpha_2 g + \alpha_3 \bar{g}; \tag{6.49}$$

where the constant parameters α are given by:

$$\alpha_1 = \frac{1}{1-\rho\bar{\rho}\xi_m\bar{\xi}_{\bar{m}}} [\nu + \lambda\rho(1 - \xi_m)\xi_\ell + \rho\xi_m\{\bar{\nu} + \bar{\lambda}\bar{\rho}(1 - \bar{\xi}_{\bar{m}})\bar{\xi}_{\bar{\ell}}\}], \tag{6.50}$$

$$\alpha_2 = \frac{-1}{1 - \rho\bar{\rho}\xi_m\bar{\xi}_{\bar{m}}} \{1 - \rho(1 - \xi_m)(1 - \xi_\ell) - \rho\bar{\rho}\xi_m\bar{\xi}_{\bar{m}}\}, \tag{6.51}$$

$$\alpha_3 = \frac{\rho\bar{\rho}\xi_m(1 - \bar{\xi}_{\bar{m}})(1 - \bar{\xi}_{\bar{\ell}})}{1 - \rho\bar{\rho}\xi_m\bar{\xi}_{\bar{m}}}. \tag{6.52}$$

The north's growth rate is a similar expression in $\bar{\alpha}_1$, $\bar{\alpha}_2$, $\bar{\alpha}_3$, defined symmetrically to α_1, α_2 and α_3. Apart from $\bar{g} = g = 0$, the system has on equilibrium point, given by:

$$\chi = \frac{\alpha_3\bar{\alpha}_1 - \alpha_1\bar{\alpha}_2}{\alpha_2\bar{\alpha}_2 - \alpha_3\bar{\alpha}_3}; \quad \bar{\chi} = \frac{\bar{\alpha}_3\alpha_1 - \bar{\alpha}_1\alpha_2}{\alpha_2\bar{\alpha}_2 - \alpha_3\bar{\alpha}_3}, \tag{6.53}$$

provided the right-hand sides of (6.53) are positive. The latter are se to boil down to (6.45) and its southern equivalent, respectively. Thus have to show (6.45) to be positive. Clearly (6.44) implies:

$$1 - \rho(1 - \xi_m)(1 - \xi_\ell) > 0.$$

Hence the term between square brackets in (6.45) is positive. Furthermo (6.44) implies

$$\{1 - \rho(1 - \xi_m)(1 - \xi_\ell)\} > \rho\xi_m. \tag{6.54}$$

Clearly (6.54) and its equivalent for the south imply positivety of ϕ; hence the right-hand side of (6.45), equal to that of the north's growth rate in (6.53), is positive; symmetrically, the same applies to that of the south.

It remains to be shown that the two growth rates given by (6.53) are stable. To begin with we write the system in its polar form:

$$\frac{\dot{g}}{g} = \alpha_2(g - \chi) + \alpha_3(\bar{g} - \bar{\chi}). \tag{6.55}$$

$$\frac{\dot{\bar{g}}}{\bar{g}} = \bar{\alpha}_2(\bar{g} - \bar{\chi}) + \bar{\alpha}_3(g - \chi). \tag{6.56}$$

To examine the stability of this system we construct a phase diagram. The linear curves where $\dot{g}$ and $\dot{\bar{g}}$ are zero, are given by:

$$g = -\frac{\alpha_3}{\alpha_2}(\bar{g} - \bar{\chi}) + \chi; \quad (\dot{g} = 0) \tag{6.57}$$

$$g = -\frac{\bar{\alpha}_2}{\bar{\alpha}_3}(\bar{g} - \bar{\chi}) + \chi. \quad (\dot{\bar{g}} = 0) \tag{6.58}$$

Since (6.44) and its southern equivalent imply $\rho\xi_m < 1$ and $\bar{\rho}\bar{\xi}_{\bar{m}} < 1$, the signs of α_2, α_3 and of $\bar{\alpha}_2$, $\bar{\alpha}_3$ are readily inferred:

$$\alpha_2, \bar{\alpha}_2 < 0. \tag{6.59}$$

$$\alpha_3, \bar{\alpha}_3 > 0. \tag{6.60}$$

Moreover:

$$-\frac{\alpha_3}{\alpha_2} + \frac{\bar{\alpha}_2}{\bar{\alpha}_3} = \frac{-(1 - \rho\bar{\rho}\xi_m\bar{\xi}_{\bar{m}})\phi}{\rho\bar{\rho}\bar{\xi}_{\bar{m}}(1 - \xi_m)(1 - \xi_\ell)\{1 - \rho(1 - \xi_m)(1 - \xi_\ell) - \rho\bar{\rho}\xi_m\bar{\xi}_{\bar{m}}\}} < 0 \tag{6.61}$$

The right-hand side of (6.61) is negative; therefore the slope of the

$\dot{\bar{g}} = 0$ line (6.58) exceeds that of the $\dot{g} = 0$ line (6.57). In addition, a
is immediately seen from (6.49) and its equivalent for the south, we fi
for the intercepts of the lines in (6.57) and (6.58):

$$g(\bar{g} = 0, \dot{g} = 0) = -\frac{\alpha_1}{\alpha_2} > 0. \tag{6.62}$$

$$g(\bar{g} = 0, \dot{\bar{g}} = 0) = -\frac{\bar{\alpha}_1}{\bar{\alpha}_3} < 0. \tag{6.63}$$

Combining this with (6.61), we find that the $\dot{g} = 0$ and $\dot{\bar{g}} = 0$ lines can drawn in the $(g,\bar{g})$ plane as in figure 6.1: both linear, upward sloping, the slope of the $\dot{\bar{g}} = 0$ line exceeding that of the $\dot{g} = 0$ line and the $\dot{\bar{g}} = 0$ line having a negative, the $\dot{g} = 0$ line a positive intercept.

From (6.55) and (6.56) we have $\dot{g} < 0$ if g is above the $\dot{g} = 0$ line (since $\alpha_2 < 0$). Similarly $\dot{g} > 0$ if g is below the $\dot{g} = 0$ line. The situation with respect to $\dot{\bar{g}}$ is symmetrical. Thus the movement of the system is as indicated in figure 6.1.

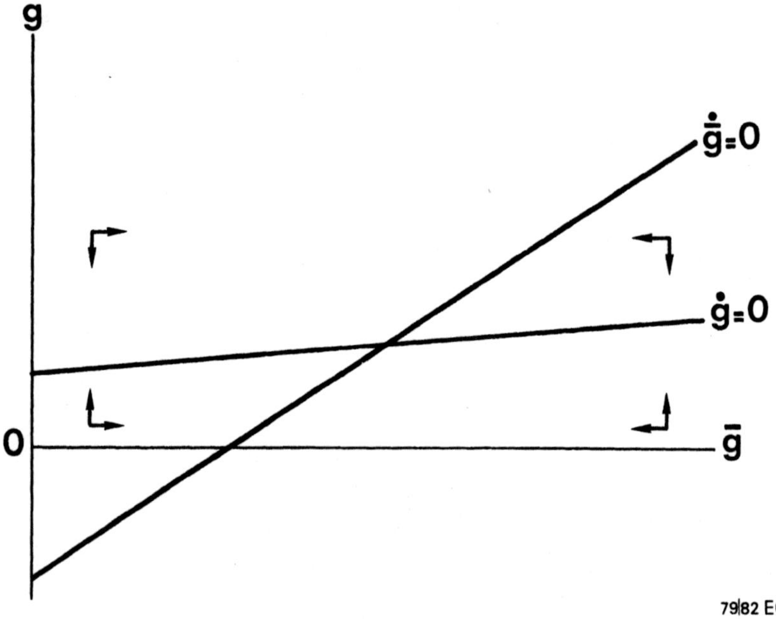

Figure 6.1. Phase-diagram of north's and south's growth rates, g and $\bar{g}$

Since g and $\bar{g}$ are strictly positive initially, figure 6.1 immediately shows the growth rates to converge to the steady rate (6.45) and its southern equivalent, respectively.

Q.E.D.

6.4. Determinants of the north's and south's long-run growth rates

As in the single-country analysis of chapter 4, it is convenient to consider the difference between each region's growth rate and its 'autarkic' rate. The 'autarkic' rate is defined in the same way as in the single-country case (cf. 4.54). Thus for the north this rate, χ_{au}, is:

$$\chi_{au} = \frac{\nu + \lambda\rho\xi_{\ell}}{\theta_{au}}, \tag{6.64}$$

with

$$\theta_{au} = 1 - \rho(1 - \xi_{\ell}); \tag{6.65}$$

and symmetrically for the south. Once again a necessary condition for existence and stability of the 'autarkic' rates is positivity of θ_{au} and $\bar{\theta}_{au}$.

Using (6.64), (6.65), we may write the steady-growth rates in a very instructive form; for the north:

$$\chi = \chi_{au} + \frac{\rho\xi_m}{\phi}\,[\{1 - \bar{\rho}(1 - \bar{\xi}_m)(1 - \bar{\xi}_{\ell}) - \bar{\rho}\bar{\xi}_m\}(\bar{\chi}_{au} - \chi_{au})$$

$$+ \xi_{\ell}\{1 - \bar{\rho}(1 - \bar{\xi}_m)(1 - \bar{\xi}_{\ell})\}(\chi_{au} - \lambda) + \bar{\rho}\bar{\xi}_{\ell}\bar{\xi}_m(\bar{\chi}_{au} - \bar{\lambda})]. \tag{6.66}$$

For the north the expression is again symmetrical, all variables with bars being replaced by the same ones without a bar and vice versa.

Just like (4.56) in the single-country case, equation (6.66) and its southern equivalent decompose each region's growth rate in its 'autarkic' rate and a 'gains' term. Once again the latter consists of a positive <u>multiplier</u> ($\rho\xi_m/\phi$, and $\bar{\rho}\bar{\xi}_m/\phi$, respectively) and a <u>'sign indicator'</u>. If the latter is positive, the region's growth rate exceeds the value predicted by closed-economy analysis. Equation (6.66) shows that there are three sources for such a 'gain'.

The first of these is - since the terms between braces are positive due to (6.44) and its southern equivalent - excess of the foreign region's 'autarkic' growth rate over that of the home region: in the case of the north: $\bar{\chi}_{au} > \chi_{au}$. Clearly this source does not work both ways simultaneously: a northern 'gain' due to a relatively high 'autarkic' growth rate of the south, implies a southern 'loss' and vice versa. Thus, when the growth of the north-south trade system is compared to the growth that closed-economy analysis of both regions predicts, explicit recognition of north-south trade shows transmission of growth from the fastest to the slower growing region. But in addition extra growth is generated in both hemispheres. For in (6.66) there are two other sources for a 'gain': rising 'autarkic' per capita incomes in the home region and abroad ($\chi_{au} - \lambda > 0$, $\bar{\chi}_{au} - \bar{\lambda} > 0$). Clearly therefore, as long as both regions' 'autarkic' per capita growth rates are high, and do not differ too much, both regions grow faster than should be expected without north-south trade.

Table 6.1. Numerical illustration of the long-run growth rates of north and south: the central position.

λ	$\bar{\lambda}$	ν	$\bar{\nu}$	ξ_ℓ	$\bar{\xi}_{\bar{\ell}}$	ρ	$\bar{\rho}$	ξ_m	$\bar{\xi}_{\bar{m}}$	χ_{au}	χ	$\bar{\chi}_{au}$	$\bar{\chi}$
(%)	(%)	(%)	(%)	(%)	(%)			(%)	(%)	(%)	(%)	(%)	(%)
0.75	2.5	1.0	1.0	75.0	75.0	1.1	1.1	4.0	13.0	2.23	2.41	4.22	4.13

To analyse the causes and extent of both the transmission and the generation of growth by north-south trade, we discuss the influence of each of the parameters of the system; the results are summarized at the end of this section. As in chapter 4, we illustrate our results numerically. The central case is presented in table 6.1; in subsequent tables only the parameter values that differ from those in table 6.1 are presented. The parameter values in table 6.1 correspond mainly to the actual data for developed and less-developed market economies around

1976/77. Thus the north's labour force expands at 3/4 of one percent, but that of the south at 2½ percent; the two regions' import shares also are the 1976/77 ones. The other parameters are less easy to measure and we have simply assigned them the same values as in table 4.1, the central position of the single-country case. With these parameter values, the north's 'autarkic' growth rate is much lower than the south's (a 2% difference); but with trade the difference is somewhat less pronounced (1.7%); this is because the north enjoys a slight 'gain', whereas the south's growth rate is slightly lower than closed-economy theory predicts. In view of (6.66) the explanation is not difficult: the huge excess of the south's natural rate over that of the north causes the north's demand for the south's output to be sluggish relative to the south's 'autarkic' growth; though the growth of 'autarkic' per capita income in both regions causes trade to generate some additional growth, this is insufficient to offset the negative effect of the sluggish growth of demand. Naturally, for the north the situation is the reverse of that in the case of the south.

The rates of technical progress

Provided θ_{au} and $\bar{\theta}_{au}$ are positive, the two regions' 'autarkic' growth rates are increasing functions of their rate of technical progress. Again assuming $\theta_{au}, \bar{\theta}_{au} > 0$, the 'gains' term of each region is an increasing function of the region's rate of technical progress if (cf. appendix 6.1), in the case of the north:

$$(1 - \xi_{\ell})\{1 - \bar{\rho}(1 - \bar{\xi}_{\bar{m}})(1 - \bar{\xi}_{\bar{\ell}})\} - \bar{\bar{\rho}}\bar{\xi}_{\bar{m}} < 0. \qquad (6.67)$$

If this condition is violated, the 'gains' term of the north is a decreasing function of the rate of returns to scale; the same applies to the south if the condition symmetrical to (6.67) is violated. Condition (6.67) is not trivial. Since the term between braces is positive but smaller than unity, a sufficient condition for (6.67) to be satisfied is:

$$\frac{\xi_{\ell}}{1 - \bar{\bar{\rho}}\bar{\xi}_{\bar{m}}} > 1. \qquad (6.68)$$

Using (3.15) this condition boils down to $\bar{\varepsilon}\xi_{\ell} < -1$, which is precisely th same condition that was shown to imply a positive relation between the 'gains' term and the rate of technical progress in the individual-country analysis (cf. 4.59). In the present two-region case, however, the condition is less likely to be satisfied. Only if the south's import shar is fairly high, (6.68) is met. In the mid-1970's this share was still too small, circa 13%; with a labour share of, say, 75%, this implies that (6.68) is violated.

Of course the original condition, (6.67), can still be satisfied even i (6.68) is violated, viz. if the term between braces is small; this happen if both the south's import share and its labour share are small. But its labour share is not small. Thus (6.67) is at least as likely to be violated as to be met. Actually, in the numerical example of table 6.1, the left-hand side of (6.67) takes the value 0.047, and the symmetrical one for the south 0.14: both conditions are violated. Thus, with the parameter values of the mid-1970's technical progress in a hemisphere probably has a negative impact on that hemisphere's 'gain from north-soutl trade'. The basic reason for this is that foreign demand is not very elastic because the import share is low. The latter diminishes the impact of an acceleration of technical progress because the main effect of such an accelaration is to lower the relative export price of the region concerned. If this fails to raise foreign demand substantially, the availability of imported inputs is not improved by the additional technical progress. Hence the positive impact of a rise in the rate of technical progress is not supplemented by a subsidiary effect through foreign trade. It should however be noted that our numerical exercise in table 6.2 below indicates that this negative impact on the 'gain' is minor, quantitatively.

Unlike the effect of a rise in a region's own rate of technical progres on that region's 'gain', the influence of an acceleration of the foreign rate of technical progress is firmly positive; the derivatives of the 'gains' term, equal to those of the open-economy rates proper, of north and south are respectively:

$$\frac{\rho\xi_m}{\phi}, \frac{\bar{\bar{\rho}}\bar{\bar{\xi}}_{\bar{m}}}{\phi} > 0. \qquad (6.69)$$

Table 6.2. Impact of variations in the rates of technical progress of north and south.

Technical progress		The north's			The south's		
North	South	'Autarkic' growth	'Gain'	Open-economy growth	'Autarkic' growth	'Gain'	Open-economy growth
ν	$\bar{\nu}$	χ_{au}	$\chi-\chi_{au}$	χ	$\bar{\chi}_{au}$	$\bar{\chi}-\bar{\chi}_{au}$	$\bar{\chi}$
(%)	(%)	(%)	(%)	(%)	(%)	(%)	(%)
1.0	1.0	2.233	0.180	2.413	4.224	-0.097	4.127
2.0	1.0	3.612	0.175	3.787	4.224	0.163	4.385
1.0	2.0	2.223	0.269	2.492	5.604	-0.146	5.456
0.0	0.0	0.853	0.105	0.959	2.844	-0.306	2.539
2.0	2.0	3.612	0.254	3.866	5.604	0.111	5.114

The role of the two rates of technical progress is illustrated in table 6.2. The first line repeats the central position of table 6.1. The second line shows that an increase in the north's rate of technical progress slightly decreases the north's 'gain', but substantially improves the south's growth rate, converting the initial 'loss' to a 'gain'. A similar effect in the other direction is displayed in the next line, where the south's rate of technical progress is higher. The last two lines show how a simultaneous improvement of both regions' technical progress from zero to two percent improves both regions' growth rates and both 'gains'; particularly for the south the difference is pronounced: one-half of a percent.

The natural rates

Growth of the labour forces is the other basic source of growth, next to technical progress. As shown in appendix 6.1, the 'gain' is inversely related to each region's natural rate if

$$1 - \rho\bar{\rho}\bar{\xi}_{\bar{m}} > 0, \qquad 1 - \rho\bar{\rho}\xi_m > 0. \tag{6.70}$$

These conditions cannot fail to hold for alle practical purposes. It should be noted that e.g. the first condition in (6.70) can be written as $\gamma > 0$, using (3.15) and defining γ by $\bar{\varepsilon}(\rho-1) + \rho$; the condition $\gamma > 0$ is the same one required to obtain a negative relation between the natural rate and the 'gain' in the single-country case. The explanation of the negative relation is the same in both cases: the higher a region's natural rate, the larger the region becomes relative to the trade partner. Hence, any positive effect of trade on the growth rate must be smaller with a higher natural rate; the negative effect of unfavourable conditions is increased by a high natural rate, because the scarcity of imported inputs becomes a more serious bottleneck than with a low natural rate.

The impact, on both the 'gain' and the growth rate proper, of a rise in the foreign natural rate is always positive (cf. appendix 6.1), just as is the case with foreign technical progress. The reason is perfectly clear: foreign-demand growth is raised this way and this is very beneficial to a

Table 6.3. Impact of variations in the natural rates.

Natural rates		The north's			The south's		
North	South	'Autarkic' growth	'Gain'	Open-economy growth	'Autarkic' growth	'Gain'	Open-economy growth
λ (%)	$\bar{\lambda}$ (%)	χ_{au} (%)	$\chi-\chi_{au}$ (%)	χ (%)	$\bar{\chi}_{au}$ (%)	$\bar{\chi}-\bar{\chi}_{au}$ (%)	$\bar{\chi}$ (%)
0.75	2.5	2.23	0.18	2.41	4.22	-0.10	4.13
0.75	3.5	2.23	0.24	2.47	5.36	-0.28	5.08
0.75	1.5	2.23	0.12	2.36	3.09	0.09	3.17
0.75	0.75	2.23	0.08	2.32	2.23	0.22	2.46
0.0	2.5	1.38	0.22	1.60	4.22	-0.25	3.97
1.5	2.5	3.09	0.14	3.23	4.22	0.06	4.28
0.0	0.0	1.38	0.07	1.45	1.38	0.21	1.59

region's growth rate, as we demonstrated in chapter 4. The impact of variations in the natural rates is illustrated in table 6.3. The first line again displays the central position, with natural rates equal to the current ones of north and south. The next three lines show the effect of decline of the south's natural rate, from an explosive 3.5% to the ¾% of the north. Because of the north's small import share, the effect on the north's growth rate is marginal; but the south's 'gain' is increased considerably. One very interesting result is that per capita income growt is slightly improved, from 1.58% at the 3.5% natural rate to 1.71% at the ¾% rate. This in spite of the presence of increasing returns that causes the 'autarkic' per capita growth rate to fall from 1.86 to 1.48%. Thus du to north-south trade lowering the south's natural rate increases its per capita income growth. It can be shown that this is not only true in the numerical example, but quite generally as long as the shares of imports i north and south are not too high and that of labour in local factors fairly high.(5)

The next two lines of table 6.3 show that the impact of a change in the north's natural rate on the south's growth rate is not negligible either. Finally, the last line displays the consequences of zero labour growth in both regions. Here one-sixth of the south's growth is generated by north-south trade.

The rates of returns to scale

Of course the 'autarkic' growth rate of each region is an increasing function of the region's own rate of returns to scale. Appendix 6.1 shows that the same applies to the region's 'gains' multiplier. However the relation with the sign indicator is ambiguous: the latter is an increasir function of the rate as long and only as long as (6.67) and its southern counterpart hold, but we noted above that these conditions may well be violated. For the regular case of our numerical examples, the derivative of the sign indicator is therefore negative, but not too strongly so. Th the effect on the multiplier should dominate. Consequently, if trade conditions are unfavourable (i.e. a negative sign indicator), their impa on the growth rate is highest if there are strong increasing returns and minimal if decreasing returns prevail; similarly, under favourable trade conditions, increasing returns cause the growth rate to be improved more

Table 6.4. Impact of variations in rates of returns to scale.

Rates of returns to scale		The north's			The south's		
North	South	'Autarkic' growth	'Gain'	Open-economy growth	'Autarkic' growth	'Gain'	Open-economy growth
ρ	$\bar{\rho}$	χ_{au}	$\chi-\chi_{au}$	χ	$\bar{\chi}_{au}$	$\bar{\chi}-\bar{\chi}_{au}$	$\bar{\chi}$
(%)	(%)	(%)	(%)	(%)	(%)	(%)	(%)
0.9	0.9	1.94	.11	2.05	3.47	-0.10	3.37
1.0	1.0	2.08	.14	2.22	3.83	-0.10	3.73
1.1	1.1	2.23	.18	2.41	4.22	-0.10	4.13
1.1	0.9	2.23	.14	2.37	3.47	-0.05	3.41
0.9	1.1	1.94	.14	2.08	4.22	-0.16	4.06

by trade than would by the case under decreasing returns.

The sign indicator and multiplier are both increasing functions of the foreign rate of returns to scale. Thus a high rate of returns abroad improves the potential 'gain' (i.e. a positive sign indicator) and the actual 'gain' is highest under strong increasing returns abroad too. But if there is a potential 'loss', the actual 'loss' too is highest under increasing returns abroad. Thus as long as the sign indicator is negative, the role of increasing returns abroad is ambiguous.

A numerical illustration of changes in the rates of returns to scale is given in table 6.4. The first three lines show the effect of a rise of both regions' rates of returns to scale. Since the north's trade circumstances are favourable, due to the high natural rate of the south, increases of both regions' rates of returns to scale affect the north's gain in the same direction, raising it somewhat. With respect to the south, the increase in the north's rate of returns raises the south's 'gain' but the rise in the south's own rate inflates the 'loss'; in the table 6.4 example the two effects are balanced. In the last two lines both regions' rates of returns to scale vary in opposite directions; as should be expected this yields results conforming to those above.

Labour's shares

Provided $\nu+\lambda(\rho-1) > 0$ and $\bar{\nu}+\bar{\lambda}(\bar{\rho}-1) > 0$, both regions' 'autarkic' growth rates are decreasing functions of their own labour share. The derivative of the north's sign indicator with respect to the north's labour share is positive if (cf. appendix 6.1):

$$\{\lambda(\rho - 1) + \nu\}\{1 - \bar{\rho}(1 - \bar{\xi}_{\underline{m}})(1 - \bar{\xi}_{\underline{\ell}}) - \rho\bar{\rho}\bar{\xi}_{\underline{m}}\} > 0. \tag{6.71}$$

The second part of the left-hand side is almost equivalent to the terms in the southern equivalent of (6.44), the only difference being the pre-multiplier ρ of $\bar{\rho}\bar{\xi}_{\underline{m}}$. Since we assumed (6.44) to be satisfied it is reasonable to assume that (6.71) holds. Appendix 6.1 shows the north's multiplier to be a decreasing function of its labour share. Under favourable trade conditions therefore the effect of a rise in the own share of labour on the regions' 'gain' is ambiguous; but under un-favourable conditions (a negative but increasing sign indicator), an

Table 6.5. Impact of variations in north's and south's labour shares.

Labour shares		The north's			The south's		
North	South	'Autarkic' growth	'Gain'	Open-economy growth	'Autarkic' growth	'Gain'	Open-economy growth
ξ_ℓ (%)	$\bar{\xi}_{\bar{\ell}}$ (%)	χ_{au} (%)	$\chi-\chi_{au}$ (%)	χ (%)	$\bar{\chi}_{au}$ (%)	$\bar{\chi}-\bar{\chi}_{au}$ (%)	$\bar{\chi}$ (%)
60	75	2.67	0.21	2.88	4.22	-0.01	4.21
90	75	1.96	0.16	2.12	4.22	-0.15	4.07
75	60	2.23	0.20	2.44	4.73	-0.22	4.51
75	90	2.23	0.17	2.40	3.90	-0.04	3.87
60	60	2.67	0.24	2.91	4.73	-0.11	4.62
75	75	2.23	0.18	2.41	4.22	-0.10	4.13
90	90	1.96	0.14	2.10	3.90	-0.09	3.82

increase in labour's share limits the 'loss' unambiguously. Thus in the latter case a rising share of labour is less disadvantageous than closed-economy analysis predicts.

Both the sign indicator and the multiplier are decreasing functions of the foreign labour share (cf. appendix 6.1). Consequently, if trade circumstances are favourable, increasing the foreign labour share lowers the growth rate. If trade circumstances are unfavourable, the effect of a rise in the foreign labour share is ambiguous.

Table 6.5 provides a numerical illustration. In the first two lines an increase in the north's labour share affects the north's gain only marginally; but the south's 'loss' increases markedly. Apparently the effect on the south's sign indicator (an increase of the potential 'loss') dominates that on the multiplier - a decrease of the 'losses'' impact. A similar effect is obtained if the south's labour share decreases from 90% to 60%: the south's 'loss' is substantially increased, the north's gain is only marginally affected. The last three lines combine both movements: if both regions' labour shares increase, both lower the north's 'gain' a bit and accordingly reinforce each other's impact; but since both affect the south's 'loss' in a different direction, the latter remains fairly constant.

Consequently, table 6.5 shows that a tendency towards more skill-intensive production (with higher labour shares) in north and south, affects both hemispheres' growth rates only insofar as it affects the 'autarkic' growth rates; north-south trade does not transmit these effects to any substantial degree.

The import shares

Each region's own import share occurs only in its 'gain' multiplier. The multiplier is an increasing function of the share, as shown in appendix 6.1. Thus we find, just as in the single-country analysis, that the import share does not affect the direction of the influence of north-south trade on the growth rate, but only the extent of its influence.

The north's growth rate is an increasing function of the south's import share if:

$$\{1 - \rho(1 - \xi_\ell)(1 - \xi_m) - \rho\xi_m\}(\chi_{au} - \bar{\chi}_{au}) + \xi_\ell\rho\xi_m(\chi_{au} - \lambda)$$

$$+ \bar{\xi}_{\bar{\ell}}\{1 - \rho(1 - \xi_m)(1 - \xi_\ell)\}(\bar{\chi}_{au} - \bar{\lambda}) > 0, \qquad (6.72)$$

and a decreasing function if (6.72) is violated; of course a symmetrical condition holds for the relation between the south's growth rate and the north's import share.

In (6.72) the multiplier of $\chi_{au} - \bar{\chi}_{au}$ is positive as a consequence of (6.44); those of the two per capita 'autarkic' growth rates $\chi_{au} - \lambda$ and $\bar{\chi}_{au} - \bar{\lambda}$ are positive. Thus, first of all, (6.72) indicates that a high import share in the trade partner's market is advantageous if the latter's 'autarkic' growth is slower than that of the home region. This result is comparable to that obtained in the single-country case regarding the role of the terms of trade elasticity of foreign-demand: elasticity of foreign demand is favourable if non-price foreign demand growth is relatively slow and unfavourable if foreign demand grows rapidly (cf. conclusion 2, section 4.4). In the present case the terms of trade elasticity of foreign demand for e.g. the north's exports, $\bar{\varepsilon}$, is given by $-1/(1 - \bar{\rho}\bar{\xi}_m)$, cf. (3.15). Thus the absolute value of $\bar{\varepsilon}$ is an increasing function of the south's import share, $\bar{\xi}_m$, implying that the results with respect to $\bar{\varepsilon}$ in the single-country case and with respect to $\bar{\xi}_m$ in the present two-region analysis are analogous. Intuitively speaking, the rationale for the inverse relation between the growth rate and the foreign import share in the case of rapid foreign 'autarkic' growth is not difficult to grasp. For a small region can easily hook in to the fast growth of its large trade partner. But if the slower region is large, it starts functioning as a drag on the faster region; this in turn must diminish the gain of the slower region. The consequence is that if we consider only the difference of the two 'autarkic' growth rates, it is advantageous for the south to expand its import share in the north, but not for the north to expand its share in the south - at least as long as χ_{au} is indeed smaller than $\bar{\chi}_{au}$.

The difference between the two 'autarkic' growth rates, however, is not the only factor to consider. For condition (6.72) shows that even if foreign 'autarkic' growth is faster, a large import share abroad is still favourable as long as the level of per capita 'autarkic' growth is high both at home and abroad. In that case the optimal rate of expansion of imports is high because of the rapid 'autarkic' growth at home; the

Table 6.6. Impact of variations in the two hemispheres' import shares.

Import shares		The north's		The south's	
North	South	'Gain'	Open-economy* growth	'Gain'	Open-economy* growth
ξ_m (%)	$\bar{\xi}_{\bar{m}}$ (%)	$\chi-\chi_{au}$ (%)	χ (%)	$\bar{\chi}-\bar{\chi}_{au}$ (%)	$\bar{\chi}$ (%)
2.0	13.0	0.09	2.32	-0.11	4.11
4.0	13.0	0.18	2.41	-0.10	4.13
13.0	13.0	0.58	2.81	-0.02	4.20
33.0	13.0	1.44	3.68	0.14	4.36
4.0	4.0	0.18	2.42	-0.03	4.19
4.0	13.0	0.18	2.41	-0.10	4.13
4.0	25.0	0.17	2.41	-0.18	4.04
4.0	33.0	0.17	2.40	-0.23	3.99
4.0	13.0	0.18	2.41	-0.10	4.13
13.0	25.0	0.58	2.81	-0.04	4.18
25.0	30.0	1.14	3.37	0.18	4.40
33.0	33.0	1.55	3.78	0.38	4.60

* The 'autarkic' growth rates are 2.23 (north) and 4.22 (south).

foreign region is capable of sustaining rapid growth of its exports because of its high 'autarkic' rate; and the higher the foreign import share, the greater the extent to which favourable conditions can actually affect the two regions' growth rates. Put briefly, an increase in the foreign import share raises the growth rate of the faster growing region both by diminishing the negative impact of transmission of growth on the faster region and by increasing the impact of generation of growth.

Table 6.6 demonstrates the role of the import shares. The first four lines show how an increase in the north's import share raises both the north's own growth rate and that of the south. The reverse happens if the dependence of the south on the north increases (in the next four lines) without simultaneous increase in the share of imports in the north's economy: the south's growth rate declines, that of the north too, though only marginally. In the last four lines it becomes clear that a simultaneous rise of both regions' import shares increases both growth rates even more than happens if just that of the north is raised.

Summary and conclusions

Prior to summarizing our conclusions we must again emphasize a caveat. Our basic hypothesis is that north-south trade is indispensable to both regions: neither can do without this trade, at least not without great losses and considerable restructuring of the economy. Accordingly our term 'autarkic growth rate' refers only to the rate that closed-economy theory predicts given all relevant parameters of the trading system; it does not refer to the growth rate that would be achieved if north-south trade were eliminated: the latter entails structural changes in the two regions' economies that are not taken into account by our analysis. Similarly, the term 'effect of north-south trade' does not refer to causal implications of introducing north-south trade in a non-trading system, but only to the difference between an analysis where north-south trade is explicitly taken into account and the results closed-economy theory predicts given the observed values of the parameters of the actual, open, system.

With this understanding our conclusions can be summarized as follows.

1. North-south trade has two basic effects on the two hemispheres' long-run growth rates. First it transmits growth from the region with the

highest 'autarkic' growth rate to the other one, leaving the former worse and the latter better off than closed-economy analysis stipulates. Second it generates growth in both regions as soon as both hemispheres' per capita 'autarkic' incomes grow. As a consequence both regions' growth rates are higher than closed-economy analysis predicts if the two 'autarkic' growth rates do not differ too much and exceed their respective natural rates substantially.

2. The long-run growth rates of north and south are increasing functions of their own rate of technical progress; the presence of north-south trade does not make much difference to the impact of technical progress. However, both growth rates are increasing functions of the rate of technical progress in the other hemisphere.

3. A fall in a region's natural rate decreases this region's growth rate, but to a lesser extent than closed-economy analysis predicts. On the contrary, a fall in the south's natural rate increases, even under increasing returns, the growth rate of the south's per capita income, at least as long as the share of north-south trade is as moderate as it was in the mid-1970's.

   Each hemisphere's growth rate is an increasing function of the other hemisphere's natural rate.

4. Favourable trade conditions - specifically rapid 'autarkic' growth of the partner - improve a region's growth rate more, the stronger increasing returns prevail in the home region; similarly, unfavourable trade conditions hurt most under increasing returns.

   Increasing returns in the partner region improve the conditions of trade and intensify the impact of north-south trade on the home region's growth rate.

5. With unfavourable conditions of trade, a high share of labour in a region's capital plus labour limits the region's 'loss' from north-south trade; under favourable trade conditions, the role of this labour share is ambiguous.

   Under favourable trade conditions a low labour share abroad is favourable to a region's growth rate; with unfavourable circumstances the role of the foreign labour share is ambiguous.

6. As in the single-country case, the value of a region's import share is irrelevant to the question whether the open-economy growth rate exceeds the one predicted by closed-economy analysis. But the absolute value of

the difference between the two is an increasing function of the region's import share.

A high share of imports in the partner region's economy is favourable if that region's 'autarkic' growth rate is low relative to that of the home region and if both regions' 'autarkic' per capita growth rates are high: then the negative impact of the transmission of growth from the faster to the slower region is diminished whereas that of the generation of growth is improved by a high foreign import share.

7. Due to the much higher share of north-south trade in the south than in the north, the south's growth rate is more sensitive to developments in the north than vice versa.

6.5. Implications

In north-south trade relations there are two important issues. The first one concerns the south's opportunities for development and in particular the question whether the conditions of north-south trade are unfavourable to the south's growth. The other one is whether rapid industrialization and growth of the south will hurt the north. Our analysis of the preceding sections provides a firmer theoretical base to discuss these questions in the aggregate than has hitherto been available. To apply the analysis, we need at least some indication of the values of the parameters of the system. Therefore we first provide some crude estimates of these.

The growth of the north-south system, 1955 - 1979

We need estimates of the two regions' natural rates, λ and $\bar{\lambda}$, rates of technical progress, ν and $\bar{\nu}$, of returns to scale ρ and $\bar{\rho}$, the shares of imports in total output, ξ_m and $\bar{\xi}_{\bar{m}}$, and of the value shares of labour in the two regional factors (labour and capital), ξ_ℓ and $\bar{\xi}_{\bar{\ell}}$. Table 6.7 provides the basic data that are available for four subperiods of the past quarter of a century: the two regions' growth rates of real GDP and population and the value shares of north-south trade in each region's total output.

We adopt these averages for each subperiod as estimates of the steady-growth rates χ and $\bar{\chi}$ and for the parameters λ, $\bar{\lambda}$ and ξ_m, $\bar{\xi}_{\bar{m}}$. Then our

Table 6.7. North and south's growth rates of real G.D.P. and population and the shares of north-south trade in total output, 1955-1979.

	The north's			The south's		
	Real GDP growth	Population growth	Share of imports from the south in total output	Real GDP growth	Population growth	Share of imports from the north in total output
	χ (%)	λ (%)	ξ_m (%)	$\bar{\chi}$ (%)	$\bar{\lambda}$ (%)	$\bar{\xi}_{\bar{m}}$ (%)
1955-60	3.3	1.2	2.4	4.7	2.4	12.0
1960-65	5.2	1.2	1.9	5.6	2.4	9.7
1965-73	4.6	1.0	1.9	5.8	2.5	9.8
1973-79	2.4	0.7	3.7	5.4	2.6	12.4

Sources: compare appendix 6.2.

Table 6.8. Estimates* of north's and south's rates of technical progress, 'autarkic' growth rates and the growth rates' 'gain' from north-south trade, 1955-1979.

	The north's			The south's		
	Technical progress ν (%)	'Autarkic' growth χ_{au} (%)	'Gain' $\chi-\chi_{au}$ (%)	Technical progress $\bar{\nu}$ (%)	'Autarkic' growth $\bar{\chi}_{au}$ (%)	'Gain' $\bar{\chi}-\bar{\chi}_{au}$ (%)
1955-60	1.32	3.19	0.11	1.38	4.64	0.06
1960-65	2.71	5.10	0.10	1.87	5.31	0.29
1965-73	2.43	4.49	0.11	2.01	5.61	0.19
1973-79	0.99	2.16	0.24	1.89	5.57	-0.17

*Postulating $\rho = \bar{\rho} = 1.1$ and $\xi_\ell = \bar{\xi}_{\bar{\ell}} = .75$. Sources are given in the text.

steady-growth equations (6.45) - (6.46) allow the calculation of estimat for two of the six remaining parameters, ρ, $\bar{\rho}$, ξ_ℓ, $\bar{\xi}_\ell$, ν, $\bar{\nu}$, once four o these are given. We take the rates of returns to scale, ρ and $\bar{\rho}$, at thei standard value 1.1 employed above; similarly the labour shares ξ_ℓ and $\bar{\xi}_\ell$ are assigned the standard 75% value. This way estimates of both regions' rates of technical progress and of their 'autarkic' growth rates are obtained from the steady-growth equations; these are shown in table 6.8. An assumption underlying this procedure is that the production functions are constant in each period, but may differ from one period to another.

Of course the 'guesstimates' thus obtained can provide only a very cru indication. There are several sources of errors. *First*, the postulated values of the rates of returns to scale and the labour shares may be off the mark. However, as some exercises reported in table 6.11 in appendix 6.2 show, the estimates of the rates of technical progress and, in particular, of the two 'autarkic' growth rates, are fairly insensitive t variations in the rates of returns to scale and the labour shares. A *second* source of error is the approximation of the natural rate, that is of the growth of employment, by that of total population. Clearly, gradually rising unemployment as e.g. in the 1973-79 period, biases the estimates of λ and $\bar{\lambda}$ upward, whereas a rising degree of participation in the labour forces biases them downward. *Third*, we have abstracted from t business cycle. However, each of the subperiods selected is fairly homogeneous in this respect; thus this assumption should not be too harmful. *Fourth*, a maintained hypothesis is that the system is on, or fluctuates around, its steady-growth path. But this hypothesis should no be too harmful either, because none of the subperiods is immediately subsequent to large-scale destruction of capital such as is caused by global warfare. A *final caveat* concerns the data: considerable conceptua and statistical problems still surround the real-income growth rates, particularly those for less-developed countries, cf. e.g. Kuznets (1972), Bairoch (1975, pp. 183-186), Gilbert (1980), Giarini (1980).

In view of those reservations, some attention should be paid to the plausibility of the results in table 6.8, particularly those on the two hemispheres' rates of technical progress. The most prominent feature of the estimates is the considerable, 1½ percent, drop of the north's rate technical progress from the 1965-73 period to the 1973-79 years - contrasting sharply with the constancy of the south's rate. How plausibl is this result? The estimates of technical progress have two main drawbacks. First, under the heading 'technical progress' our definition lumps together the growth of all other factors of production than (homogeneous) capital, labour and imports, along with all other systematic shifts in output. Second, we impose steady growth. Thus a fall in our estimate of the rate of technical progress need not represent a deceleration of the rate of application of new technologies to the productive process, but may be caused both by a host of influences on output (e.g. depletion of natural resources, diversion of capital resources to cope with environmental pollution, depression of entre-preneurial spirits) and simply by a stagnation of investment at a level below its steady-growth value.

One way to test this, is to apply 'growth accounting' to the two hemispheres' growth rates. By specifying the relevant production factors in sufficient detail, an alternative estimate of the rate of technical progress can be computed, once again as a residual. For the two hemispheres, lack of data prevents this exercise, but recently Dennison (1979) updated his accounting of US growth to cover the 1973-76 period. He estimates that the US rate of technical progress is 2.2% below the value it had prior to this period. Thus Dennison's estimate, based on detailed examination of inputs and not burdened by either the assumption of steady growth or that of full-capacity growth, yields substantially the same result as our approach.

An alternative way to check the values of the rates of technical progress, would be to obtain some direct data on the rate at which new technology is applied in production. However, nothing of this kind is readily available even for individual countries, let alone for the vast aggregates we consider. Nevertheless one suggestive indicator can be constructed without difficulty: the rate at which each hemisphere's growth of intra-bloc trade in manufacturing exceeds the growth of its manufacturing output. If trade grows faster than output this must imply that production of export goods is expanded and of other products contracted, domestic production of the latter being replaced by imports. Hence an increasing ratio of intra-bloc trade to output signifies increased specialization of the countries of the bloc. And with this increased specialization come the benefits of economies of scale, learning by doing and the traditional 'static' gains from trade. Thus if intra-bloc

<u>Table 6.9</u>. Volume growth of industrial output and intra-bloc trade in manufacturing, 1960–1977, north and south.*

	The north's growth rate of			The south's growth rate of		
	Volume of industrial output	Volume of intra-bloc trade in manufacturing	Degree of specialization** in manufacturing	Volume of industrial output	Volume of intra-bloc trade in manufacturing	Degree of specialization** in manufacturing
1960–65	6.2	10.8	4.6	7.3	9.9	2.6
1965–73	5.7	11.1	5.4	7.6	13.2	5.6
1973–77	1.2	4.0	2.8	4.9	14.7	9.8

* Sources: cf. appendix 6.1.

** Second column less first one and fifth less fourth one, respectively.

trade grows faster than output, particularly in manufacturing, this must both cause and be caused by technical progress.[6] Table 6.9 shows the growth rates of manufacturing output, intra-bloc trade in manufacturing and the difference between the two for 1960-65, 1965-73 and 1973-77.

For the north, the degree of specialization in manufacturing does indeed exhibit the same drop from the sixties to the seventies that we found in table 6.8 for the north's rate of technical progress; for the two subperiods of the sixties both rates are roughly constant. The south's rate of growth of specialization increases steadily throughout the three subperiods; here there is no decline in the seventies at all. On the contrary, the rapid increase in the degree of specialization even leads to the question why technical progress in the south was not faster than in the sixties. Probably the reason for this is the still small share of manufacturing in the south's GDP: this implies that the technical progress in manufacturing generated by and generating increased specialization still translates into a relatively moderate technical progress for the economy as a whole.[7]

These results imply that the estimates of table 6.8 for the rates of technical progress yield a picture that is perfectly compatible with both Dennison's detailed, but indirect, measurement of technical progress by growth accounting and with available direct evidence. It is therefore acceptable to base our discussion of north-south issues on the estimates in tables 6.7 and 6.8.

North-south trade and the south's growth rate, 1955-1979

A central issue in north-south relations is the extent to which the south's development depends on the growth of the north and on the conditions of north-south trade. Our analysis can throw some light on this issue. In view, however, of the strong political overtones in the debate on it[8] we should first emphasize again what our analysis cannot and what it can do. Our analysis is not suited to show what the effects will be if the south would largely abandon imports from the north. Our 'autarkic' growth rate does not refer to the situation this would generate, but just to the hypothetical case where imports are absent but the basic parameters of the trading system are retained. The latter is obviously impossible. Consider the example of the rate of technical progress. The south's rate of technical progress is maintained to an unknown extent by importing technology from the north. On the other hand, infant capital industries i the south may be prevented from maturing precisely by competition from tl north. The total effect of imports is therefore obviously undeterminable with our tools. What, however, our analysis is well suited to deal with i the impact of developments in the north on the south, given 'normal' trac relations. In addition our analysis is quite capable of dealing with not too large changes in the intensity of north-south trade. Finally, it enables us to compare the trading system's growth rates with that in the no-trade situation, under the hypothesis that the structural parameters are the same in both cases; the relevance of this exercise is purely theoretical: it shows to what extent a bias is obtained if the south's growth rate is analysed using real-world parameter estimates in closed-economy models, or, for that matter, in HOS-type and (neo-) Ricardian one where imports are thought to have perfect domestic substitutes.

With these qualifications in mind, the estimates in table 6.8 yield son interesting results. One of the core features emerging from the table is that the south's 'autarkic' growth rate consistently, and frequently substantially, exceeded that of the north. By conclusion 1 of section 6.4 this implies that the transmission of growth was from south to north throughout the last quarter of a century. This, however, was compensated by the generation of growth that occurs if both regions' per capita 'autarkic' growth rates are high. Until 1973 this generation of growth completely offset the negative impact of the transmission on the south's growth rate, leaving the south better of than closed-economy theory woulc have indicated. This was particularly true from 1960 to 1973. In this period the south actually benefitted more from north-south trade than the north: the ratio of the south's growth rate to the north's exceeded the ratio of their 'autarkic' growth rates. After 1973, however, when the north's 'autarkic' growth slackened, the south's rate of expansion was lower than closed-economy analysis would lead to expect. However, table 6.8 indicates that this 'loss', like the 'gain' in the pre-1973 period, was minor.

To summarize, the conclusion must be that in the past 25 years the south's growth rate was only marginally affected by changes in the conditions of north-south trade and in the rate of growth of the north. I is interesting to know how the south's 'gain' from north-south trade cou be enlarged.

One way to do this, is to diminish the negative effect of the south-north transmission of growth caused by the excess of the south's 'autarkic' growth rate over that of the north. This, in turn, can be achieved in two ways. The first is, obviously, lowering the south's natural rate. If, for example, in the past twenty-five years the south's natural rate would have been one percent lower than it actually was, with all other parameters of table 6.8 unchanged, the total 'gain' from north-south trade for the south would have been 6.2% instead of the meagre 2.3% it actually was according to the figures in table 6.8. However, as long as the assumption of 10% increasing returns made in table 6.8 is correct, this would not have made much difference to the south's per capita income: the lower natural rate, though increasing the 'gain', lowers the 'autarkic' growth rate, which would on balance result in a mere 0.5 percent per capita income improvement for the period as a whole. A much more effective way to improve the south's 'gain' is to increase the north's rate of technical progress. The beneficial effect of this for the south is quite evident from table 6.8 and also from table 6.10 below. Thus, ironically, the south 'gains' more from north-south trade if the north's growth is stepped up.

Another way to improve the south's 'gain' is to increase the impact of the generation of growth on the south's growth rate. This is already achieved if the north's rate of technical progress increases, but in addition if the north increases the share of southern imports in its total imports; incidentally, this also diminishes the negative impact of the transmission of growth on the south. This result follows from conclusion 6 of section 6.4 and is illustrated numerically in table 6.6.

It would be false to hope that even the combination of all the changes in the parameters of the north-south system discussed above would raise the south's growth rate really substantially. Each of these parameter changes raises the rate by only a little and combined they can at best achieve an improvement of one or one and a half percent. The south's growth depends, at least until north-south trade becomes much more intensive, mainly on internal influences, not on the conditions of north-south trade or the rate of growth of the north.

Impact of the south's development on the growth of the north, 1980-2050

Traditionally there has been much concern in the developed world that i would be adversely affected by development of the south. Thus during the colonial period industrialization of colonies was sometimes downright prohibited. It is to a close empirical examination of the validity of thi concern that Hilgerdt's (1945) landmark study for the League of Nations was devoted. His conclusion is that industrialization of new countries reinvigorates rather than retards growth of the old developed countries, by providing them with growing export markets that more than compensate the loss due to competitive imports. During the period of rapid expansior after the second world war, Hilgerdt's position was generally unchallenged. But since the north's growth slowed down after 1973, the traditional fears have once again emerged (for a number of references cf. Stein, 1981; also compare Anell and Nygren, 1980, pp. 71-74). Therefore i is useful to examine the issue within the framework of our theory of the growth of the north-south system. To this end we construct an illustrati scenario for the next 70 years. This scenario is not a prediction, but merely a tool to point out what the consequences will be of rapid development of the south combined with 'autarkic' growth of the north th does not differ too much from its experience in the past 25 years. The scenario simply <u>assumes</u> both of the latter developments and brings out their consequences. To do this, the two assumptions must of course be translated into values for the parameters of our system. We discuss thes parameter values first.

Development is reflected in several ways by the aggregate variables to which our analysis is confined. The value of per capita income is the obvious prime indicator of the level of development. As such, however, tl south's per capita income is irrelevant to the north's growth rate. What matters is, first, its implications in the very long run for the growth rates of population and technology and next the relative income level compared to that of the north.

A fairly clearcut picture has emerged of the influence of per capita income on the growth rate of population (for a wealth of empirical evidence, cf. Rostow, 1978, pp. 1-44). At very low levels of per capita income, population growth appears to be slow, but not nil. As income rises, so does the natural rate, but at high income levels population growth is clearly declining and may well be heading to zero. That of the south is still accelerating slightly; but fertility rates in the south are now declining. Because, however, a very large percentage of the south's population is still under the age of twenty, the decline of the fertility rates will not lead to a decline in the growth of population before the end of the present century. Thereafter a gradual decline should be possible; our scenario is as optimistic as to postulate a one-percent growth rate from the 2020's onward. For the north we postulate a decline to zero in the last decade of the present century.

Per capita income's growth rate exhibits a similar pattern as the natural rate, accelerating up to a certain level of income and decelerating above that level. Here, however, the relation must be cast in relative rather than absolute terms, the dependent variable being the country's growth rate compared to that of the whole world economy - and possibly the independent variable too should be relative rather than absolute real income per capita. A recent authoritative statement of the evidence is Rostow (1980, pp. 259-301). Our data for the 1960's do not adequately reflect this tendency, because the aggregation of the 'south' lumps together slowly growing countries from the low-income brackets with fast ones in the medium range; briefly the 'north' aggregates rapid-growth countries that were, originally, in the medium range (Japan!) with slower advanced ones. In the 1970's however, the south's growth rate and the rate of technical progress we computed, clearly exceed that of the north.

A plausible explanation of this picture is that at the highest income levels further technical progress is more difficult because basic scientific breakthroughs and inventions are necessary to develop new 'leading sectors'; on the other end of the scale, at very low income levels, the economy is still insufficiently integrated and market oriented for fast diffusion of available technical improvements.(9) The transitional and newly industrialized countries between these extremes are capable of spreading and applying innovations rapidly and have a vast stock of still unutilized technological knowledge to draw from. If this explanation of the relation between income growth and income level is accepted, it can be used to obtain hints as to the future development of technical progress. As Chenery (1977) shows, a large number of countries in the south are now in the intermediate range; in 1973 their population

Table 6.10. Growth of the north-south system: scenario 1980-2050.

		1980-'89	1990-'99	2000-'09	2010-'19	2020-'29	2030-'39	2040-2050
Rates of technical	north, ν	1.3	1.3	2.0	2.5	1.3	1.3	2.5
progress (%)	south, $\bar{\nu}$	2.0	2.5	2.5	3.0	3.0	3.0	3.0
Natural	north, λ	0.5	0.0	0.0	0.0	0.0	0.0	0.0
rates (%)	south, $\bar{\lambda}$	2.5	2.5	2.0	1.5	1.0	1.0	1.0
Share of imports in	north, ξ_m	3.7	5.0	8.0	12.0	16.0	20.0	20.0
total output (%)	south, $\bar{\xi}_{\bar{m}}$	12.4	13.0	15.0	17.0	19.0	20.0	20.0
'Autarkic' growth	north, χ_{au}	2.36	1.79	2.76	3.45	1.79	1.79	3.45
rates (%)	south, $\bar{\chi}_{au}$	5.60	6.29	5.72	5.84	5.28	5.28	5.28
'Gain' (%)	north, $\chi-\chi_{au}$	0.25	0.31	0.60	0.94	1.16	1.46	1.47
	south, $\bar{\chi}-\bar{\chi}_{au}$	-0.12	-0.24	0.09	0.44	0.24	0.33	0.80
Total growth	north, χ	2.61	2.10	3.36	4.39	2.95	3.25	4.92
rate (%)	south, $\bar{\chi}$	5.48	6.05	5.82	6.28	5.51	5.61	6.08

The south's real GDP as percent of the north's* (end of period)		'autarkic'	32	51	68	87	123	174	209
		total	31	46	59	71	92	117	131
Per capita GDP, in 1979 US$ (end of period)**	north	'autarkic'	9 878	11 818	15 573	21 985	26 302	31 468	45 983
		total	10 129	12 500	17 596	27 145	36 467	50 465	86 701
	south	'autarkic'	1 009	1 475	2 140	3 305	5 068	7 773	12 441
		total	997	1 423	2 083	3 362	5 579	8 370	14 635
The south's real GDP per capita as % of the north's (end of period)**		'autarkic'	10.2	12.5	13.7	15.3	19.3	24.7	27.1
		total	9.8	11.4	11.8	12.4	15.3	16.6	16.9

* 1979: 23%

** 1979: north 8200, south 740, south as % of north 9.0%.

constituted 27% and their GDP 61% of the south's total. This means that under our basic assumption of rapid development(10) in the next few decades, the south's rate of technical progress will probably exceed that of the north, as it has already done in the seventies by our evidence. Probably the same remains true well into the next century as wave after wave of poor countries enter the transitional phase. For the north our scenario postulates a rate of technical progress for the next two decades that exceeds that of the late seventies somewhat: the 1.3% we found for the late fifties. After that we postulate some long swings in the rate of technical progress, in order to show how differences in this rate affect the impact of the south's development.

The combined result of a higher natural rate and a higher rate of technical progress in the south than in the north is that the size of the south's economy grows relative to that of the north. In our steady-growth model this has no influence as such, because the share of southern goods in the north is constant under the Cobb-Douglas assumption. In reality on may assume that as the south's relative size grows, the increased opportunities for north-south specialization in manufacturing will raise the north's import share; of course this does not have to happen, as protective policies may prevent it, but it seems reasonable to postulate rise as the normal development of the Cobb-Douglas technology. Thus we take the share of southern goods in the north's total imports to increase gradually from its present 3.7% to 20% at mid-century; we postulate this process to be acompanied by a slight rise of the share of northern goods in the south, also to 20%.

For the remaining parameters, the rates of returns to scale and the labour shares, we simply adopt the standard values of tables 6.1 and 6.8.

Table 6.10 shows that with this scenario, the north consistently 'gains from the development of the south: its 'gain' from north-south trade gradually increases as the relative size of the south's economy, and witl it the share of the south's goods in the north, grows. This remains true even when the south's natural rate declines - because of the high rate o: technical progress in the south. For the south, the picture is different In the last decades of the present century, the scenario envisages a slight 'loss' from north-south trade. In the early 21'st century, this 'loss' is reversed and an, initially small, 'gain' emerges. This is due both to the decline of the south's natural rate and to the increase of tl share of the south's goods in the north's economy (cf. the last part of conclusion 6, section 6.4). Table 6.11 shows that the south's 'gain' is considerably higher in the periods where we assigned a high rate of technical progress to the north, than in the decades where a lower rate is postulated.

The consequence of the south's development is that its total income grows relative to that of the north. However, because the same development of the south boosts the north's growth through north-south trade, the ratio of the two hemispheres' incomes, both total and per capita, grows much slower than should be expected without trade. Initially, the north's total income is four times that of the south; under the 'autarky' scheme both are equal in the early 2020's, whereas this point is reached a decade later in the trade scenario. The effect of trade on per capita incomes is even more pronounced. Until around 2015 the scenario assignes the south a lower per capita income than it would have if it could do without north-south trade. In contradistinction, the north's per capita income growth is considerably faster due to trade; at midcentury it is almost twice as high as it would have been without the impact of the south's development. As a result, the north's lead in per capita income remains considerable, the ratio of the two regions' incomes rising only from 9% in 1979 to 17% in 2050.(11)

The central conclusion that emerges with respect to the impact of the south's development on the north, is that the north can benefit greatly from it. Of course this conclusion must be regarded with great caution. For one of the two basic assumptions from which the scenario starts in the first place, is that the north continues to grow in the same way, though not quite as fast, as the past 25 years. This in turn presupposes that the north's natural rate, its rate of capital accumulation and its rate of technical progress are not lowered by the south's development. The first happens if the south's competition destroys more jobs than are created by the new output generated by exports to the south. The north's rate of technical progress may be retarded by the south's development, if the latter discourages innovative investments. The scenario therefore presupposes that the north succeeds in creating new technologies and new leading sectors as the south learns to master the older ones. Our analysis shows that, if the north succeeds, it will also gain considerably from the south's development through north-south trade.

Appendix 6.1. Parameter variations and the steady-growth rates

In this appendix we give the derivatives of the steady-growth rates wi respect to the parameters of the system. We give these for the north onl as those for the south are symmetrical.

The derivative of the sign indicator with respect to the north's rate technical progress, ν, is:

$$-\frac{1}{\theta_{au}}[(1-\xi_{\ell})\{1-\bar{\rho}(1-\bar{\xi}_{\bar{m}})(1-\bar{\xi}_{\bar{\ell}})\}-\bar{\rho}\bar{\xi}_{\bar{m}}]; \tag{6.73}$$

that with respect to the south's rate of technical progress, $\bar{\nu}$, is unit: The sign indicators' derivatives with respect to the north's and the south's natural rates, λ and $\bar{\lambda}$, are, respectively:

$$\frac{-\xi_{\ell}(1-\rho\bar{\rho}\bar{\xi}_{\bar{m}})}{\theta_{au}}, \tag{6.74}$$

and:

$$\bar{\rho}\bar{\xi}_{\bar{\ell}}(1-\bar{\xi}_{\bar{m}}). \tag{6.75}$$

Note that the 'gains' multiplier is independent of both ν, $\bar{\nu}$ and of λ, the 'autarkic' growth rate of the north does not depend on $\bar{\nu}$ and $\bar{\lambda}$ and as is shown in chapter 4, an increasing function of λ and ν.

The multiplier's derivative to the north's rate of returns to scale, ρ, is:

$$\frac{\xi_m\{1-\bar{\rho}(1-\bar{\xi}_{\bar{m}})(1-\bar{\xi}_{\bar{\ell}})\}}{\phi^2}; \tag{6.76}$$

that of the sign indicator is:

$$\frac{[\lambda\xi_{\ell}+\nu(1-\xi_{\ell})][(1-\xi_{\ell})\{-1+\bar{\rho}(1-\bar{\xi}_{\bar{m}})(1-\bar{\xi}_{\bar{\ell}})\}+\bar{\rho}\bar{\xi}_{\bar{m}}]}{\theta_{au}^2} \tag{6.77}$$

The multiplier's derivative to the south's rate of returns to scale, is:

$$\frac{\rho\xi_m}{\phi^2}\,[(1-\bar{\xi}_{\bar{m}})(1-\bar{\xi}_{\bar{\ell}})\{1-\rho(1-\xi_m)(1-\xi_\ell)\}+\rho\xi_m\bar{\xi}_{\bar{m}}]\ , \tag{6.78}$$

and that of the sign indicator:

$$\bar{\lambda}\bar{\xi}_{\bar{\ell}}(1-\bar{\xi}_{\bar{m}})+\chi_{au}\bar{\xi}_{\bar{m}}+\frac{(1-\bar{\xi}_{\bar{m}})(1-\bar{\xi}_{\bar{\ell}})}{\theta_{au}}\{\lambda\xi_\ell+\nu(1-\xi_\ell)\}, \tag{6.79}$$

The derivative of the sign indicator with respect to the north's labour share, ξ_ℓ, is:

$$\frac{\lambda(\rho-1)+\nu}{\theta_{au}^2}\,[1-\bar{\rho}(1-\bar{\xi}_{\bar{m}})(1-\bar{\xi}_{\bar{\ell}})-\rho\bar{\rho}\bar{\xi}_{\bar{m}}]\ , \tag{6.80}$$

and that of the multiplier:

$$\frac{-\rho\xi_m}{\phi^2}\,\{1-\bar{\rho}(1-\bar{\xi}_{\bar{m}})(1-\bar{\xi}_{\bar{\ell}})\}\rho(1-\xi_m). \tag{6.81}$$

The sign indicator's derivative to the south's labour share, $\bar{\xi}_{\bar{\ell}}$, is:

$$-\frac{1}{\theta_{au}}\,\bar{\rho}(1-\bar{\xi}_{\bar{m}})(1-\xi_\ell)\{\nu+\lambda(\rho-1)\}, \tag{6.82}$$

and that of the multiplier:

$$-\frac{\rho\xi_m}{\phi^2}\,\{1-\rho(1-\xi_m)(1-\xi_\ell)\}\bar{\rho}(1-\bar{\xi}_{\bar{m}}). \tag{6.83}$$

The derivative of the south's multiplier to the north's import share, ξ_m, is:

$$\rho\{1-\bar{\rho}(1-\bar{\xi}_{\bar{m}})(1-\bar{\xi}_{\bar{\ell}})\}\{1-\rho(1-\xi_\ell)\}+\rho^2\bar{\rho}\xi_m\bar{\xi}_{\bar{m}}\ . \tag{6.84}$$

The derivative of the growth rate with respect to the south's import share given in (6.72) is obtained from:

$$\frac{\rho\bar{\rho}\xi_m}{\phi^2}\,\big[-\bar{\nu}\{-\rho\xi_m+(1-\bar{\xi}_{\bar{\ell}})\{1-\rho(1-\xi_\ell)(1-\xi_m)\}\}+\bar{\xi}_{\bar{\ell}}\bar{\lambda}\{\rho\bar{\rho}\xi_m-\{1-\rho(1-\xi_\ell)(1-\xi_m)\}\}+\lambda\xi_\ell\rho\bar{\theta}_{au}(1-\xi_m)+\nu\bar{\theta}_{au}\big]. \tag{6.85}$$

Appendix 6.2. Sources of tables 6.7, 6.8 and 6.9

In table 6.7, sources for the growth rates of real GDP and of populati are:

1955-60 UNCTAD, Handbook of International Trade and Development Statistics, 1969, provides growth rates of total and per capita rea GDP. The growth rate of population is calculated as the difference between the two.

1960-73 World Bank, World Tables, 1976.

1973-79 UNCTAD, Handbook of International Trade and Development Statistics, 1979, provides growth rates of total and per capita rea GDP for 1970-73.
Ditto, 1980 provides them for 1970-79; for the period 1973-79 the rates are calculated from these two data. Growth rates of populatio are the difference of total and per capita GDP growth.

Sources for the import shares in table 6.7 are:

For 1958, 1960, 1963, 1965, 1967-1978 total GDP in millions of current dollars is provided for north and south by UNO, Yearbook of National Account Statistics, various issues. For 1979 the total GDP has been estimated by adding to the 1978 data the real growth (source: see above) and US inflation (source: Federal Reserve Bulletin). For all years, sources for the value of north-south trade are various issues of UNCTAD' Handbook. The shares of imports in total output are then calculated as $\frac{a}{1+a}$, where a is the ratio of the import flow to the GDP of the region concerned; strictly speaking, this is only correct if trade is balanced, but the differences are minor. The data for 1955-60 refer to 1958; thos for 1960-65 to the average of 1960, 1963, 1965; those for 1965-73 to th average for 1965, 1967-1973; those for 1973-1979 to the average of all years of the period.

For all data in table 6.7, 'north' refers to developed market economi 'south' to developing market economies, both groups defined in the usua UNO sense.

Sources for table 6.8 have been described in the main text. Here we sl that variations in the postulated values of the rates of returns to scale, ρ and $\bar{\rho}$, and of the two regions' labour shares, ξ_ℓ, $\bar{\xi}_\ell$, have a minor impact only on the estimates of the parameters provided by table 6.8. This is shown in table 6.11: the differences in the estimates of ν and $\bar{\nu}$ are at most in the order of magnitude of one-half of a percent. Those in the estimates of the 'gains' $\chi - \chi_{au}$ and $\bar{\chi} - \bar{\chi}_{au}$ are still smaller, not exceeding 0.08%. The qualitative conclusions of the main text hold for all postulated parameter values: in the periods 55-60 and 73-79 the south's technical progress consistenly exceeds that of the north, in the intermediate periods this situation is always reversed. The same applies to the relative values of the two regions' 'gains'.

Sources for table 6.9 are UNCTAD's (1980) Handbook (manufacturing output) and UNO's (1978) Yearbook of International Trade Statistics (volume of trade in manufacturing).

Table 6.11. Impacts of variations in postulated values of rates of retur to scale and labour shares on estimates of technical progres and 'gains'.

		ν (%)		$\chi-\chi_{au}$ (%)		$\bar{\nu}$ (%)		$\bar{\chi}-\bar{\chi}_{au}$ (%)	
	$\xi_{\ell}=\bar{\xi}_{\bar{\ell}}$ (%)	75	85	75	85	75	85	75	85
	$\rho=\rho$								
55-60	1.1	1.32	1.54	0.11	0.10	1.38	1.61	0.06	0.0
	1.0	1.50	1.71	0.10	0.09	1.69	1.89	0.05	0.0
60-65	1.1	2.71	3.14	0.10	0.10	1.87	2.18	0.29	0.3
	1.0	2.94	3.33	0.09	0.08	2.21	2.49	0.26	0.2
65-73	1.1	2.43	2.82	0.11	0.11	2.01	2.33	0.19	0.2
	1.0	2.62	2.98	0.10	0.10	2.35	2.65	0.17	0.1
73-79	1.1	0.99	1.17	0.24	0.22	1.89	2.16	-0.17	-0.1
	1.0	1.11	1.13	0.21	0.19	2.21	2.46	-0.15	-0.0

7. NORTH-SOUTH AID AND THE NORTH'S INCOME

One of the central conclusions of chapter 6 is that growth of one region is beneficial to its trade partners' 'long-run' growth rate of income. This result is obtained for the case of a closed balance of trade without international aid. This raises the question whether direct aid, being meant to induce growth in the receiving region, may also have positive effects on the donor region's income. This question is not satisfactorily dealt with in the literature. The relevant literature, briefly surveyed in section 7.1, does analyse the 'short-run' effects of aid flows ('transfers'): the adjustment of trade flows, terms of trade, and income with *given* stocks of capital. These are usually dubbed the 'secondary' effects, the 'primary' one being the immediate cost of the transfer proper; the combined primary and secondary effect on the donor's income is usually thought to be negative. However, the literature does not analyse the consequences of the aid-induced accumulation in the receiving region for the donor's income. This in spite of the fact that aid is meant precisely to facilitate the recipient's development and accumulation. Therefore this chapter tackles these capital-accumulation (or 'tertiary') effects of aid. Here we no longer employ the main tool of preceding chapters: the analysis of steady-growth paths and their stability. As the need for aid is, hopefully, a transitional phenomenon it should be treated as such.

Section 7.2 treats the question without even an explicitly dynamic analysis. We just consider the effect of aid on the recipient's accumulation - allowing for adjustment of trade-flows and terms of trade - and the immediate impact of this induced accumulation on the donor's income. The result is that the tertiary effects on the donor's income and terms of trade are positive as long as the receiving region's capital stock is small relative to the donor region's. Thus this 'tertiary blessing' offsets the 'primary *cum* secondary burden' at least partially. The extent of the tertiary blessing is positively influenced by three factors: the share of aid funds the recipient devotes to accumulation instead of consumption, the share of aid that the donor finances out of consumption instead of saving and investment, and the ratio of the donor's capital stock to that of the recipient. If the donor region's capital stock is sufficiently sizeable compared to the recipient's, the tertiary blessing may even completely offset the primary cum secondary burden, the total effect of aid on the donor's income being positive. Thus in a two-region system aid of a rich to a poor region is less costly to the donor than traditional theory suggests, even to the extent that it may be profitable.

Section 7.3 carries the analysis one step further to an explicitly dynamic treatment in order to elaborate on the possibility that aid is beneficial to the donor. To do this we analyse what the latter's optimal policy should be if it wishes to maximize its consumption over some planning period. Of course its first instrument is domestic investment financed out of current production; but we are interested mainly in the second possible instrument: aid to the trade partner. Should, in any part of the planning period, the region aid its partner if it just wants to maximize its own consumption? The answer is yes. Provided the partner's capital stock is originally small enough relative to the home region's it is optimal for the latter to give aid in the initial part of a sufficiently long planning period. Admittedly we achieve this result only with simplifying assumptions on the production functions but more realistic assumptions will not alter the qualitative result.

As to the relevance of our analysis, the two-region model can first of all serve as a prelude to a multi-region system. It should perhaps be noted that, when generalizing our analysis to a multi-region system, the question whether aid must be spent in the donor country, or whether it may also be spent in third countries becomes relevant. In the present two-region system this point is irrelevant because there are no third regions implying that the whole transfer is always spent in the donor region. Clearly, our analysis is directly applicable to situations where the effects of trade with third regions are not too sizeable. Good examples of this are aid flows of rich regions of a large economy to its poorer regions, for instance aid within the European Community and between the states of the U.S. Historically US Marshall-aid to Europe may well fit the requirements. However, the most immediate application of our model is of course north-south aid. Therefore we once again, as in chapter six, label the two regions as 'north' and 'south'. Of course it is not clear without empirical work what the extent of the tertiary blessing is in the case of north-south aid. Nevertheless it is certain that the north's capital stock is quite sizeable compared to the south's. Thus our analysis can leave no doubt that north-south aid is less costly to the north than traditionally thought.

7.1. The transfer problem

Aid is a specific case of an international transfer of purchasing power. This subject has enjoyed a good deal of interest by economists. In the nineteenth century interest was stimulated by the phenomenon of absentee landlords which was politically relevant in Britain because of the Irish question; cf. e.g. Mill (1844, pp. 258-261, 1848 pp. 638/639) and Marshall (circa 1873). In the early twentieth century Viner (1924) discussed the subject in connection with capital exports to Canada. Keynes (1929) and Ohlin (1929) debated the effects of German reparations payments. After the Second World War American Marshall-aid to Europe inspired (1) Samuelson's (1952, 1954, 1968) classic treatment of the subject. Presently the subject is not only relevant because of north-south aid but also because of transfers by foreign labourers to their home countries and, as noted by Jones (1976), of OPEC surplusses.

The primary effect of a transfer is a displacement of purchasing power from the paying to the receiving region. To this are immediately added secondary effects because the terms of trade adjust. This causes changes in trade flows, consumption, output and income of both regions. In turn, these initial 'direct' effects give rise to changes in each region's capital stock, because both the transfer itself and the resulting income changes affect investments in both regions. To judge the effect of a transfer one must therefore add resulting changes in incomes to the immediate effects.

Most of the literature has dealt with the immediate effect of a transfer on the terms of trade; that is with given capital stocks and full employment. This issue is referred to as the 'transfer problem'. Mill, Marshall, Viner, Taussig (1912, chapter 33), Keynes, et al., advocated what Ohlin dubbed (cf. Chipman, 1974) the 'orthodox view'. In Mill's (1848, p. 638) words: 'The result is that a country which makes regular payments to foreign countries besides losing what it pays, looses also something more, by the less advantageous terms on which it is forced to exchange its productions for foreign commodities'. The alternative view o: Ohlin (1929) is that no presumption is possible. For the case of no trade impediments Ohlin's view is vindicated by Samuelson (1952) who shows that the outcome depends crucially on the marginal income propensities to consume. However, a presumption becomes once again possible if something can be said *a priori* about these marginal income propensities. Jones (1970) argues that if there are random differences in tastes and comparative advantage, independent of each other, this implies a tendency to import goods towards which the country's tastes are biased. As Samuelson (1971) puts it: 'If I am a drunkard and you are a fop, I am mor‹ likely to export cloth and import rye than vice versa'. The resulting bia: in the marginal income propensities yields, according to Samuelson's (1952) calculations, an *anti-orthodox* presumption of a change of the term: of trade in favour of the paying country.

If trade impediments are present, things are more complicated and depen‹ on the precise way in which the impediments are introduced. Samuelson (1954) assumes a certain portion of each good to be lost in transit but currently a more popular approach is to postulate the existence of a non-traded goods sector. This idea goes back not only to Taussig (1906), as Chipman (1974) notes, but even to Marshall (*circa* 1873), a paper recently uncovered by Whitaker. The modern contributions have been made by McDougall (1965), Samuelson (1971, whose non-traded good is leasure) Chipman (1974) and Jones (1975, 1976, 1979). Jones' (1975, p. 263) summar of the results is: 'First, the question of presumption hinges in large part on the underlying causes of trade. In particular the presumed direction of change of the terms of trade depends upon whether demand differences between countries are more or less pronounced than supply differences. Secondly, if trade is explained by differences both in deman and supply, much depends upon the degree of sensitivity to price changes of demanders, on the one hand, and producers on the other'.

All this concerns the (immediate) effect of a transfer on the terms of trade. This question derives its interest from the repercussions for the national incomes. If the terms of trade deteriorate, this implies an additional transfer cost, a 'secondary burden', for the income of the paying country. If they improve, the primary burden is partially alleviated by a 'secondary blessing'. This poses the question whether the secondary blessing can be large enough to compensate the primary burden fully; in this case the total effect of a transfer would be a real income gain of the paying country. Leontief (1936) first pointed out this possibility; hence it is sometimes referred to as a 'Leontief-effect'. There are, in the context of the two-good model with perfect domestic substitutes for imports and with fixed capital stocks, only three cases in which a Leontief-effect has been shown to occur.

First, Leontief's (1936) own example showed real income to improve locally in a special case. Samuelson (1947, footnote 7, p. 29), however, notes that in Leontief's special case 'an increase in demand for a commodity lowers rather than raises its price'. Thus in this case the Marshall-Lerner condition is violated. According to Samuelson (ibid; 1952, footnote, p. 284) the equilibrium is unstable in this case. Then the equilibrium is irrelevant for all practical purposes and so is the Leontief-effect. This is an application of Samuelson's Correspondence Principle: an equilibrium with perverse comparative-static properties is usually unstable. However, in the present case, the stability or instability of the equilibrium depends crucially on the adjustment process involved. If not exports or the terms of trade are the adjusting variable but imports instead, the equilibrium is stable precisely if the Marshall-Lerner condition is violated (cf. Van Bochove, 1981, and also chapter 8). This adjustment of imports is relevant because the main part of trade is in inputs. Thus the Correspondence Principle breaks down and there are no *a priori* grounds to preclude the existence of a Leontief-effect. Whether or not a particular transfer will have as immediate effect a rise of the paying country's income is therefore an empirical issue: no presumption is possible.

Second, even if the Marshall-Lerner condition is satisfied locally, near the pre-transfer equilibrium, a global Leontief-effect may yet exist if there are multiple equilibria. Then a transfer may kick the system from one locally stable equilibrium to another, causing a quantum jump in the terms of trade such that the paying country's income rises. This possibility is recognized by Samuelson (1952, p. 284) and rigorously proved by Balasko (1978).

A third possibility for a Leontief-effect was recently pointed out by Chichilnisky (1980). She analyses the transfer problem in a three-country world. Then, in a particular case,(2) a transfer may result in a deterioration of the receiving country's welfare and an increase in that of the donor country and the third one combined - even if the equilibrium satisfies Walrasian stability conditions.

All these instances of a Leontief-effect require the international trade system to be a bit un-wellbehaved. If it is a wellbehaved bilateral system with a unique equilibrium satisfying the Marshall-Lerner condition the initial effect of a transfer is to lower the paying country's income. This however does not have to be true in the long run. For both the transfer itself and the additional income generated by the transfer in the receiving country give rise to incremental investment in the latter country. This, in turn, raises the productive capacity and the income of this country still further and this has a positive impact on the paying country's income, say a 'tertiary blessing'. It therefore remains to be seen what the eventual result is. The literature ignores this question. There is of course a great deal of attention devoted to international investment but there the analysis concentrates on the effects of mobility of physical capital and of interest payments and repatriation. In the case of a transfer there is just a displacement of purchasing power, not of physical capital. One exception in the literature is Ruffin (1979, pp. 837-840) who does analyse the effect of a transfer allowing for investment in the receiving and the paying country alike. He concludes that an eventual rise of the paying country's income is extremely unlikely. Ruffin, however, employs a model that does not incorporate international trade but only international capital movements. In his model a rise in the paying country's income can only be generated by changes the transfer causes in the rate of interest and with it in the interest received on foreign investments. Thus a rise in the receiving country's income cannot by generating trade positively affect the donor country. In the next sections we show that it is precisely this trade-transmitted growth that may cause a blessing to the donor country.

7.2. North-south aid: a tertiary blessing for the north

The results of a once and for all, lump sum, transfer from north to south can, as already noted, be broken down in a sequence of effects. First, the transfer raises the south's income and lowers that of the north. Second, the terms of trade adjustment mitigates these income changes, the eventual result normally still being a rise in the south's income and a decrease of the north's. Third, these income changes affect both regions' investment. That of the south is raised, of the north lowered. The extent of this impulse on investments depends on the way the transfer is financed in the north and influences saving in the south. If it is financed mainly out of the north's saving it depresses the north's investment more than if its funding is distributed over saving and consumption in the same proportion as all expenditure or if consumption is the main contribuant. In the south a larger part of the transfer may be saved than of ordinary income, implying that the transfer's impact on the south's investment is amplified. The fourth stage begins when the changes in the two regions' capital stocks caused by the changes in investment have their impact on output and income: in the north the latter are once again lower than they would have been without transfer, in the south higher. Fifth, however, these additional changes in output affect trade and are thus transmitted between the two hemispheres. By making the south's goods more abundant vis-à-vis those of the north, this may increase the north's income. It is from this effect, which may be dubbed a 'tertiary blessing', that the possibility of an eventual income gain in the north arises.

Of course the chain of events does not break off at this point, since investments are once again affected and so on. However, to demonstrate that the north's income loss may be less than traditional theory suggests and that even an eventual income gain in the north can be generated it suffices to show that the 'tertiary blessing' is large enough. One way to do this is to describe the dynamics explicitly either in continuous or in discrete time. However, for simplicity we prefer to telescope all five stages into one, treating them as though they occur simultaneously. Comparative statics therefore suffices as analytical tool.

Modelling a north-south transfer

We employ the same north-south model as in chapter 6 but can leave out technical progress since we do not explicitly describe the dynamics of the system. Thus the production functions of north and south are, respectively:

$$v = v(z(\ell, k), m). \qquad (7.1)$$

$$\bar{v} = \bar{v}(\bar{z}(\bar{\ell}, \bar{k}), m). \qquad (7.2)$$

The notation is the same as in chapter 6: v denotes output, z is a linear homogeneous function of capital, k, and labour, ℓ; m is imports. Without bar the variable relates to the north, with bar to the south. The production functions v and $\bar{v}$ are homogeneous of degree one; the generalization to increasing and decreasing returns provides no basic difficulties but clutters the formulas. We take the production functions to satisfy the standard assumptions of positive marginal factor products and strict quasi-concavity.

Import demand is given by:

$$v_m = P^{-1}. \qquad (7.3)$$

$$\bar{v}_{\bar{m}} = P. \qquad (7.4)$$

Here v_m is v's derivative to m, and P the north's terms of trade, the ratio of its export price to its import price.

The balance of trade equation is:

$$\bar{m} = mP^{-1} + n, \qquad (7.5)$$

the south's imports being equal to the sum of the value of its exports mP^{-1} and the transfer n; the latter is measured in units of the north's output.

Finally, the two regions' income are:(3)

$$y = v - \bar{m}. \qquad (7.6)$$

$$\bar{y} = \bar{v} - m. \qquad (7.7)$$

We calculate the impact of the transfer by transforming the system into logarithmic differentials and applying some 'hat calculus'. For convenience we take the transfer's initial value to be zero; generalization to non-zero values yields no new insight and is cumbersome

With labour forces constant the two production functions are transformed to:

$$\hat{v} = q_m\hat{m} + (1 - q_m)(1 - q_\ell)\hat{k}. \tag{7.8}$$

$$\hat{\bar{v}} = \bar{q}_{\bar{m}}\hat{\bar{m}} + (1 - \bar{q}_{\bar{m}})(1 - \bar{q}_{\bar{\ell}})\hat{\bar{k}}. \tag{7.9}$$

Hats indicate relative total differentials, e.g. $\hat{v} = \frac{dv}{v}$; q_m is defined in (3.8) and equals, with optimal allocation of inputs, imports' value share in total inputs; similarly q_ℓ, defined in (3.9), is labour's value share in the total input of the two regional factors capital and labour.

For the import-demand equations we obtain analogously to (4.28):

$$\frac{1}{e}\hat{m} - \frac{1 - q_\ell}{e}\hat{k} = - \hat{P}. \tag{7.10}$$

$$\frac{1}{\bar{e}}\hat{\bar{m}} - \frac{1 - \bar{q}_{\bar{\ell}}}{\bar{e}}\hat{\bar{k}} = \hat{P}. \tag{7.11}$$

Here e is the terms of trade elasticity of import demand (cf. 3.12).

The balance of trade equation is transformed to (using n = 0):

$$\hat{\bar{m}} = \hat{m} - \hat{P} + \frac{dn}{\bar{m}} . \tag{7.12}$$

From (7.10)-(7.12) the change in the terms of trade due to changes in the transfer and the capital stocks is found to be:

$$\hat{P} = \frac{1}{1+e+\bar{e}} \{\frac{dn}{\bar{m}} - (1 - \bar{q}_{\bar{\ell}})\hat{\bar{k}} + (1 - q_\ell)\hat{k}\}. \tag{7.13}$$

Thus the direct effect of a transfer on the terms of trade is negative (under the standard assumption $1 + e + \bar{e} < 0$), the orthodox result of a secondary burden. In the present case the multiplier is $1/(1+e+\bar{e})$. This differs from Samuelson's result which can be written as:

$$\hat{P} = \frac{1-x-\bar{x}}{1+e+\bar{e}} \frac{dn}{\bar{m}} , \tag{7.14}$$

where x is the marginal propensity to consume importables. In (7.13) these propensities do not occur because we have not incorporated income effects in the import-demand equations; these could be introduced by e.g. describing joint production of two goods instead of just a single one.

The change in incomes is:

$$\frac{dy}{v} = (1-q_\ell)(1-q_m)\hat{k} + \frac{q_m}{1+e+\bar{e}}\left[-(e+\bar{e})\frac{dn}{\bar{m}} + (1-q_\ell)\hat{k} - (1-\bar{q}_{\bar{\ell}})\hat{\bar{k}}\right]. \quad (7.15)$$

$$\frac{d\bar{y}}{\bar{v}} = (1-\bar{q}_{\bar{\ell}})(1-\bar{q}_{\bar{m}})\hat{\bar{k}} + \frac{\bar{q}_{\bar{m}}}{1+e+\bar{e}}\left[(e+\bar{e})\frac{dn}{\bar{m}} + (1-\bar{q}_{\bar{\ell}})\hat{\bar{k}} - (1-q_\ell)\hat{k}\right]. \quad (7.16)$$

The direct effect of a transfer on the north's income is negative, that of the south's income positive.

To obtain the tertiary effects of a transfer, the change in the two regions' capital stocks must be specified. We assume that a fraction $\bar{\sigma}$ of the direct income gain of the south is saved and invested:

$$d\bar{k} = \bar{\sigma}\,\frac{\bar{q}_{\bar{m}}(e+\bar{e})}{1+e+\bar{e}}\,\frac{dn}{\bar{m}}\,\bar{v}. \quad (7.17)$$

Similarly, a fraction σ of the north's direct income loss would have been invested without transfer:

$$dk = -\sigma\,\frac{q_m(e+\bar{e})}{1+e+\bar{e}}\,\frac{dn}{\bar{m}}\,v. \quad (7.18)$$

The tertiary effects of the transfer are now easily obtained by substituting (7.17) and (7.18) into the terms of trade equation (7.13) and the two income equations (7.15) and (7.16).

<u>The tertiary effects of a north-south transfer</u>

For the total effect (direct primary <u>cum</u> secondary and the tertiary one) of the transfer on the <u>terms of trade</u> we find:

$$\hat{p} = \frac{1}{1+e+\bar{e}} - \frac{e+\bar{e}}{(1+e+\bar{e})^2}\left\{\bar{\sigma}\bar{q}_{\bar{m}}(1-\bar{q}_{\bar{\ell}})\frac{\bar{v}}{\bar{k}} + \sigma q_m(1-q_\ell)\frac{v}{k}\right\}. \quad (7.19)$$

The second term on the right-hand side represents the tertiary effect of a transfer on the terms of trade. In contradistinction to the direct effect - the first term - it is positive. Thus the tertiary effect is anti-orthodox and compensates at least partially for the initial movement of the terms of trade against the north. This is caused both by the transfer-induced increase in the south's capital stock and by the decrease of accumulation in the north: both increase the abundance of the south's goods relative to those of the north.

Equation (7.19) clearly shows what determines the extent of the tertiary movement. It is an increasing function of the two hemispheres' rates of saving out of transfer-generated income - the latter negative in case of the north. If the south uses the transfer primarily to finance development projects and if its saving out of ordinary income is not depressed too much by the transfer,[(4)] the tertiary effect is higher than if the transfer is given in the form of e.g. food aid. The north's rate of saving from the transfer-generated income loss depends on whether the transfer is financed largely out of consumption or out of saving. If the latter is the case the loss of income due to a decrease of capital accumulation is higher but this is compensated by an improvement of the terms of trade.

The tertiary effect is also an increasing function of the two regions' capital shares in domestic factors: the higher these are the more sizeable the capital accumulation's impact on output and thence on the terms of trade. Similarly the tertiary effect is an increasing function of the import shares: the higher these are the stronger the impulse of rising outputs on trade flows and terms of trade is. Finally the tertiary effect is an increasing function of the two output-capital ratios.

A central question is whether the south's poverty makes it more, or less, likely that the tertiary blessing for the north's terms of trade is sizeable. The obvious yardstick of 'poverty' is the size of the south's capital stock, its population being given. Appendix 7.1 derives the relation between the terms describing the tertiary effect in (7.19) and both regions' capital stocks. We assume the north's imports from the south to be almost complementary to its own factors: an elasticity of substitution between imports and regional factors, E, between zero and minus unity. Since most of the north's imports are raw materials, and we do not deal in the present case with really long-run effects, this assumption is justified. On the other hand, the south's elasticity of substitution between imports and regional factors, E, is likely to be smaller than minus unity since the south's imports from the north consist mainly of manufactures. In addition we assume that changes in the elasticities of substitution as the ratios of imports to domestic factors, of which they are functions, change, are small compared to those in the import shares. Since the latter are derivatives of the second order, but the former of the third order, this assumption is fairly innocuous. Finally, we take the value shares of labour in regional factors to exceed one half and assume that the absolute value of the elasticity of substitution between capital and labour is not excessively large: it may exceed unity but not too much.

Under these assumptions the term between braces in (7.19) is a strictly decreasing function of the south's capital stock. Thus the poorer the south the larger this term. This does not immediately imply that the extent to which the tertiary effects compensate the negative direct transfer effects is also greater if the south's capital stock is small; the relevant part of the multiplier of the tertiary effect, $(e+\bar{e})/(1+e+\bar{e})$, is an increasing function of $\bar{k}$ and is therefore smaller at low $\bar{k}$ values. However, this term consists of second-order derivatives of v and $\bar{v}$ and is therefore less sensitive to changes in k than v itself and than the other terms between braces. Besides, $(e+\bar{e})/(1+e+\bar{e})$ is bounded below by unity. Accordingly the compensation of the initial adverse movement of the terms of trade by the tertiary effect is the larger the smaller the south's capital stock. If the latter is small enough the tertiary effect surpasses the initial one and the orthodox result of a decline in the north's terms of trade is reversed to an increase.

Both the multiplier $(e+\bar{e})/(1+e+\bar{e})$ and the term between braces are decreasing functions of the north's capital stock k. The reason for this is intuitively clear: the larger the north's capital stock, *ceteris paribus*, the smaller the impact of the initial accumulation loss on output - and hence on the terms of trade - given decreasing returns to capital; similarly the effect of increased imports from the south is the smaller the larger the north's capital stock, given constancy of the labour force and decreasing returns to imports and capital.

The total effect of the transfer on the north's income is:

$$\frac{dy}{v} = \frac{dn}{\bar{m}} \cdot \frac{q_m(e+\bar{e})}{1+e+\bar{e}} \left[-1 + \left\{-\sigma(1-q_\ell)\frac{v}{k}\left(1 - q_m + \frac{q_m}{1+e+\bar{e}}\right) + \right.\right.$$

$$\left.\left. - \bar{\sigma}(1-\bar{q}_{\bar{\ell}})\frac{\bar{v}}{\bar{k}}\frac{\bar{q}_{\bar{m}}}{1+e+\bar{e}}\right\}\right]. \qquad (7.20)$$

The multiplier in (7.20) is positive; therefore the impact of the transfer on income has the same sign as the term between square brackets; to determine whether the tertiary effect compensates partially or fully for the primary and secondary burden it suffices to analyse this bracketed term. The minus unity between square brackets represents the direct transfer effect (primary and secondary) which is of course negative. The term between braces represents the tertiary effect. Of this tertiary effect the first part is the negative [(5)] impact of decreased accumulation in the north, the second one the positive impact of accumulation in the south. If the latter surpasses the absolute value of the former there is a tertiary blessing; if not there is a tertiary burden.

The impact of decreased accumulation in the north has, as we saw above, a positive influence on the north's terms of trade; but (7.20) shows that this is insufficient to prevent this decrease in accumulation from having a negative impact on the north's income. As a consequence the rate of saving from the income lost by the initial transfer effects negatively affects the tertiary effect on income: the smaller the fraction of the transfer that is financed from saving the less the tertiary income loss. The same applies to the north's share of capital in regional factors capital and labour, and to its output-capital ratio.

In contrast, a high rate of saving from the transfer-generated income in the south is favourable to the north's income and the same applies to the south's capital share, its import share and its output-capital ratio.

In (7.20) the term between square brackets is negatively related to the south's capital stock, as shown in appendix 7.1. Then, the smaller the south's capital stock, the more likely a tertiary blessing for the north. This implies that the same poverty of the south that is the reason for north-south aid in the first place, also lessens the real-income cost of the aid for the north.

If the south's capital stock is small there is a tertiary blessing for the north provided the import shares and elasticities are non-vanishing.[(6)] If the south's capital stock is small enough this tertiary blessing even exceeds the primary cum secondary burden and the north's income is actually raised by aid to the south.

Of course, without empirical knowledge on the production functions and capital stocks of north and south, it is not possible to determine whether this income raising effect is practically relevant. This analysis is fairly difficult, because it requires measurement of both regions' capital stocks; in addition, either the latter must include human capital, or labour inputs must be corrected for the north-south difference in quality. Besides, our model does not incorporate the spin-offs from pure capital accumulation in the south. These take the form of accelerated technical progress and improved training of labour. For a given amount of capital accumulation, these spin-offs are much higher in the south than in the north because the south can draw on a vast existing pool of technologies and training programs it does not yet utilize whereas the north can only advance further in technology and training by the laborious creation of new technology and by slow advances in education and skills. To obtain a reliable empirical picture all these effects should be explicitly recognized. This is beyond the scope of our analysis. Therefore we remain content with noting the possibility that aid to the south raises the north's income and with the observation that the costs of aid are, anyway, lower than traditional analysis infers.

The term between square brackets in (7.20) is an increasing function of the north's capital stock. Thus it is the relative rather than the absolute size of the region's capital stocks that determines the existence of a tertiary blessing for the north. This reinforces our conclusion that the poverty of the south lessens north-south aid's real-income costs to the north.

The total effect of a north-south transfer on the south's income is given by:

$$\frac{d\bar{y}}{\bar{v}} = \frac{dn}{\bar{m}} \cdot \frac{\bar{q}_{\bar{m}}(e+\bar{e})}{1+e+\bar{e}} \Big[1 + \Big\{\bar{\sigma}(1 - \bar{q}_{\bar{\ell}}) \frac{\bar{v}}{\bar{k}} \Big(1 - \bar{q}_{\bar{m}} + \frac{\bar{q}_{\bar{m}}}{1+e+\bar{e}}\Big) + \sigma(1 - q_{\ell}) \frac{v}{k} \frac{q_m}{1+e+\bar{e}} \Big\}\Big]. \tag{7.21}$$

Again the multiplier is positive and the impact of the tertiary effect hinges on the bracketed terms. Here too a high rate of saving from transfer-generated income in the south raises income and once again the same applies to the south's capital share and its output-capital ratio. Again a high rate of saving, a high capital share and a high output-capital ratio in the north lower income. Thus all these parameters and variables affect income in north and south in the same direction.

As in case of the north the south's tertiary effect is negatively related to the south's capital stock and positively to that of the north. Thus the poverty of the south not only diminishes aid's cost to the north but also improves its positive effect on the south's income.

The central conclusion of this section is that neglection of the capital-accumulation impact of north-south aid leads to overestimation of the costs of this aid for the north and underestimation of its impact on the south. To give aid, especially to the very poor countries, is more compatible with the north's own interests than traditional analysis of transfer payments indicates.

7.3. The trajectory of north-south aid maximizing the north's consumption

The conclusion of the preceding section is a strong argument in favour of aid next to the traditional ethical arguments. Presently the ethical reasons to aid the south appear to carry less weight in some major rich countries than before; therefore it is worthwhile to investigate the possibility of aid that yields a bonus for the paying region more thoroughly. Accordingly the present section is addressed directly to the question what the optimal aid is from the viewpoint of the donor region's consumption. To do this we carry the analysis of the preceding section one step further. In that section we took only the 'immediate' impact of aid on capital accumulation into account and ignored the feedbacks that take more time and the effect of a sustained flow of aid. Capturing the latter requires an explicitly dynamic treatment. Therefore we now consider the choice between investment in the north and aid to the south in order to maximize the north's consumption over some planning horizon.

Unfortunately, the analysis turns out to be rather involved. Therefore we reduce the problem to its bare bones and simplify the description of both regions' production processes considerably. Thus we assign both regions symmetrical, linear homogeneous, Cobb-Douglas production functions and we ignore both technical progress and labour. The first subsection gives the model and presents the resulting optimal-control theorem and its implications; the second subsection provides the proof for this theorem.

An optimal aid and investment theorem

With the simplifying assumptions listed above, the two regions differ only in the size of their capital stocks. The two production functions are:

$$v = m^{\xi_m} k^{1-\xi_m}. \tag{7.22}$$

$$\bar{v} = \bar{m}^{\xi_m} \bar{k}^{1-\xi_m}. \tag{7.23}$$

Here units have been chosen such as to have unit-valued multiplicative constants. Inserting the balance of trade equation (7.5) into the import-demand equations (7.3) and (7.4), we obtain for both regions' equilibrium trade flows:

$$\bar{m} - n = \xi_m v. \tag{7.24}$$

$$\frac{m}{\bar{m}-n} = \xi_m \frac{\bar{v}}{\bar{m}}. \tag{7.25}$$

The north's consumption is:

$$c = v - \bar{m} - s, \tag{7.26}$$

where s is the north's savings, equal to its investment; thus s is define such that it excludes aid. Accumulation in both regions is given by:

$$\dot{k} = s. \tag{7.27}$$

$$\dot{\bar{k}} = \bar{\sigma}(\bar{v} - m). \tag{7.28}$$

Thus the south's accumulation is strictly proportional to its income.

Equations (7.22)-(7.28) determine the time path of the system as a function of the north's saving, s(t), and north-south aid, n(t). The latter are used to maximize the north's consumption. We assume that s and n may not exceed certain boundaries: it is unreasonable to allow investment to fall to zero in a finite planning period - because the economy has to live on after the planning period; similarly it is not realistic to allow investment and aid to absorp all income - a minimum consumption should be allowed for at each moment. Therefore we restrict investment to be at least a fraction σ_1, and at most a fraction σ_2, of the north's income; aid may not exceed a fraction α_0 of the north's income. Adding non-negativity constraints this yields:

$$0 \leq n \leq \alpha_0(v - \bar{m}'). \tag{7.29}$$

$$\sigma_1(v - \bar{m}) \leq s \leq \sigma_2(v - \bar{m}). \tag{7.30}$$

Here $\bar{m}'$ represents regular exports, that is total exports less the aid part ($\bar{m}' = \bar{m} - n$). The objective is to maximize total consumption in a planning period $[t_0, T]$. For simplicity we do not discount; the consequence of discounting is discussed below. The optimal-control problem now is:

$$\text{Maximize} \int_{t_0}^{T} c[k(t), \bar{k}(t), s(t), n(t)]dt, \tag{7.31}$$

subject to (7.27) - (7.30).

Theorem 7.1: If a solution to the above problem exists, it satisfies the following properties:

1. In the final part of the trajectory aid is zero ($n=0$) and saving minimal ($s = \sigma_1\{v - \bar{m}\}$).
2. If the horizon is long enough, saving is maximal in the initial part of the trajectory.
3. If the horizon is long enough and at the initial point the condition holds that

$$\frac{\bar{k}}{k} < \left(\frac{\bar{\sigma}}{\sigma_2}\right)^{\frac{\xi_m+1}{2\xi_m}}, \tag{7.32}$$

then aid is positive ($n>0$) in the initial part of the trajectory.

If no solution to the above problem exists, there is at least one path with non-zero aid at some point(s) of the planning period that yields a higher value of the objective function than all trajectories where aid is zero throughout.

The theorem breaks down in two parts. The first one deals with the case that an optimal path exists, the second one with the case where this is not true. This distinction is necessary because it has not been possible to establish the existence of an optimal path: all the standard existence theorems require some concavity conditions which are not satisfied in the present case. Thus a 'chattering control' where the control variables oscillate infinitely rapidly cannot be precluded.

The first part of the theorem deals with the regular case where an optimal path exists. Here the third statement is the core result: for a planning period that is long enough, it is optimal to aid the south if (7.32) is satisfied initially. This result confirms our findings of the preceding section. For (7.32) shows aid to the south to be optimal to the north's consumption if the south's capital stock is small relative to that of the north. Thus, once again, we find that north-south aid need not be based on altruism alone: precisely because the south is relatively poor, aid yields potential benefits for the north in addition to improving the south's lot.

In section 7.2 we found that a high rate of saving in the south - from transfer-generated income - is beneficial to the north. This result is confirmed here too: if the south's rate of saving is high, (7.32) is satisfied sooner than if it is low. Similarly, our result of section 7.2 with respect to the north's rate of saving is confirmed: the lower the maximum rate σ_2 is, the sooner (7.32) is satisfied. An interesting special case is the one where the south's rate of saving and the north's maximum rate are equal: in this case aid is optimal as soon as the south's capital stock is smaller than the north's.

If the south's rate of saving is smaller than the north's maximal one, the south's capital stock must be considerably smaller than the north's for aid to be optimal. This is because the exponent of the right-hand side of (7.32) exceeds unity. This exponent is inversely related to the import share, ξ_m. Thus if trade is intensive, and $\bar{\sigma} < \sigma_2$, aid is optimal at higher initial values of the capital stock of the south than if trade is minor. This result implies that, because of the still minor share of north-south trade in both region's output, the south's capital stock must be fairly small. But, in view of the poverty of the south, the ratio of the two capital stocks <u>is</u> quite low, implying that (7.32) may well be satisfied in spite of the low value of ξ_m.

The case where no optimal path exists is covered by the second part of theorem 7.1. This statement leaves the major qualitative result intact: some aid is better than no aid throughout as long as (7.32) holds.

Our simplifying assumptions yield a clearcut result that corresponds quite well with the one obtained in the preceding section. How serious are our simplifications and how would more realistic assumptions affect the result? The first point requiring attention is the objective function. We choose, for analytical convenience, to maximize total consumption. Instead, we could have maximized a function, u, of consumption satisfying the usual assumptions $u > 0$, $u' > 0$, $u'' < 0$, $u'(0) = \infty$, $u'(\infty) = 0$. However, by introducing boundaries on the controls we achieved much the same effect and there is no reason to assume that introducing a function u (c) would have altered our result qualitatively. A more serious omission is not to discount. Introduction of a positive rate of discount would alter the impact of aid and saving in the initial period on the objective function. This will result in a stronger condition for positive aid to be optimal than (7.32). But the essential point - if the south is poor it is optimal to give aid - should not be altered. Second, we considerably simplified the production functions, assuming them to be strictly symmetrical Cobb-Douglas functions and omitting labour. The latter is the more serious omission: with labour added the role of both capital and trade diminishes and once again a stronger condition than (7.32) should be the result. However, this effect is offset to some extent because labour grows faster in the south than in the north: this results in a higher marginal efficiency of aid-generated capital accumulation in the south, and this in turn is favourable to the north as it is transmitted by trade. The assumption of strictly symmetrical Cobb-Douglas functions should not be too serious: in the preceding section we obtained qualitatively comparable results for functions with elasticities of substitution differing from unity and not symmetrical for north and south.

Thus it seems reasonable to assume that though more realistic assumptions might result in more restrictive conditions, the qualitative result remains unaffected: because the south is relatively poor in capital north-south aid may well be optimal from the viewpoint of the north's long-run consumption.

Proof of the optimal-path theorem

The formulation (7.22) - (7.28) of the model has the disadvantage that the control variables n and s are additive to total exports and consumption in a model where most relations are multiplicative. Therefor we reformulate the model in terms of the rate of savings S and the ratio of total exports to exports without the transfer, A. Thus:

$$S = \frac{s}{v-\bar{m}} \; ; \; A = \frac{\bar{m}}{\bar{m}-n} \; . \tag{7.33}$$

Then equations (7.22) - (7.28) are transformed to:

$$\bar{m} = A\left(\frac{1+\varepsilon}{\varepsilon}\right)v, \tag{7.34}$$

$$m = \frac{1+\varepsilon}{A\ \varepsilon}\,\bar{v} \; , \tag{7.35}$$

$$c = (1-S)\left\{\frac{\varepsilon - A(1+\varepsilon)}{\varepsilon}\right\}v \; , \tag{7.36}$$

$$\dot{k} = S\left\{\frac{\varepsilon - A(1+\varepsilon)}{\varepsilon}\right\}v \; , \tag{7.37}$$

$$\dot{\bar{k}} = \bar{\sigma}\left\{\frac{A\varepsilon - (1+\varepsilon)}{A\varepsilon}\right\}\bar{v} \; , \tag{7.38}$$

where $\varepsilon = -\frac{1}{1-\xi_m} < -1$. Restrictions (7.30) and (7.31) are transformed to

$$\sigma_1 \leq S \leq \sigma_2 \; , \tag{7.39}$$

$$1 \leq A \leq \alpha < \frac{\varepsilon}{1+\varepsilon} \; , \tag{7.40}$$

where:

$$\alpha = \frac{1+\varepsilon-\alpha_0}{1+\varepsilon} \; . \tag{7.41}$$

These restrictions imply:

$$\begin{aligned} &-1 < \varepsilon - A(1+\varepsilon) < \varepsilon - \alpha(1+\varepsilon) < 0; \\ &-\frac{\omega}{1+\varepsilon} < A\varepsilon - (1+\varepsilon) < -1 \; . \end{aligned} \tag{7.42}$$

Clearly, as long as (7.42) is satisfied both $\dot{k}$ and $\dot{\bar{k}}$ are strictly positive.

The model is now easy to solve:

$$v = \gamma' \{k^{\varepsilon} \bar{k}^{1+\varepsilon} A^{-(1+\varepsilon)}\}^{1/\omega} , \tag{7.43}$$

$$\bar{v} = \gamma' \{\bar{k}^{\varepsilon} k^{1+\varepsilon} A^{1+\varepsilon}\}^{1/\omega} ,$$

where $\gamma' = \gamma^{-\varepsilon}(\frac{1+\varepsilon}{\varepsilon})^{-(1+\varepsilon)}$ and $\omega = 1 + 2\varepsilon < -1$. The solutions for m, $\bar{m}$ and c easily follow. The problem is now to maximize:

$$\int_{t_0}^{T} c(k,\bar{k},S,A)dt, \tag{7.44}$$

subject to (7.37) - (7.40).

It is easily seen that c is not concave in k, $\bar{k}$, S and A. Hence existence of an optimal path is difficult to prove. Therefore we limit the analysis to the properties of an optimal path given the assumption that it exists and to showing that, if no optimal path exists, to give no aid is always bad.

To obtain the necessary maximum conditions, we use Pontryagin's (1961) maximum principle and apply Takayama's (1974, p.648) convenient theorem 8 C.1. Note that the constraint qualification is satisfied. The Hamiltonian H is defined as:

$$H = c + Sp_k \frac{\{\varepsilon - A(1+\varepsilon)\}}{\varepsilon} v + \bar{\sigma}\bar{p}_{\bar{k}} \frac{\{A\varepsilon - 1 - \varepsilon\}}{A\varepsilon} \bar{v} . \tag{7.45}$$

Here p_k and $\bar{p}_k$ are the continuous auxiliary variables. The generalized Hamiltonian is:

$$L = H + r_1(S - \sigma_1) + r_2(\sigma_2 - S) + r_3(A - 1) + r_4(\alpha - A) . \tag{7.46}$$

Necessary conditions for S*(t) and A*(t) to be piecewise continuous optimal controls are:

$$\dot{p}_k = - L_k \; ; \; \dot{\bar{p}}_{\bar{k}} = - L_{\bar{k}} . \tag{7.47}$$

$$H(k^*, \bar{k}^*, S^*, A^*, p_k, \bar{p}_{\bar{k}}) \geq H(k^*, \bar{k}^*, S, A, p_k, \bar{p}_{\bar{k}}) . \qquad (7.48)$$

$$L_S = 0, \; L_A = 0. \; (A = A^*, \; S = S^*) \qquad (7.49)$$

$$r_1(S^*-\sigma_1) = r_2(\sigma_2-S^*) = r_3(A^*-1) = r_4(\alpha-A^*) \doteq 0; \quad r_1, r_2, r_3, r_4 \geq 0. \qquad (7.50)$$

$$\dot{r}_1(S^*-\sigma_1) = \dot{r}_2(\sigma_2-S^*) = \dot{r}_3(A^*-1) = \dot{r}_4(\alpha-A^*) = 0. \qquad (7.51)$$

$$p_k(T) = \bar{p}_{\bar{k}}(T) = 0. \qquad (7.52)$$

Here r_1, r_2, r_3, r_4 are piecewise continuous and continuous at every poi[nt] where S^* and A^* are continuous. Asterisks denote optimal-path values; below we drop these and S and A throughout denote the optimal-path value[s] of the controls. Here we refer to the Pontryagin path as the 'optimal path', though it should be borne in mind that this is only correct if an optimal path does indeed exist. In (7.47) L_S is L's derivative to S; L_A the derivative to A. From (7.47) and (7.49) we obtain:

$$\dot{p}_k = -\frac{v}{k}\frac{\{\varepsilon-A(1+\varepsilon)\}}{\omega}\{1+S(p_k-1)\} - \overline{\sigma v p}_{\bar{k}}\{\frac{1+\varepsilon}{\varepsilon\;\omega}\}\frac{\{A\varepsilon-1-\varepsilon\}}{Ak} . \qquad (7.53)$$

$$\dot{\bar{p}}_{\bar{k}} = -(1+\varepsilon)\frac{v}{\bar{k}}\frac{\{\varepsilon-A(1+\varepsilon)\}}{\varepsilon\omega}\{1 + S(p_k-1)\} - \overline{\sigma v p}_{\bar{k}}\frac{\{A\varepsilon-1-\varepsilon\}}{\omega\;\bar{k}\;A} . \qquad (7.54)$$

$$\frac{(p_k-1)v\{\varepsilon-A(1+\varepsilon)\}}{\varepsilon} = r_2 - r_1 . \qquad (7.55)$$

$$\frac{(A+1)(\varepsilon+1)}{A\omega}\left[-v\{1 + S(p_k-1)\} + \frac{\overline{\sigma v p}_{\bar{k}}}{A}\right] = r_4 - r_3. \qquad (7.56)$$

We now obtain:

<u>Lemma 7.1</u>: For each $t_0 \leq t < T$ the auxiliary variables p_k and $\bar{p}_{\bar{k}}$ are strictly positive and $\dot{p}_k$, $\dot{\bar{p}}_{\bar{k}} < -\Delta$, where Δ is a positive constant, its value independent of the length of the planning period.

<u>Proof</u>: Because ε, ω, $1+\varepsilon$, $\varepsilon - A(1+\varepsilon)$ and $A\varepsilon-1-\varepsilon$ are all negative, (7.53) and (7.54) imply negativity of $\dot{p}_k$ and $\dot{\bar{p}}_{\bar{k}}$ as long as $1+S(p_k-1) > 0$ and

$p_K > 0$. The transversality condition (7.52) implies that the latter conditions are satisfied at T; thus $1 + S(p_k(T) - 1) = 1-S > 1-\sigma_2 > 0$. Hence $\dot{p}_k$ and $\dot{\bar{p}}_{\bar{k}}$ are negative at T. Since $p_k(T) = \bar{p}_{\bar{k}}(T) = 0$, this implies

positivity of $\bar{p}_{\bar{k}}$ and p_k - hence of $1 + S(p_k-1)$ - immediately prior to T.

Thus in some interval ending at T, $\dot{p}_k$ and $\dot{\bar{p}}_{\bar{k}}$ are negative too. The same reasoning implies positivity of $\bar{p}_{\bar{k}}$ and p_k and negativity of $\dot{\bar{p}}_{\bar{k}}$ and $\dot{p}_k$ throughout the planning period.

To show that the time derivatives of p_k and $\bar{p}_{\bar{k}}$ are not only negative, but smaller than a negative constant, independent of the length of (t_0, T), consider the maximum value of $\dot{p}_k$. Since $p_k, \bar{p}_{\bar{k}} > 0$ throughout, this value is attained at T, with $p_k = \bar{p}_{\bar{k}} = 0$. Then the maximum of $\dot{p}_k$ in A and S is given by:

$$\dot{p}_k = -\frac{v}{k}\frac{\{\varepsilon - \alpha(1+\varepsilon)\}}{\omega}(1-\sigma_1). \tag{7.57}$$

In the right-hand side of (7.57) all terms are constants, independent of (t_0, T), except v/k. The latter can be written as:

$$\frac{v}{k} = \gamma'\alpha^{-\frac{1+\varepsilon}{\omega}}\left(\frac{k}{\bar{k}}\right)^{-\frac{1+\varepsilon}{\omega}}. \tag{7.58}$$

Clearly, to show that $\dot{p}_k$ (and similarly $\bar{p}_{\bar{k}}$) is bounded above by a strictly negative constant, it suffices to show that $\bar{k}/k$ is bounded below by a value that is independent of (t_0, T). To this end, consider the rate of change of $\bar{k}/k$:

$$\frac{\dot{\bar{k}}}{\bar{k}} - \frac{\dot{k}}{k} = -\frac{\gamma'}{\varepsilon}S\{\varepsilon - A(1+\varepsilon)\}A^{-\frac{\omega+1}{\omega}}\left(\frac{k}{\bar{k}}\right)^{\frac{\varepsilon+1}{\omega}}\left\{\left(\frac{\bar{k}}{k}\right)^{-\frac{\omega+1}{\omega}} - \frac{\bar{\sigma}}{\sigma_2}\frac{\{A\varepsilon-1-\varepsilon\}}{\{\varepsilon-A(1+\varepsilon)\}}A^{\frac{1}{\omega}}\right\}. \tag{7.59}$$

Hence:

$$\frac{\dot{\bar{k}}}{\bar{k}} \gtrless \frac{\dot{k}}{k} \text{ according to } \frac{\bar{k}}{k} \lessgtr \left(\frac{\bar{\sigma}}{S}\right)^{\frac{\omega}{\omega+1}}\left\{\frac{A\varepsilon-1-\varepsilon}{\varepsilon-A(1+\varepsilon)}A^{\frac{1}{\omega}}\right\}^{\frac{\omega}{1+\omega}}. \tag{7.60}$$

Clearly, $\bar{k}/k$ increases whenever its value is below the minimum in A and S of the extreme right-hand side of (7.60). Since both A and S are bounded by non-zero, finite constants, this minimum is finite (noting that $A\varepsilon-1-\varepsilon$ and $\varepsilon-A(1+\varepsilon)$ are non-zero and finite too). Thus $\bar{k}/k$ is bounded from below by the minimum of $\bar{k}/k$ ($t = t_0$) and the minimum of the extreme right-hand side of (7.60).

Q.E.D.

We now determine the optimal values of the controls S and A as functic of the auxiliary variables.

Lemma 7.2: The values of S and A that satisfy (7.55) and (7.56) and maximize the Hamiltonian are:

$$S = \begin{array}{ll} \sigma_1 & (p_k < 1). \\ \sigma_2 & (p_k > 1). \end{array} \tag{7.61}$$

$$A = \begin{array}{ll} 1 & (X < 1), \\ X & (1 < X < \alpha), \\ \alpha & (X > \alpha), \end{array} \tag{7.62}$$

where

$$X = \frac{\bar{k}}{k} \left\{\frac{\bar{\sigma}\, \bar{p}_{\bar{k}}}{1 + S(p_k - 1)}\right\}^{-\omega}, \tag{7.63}$$

with S in (7.63) determined by (7.61).

Proof: The Hamiltonian is linear in S and the sign of the derivative of to S, H_S, displayed in the left-hand side of (7.55), is independent of the value of A: since $\varepsilon - A(1+\varepsilon)$ and ε are negative for all A, H_S is positive if $p_k > 1$ and negative if $p_k < 1$. Since $\sigma_1 < S < \sigma_2$, the value of S maximizing the Hamiltonian are those given by (7.61). Clearly thes also satisfy (7.55), since $r_2 - r_1 < 0$ if $S = \sigma_1$ and $r_2 - r_1 > 0$ if $S = \sigma_2$.

Because $r_4 - r_3$ is positive if $A = \alpha$, negative if $A = 1$ and zero if A is intermediate valued, the term between square brackets in (7.56) shou be positive, negative and zero, respectively. This corresponds to $X > \alpha$, $X < 1$ and $X = A$, respectively. It remains to show that (7.62) also maximizes the Hamiltonian. The latter's derivative to A, H_A, is shown i the left-hand side of (7.56). Its derivative to A, H_{AA}, evaluated at a point where $H_A = 0$, is:

$$H_{AA}\ (H_A = 0) = \frac{(1+\varepsilon)(1+A)\overline{\sigma v p}_{\bar{k}}}{A^3\omega^2} . \tag{7.64}$$

This expression is negative because $\bar{p}_{\bar{k}} > 0$ (lemma 7.1), implying $A = X$ $(1 < X < \alpha)$ is indeed the maximum of the Hamiltonian; the maximum is unique because H_{AA} is negative whenever $H_A = 0$, implying that there can be only one value of A with $H_A = 0$. From the negativity of H_{AA} at $H_A = 0$ it is readily inferred that $A = 1$ $(X < 1)$ and $A = \alpha$ $(X > \alpha)$ also maximize H.

Q.E.D.

Lemma 7.3: In an interval ending at T, the optimal controls are $S = \sigma$, $A = 1$. This interval is, provided the planning period is long enough, preceded by one with $S = \sigma_2$; the latter interval extends backward to the initial point of the planning period.

Proof: At T, we have $p_k = \bar{p}_{\bar{k}} = 0$ and, by lemma 7.2, this implies $A(T) = 1$, $S(T) = \sigma_1$; since the auxiliary variables are continuous, the same must be true for some time prior to T. To obtain the second part of the lemma note that $p_k(T) = 0$ implies:

$$p_k(t_1) = - \int_{t_1}^{T} \dot{p}_k dt. \tag{7.65}$$

Lemma 7.1 states $-\dot{p}_k > \Delta > 0$ for each t in (t_0, T). Since $p_k(T) = 0$ this implies that there is a t_1 $(t_0 < t_1 < T)$ such that $p_k(t_1) = 1$ and $p_k(T) > 1$ for $t < t_1$, provided (t_0, T) is long enough. Applying (7.61) the lemma's proof is complete.

Lemma 7.4: Throughout the interval where $s = \sigma_2$, the inequality

$$\frac{\bar{k}}{k} < \left(\frac{\bar{\sigma}}{\sigma_2}\right)^{\frac{\omega}{\omega+1}} \tag{7.66}$$

holds true.

Proof: (7.66) is equivalent to (7.32). Thus at $t = t_0$ the inequality holds. Now again consider (7.60), noting that $s = \sigma_2$. The term between braces in the extreme right-hand side of (7.60) has a positive exponent and is smaller than unity if $A > 1$ and equal to unity if $A = 1$. Thus th extreme right-hand side of (7.60) is smaller than or equal to the right hand side of (7.66). Since $\bar{k}/k$ is smaller than the latter at $t = t_0$, there are two possibilities at t_0. Firstly, $\bar{k}/k$ may be smaller than the extreme right-hand side of (7.60). In that case, by (7.60), $\bar{k}/k$ increases, but never quite up to the value of (7.60)'s extreme right-hand side since at that value its rate of change is zero and the time interval is finite. This result implies that $\bar{k}/k$ must rema smaller than the right-hand side of (7.66), since the latter is the maximum in A of the extreme right-hand side of (7.60). Second, at t_0 th value of $\bar{k}/k$ may ly between the right-hand sides of (7.60) and of (7.66 In that case $\bar{k}/k$ declines and thus moves away from the right-hand side (7.66); this case occurs only if $A > 1$ at t_0. Clearly, in both cases $\bar{k}/k$ can never equal, let alone surpass, the right-hand side of (7.66) in a finite interval where $S=\sigma_2$.

Q.E.D.

Lemma 7.5: If the planning period is long enough, the optimal value of A in its initial interval exceeds unity.

Proof: From lemma 7.3 we know $S = \sigma_2$ in the first part of the planning period, say (t_0, t_1). It is easily seen from the proof of lemma 7.3 tha (t_0, t_1) can be made arbitrarily long by selecting (t_0, T) long enough. Lemma 7.4 implies that (7.66) is satisfied throughout (t_0, t_1). Using this property, we first show that in (t_0, t_1) an interval where $A > 1$ cannot be preceded by one with $A = 1$. Next we demonstrate that there is at least one point t_2 $(t_0 < t_2 < t_1)$ where A indeed exceeds unity, so that the same must be true for each $t_0 < t < t_2$.

The value of A depends on that of X, as indicated by (7.62). Therefor the movement of X must be traced out. It suffices to do this for intervals where $A = 1$ only. There the rate of change of X is:

$$\frac{\dot{X}}{X} = -\gamma'\left(\frac{1+\varepsilon}{\varepsilon}\right)\left(\frac{\bar{k}}{k}\right)^{-\frac{1+\varepsilon}{\omega}} \sigma_2\left[\frac{\bar{\sigma}}{\sigma_2}\left(X^{\frac{1}{\omega}} - X^{-\frac{1}{\omega}}\right) + \left(1 + X^{-\frac{1}{\omega}}\right)\left\{\frac{\bar{\sigma}}{\sigma_2} - \left(\frac{\bar{k}}{k}\right)^{\frac{\omega+1}{\omega}}\right\}\right] \quad (7.67)$$

It is easily seen from (7.67) that $\omega < 0$ and (7.66) imply $\dot{X} < 0$ as soon as $X < 1$. Since A can only equal unity if $X < 1$ (cf. 7.62), we therefor have $\dot{X} < 0$ at any point where A = 1. Now suppose that a section where A > 1 is preceded by one where A = 1. By (7.62) A > 1 is only possible if X > 1. If an interval where X > 1 is to be preceded by one with A = 1 (or X ≤ 1), the latter must clearly terminate with $\dot{X} > 0$. But this contradicts the conclusion just obtained. Therefore no interval where A > 1 can be preceded by one with A = 1.

To show that A exceeds unity at least at one point in (t_0, t_1), consider the situation at t_1. Suppose X ≥ 1 at t_1. Then A exceeds unity at t_1, by (7.62). Now suppose X < 1 at t_1. Then A = 1, implying that (7.67) describes the motion of X. If the terms between square brackets in (7.67) are positive, $\dot{X}/X$ is negative. Both these terms are non-negative if X < 1. If the second term is zero, $\dot{X}/X$ does not depend on the length of the planning horizon in any crucial way, just on the value of X itself. Thus, since $X^{\frac{1}{\omega}} - X^{-\frac{1}{\omega}}$ is positive if X < 1 and zero if X = 1, X is arbitrarily close to unity at t_0 if (t_0, T) is selected long enough. However, the second term is not zero, but strictly positive, and hence carries X across the unity hurdle, implying that X, and hence A, also exceeds unity in the early part of the trajectory if the latter is long enough.

Q.E.D.

Lemma 7.5 completes the proof that <u>if</u> an optimal path exists it has the properties stated in theorem 7.1. It still remains to show that, even if no optimal path exists, it still is better to give some aid than none at all. Put differently: that there is a trajectory with aid that is superior to all no-aid paths. This is done in lemma 7.6. To economize on space we give just a sketch of the proof, leaving the details to the interested reader.

<u>Lemma 7.6</u>: There is, if no solution to the optimal-control problem exists, at least one path where A > 1 somewhere, that yields a higher value of the objective function than all paths where A = 1 throughout.

<u>Sketch of proof</u>: Consider the set of trajectories where A = 1 throughout. Within this set there is an optimal one. Existence of the latter is easily shown, since with A = 1 the objective function and the capital-

accumulation equations are linear in the sole control, S.[7] Since we assumed that no optimal path exists, whereas one does if A = 1 throughout, the lemma's statement holds. This also completes the proof o theorem 7.1.

Appendix 7.1. The transfer effect and the capital stocks

This appendix analyses the influence of the value of the two regions' capital stocks on the transfer effects. To this end we calculate the derivatives of the relevant terms with respect to these stocks. Since different values of capital stocks entail different values of the other variables of the system, the impact of variations in the capital stocks can only be obtained by totally differentiating the whole system and solving. This amounts to solving the system (7.6)-(7.10) with dn = 0. For imports this yields:

$$\hat{m} = (1-q_{\ell})\hat{k} - \frac{e}{1+e+\bar{e}}\, x, \qquad (7.68)$$

where

$$x = (1-q_{\ell})\hat{k} - (1-\bar{q}_{\bar{\ell}})\hat{\bar{k}}. \qquad (7.69)$$

A symmetric equation holds for the south; note that $\bar{x}$ equals $-x$.

For total output we find:

$$\hat{v} = (1-q_{\ell})\hat{k} - \frac{eq_m}{1+e+\bar{e}}\, x. \qquad (7.70)$$

We also need information on some shares and elasticities. For $\hat{q}_m$ we obtain from (7.68) and (3.20):

$$\hat{q}_m = -\frac{1+E}{1+e+\bar{e}}\, x. \qquad (7.71)$$

For the labour share, using (3.21):

$$\hat{q}_{\ell} = (1-q_{\ell})\left(\frac{1+H}{H}\right)\hat{k}. \qquad (7.72)$$

Finally we obtain, using $e = E/(1-q_m)$:

$$d\,\ln(1+e+\bar{e}) = \frac{x}{(1+e+\bar{e})^2}\left\{e(1+E)\,\frac{q_m}{1-q_m} - \bar{e}(1+\bar{E})\,\frac{\bar{q}_{\bar{m}}}{1-\bar{q}_{\bar{m}}}\right\}, \qquad (7.73)$$

where it has been assumed that changes in the elasticities of substitution, being third-order derivatives, can be neglected: $dE = d\bar{E} = 0$.

In order to obtain definite results, we assume $E > -1$ and $\bar{E} < -1$. This immediately implies $\bar{e} < -1$; moreover, since $e = E/(1-q_m)$, we have $e > -1$ as long as q_m is sufficiently small. With $E > -1$, (7.71) implies that q_m declines if x is positive. Thus if k is large and/or $\bar{k}$ small, q_m is alwa small enough for e to exceed minus unity; in addition, the present value of q_m is only 4% implying that, as long E is indeed smaller than unity i absolute value, we have $e > -1$. Consequently we throughout assume:

$$\begin{aligned} &E,\ e > -1 \\ &\bar{E},\ \bar{e} < -1. \end{aligned} \tag{7.74}$$

We are now in a position to determine the effect of changes in the capital stocks on the transfer effects. In the logarithmic differentials of the terms in (7.19) we find from (7.68)-(7.73)

$$d \ln \frac{e+\bar{e}}{1+e+\bar{e}} = \frac{x(e+\bar{e})}{(1+e+\bar{e})^3} \left\{ e(1+E) \frac{q_m}{1-q_m} - \bar{e}(1+\bar{E}) \frac{\bar{q}_{\bar{m}}}{1-\bar{q}_{\bar{m}}} \right\} . \tag{7.75}$$

Using (7.74), (7.75) implies that $(e+\bar{e})/(1+e+\bar{e})$ is positively related to $\bar{k}$ and negatively to k.

$$d \ln \bar{\sigma}\bar{q}_{\bar{m}}(1-\bar{q}_{\bar{\ell}}) \frac{\bar{v}}{\bar{k}} = \frac{\bar{e}+1}{1+e+\bar{e}} x + \bar{q}_{\bar{\ell}} \frac{\hat{\bar{k}}}{\bar{H}} . \tag{7.76}$$

Since $\bar{H} < 0$, (7.76) implies that $\bar{\sigma}\bar{q}_{\bar{m}}(1-\bar{q}_{\bar{\ell}})\ \bar{v}/\bar{k}$ is negatively related to $\bar{k}$ and positively to k.

$$d \ln \sigma q_m(1-q_\ell) \frac{v}{k} = - \frac{e+1}{1+e+\bar{e}} x + q_\ell \frac{\hat{k}}{H} . \tag{7.77}$$

Thus $\sigma q_m(1-q_\ell)\ v/k$ is negatively related to $\bar{k}$; by writing out x, noting that q_ℓ normally exceeds one half and that $-(e+1)/(1+e+\bar{e})$ is smaller th unity, it is clear that $\sigma q_m(1-q_\ell)\ v/k$ is also negatively related to k as long as H is not too large in absolute value.

To determine the impact of changes in k and $\bar{k}$ on the transfer's impact on income, we calculate the total differential of the terms between squa brackets in (7.20) as k and $\bar{k}$ change. This yields:

$$-\sigma(1-q_\ell)\,\frac{v}{k}\Big[\Big(1-q_m+\frac{q_m}{1+e+\bar e}\Big)\Big\{\frac{q_\ell}{H}\,\hat k-\frac{eq_m}{1+e+\bar e}\,x\Big\}$$

$$+\frac{q_m x}{(1+e+\bar e)^2}\Big\{(e+\bar e)(1+E)-\frac{1}{1+e+\bar e}\Big(e(1+E)\,\frac{q_m}{1-q_m}-\bar e(1+\bar E)\,\frac{\bar q_{\bar m}}{1-\bar q_{\bar m}}\Big)\Big\}\Big]$$

$$+\,\bar\sigma(1-\bar q_{\bar\ell})\,\frac{\bar v}{\bar k}\,\frac{\bar q_{\bar m}}{1+e+\bar e}\Big[\frac{\bar q_{\bar\ell}\hat{\bar k}}{\bar H}+\frac{(1+\bar e)x}{1+e+\bar e}-\frac{x}{(1+e+\bar e)^2}$$

$$\Big\{e(1+E)\,\frac{q_m}{1-q_m}-\bar e(1+\bar E)\,\frac{\bar q_{\bar m}}{1-\bar q_{\bar m}}\Big\}\Big]. \qquad (7.78)$$

Using H, $\bar H < 0$, and (7.74), we find that the term between brackets in (7.20) is negatively related to $\bar k$ and positively to k, as long as $1-q_m + q_m/(1+e+\bar e) > 0$. This term can be written as

$$1-q_m+\frac{q_m}{1+e+\bar e}=\frac{(\bar E+1)(1-q_m)+q_m-\bar q_{\bar m}+E(1-\bar q_{\bar m})}{(1+e+\bar e)(1-\bar q_{\bar m})}. \qquad (7.79)$$

The right-hand side's numerator is negative as soon as the south's import share $\bar q_{\bar m}$ exceeds that of the north, a trivial condition. Thus the right-hand side of (7.79) as a whole is positive and the conclusions with respect to the relation between the bracketed term in (7.20) and the capital stocks are valid.

If all shares and elasticities are nonvanishing, the multiplier of $\hat{\bar k}$ in (7.78) is bounded by some strictly negative constant if $\bar k$ declines and k rises - since v/k and $\bar v/\bar k$ are decreasing in k and $\bar k$, respectively. Accordingly, the term between square brackets in (7.20) becomes arbitrarily large if $\bar k$ is sufficiently small. Mutatis mutandis the same applies if k is large enough.

Since the term between square brackets in (7.21) is, apart from a change of sign, symmetric to the one in (7.20), it follows that this bracketed term in (7.21) is negatively related to $\bar k$ and positively to k.

8. STABILITY OF THE GOODS MARKET AND THE BALANCE OF TRADE WHEN IMPORTS ARE INDISPENSABLE INPUTS

In this work we have stressed that most imports are inputs without perfect domestic substitutes. This implies that import demand is generate in a different way than most trade theory postulates: it derives directly from a macro production function and not from excess-demand functions. Throughout we imposed equilibrium on the import market, i.e. equality of actual imports to import demand. For this to be justified the equilibrium must be stable. The standard condition for stability of international equilibria is the Marshall-Lerner condition; in our analysis of growth we consistently took this condition to hold. But it remains to be seen whether international equilibria with indispensable imported inputs are also stable under the Marshall-Lerner condition: since import demand is generated differently than in traditional trade theory there is no guarantee that the standard stability results carry over. This applies no only to the equilibrium on the goods market but also to that of the balance of trade. Therefore we devote this chapter to an investigation of the stability properties of trade systems where trade consists of indispensable inputs. The adjustment processes concerned are short-run adjustments. Thus in the present chapter we do not have to deal with economic growth but can simply take the stocks of capital, labour and technology as fixed.

The <u>first</u> section, after briefly surveying the relevant literature, analyses the stability of the goods market equilibrium for the case of balanced trade. The basic adjustment process involved is a quantity adjustment: if there is a disequilibrium entrepreneurs adjust their imports in the direction of the import demand generated by the requiremen of efficiency in production. The upshot is that an equilibrium is stable if the Marshall-Lerner condition does <u>not</u> hold and unstable if it holds. Thus the stability properties of an international equilibrium where trade consists of indispensable inputs are the reverse of those of equilibria a described by traditional trade theory. Does this mean that the results obtained in preceding chapters, where equilibrium was assumed under the Marshall-Lerner condition, are invalid? The <u>second</u> section shows that thi does not have to be true. In that section we replace the assumption of balanced trade by the more realistic one of gradual adjustment of the terms of trade when the trade balance is not in equilibrium. Thus in this case there are simultaneously two adjustment processes: quantity adjustment to disequilibira on the goods market and terms of trade adjustment to disequilibria of the balance of trade. It turns out that then the system is stable if the Marshall-Lerner condition holds provided the adjustment process of the terms of trade is slow relative to that of the trade flows.

This result has an important policy implication: in view of the sizeable share of indispensable inputs in modern trade, fixed, or crawling, exchange rates must be preferred to flexible ones. For flexible exchange rates increase the speed of adjustment of the terms of trade and this renders the system, both the goods market and the balance of trade, unstable in the normal case where the Marshall-Lerner condition is satisfied.

8.1. Stability of the goods market with balanced trade

We first briefly discuss how the stability of demand-supply equilibria in international trade has been treated in the literature and next show how it works out in the case where imports consist of indispensable inputs.

Treatment in the literature

The question of the stability of an equilibrium of demand and supply for internationally traded goods was ostensibly settled long ago. The analysis was pioneered by Marshall (*circa* 1874, 1879, 1923 appendix J). His approach is to postulate a country's export supply to be a function of its actual imports. This relation has come to be called '*offercurve*'. In the standard two-region case the intersection of both regions' offercurves is the 'demand-supply equilibrium'. Marshall's approach to the stability issue is to assume that actual exports adjust towards export supply if the two differ from each other as a consequence of external shocks. He analyses the resulting dynamic system with phase diagrams, the first use of this tool in economics. He shows that a two-region equilibrium is locally stable if, at the equilibrium, the product of the slopes of the two offercurves is smaller than unity. (1) This condition can be recast in terms of the terms of trade elasticity of imports; if both regions' elasticities are negative Marshall's condition boils down to the requirement that the absolute value of the sum of the two regions' elasticities exceed unity. Since Lerner (1944, p. 378) gave the same condition for the stability of the balance of trade, the inequality has come to be called 'Marshall-Lerner condition'. This label is, however, inappropriate if only because the elasticity condition is not necessary for Marshall's condition to be met.(2)

Marshall's analysis poses quite a few questions and has been followed by a lot of discussion. A first issue is why export supply should be a function of imports and not of the terms of trade. Therefore Kemp (1964, p. 64; 1969, p.85) analyses the latter case. In his dynamic assumptions he follows Marshall closely, once again assuming exports to adjust towards the export-supply curve. In this case the stability condition is precisely the Marshall-Lerner elasticity condition; thus the condition is somewhat stronger than in Marshall's case but the result is not greatly different. A second issue is why there is only an export-supply curve and not an import-demand curve: if export supply is a function of actual imports, one may just as well postulate import demand to be a function of actual exports. In the latter case the counterpart of Marshall's adjustment is adjustment of imports towards import demand. As shown elsewhere (Van Bochove, 1981) the stability condition this yields is precisely the reverse of Marshall's; in the regular case of negative elasticities of imports with respect to the terms of trade, the equilibrium is unstable if the Marshall-Lerner condition holds. A third issue is how the offercurve can be generated. To know this, one has to specify the underlying relations regarding consumption and production; only if these are known it is possible to decide which of the formulations of import demand and export supply mentioned above should be adopted. This was noted long ago by Edgeworth (1894, pp. 424/425): 'A movement along a supply-and-demand curve of international trade should be considered as attended with rearrangements of internal trade; as the movement of the hand of a clock corresponds to considerable unseen movements of the machinery.' Of course many specifications of consumption and production are possible. One may use the standard two-good H O S model, amend this model to include non-traded goods, intermediates, add unemployment, etc. But even if a specification has been selected there still is a fourth issue to deal with: the assumptions on the adjustment process. Amano (1968) employs a standard H O S model, postulates a tâtonnement in the short run, where production is given, and a quantity adjustment of production in the long run; this yields stability conditions that are not too different from Marshall's. Chipman (1978) introduces a non-traded good and assumes excess supplies of tradables to adjust in the direction of the difference between relative cost of production and relative price. His stability conditions again are not too different, essentially, from Marshall's.

We conclude that stability of an international demand-supply equilibrium usually involves the Marshall-Lerner condition or something close to it. Only if imports adjust towards an import-demand curve is the equilibrium stable precisely if the Marshall-Lerner condition does not hold.

The case where imports are indispensable inputs

Unfortunately, when imports are indispensable inputs, the natural adjustment process is one where imports adjust towards the import-demand curve; and in this case the equilibrium is stable if and only if the Marshall-Lerner condition does not hold.

Formally the model is the same as in chapters 6 and 7; for convenience we once again refer to the two regions as 'north' and 'south'; but here the interpretation may equally well be that of an individual country and the rest of the world. The two production functions are, respectively:

$$v = v(\ell, k, m), \tag{8.1}$$

$$\bar{v} = \bar{v}(\bar{\ell}, \bar{k}, \bar{m}), \tag{8.2}$$

where v is output, ℓ labour, k capital, m imports and bars indicate that a variable refes to the south. We take, throughout the present chapter, capital and labour to be given. For convenience we assume constant returns; generalization to non-constant returns encounters no difficulties. The production functions are assumed to have the usual properties, particularly positive first-order derivatives and negative direct second-order ones. The import-demand equations are given by:

$$v_{m^d} = P^{-1}. \tag{8.3}$$

$$\bar{v}_{\bar{m}^d} = P. \tag{8.4}$$

Here v_{m^d} is v's derivative to m; the superscript d has been added to m in order to indicate that (8.3) and (8.4) give the import demand equations. In preceding chapters this superscript was redundant because import demand was assumed to equal actual imports throughout. In (8.3) and (8.4) P represents the north's terms of trade, the ratio of its export price to its import price. For the time being we follow Marshall in assuming balanced trade:

$$\bar{m} = mP^{-1}; \tag{8.5}$$

this assumption is relaxed in section 8.2.

Suppose actual imports differ from import demand as given by (8.3) and (8.4). To what adjustment process does this lead? The natural process is that where producers gradually adjust their actual imports in the direction of their import demand. Thus:

$$\dot{m} = f(m^d(P^{-1}) - m). \tag{8.6}$$

$$\dot{\bar{m}} = \bar{f}(\bar{m}^d(P) - \bar{m}). \tag{8.7}$$

Here f and $\bar{f}$ are the speeds of adjustment; the arguments of these functions are the excesses of import demand over actual imports. The functions f satisfy:

$$f(0),\ \bar{f}(0) = 0;\ f' > 0,\ \bar{f}' > 0, \tag{8.8}$$

where f' is f's derivative.

The model now obtained resembles Kemp's modification of Marshall's system: quantities are functions of the terms of trade and they adjust towards the thus generated curve. The difference with Kemp's analysis is that here imports adjust towards import demand, whereas in Kemp's case exports adjust towards export supply.

Denote $\partial \ln m^d / \partial \ln P^{-1}$, the terms of trade elasticity of import demand, by e; similarly the south's elasticity, $\partial \ln \bar{m}^d / \partial \ln P$ is $\bar{e}$. As shown in chapter 3 we have $e = v_m / m v_{mm}$, and similarly for $\bar{e}$. We now obtain:

Theorem 8.1: An equilibrium of the system (8.3)-(8.7) is locally stable if:

$$1+e+\bar{e} > 0, \qquad (8.9)$$

where the elasticities are evaluated at the equilibrium; and unstable if the Marshall-Lerner condition holds:

$$1+e+\bar{e} < 0. \qquad (8.10)$$

Proof: The first-order approximation of (8.6) and (8.7) at an equilibrium is:

$$\dot{m} = (m - m_0)f'(0)(-e_0 - 1) + (\bar{m} - \bar{m}_0)f'(0)e_0P_0. \qquad (8.11)$$

$$\dot{\bar{m}} = (m - m_0)\bar{f}'(0)\bar{e}_0P_0^{-1} + (\bar{m} - \bar{m}_0)\bar{f}'(0)(-\bar{e}_0 - 1). \qquad (8.12)$$

Here the subscript 0 indicates that the variable is evaluated at the equilibrium. The characteristic equation of the Jacobian of (8.11) and (8.12) reduces to:

$$x^2 + x\{f'(0)(e_0 + 1) + \bar{f}'(0)(\bar{e}_0 + 1)\} + f'(0)\bar{f}'(0)(1+e_0+\bar{e}_0) = 0, \qquad (8.13)$$

where x represents the eigenvalues. For (8.11) and (8.12) to be globally stable the roots of (8.13) must have negative real parts only. A necessary and sufficient condition for this is:

$$\begin{aligned} &f'(0)(e_0 + 1) + \bar{f}'(0)(\bar{e}_0 + 1) > 0. \\ &f'(0)\bar{f}'(0)(1 + e_0 + \bar{e}_0) > 0. \end{aligned} \qquad (8.14)$$

Clearly $1 + e_0 + \bar{e}_0 > 0$, is a necessary and sufficient condition for (8.14), as $f'(0)$ and $\bar{f}'(0)$ are positive. If this condition does not hold, and provided $1 + e_0 + \bar{e}_0 \neq 0$, (8.13) has at least one positive real root. Thus for $1 + e_0 + \bar{e}_0 < 0$ the original system (8.3)-(8.7) is unstable, for $1 + e_0 + \bar{e}_0 > 0$ it is locally stable (cf. Hahn, 1967, theorem 28.1, p.122).

Q.E.D.

This result is troublesome. For throughout the present work a maintained hypothesis has been that the Marshall-Lerner condition holds. But now we find that under this condition the market for imports is unstable, implying that the other hypothesis maintained throughout, equality of actual imports to import demand, is invalidated. The theorem is also troubling from a theoretical point of view: it implies that Samuelson's (1942, 1947) Correspondence Principle breaks down in the present case. This Principle states that the results of dynamics and comparative statics are intimately related in two ways. Firstly the analysis of the properties of dynamically unstable equilibria is pointless; thus the stability conditions obtained from dynamic analysis can be used as input for comparative-static analysis. Secondly, comparative-static results are often useful to dynamic analysis: equilibria with perverse comparative-static properties are usually dynamically unstable. In our case the principle breaks down because the comparative static properties of our system are perverse if the equilibrium is <u>stable</u>, i.e. if the Marshall-Lerner condition does <u>not</u> hold; reversely the comparative static properties of unstable equilibria are regular.

This raises two issues. First, without the Correspondence Principle, there is no <u>a priori</u> reason for the Marshall-Lerner condition to hold. Therefore, if we assume it to hold nevertheless, this assumption must be founded on direct empirical evidence. Fortunately the empirical evidence available for individual countries clearly indicates that the Marshall-Lerner condition is generally satisfied: the foreign-demand elasticities are centered around minus two. For the north-south system the condition is probably satisfied even where short-run elasticities are concerned: the north's imports from the south are fairly complementary to its own goods, implying a low absolute value of the import-demand elasticity, but the south's imports from the north are more elastic, consisting mainly of industrial products. The long-run elasticities that are relevant in the context of growth have still higher absolute values implying that the

Marshall-Lerner condition is still more likely to be satisfied.

The second issue raised is how relevant the analysis of trading systems under the Marshall-Lerner condition is. This issue hinges on the question how realistic the adjustment process specified above is. Clearly, the major unrealistic assumption made is that of a perpetually closed balance of trade. Therefore we devote the next section to relaxing this assumption and examining the way this influences the stability properties of the system.

8.2. Stability of the balance of trade

Instead of postulating a closed balance of trade we now admit deficits and surplusses: the terms of trade then rise if there is a surplus of the value of exports over imports and fall in the case of a deficit:

$$\dot{P} = h(P - \frac{m}{\bar{m}}); \; h(0) = 0, \; h' > 0. \qquad (8.15)$$

For the goods markets we specify the same adjustment process as in the preceding section:

$$\dot{m} = f(m^d(P^{-1}) - m). \qquad (8.6)$$

$$\dot{\bar{m}} = \bar{f}(\bar{m}^d(P) - \bar{m}). \qquad (8.7)$$

To some extent the system (8.15), (8.6), (8.7) resembles that of Chipman (1978, p.58). He too combines quantity adjustment on the goods markets with adjustment of the terms of trade and rate of exchange to deficits and surplusses in the balance of trade. But there are important differences. Chipman employs a Heckscher-Ohlin-Samuelson model, adding domestic goods, whereas we treat imports as a factor of production. Still more important is the difference noted above: in Chipman's system quantities adjust in the direction of the difference between price ratios, whereas in our case they adjust towards the import-demand curves. This means that there is a tension in our system that is absent in Chipman's. This is caused by the difference in the stability conditions for the goods markets and the balance of trade. As is well known (Lerner, 1944; Mundell, 1960, p.73; 1968, p.13), if the goods market is frictionless, the stability condition for the balance of trade is simply the Marshall-Lerner condition. If the balance of trade is frictionless, the stability condition for the goods market is not too different from the Marshall-Lerner condition in Chipman's system but in our system (cf. section 8.1) it is precisely the reverse of this condition. Therefore we should expect that the stability properties of an equilibrium of (8.15), (8.6), (8.7) depend on the relative speeds of adjustment of the goods market and the balance of trade; in Chipman's system stability is independent of the speeds of adjustment.

Theorem 8.2 establishes that the speeds of adjustment do indeed matter; in particular that the acceleration of the adjustment speed at the equilibrium is crucial. The acceleration is given by the derivatives of h, f and $\bar{f}$ at equilibrium. For convenience we select the units of measurement of one of the two trade flows such that the acceleration to both import demand curves is equal at equilibrium:(3) $f'(0) = \bar{f}'(0)$. In addition, define η as the ratio of acceleration of the terms of trade towards balance of trade equilibrium to the acceleration of trade flows towards import demand. We then obtain:

Theorem 8.2: Select the unit of measurement of either m or $\bar{m}$ such as to have $f'(0) = \bar{f}'(0)$ and define $\eta = h'(0)/f'(0)$. Then an equilibrium of the system (8.15), (8.6), (8.7) is locally stable if:

$$1+e+\bar{e} < 0, \tag{8.10}$$

$$\eta < \tfrac{1}{2}, \tag{8.16}$$

$$e+\bar{e} > -\frac{2(\eta-1)^2}{\eta}, \tag{8.17}$$

where e is evaluated at equilibrium. If at least one of the inequality signs in (8.10), (8.16) or (8.17) is reversed the equilibrium is unstable.

Proof: The first-order approximation of (8.15), (8.6) and (8.7) at equilibrium is:

$$\dot{P} = h'(0)\{P - P_0 - (m-m_0)\bar{m}_0^{-1} + (\bar{m}-\bar{m}_0)\frac{P_0}{\bar{m}_0}\}. \tag{8.18}$$

$$\dot{m} = -f'(0)\{(P-P_0)e_0\frac{m_0}{P_0} + m - m_0\}. \tag{8.19}$$

$$\dot{\bar{m}} = \bar{f}'(0)\{(P-P_0)\bar{e}_0 \frac{m_0}{P_0} - (\bar{m} - \bar{m}_0)\}. \tag{8.20}$$

Here the subscript 0 again indicates that a variable is evaluated at equilibrium; use has been made of $P_0 = m_0/\bar{m}_0$. The characteristic equation of the Jacobian is:

$$\begin{aligned} &x^3 + x^2(f' + \bar{f}' - h') + x(f'\bar{f}' - f'h' - \bar{f}'h') \\ &-h'f'\bar{f}'(1 + e_0 + \bar{e}_0) = 0, \end{aligned} \tag{8.21}$$

where x represents the characteristic roots; f' is shorthand for f'(0). The Routh-Hurwitz conditions for all roots of (8.21) to have negative real parts only are:

$$f' + \bar{f}' - h' > 0. \tag{8.22}$$

$$f'\bar{f}' - f'h' - \bar{f}'h' > 0. \tag{8.23}$$

$$-h'f'\bar{f}'(1 + e_0 + \bar{e}_0) > 0. \tag{8.24}$$

$$(f' + \bar{f}' - h')(f'\bar{f}' - f'h' - \bar{f}'h') > -f'h'\bar{f}'(1 + e_0 + \bar{e}_0). \tag{8.25}$$

Inserting $f' = \bar{f}'$ and $h' = \eta f'$, (8.22)-(8.25) are easily seen to reduce to (8.10), (8.16), (8.17). Thus under these conditions the equilibrium of (8.15), (8.6), (8.7) is locally stable.

If one of the inequalities (8.22)-(8.25) is violated, there is at least one root non-negative. If such a root is positive both the linearized and the original system are unstable (Hahn, 1967, p.122), but if there is only a zero root, with all others negative, no inference on the original system is possible. Suppose there is one zero root. Clearly this requires $e_0 + \bar{e}_0 = -1$. Thus, as long as the inequality sign in (8.24) holds or is reversed, there is no zero root. The Routh-Hurwitz conditions are not only necessary but also sufficient for (8.21) to have only roots with negative real parts. Consequently, as soon as either of the inequality signs in (8.22)-(8.25) is reversed at least one root has a positive real part and the equilibrium is unstable.

Q.E.D.

The *first* condition of theorem 8.2 is the Marshall-Lerner condition. Thus, if friction in the balance of trade is accounted for, stability of both the goods market and the balance of trade is once again possible under this condition. This means that the results of preceding chapters, obtained under the Marshall-Lerner condition, are compatible with equality of imports to import demand. Hence these results are not invalidated: the troubling outcome of the stability analysis in the preceding section is caused by neglecting friction in the balance of trade.

The *second* condition, (8.16), states that the acceleration of the adjustment of imports towards import demand should be at least twice as fast as that of the terms of trade towards balance of trade equilibrium. The *third* condition reinforces this result: since the right-hand side is a decreasing function of η, provided (8.16) holds, the right-hand side of (8.17) is smaller than the left-hand side if η is small enough.

In short, theorem 8.2 establishes that both the goods market and the balance of trade are stable under the Marshall-Lerner condition, provided the adjustment of the terms of trade to balance of trade disequilibria is slow relative to the quantity adjustment on the goods market.

The reason for this result is not difficult to see. From (8.6) and (8.7) it is clear that if the terms of trade do not change at all, import demands are fixed and imports adjust monotonically to their equilibrium values. In this case entrepreneurs simply know what the equilibrium value, i.e. optimal value, of imported inputs is and have no trouble adjusting their actual input to that value. But if the terms of trade are perfectly flexible, as in section 8.1, entrepreneurs do not know what the equilibrium value of imports will be; they can only chase the temporary optimal value of imports, a value that keeps on changing as a consequence of the movement of the terms of trade. In the regular case of the Marshall-Lerner condition this chase is endless and no equilibrium is attained. Clearly then, between these extremes of rigid terms of trade and perfectly flexible ones, matters depend on the relative speeds of adjustment. If the terms of trade are too flexible no equilibrium is attained.

This result has an important policy implication: it provides a strong argument for fixed exchange rates. The reason for this is that the terms of trade is the product of two components: the ratio of the two region's prices of exports expressed in the national currency and the exchange rate. Usually the former is not perfectly flexible but rigid to some extent. If the ratio adjusts sufficiently slowly this generates, by our results, a tendency to stability. However, with a flexible exchange rate this tendency is upset as in this case the exchange-rate changes cause the terms of trade to be flexible as well. Thus if the stickiness of nominal prices is to have its stabilizing influence, the exchange rates should be fairly rigid.

Of course our analysis must be applied with some care. The reason for this is that we have neglected both all non-trade components of the balance of payments and internal monetary phenomena such as the rate of growth of money supply. This is especially tricky because we admit balance of trade disequilibrium. The latter generates capital flows and hence reflects back on the nominal prices and the terms of trade. In addition, differing rates of growth of money supply between both regions and differences in rates of interest exert autonomous pressure on exchange rates and nominal prices and make permanently fixed exchange rates unfeasible. Therefore it would be interesting to incorporate our dynamic system in a comprehensive monetary framework; but this is beyond the scope of the present book. Nevertheless it is not likely that the feedbacks caused by disequilibrium of the balance of trade will affect our results qualitatively since these feedbacks are of a secondary order of magnitude. Therefore the conclusion remains that the overwhelmingly large amount of indispensable imported inputs in modern trade makes perfectly flexible exchange rates an inefficient policy for maintaining external and internal equilibrium; ad hoc devaluations and revaluations, or schemes like crawling pegs, must be preferred.

NOTES

Chapter 1

1. Next, however, Díaz Alejandro suggests a rather complicated four-sector model of Corden (1971), instead of our more direct approach.
2. These models allow for easy empirical application and are therefore widely used in practical work. For two important recent examples, cf. Waelbroeck (1976) and Sawyer (1979).
3. For an elaboration cf. section 2.5.
4. The term is used here in a broad sense and includes, as a special case, the Harrod-Domar model.
5. This result appears to contradict empirical evidence displaying a clearcut positive correlation between income growth and the rate of saving, particularly in cross-section analysis. However, Sato's result is obtained in a model where technical progress is absent. It is more realistic to assume a positive association between technical progress and the rate of investment. Incorporated in a neoclassical growth model, this association causes the rate of saving to turn up in the steady-growth rate. Thus if, with a Cobb-Douglas production function, the rate of technical progress, ν, is linearly dependent on the rate of saving σ : $\nu = \nu_0 + \nu_1\sigma$, the steady-growth rate of income is:

$$\frac{\nu_0 + \nu_1\sigma + \xi_\ell\lambda}{\xi_\ell},$$

where the production function is taken to be linear homogeneous, λ is the natural rate and ξ_ℓ labour's exponent in the production function.

In view of this result, the steady-growth rate remains a good approximation of income's growth off the steady-growth path.

In the models we employ it is not necessary to specify an explicit relation between technical progress and the rate of saving, since we assume both to be constant and exogenous, so that a relation between the two does not affect our results.

Chapter 2

1. The simplest two-country version of the model is: $m = \mu y$; $\bar{m} = \bar{\mu}\bar{y}$; $m = \bar{m}$, where m is imports, y income, μ a multiplicative constant; bars indicate the foreign country. This yields $y = \frac{\bar{\mu}}{\mu} y$. Thus both countries' growth rates are equal. This little model is taken from Seers (1962), but originally the multiplier theory of foreign trade has been introduced by Harrod (1936, pp. 145-148) and elaborated by Metzler (1942) and Machlup (1943). The approach can be made slightly more sophisticated by adding terms of trade effects, an approach pioneered in Tinbergen's (1941) largely neglected paper, and subsequently by Meade (1948, 1949, 1951). The same type of results as in Seers' model are then obtained if the terms of trade are rigid or if foreign supply is not perfectly elastic.
2. Oddly, early in the nineteenth century suitable theories were available: a coupling of the classical theory of trade to what Samuelson (1978a) calls the canonical classical model of growth might yield an interesting theory of trade and growth. Classical growth theory emphasizes that land is an exhaustible factor and concludes that labour and capital eventually move to stationary values, with the wage and profit rates declining to subsistence levels. Clearly, trade lengthens the adjustment period in which wages and profits are above subsistence levels. If, instead of land, natural resources are the exhaustible input, we are back at current issues. Kemp and Long's (1979, 1980 essays 13 and 14) recent models could be turned into a neoclassical version of such a model by adding capital accumulation and an endogenous growth rate of labour.
3. Sato (1969) collects a number of possibilities (for general saving).
4. Trade reversals are investigated by Deardorff (1974a). He shows that they can only occur if the autarkic steady state from which the country started was unstable. Thus as long as the latter is stable to begin with, the pattern of trade in the long run is the same as that immediately after the opening up to trade. Further details about the pattern of specialization are given in Smallwood's (1975) lucid paper, and by Dixit (1978), who corrects Petith (1974).
5. Of course this does not mean that the <u>level</u> of income, or, more relevant, of consumption, cannot be improved by trade. Stiglitz (1970)

and Bertrand (1975) show that trade improves the consumption possibilities. This does not imply that steady-state consumption is actually improved. It is, if the rate of saving equals the golden-rule rate - that is, the one maximizing per capita steady-state consumption in autarky - cf. Deardorff (1973). However, if the rate of time preference is high in the case of rational savings (cf. section 2.2), or if the rate of saving is high for other reasons, steady-state consumption may be lower than it would have been without trade. A detailed exposé of the development of steady-state consumption is given by Smith (1977).

Similarly, Smallwood (1975) demonstrates that trade may raise (if the capital good is capital intensive) or lower (if the consumption good is capital intensive) the growth rate in the transition to the steady state - but not, of course, in the steady state. A detailed analysis of the gains from trade is given by Togan (1975).

6. Takayama (1972, p. 431) raises doubt about the validity of this conclusion, noting that Oniki and Uzawa appear to assume incorrectly that specialization is either complete, or that both countries do not specialize. However, Oniki and Uzawa do not assume this: to obtain figure (2.1) they just have to consider the regions where one of the countries is specialized in capital goods; what happens to consumption goods is irrelevant. Thus they show that the equilibrium is unique and stable, the system moving towards equilibrium independently of the pattern of specialization on the way. In contrast, Takayama's critique is valid for Bardhan's (1965, a) treatment (of the classical saving case): the latter considers only a few of the possible patterns of specialization and does not show that the equilibrium is unique and the basic motion the same for all cases. Thus his results are only locally valid, not globally.

A related controversy concerns the pattern of specialization in equilibrium. Oniki and Uzawa show in two illustrations (pp. 36, 37) equilibria in the region where no country is specialized. Takayama (1972, p. 431) says this is, barring accidental, knife-edge, cases, impossible. But here the saving behaviour is crucial. Takayama assumes classical saving, but as Bardhan (1973) emphasizes, Oniki and Uzawa proportional saving. In the latter case incomplete specialization is compatible with equilibrium (this is clear from Oniki and Uzawa's equation (68), p. 33, which shows that the curve of a constant capital-labour ratio for one country is not, as in Takayama, eq. 14-66, p. 427, parallel to that of the other). If, however, saving is classical or rational, this can only be true in a special, knife-edge, case that coincides with equality of the price of capital and of wages in both countries (cf. Stiglitz, 1970).

A comprehensive treatment of the pattern of specialization in the long-run equilibrium is given by Petith (1976) and, in a very lucid paper, by Deardorff and Hanson (1978).

7. The mechanism involved is not difficult to understand intuitively. If one country has a higher natural rate than the other, it tends to grow faster and becomes large in the sense of completely determining the international terms of trade. The latter therefore converge to the long-run equilibrium value for this country and the country with the lower natural rate is in precisely the same position as the small country discussed above.

8. Inada (1971) focuses on another topic than long-run growth: the development of a monocultural economy. He is not primarily concerned with long-run growth, but rather with the transition of an under-developed economy, dominated by a plantation sector with inelastic foreign demand, to industrialization. Increasing returns in manufacturing, making infant industries relatively ineffective compared to mature ones, hinder a take-off.

   Zarembka (1972) ostensibly describes the long-run growth of a three-sector economy with neoclassical production functions. But the model does not describe the production of capital goods and the process of saving.

9. Here, however, unlike the situation with proportional saving, the short-run equilibrium on the investment-goods market might be unstable; to eliminate this possibility, the elasticities of substitution in production must be sufficiently large (Drandankis, 1963).

10. This condition also guarantees that the pattern of specialization can be unambiguously traced out; this was pointed out by Bardhan (1966, p. 43). Incidentally, Stiglitz' (1970, p. 486) phase diagrams state that the elasticity must exceed the <u>profit</u>-share, but this appears to be a slip of the pen (apparently $1-\alpha$ should be substituted for α).

11. In this important, but neglected, paper, Atsumi tackles the stability issue from a new angle, obtaining a much closer correspondence to the usual methodology of trade theory by utilizing 'short-run' and 'long-run' reciprocal-demand functions.
12. Disregarding internal transport costs; if these are present they can cause two-way trade, as noted by Taussig (1915, p. 191) - also compar Van Bochove and De Vries (1977, p. 188).
13. The theory of international trade with intermediate goods and inter-industry flows has attracted a lot of authors, but the literature is somewhat fragmented and not yet surveyed comprehensively. Chacoliades (1979) recent survey pays little attention to the intermediate-goods literature proper, but instead concentrates on the connection with th neo-Ricardian theory (discussed by us in section 2.5). For further references cf. Chipman (1966, p. 42), Woodland (1977) and Der (1979); also compare Kemp and Khang (1977) for some properties of the gross outputs.
14. Johnson (1958, p. 125) erroneously reports the reverse.
15. This rate is composed of both an autonomous, non-price, movement and an exogenous change in import prices compared to the general price level abroad. The third price, that of exports, endogenously adjusts to effectuate balanced trade.
16. In contrast to our use of the term 'natural rate', that is: populatio growth plus possibly growth of labour productivity, Black uses the term for the constant long-run growth rate, irrespective of its composition.
17. There is by assumption only one good in the world, implying that all trade is either unbalanced or zero: a country either exports, or imports, but there is no point in doing both things simultaneously. That there is any trade at all is a consequence of the admission of international investment and subsequent interest payments. The point made is that it may well be advantageous for both countries concerned if an international investment is made at some point and never fully repaid. Then there is a permanent one-way trade flow in the steady state to pay for the interest.
18. Contributions have been made by many authors, e.g. Emmanuel (1969, 1978), Acheson (1970), Parrinello (1970), Mainwaring, Metcalfe and Steedman (cf. the contributions in Steedman, 1979a; also compare

Steedman, 1979b), Samuelson (1973, 1975, 1976, 1978 b, c), Kemp (1973), Smith (1976b, 1979), Burmeister (1978), Ethier (1979).

19. An alternative way to model the role of time and capital is the 'Austrian' one, associated with Jevons, Böhm-Bawerk, Wicksell. In this approach time is considered as a factor of production. Findlay (1978) describes a model where an intermediate good produced in the Austrian way is traded for a final good, produced from the intermediate good in zero time by adding labour. Then, if the rate of time preference depends on consumption, but for both countries in a different way, the most impatient country imports the time-intensive intermediate good. The rate of growth, zero in Findlay's model, is not changed by trade.

20. This formulation includes final goods of which the production time from primary input to final product exceeds a single period. If e.g. a final product takes two periods to complete, the result of processing its primary inputs for one period is defined as a new, intermediate, product, and we are back at a single-period system. For a more detailed discussion, cf e.g. Takayama (1974, pp. 487-8).

21. In this case saving behaviour, the composition of final output and the actual use of the other, non-restrictive, primary factors, are such that intermediate products are fully employed. Alternatively, it could be assumed that the input-output coefficients have been adjusted to final demand and savings in such a way that full employment of the intermediates obtains. Either way, there is no need to give explicit consideration to saving behaviour or consumption functions. This is why saving functions are not specified in the literature that treats labour as scarce.

22. Except if production functions are internationally identical and hence (cf. Samuelson, 1951) input-output coefficients without trade too; they should not be altered by the opening up of trade. But many neo-Ricardian authors assume input-output coefficients to differ internationally.

23. Dixit (1981) arrives at similar conclusions in his discussion of the neo-Ricardian approach: 'In the trade-off where one can handle <u>either</u> heterogeneous capital goods <u>or</u> non-steady-state paths, for me the latter facility seems vastly more important (p. 294).

Chapter 3

1. The shares in world imports (1976) are: USA, 12.7%; FR Germany, 8.7%; Japan, 6.4%; Netherlands, 3.9%, the latter country being the world's seventh largest importer. The four countries account for 31.7% of world imports.
2. There is some slight danger involved in equating our rule: production less than 20% of imports, with lack of specific factors. The low domestic production may be caused, not by lack of the factor involved but by relatively high costs of exploitation of the factor. In e.g. The Netherlands all coal is imported, though coal is present; however current world prices do not permit competitive mining of domestic coal. Alternatively, it may be possible to substitute capital, knowledge and intermediate inputs such as energy for specific factors Thus e.g. Germany, lacking sufficiently warm territory to grow tomatoes, imports virtually all of them. But most of these come from the no less cold Netherlands, where they are grown in greenhouses.
   However, inspection of the list of commodities included in table 3. quickly shows that most products are indeed based on specific, lacking, factors; either mineral deposits, or specific climate and soil. Moreover, part of the import of manufactures also consists of products made of special-factor based materials. Thus the table 3.1 figure for the share of special-factor based imports in total imports is more likely to underestimate the true share, than to exaggerate it
3. This is of course caused by the high share of primary products in Japan's total imports: 78.8%. The other three countries' figure is only about forty percent: USA, 43.6%; FR Germany, 41.9%; Netherlands, 40.7%.
4. To mention just one example: UNIDO (1979, p. 185) found that integrated steel mills producing flat rolled products achieve a 20% cost reduction with each doubling of capacity up to 800,000 tons annually and 10% up to 1,600,000 tons.
5. An example is found in woodprocessing (UNIDO, 1979, p. 185). Saw milling and board production yield residues that can be used for e.g. pulp production (in Finland this amounts to 11% of sawmill revenues); however, if, as in many developing countries, domestic demand for residues falls short, unit costs are raised, possibly to uncompetitiv

levels.

6. Incidentally, the 20% share in 1977 is just about what should be expected from the long-term trend; the 10% share of 1972, on the contrary, is exceptionally low. Nor is the 20% share a mere statistical fluke: the volume of fuels traded had increased more than the volume of other trade until 1972; the doubling of the share thereafter was almost entirely due to what may be regarded as a catching-up of the terms of trade.
7. In 1974, for example, 71% of net energy in the US was used by the industrial and transport sectors. Similarly, in the same year 79% of oil and oil products in The Netherlands was used for intermediate purposes (Sources: Statistical Abstract of the United States, 1977, table 980, 1974 input-output table for The Netherlands, Nationale Rekeningen, 1976, Den Haag, C.B.S.).
8. Even if each individual plant operates under fixed coefficients, the input-output coefficients may differ from plant to plant; as a consequence the aggregate production function admits substitution and its shape depends on the distribution of input-output coefficients. If this distribution is Pareto, an aggregate Cobb-Douglas results, as Houthakker (1955/6) discovered. Thus, if instead of labour and capital, each plant uses labour and imported inputs in fixed proportions, this results in an aggregate Cobb-Douglas with labour and imports, to which capital could be added under the (at least partially realistic) assumption that the national capital stock is used jointly.
9. Some authors use a model with this characteristic to analyse the balance of payments, though without consideration of growth, cf. Chacoliades (1970, 1971), Schmid (1976); Elkan (1970) uses a model that incorporates scale effects to examine industrialization but he does not analyse capital accumulation.
10. Humphries (1976) uses three-factor (labour, capital, imports) Cobb-Douglas and CES functions to derive 'sources of growth equations' and estimates these for a multicountry cross-section sample. Her conclusion is that the elasticity of substitution is about 0.8, suggesting 'that global possibilities for substitution are considerably wider than might be implied by models such as the Chenery-Strout "two-gap" model where the implicit assumption is that the production function is Leontief' (p. 352).

11. Breaking-up the production of a single product in several components and locating the latters' production in different countries not only generates the traditional economies of scale associated with longer product runs. In addition it admits location of the production of ea component in the country where the factors that are used relatively intensively in its production are most abundant. Thus a higher outpu of the final product is obtained at the same total level of inputs. the aggregate this turns up as increasing returns to capital, labour and imports combined.
12. Leakey and Lewin (1979, p. 100) passionately advocate the use of thi term instead of the usual 'hunting and gathering', because in most such societies the major part of the diet is obtained by gathering, not by hunting.
13. Unless, of course, Inada's suggestion is correct that his conditions imply a unit elasticity at $K \to 0$.
14. All micro functions should have the form $v(\alpha_i \cdot k_i, \ell_i)$, where onl the constants α_i differ between firms. Obviously, because the α_i's differ, capital is heterogeneous, that is: equal money amounts of capital (measured at replacement value, or whatever, as long as the same unit of measurement is used for all firms) combined with equal amounts of (homogeneous, unfortunately) labour yield different amoun of output.
15 This presupposes constant exchange rates. Under flexible rates, imports' share exceeds its ex-ante share.
16. Verdoorn (1973) has put forward an argument in the case of increasin returns that is broadly similar to the present one.

Chapter 4

1 The terms of trade on which export demand depends are defined as the ratio of the import price to that of output; this implies absence of price discrimination between exports and domestic deliveries. The presence of such discrimination may alter trade flows considerably a notably affect the effects of economic integration, c.f. Verdoorn (1960), Verdoorn and Meyer zu Schlochtern (1964), Verdoorn and Schwartz (1972) and Verdoorn and Van Bochove (1972). Another

consequence is the emergence of two-way trade, c.f. Van Bochove and De Vries (1977).

2. From (3.13), E, e < 0 is seen to imply equivalence of $1 + e + \bar{\varepsilon} < 0$ to: $(1+\varepsilon)(1 + q_m\{E(\rho-1) - 1\}) + E < 0$. The left-hand side of this expression can be transformed to: $(1-q_m)B + q_m E\gamma$, which is negative if (4.7), (4.8) and (4.9) are satisfied, since $0 < q_m < 1$.

3. With labour constant, we have $\frac{dz}{z} = (1-q_\ell)\frac{dk}{k}$. From (3.21) it is clear that, with $H > -1$, the value of $1-q_\ell$ for high k is highest if H is close to minus unity, say at its lower bound H*. Thus z is, for high k, always smaller than it would be with H = H*. It is easily seen that a CES function with elasticity of substitution H* > -1 has a maximum where $z_k = 0$.

4. Of course there are global limits to this process, as soon as depletable natural resources in the presently underdeveloped countries are exhausted too and as soon as pollution becomes too intensive on a planetary scale. But presently the world does not yet appear to be too close to these global limits (c.f. e.g. Malinvaud, 1980). Moreover, one may speculate, somewhat science fictional, that by the time the planetary constraints begin to matter seriously, space technology will have been developed to such an extent that a way out is provided by extraterrestrial activities such as mining the asteroid belt and Mercury (c.f. e.g. Powers, 1980) for rare metals and location of major polluting and high-risk industries (e.g. nuclear power plants) in outer space. In that case outer space would play the same role vis à vis earth, now played by the less-developed countries vis à vis the industrial countries of the northern hemisphere; our model could then be applied to the planet as a whole - though the rate of growth of foreign demand in the export equation would have to be replaced by some function of the rate of accumulation of extra-terrestrial capital stock, the latter in turn being a function of the marginal productivity of 'imports' to earth.

5. Specifically we should have: $1-q_\ell > \frac{1}{\rho}$. Then $-(\rho q_\ell - \rho + 1)g > 0$. If $H < -1$, q_ℓ decreases as long as $g > 0$. Hence (c.f. 4.36) g cannot decrease to zero and keeps on growing.

6. This is seen from (4.37). With $H < -1$, the term $-(\rho q_\ell - \rho + 1)g$ tends to $(\rho-1)g$, which is positive under decreasing returns, implying that g cannot fall to zero. But initially $-(\rho q_\ell - \rho + 1)g$ may be negative,

becoming positive only if g is positive long enough to raise the capital-labour ratio to such an extent that q_{ℓ} is lowered sufficiently. The latter will happen if q_m is originally large enough: then M : strictly positive and the positivity of the second term in (4.37) prevents g from falling to zero. Of course, with E < -1, in the long run q_m and M must fall to zero, but if q_m is large initially, this ma be just enough for the transition to steady growth at a strictly positive rate.

7. To see this, first note that $(1 - \xi_{\ell\infty})\gamma\mu_i$ $(i = 0, \infty)$ is non-negative. Thus $\theta_{au} < 0$ is a necessary condition for θ_i $(i = 0, \infty)$ to be non-positive. Accordingly the condition $\theta_0 > 0$ does not have to be impose explicitly, as the case $Z \to 0$ corresponding to $\theta_{au} + (1-q_{\ell})\gamma M \to \theta_0$, can only occur for $\theta_{au} > 0$. If $\theta_{au} < 0$, θ_{∞} could be negative. The latter can be written as:

$$\theta_{\infty} = 1 - (1-\xi_{\ell\infty})(\rho-\gamma\mu_{\infty}).$$

If $E_{\infty} > -1$, $\rho-\gamma\mu_{\infty}$ takes the value $(1+E_{\infty})/E_{\infty}$, since $\xi_{m\infty} = 1$ in this case.
Since $(1+E_{\infty})/E_{\infty} < 1$, and $(1-\xi_{\ell\infty}) < 1$, θ_{∞} cannot be negative in this case. If $E_{\infty} = -1$, $\rho-\gamma\mu_{\infty}$ takes the value $\rho\bar{\varepsilon}(1-\xi_{\ell\infty})$, which is negative implying once more positivity of θ_{∞}. Only if $E_{\infty} < -1$, μ_{∞} is zero-valued, implying: $\theta_{\infty} = \theta_{au} < 0$.

8. This is immediately seen by setting $\xi_m = 0$, hence $\mu = 0$ in (4.47). Alternatively, the autarkic rate can be obtained from the time path (the closed economy, in the same way as we did for the open one. Thus one obtains a generalization of Verdoorn's (1959) analysis of the Cobb-Douglas based growth model (with non-constant returns and technical progress) to that of a variable elasticity of substitution converging to a constant value.

9. Under decreasing returns, $E = -\infty$ violates the condition $E(\rho-1) - 1 < 0$; in this case the growth rate is therefore not determined by (4.47). Instead all trade is substituted away.

10. If there is, potentially, a 'loss', $E = -\infty$ immediately implies $\xi_m = 0$, hence equality of χ to χ_{au}, regardless of the value of ρ.

11. This is not immediately evident from consideration of the long-run growth rate only: as soon as E is only slightly below minus unity,

ξ_m equals zero and the 'loss' is reduced to zero; further decreases in E have no influence whatsoever on the growth rate. However, the convergence to the long-run growth rate consumes time, and the lower E is, the more rapidly q_m drops to zero, minimizing the loss from trade during the adjustment process.

12. The latter need not be disadvantageous to OPEC in the long run: though the oil proceeds would diminish, the opportunities for industrialization of these countries are far better if world trade expands rapidly than if it is depressed. In this view lowered oil prices may well be the best way for these countries to ensure reasonable welfare in the period after their oil reserves are depleted. Besides, it is by now (1982) becoming clear that the recession in the industrial countries is harmful to OPEC too, because of the low demand for oil that threatens to interfere with the financing of their industrial development programs. Clearly, therefore, an agreement where OPEC commits itself to fixed, low, oil prices for, say, five years and the OECD countries to joint Keynesian stimulation is favourable for both parties.
13. This is the conclusion of Toynbee's (1976) last work, a world history: 'The present-day global set of local sovereign states is not capable of keeping the peace, and it is also not capable of saving the biosphere from man-made pollution or of conserving the biosphere's non-replaceable natural resources [...] What has been needed for the last 5000 years, and has been feasible technologically, if not politically, for the last hundred years, is a global body politic [...].'However: 'In the age in which mankind has acquired the command over nuclear power, political unification can be accomplished only voluntarily, and, since it is evidently going to be accepted only reluctantly, it seems probable that it will be delayed until mankind has brought upon itself further disasters of a magnitude that will induce it to acquiesce at last in global political union as being the lesser evil.' (p. 593)
14. For developing countries, hints as to the most appropriate choice of sectors to stimulate can be obtained from e.g. Chenery-type patterns of growth studies (c.f. Chenery's (1960) seminal paper and Chenery and Syrquin (1980) for further references), or from Balassa's (1980) 'stages of comparative advantage' study.

15. One example is Van der Zwan et al. (1980); Beckerman (1962) provides an excellent much earlier example.
16. A good case in point is coalmining in The Netherlands. In the early 1960's, when the price of imported oil relative to domestically produced coal was low, the country decided to cease domestic mining. The decision was made virtually irreversable because production was ceased completely, equipment sold or scrapped and the mines destroye At current, 1982, prices mining might have been competitive again if the mines would have been left intact by retaining a token productio This would have improved the flexibility of the economy: production could have been profitably stept up again with the change in conditions.

Chapter 5

1. Their estimates should, however, be interpreted with some care: in Burgess' two (1974 a, b) papers very different estimates are obtaine specifically for the capital-imports elasticity. Burgess does not comment on the differences, but they appear to be caused by the fact that the first (1974a) paper treats output as homogeneous, whereas t second one disaggregates it into investment and consumption goods. A alternative explanation might be that the first paper estimates the production function directly, whereas the second one utilizes dualit to obtain the elasticities indirectly from estimates of cost functions.
2. Theorem 5.4 omits the part of theorem 4.5 devoted to the closed economy. The reason is, that without separability there is no natura way to define a corresponding closed economy. Since the closed econo should, by definition, be independent of trade, the most obvious definition is the same one as in chapter 4, which would not alter th results of theorem 4.5.

   Theorem 5.4 also omits the part of theorem 4.5 that states that $E > -1$ implies zero growth in the long run as long as $H > -1$. This because to establish the statement, one needs to show that $\dot{g}/g$ is strictly negative if $q_m = 0$. In the case of $q_m = 0$ we obtain:

$$\frac{\dot{g}}{g} = - q_\ell' g.$$

If $\dot{g}/g$ is to be strictly negative for $g > 0$, we must have q_ℓ' non-zero. In theorem 4.5 the condition $H > -1$ is sufficient to achieve this, but here an appropriate generalization would be required, similar to (5.21) and (5.22). Since, however, the purpose of theorem 4.5 is to demonstrate that growth remains possible with $E < -1$ and not that it may be impossible with $E > -1$, we forego generalization of the latter part of the theorem.

Chapter 6

1. Sources are UNO Yearbooks of National Account Statistics and Foreign Trade Statistics; also compare appendix 6.1.
2. Since $q_m = mv_m/v$ we have:

$$\frac{\dot{v}_m}{v_m} = \frac{\dot{q}_m}{q_m} - \frac{\dot{m}}{m} + \frac{\dot{v}}{v} .$$

   Inserting (4.28) and (4.25), and noting that $\dot{v}_m/v_m$ equals $\dot{P}/P$ by (6.3), we obtain the south's import-demand equation; the north's equation is symmetric.
3. Specific conditions under which g and $\bar{g}$ indefinitely remain below λ and $\bar{\lambda}$, respectively, are complicated. It can be shown that, at least under constant returns, D and $\bar{D}$ cannot be negative simultaneously if (6.42) and its southern counterpart hold. Therefore the slow-growth path, if it exists, must be oscillating with the two growth rates rising and falling alternately, though always remaining below λ. Clearly, though, the growth rates can only fall if in (6.39) the term MD dominates, since C is always positive if $g < \lambda$. Therefore M must be 'large' and this is seen to imply high import shares combined with low absolute values of E and $\bar{E}$.
4. Constancy of labour's share in domestic factors, q_ℓ, is not necessary to obtain definite results, because the direction of the evolution of the capital-labour ratios is unambiguous. Hence extreme factor ratio conditions of the same type employed in chapter 4 (cf. 4.41) render q_ℓ constant (denoted ξ_ℓ) in the long run. Nevertheless, for simplicity we take the elasticity of capital-labour substitution H to be unity too; the reader interested in non-unit-valued elasticities

can simply replace ξ_ℓ by $\xi_{\ell\infty}$ (with $\xi_{\ell\infty} = 0$ if $H < -1$ and $\xi_{\ell\infty} = 1$ if $H > -1$), as long as the normal conditions of theorems 6.4 and 6.5 are satisfied.

5. The derivative of the per capita growth rate with respect to the natural rate is (for the north) negative if:

$$(\rho-1)\phi - \rho\xi_m\xi_\ell(1 - \rho\bar{\rho}\bar{\xi}_{\bar{m}}) < 0.$$

If $\rho > 1$ the first term is positive; however, with ξ_ℓ, $\bar{\xi}_{\bar{\ell}}$ large and ξ_m, $\bar{\xi}_{\bar{m}}$ small, it is small whereas $\xi_\ell(1 - \rho\bar{\rho}\bar{\xi}_{\bar{m}})$ is large. Of course the latter term is premultiplied by ξ_m, but in ϕ such premultiplication occurs too and there it is quadratic.

6. Only intra-bloc trade is relevant here; because we have introduced inter-bloc trade and its benefits, through economies of scale and increased productivity of capital and labour, explicitly.

7. Anyway, the high rate of increase of specialization in the south is evidence that our estimate of the south's technical progress in the seventies is not too high. A reason to suppose the latter would be th rise in oil prices. The latter might be thought to have raised the south's income without adding factor inputs and hence to be reflecte in our estimate of technical progress. However, the proceeds of the higher oil prices have been mainly used to step-up imports and these are explicitly taken account of in our approach. Thus the estimate o the rate of technical progress should not be biased by the rising oi prices.

8. Thus the issue is an essential element in the debate on the 'New International Economic Order'; for a discussion of many of the aspec of the latter and of the relevant UNO resolutions, cf. Anell and Nygren (1980).

9. This is not only true for the poorest present-day countries, but likewise applied to industrialization's pioneer Britain in the eighteenth century, cf. Pawson (1979).

10. In our steady-growth analysis the assumption of rapid per capita income growth as such already implies that a high rate of technical progress must be postulated: in non-steady growth situations the oth

main source of per capita growth, apart from expanding trade, is capital accumulation; but on the steady-growth path the rate of growth of capital has adjusted to such a value that this source of growth no longer explicitly enters income's growth rate. Therefore, under our maintained hypothesis that the average growth rates in the periods concerned can be adequately described with steady-growth methods, rapid growth must find expression in the other sources of growth.

11. Note however, that the south's real per capita income does grow, reaching by the late 2030's the level presently enjoyed by the north.

Chapter 7

1. This, at least, suggest the opening sentences of his 1952 paper; but a note states that an earlier mathematical version of the paper was prepared for Haberler's 1936-7 Harvard seminar.
2. In her model there are two goods, 'basics' and 'luxuries'. There is no production - all countries have given initial endowments of the two tradeable goods; utility functions display fixed proportions. The donor country's preferences are biased towards 'luxuries', those of the receiving country towards 'basics' and those of the third country are neutral. Both the donor country and the receiving country export 'luxuries' and import 'basics' from the third country.

   Under these conditions a transfer of luxury goods results, if the equilibrium is stable, in a fall of consumption both of luxuries and of basics in the receiving country; this implies a rise in the consumption of both goods in the donor country and the third one combined. It is not clear from Chichilnisky's paper to what extent her results depend on the extreme degree of non-substitutability she presupposes; it seems likely that both the introduction of production, and hence substitutability, on the supply side and of substitution in demand may drastically alter her results. Besides, it is peculiar to consider a transfer of luxuries to a country that already exports these. If the transfer is in basics the Leontief-effect requires once again instability of the equilibrium.
3. That is, the part of output not shipped abroad. For the north it is irrelevant whether the exports are paid for by imports, or given

freely as a transfer. Hence total exports, i.e. including the transfer, are subtracted from output in (7.6). For the south the transfer is incorporated in total output since the additional import it makes possible increase the latter.

4. Empirical evidence relating aid to rates of saving in cross-sections of less-developed countries displays a negative relation (cf. e.g. Papanek, 1972). However, as noted recently by Mosley (1980), this do not reflect a causal relationship but only the fact that the poorest countries save least in relation to their income, whereas they attra more aid precisely because of their poverty.
5. It is negative as long as $1 - q_m + q_m/(1+e+\bar{e})$ is positive; as noted appendix 7.1 the latter is the case for realistic values of the impo share and the import-demand elasticities.
6. Non-vanishing shares and elasticities are obtained by requiring $\lim E\ (Z \to 0, \infty) = -1$ and $\lim H\ (K \to 0, \infty) = -1$.
7. Our optimality problem is a simple version of the Bolza problem. Cesari's existence theorem is well suited to deal with this problem; this theorem is neatly presented by e.g. Fleming and Rishel (1975), 68.

Chapter 8

1. To be precise, let m denote the first region's imports, by definitio equal to the second region's exports; $\bar{m}$ is the first region's export Marshall postulated the first region's export supply, m^s, to be a function of m and the second region's export supply, $\bar{m}^s$, a function of $\bar{m}$. His stability condition is $(\partial\bar{m}^s/\partial m).(\partial m^s/\partial\bar{m}) < 1$.
2. The label is quite inappropriate for two reasons. First, denoting th two elasticities by e and $\bar{e}$, the inequality of the 'Marshall-Lerner condition', $1 + e + \bar{e} < 0$, is not equivalent to Marshall's condition the latter may still be satisfied if $1 + e + \bar{e} > 0$, viz. if one of t elasticities is positive and the other one smaller than minus unity. Second, the interpretation of e is different in Marshall's system an in Lerner's analysis. Lerner simply postulates total imports to be a function of the terms of trade, e being the corresponding elasticity To calculate the elasticity in Marshall's system one has to postulat a closed balance of trade, implying that the terms of trade equal th

ratio of the two trade flows, and then calculate the elasticity of the offercurve. Thus here e does not refer to a causal relationship but to an implicit equation.

As Chipman (1978, p.67) notes, the label 'Marshall-Lerner condition' was first coined by Hirschman (1949, p.52) and given currency by Haberler (1949, p.202). Curiously, the elasticities in the condition of the latter two authors are defined in a way that differs from both Marshall's and Lerner's: they are the partial elasticities of import demand (elasticities with respect to money instead of relative prices) of Bickerdyke (1906, 1907, 1920) and Robinson (1937). These elasticities have been reconciled with a general-equilibrium approach by Negishi (1968), who introduces money to make the system homogeneous in prices and money, and by Dornbusch (1975) and Chipman (1978) who arrive at homogeneity by introducing a non-traded goods sector.

3. Arrow and Hurwicz (1958, p. 525) introduced the procedure to choose units of measurement such that all derivatives of the adjustment functions are equal to unity at the equilibrium. The present case allows $f'(0)$ and $\bar{f}'(0)$ to be selected freely by suitable choice of units for m and $\bar{m}$. However, $h'(0)$ cannot be choosen freely: the units of measurement of P are fixed as soon as those of m and $\bar{m}$ are given. In theorem 8.2 we do not go as far as to select $f'(0)$ and $\bar{f}'(0)$ equal to unity; we just adopt them equal to each other. Of course this can be avoided if one wishes to retain the original units of measurement. In that case the latter turn up in the stability condition, in the form of different weights of $f'(0)$ and $\bar{f}'(0)$ in the sum of these two accelerations.

REFERENCES

Aarrestad, J. (1978) 'On the Optimal Development of Knowledge-Based Industries and the Educational Sector in a Small Open Economy', International Economic Review, 19, 379-394.

Acheson, K. (1970) 'The Aggregation of Heterogeneous Capital Goods and Various Trade Theorems', Journal of Political Economy, 78, 565-571.

Allen, R.G.D. (1938) Mathematical Analysis for Economists, London, MacMillan.

Amano, A. (1968) 'Stability Conditions in the Pure Theory of Internation Trade: a Rehabilitation of the Marshallian Approach', Quarterly Journal of Economics, 82, 326-339.

Anell, S. and B. Nygren (1980) The Developing Countries and the World Economic Order, London, Frances Pinter.

Armington, P.S. (1969) 'A Theory of Demand for Products Distinguished by Place of Production', I.M.F. Staff Papers, 16, 159-178.

Arrow, K.J. and L. Hurwicz (1958) 'On the Stability of the Competitive Equilibrium, 1', Econometrica, 26, 522-552.

Arrow, K.J., H.D. Block and L. Hurwicz (1959) 'On the Stability of the Competitive Equilibrium, 2', Econometrica, 27, 82-109.

Atsumi, H. (1971) 'The Long Run Offer Function and a Dynamic Theory of International Trade', Journal of International Economics, 1, 267-29

Bade, R. (1973) 'Optimal Foreign Investment and International Trade', Economic Record, 49, 62-75.

Bairoch, P. (1975) The Economic Development of the Third World Since 190 London, Methuen & Co.

Balasko, Y. (1978) 'The Transfer Problem and the Theory of Regular Economies', International Economic Review, 19, 687-694.

Balassa, B. (1980) 'A Stages Approach to Comparative Advantage', in I. Adelman (ed.) Economic Growth and Resources, vol. 4, National and International Policies, London, Macmillan (International Economic Association).

Bardhan, P.K. (1965a) 'Equilibrium Growth in the International Economy', Quarterly Journal of Economics, 79, 455-464.

Bardhan, P.K. (1965b) 'Optimum Accumulation and International Trade', Review of Economic Studies, 32, 241-244.

Bardhan, P.K. (1966a) 'On Factor Accumulation and the Pattern of International Specialisation', Review of Economic Studies, 33, 39-44.

Bardhan, P.K. (1966b) 'International Trade Theory in a Vintage Capital Model', Econometrica, 34, 756-767.

Bardhan, P.K. (1970) Economic Growth, Development and Foreign Trade, A Study in Pure Theory, New York, Wiley.

Bardhan, P.K. (1973) 'Review of Takayama's (1972) International Trade', Journal of International Economics, 3, 298-300.

Batra, R.N. and F.R. Casas (1973) 'Intermediate Products and the Pure Theory of International Trade: a Neo Heckscher-Ohlin Framework', American Economic Review, 63, 297-311.

Bazdarich, M.J. (1978) 'Optimal Growth and Stages in the Balance of Payments', Journal of International Economics, 8, 425-443.

Beckerman, W. (1962) 'Projecting Europe's Growth', Economic Journal, 72, 912-925.

Benhabib, J. and K. Nishimura (1979) 'The Hopf Bifurcation and the Existence and Stability of Closed Orbits in Multisector Models of Economic Growth', Journal of Economic Theory, 21, 421-444.

Benhabib, J. and K. Nishimura (1981) 'Stability of Equilibrium in Dynamic Models of Capital Theory, International Economic Review, 22, 275-293.

Bensusan-Butt, D.M. (1954) 'A Model of Trade and Accumulation', American Economic Review, 44, 511-529.

Berndt, E.R. and D.O. Wood (1979) 'Engineering and Econometric Interpretations of Energy-Capital Complementarity', American Economic Review, 69, 342-354.

Bertrand, T.J. (1973) 'Trade and Growth: a Comment', Journal of International Economics, 3, 193-196.

Bertrand, T.J. (1975) 'The Gains from Trade: an Analysis of Steady-State Solutions in an Open Economy', Quarterly Journal of Economics, 89, 556-568.

Bhagwati, J. (1969) Trade, Tariffs and Growth, Essays in International Economics, London, Weidenfeld and Nicolson.

Bickerdyke, C.F. (1906) 'The Theory of Incipient Taxes', Economic Journal, 16, 529-535.

Bickerdyke, C.F. (1907) 'Review of Pigou's "Protective and Preferential Import Duties"', Economic Journal, 17, 98-102.

Bickerdyke, C.F. (1920) 'The Instability of Foreign Exchange', Economic

Journal, 30, 118-122.

Black, J. (1970) 'Trade and the Natural Growth Rate', Oxford Economic Papers, N.S., 22, 13-23.

Blackorby, C., D. Primont and R.R. Russel (1978) Duality, Separability, and Functional Structure: Theory and Economic Applications, New York North Holland.

Brems, H. (1956) 'The Foreign Trade Accelerator and the International Transmission of Growth', Econometrica, 24, 223-238.

Brems, H. (1959) Output, Employment, Capital, and Growth, New York, Harper.

Bruce, N. (1977) 'The Effects of Trade Taxes in a Two-Sector Model of Capital Accumulation', Journal of International Economics, 7, 283-294.

Burgess, D.F. (1974a) 'Production Theory and the Derived Demand for Imports', Journal of International Economics, 4, 103-117.

Burgess, D.F. (1974b) 'A Cost Minimization Approach to Import Demand Equations', Review of Economics and Statistics, 56, 225-234.

Burmeister, E. (1978) 'An Interest Rate and Factor Price Equalization Theorem with Non-Traded Commodities', Journal of International Economics, 8, 1-9.

Cesari, L. (1966) 'Existence Theorems for Weak and Usual Optimal Solution in Lagrange Problems with Unilateral Constraints', Trans. Am. Math. Soc., 124, 369-412.

Chacoliades, M. (1970) 'Balance of Payments Equilibrium with Imports as a Factor of Production', Oxford Economic Papers, N.S., 22, 173-193.

Chacoliades, M. (1971) 'Imported Inputs under Variable Proportions', Oxford Economic Papers, N.S., 23, 169-181.

Chacoliades, M. (1978) International Trade Theory and Policy, Second Edition, New York, Mc.Graw-Hill.

Chacoliades, M. (1979) 'Intermediate Products in the Theory of International Trade', Economic Perspectives, 1, 151-172.

Chenery, H.B. (1960) 'Patterns of Industrial Growth', American Economic Review, 50, 624-654.

Chenery, H.B. and M. Bruno (1962) 'Development Alternatives in an Open Economy: the Case of Israel', Economic Journal, 72, 79-103.

Chenery, H.B. and A.M. Strout (1966) 'Foreign Assistance and Economic Development', American Economic Review, 56, 679-733.

Chenery, H.B. (1977) 'Transitional Growth and World Industrialization', in B. Ohlin, P.O. Hesselborn and P.M. Wijkman (eds.) The International Allocation of Economic Activity, London, Macmillan.

Chenery, H.B. and M. Syrquin (1980) 'A Comparative Analysis of Industrial Growth', in R.C.O. Matthews (ed.) Economic Growth and Resources, Volume 2, Trends and Factors, London, Macmillan.

Chichilnisky, G. (1980) 'Basic Goods, the Effects of Commodity Transfers and the International Economic Order', Journal of Development Economics, 7, 505-519.

Chichilnisky, G. (1981) 'Terms of Trade and Domestic Distribution, Export-Led Growth with Abundant Labour', Journal of Development Economics, 8, 163-192.

Chipman, J.S. (1965a,b, 1966) 'A Survey of the Theory of International Trade, Part 1, The Classical Theory', Econometrica, 33, 477-519, 'Part 2, The Neo-Classical Theory', Econometrica, 33, 685-760, 'Part 3, The Modern Theory', Econometrica, 34, 18-76.

Chipman, J.S. (1972) 'The Theory of Exploitative Trade and Investment Policies: a Reformulation and Synthesis', in L.E. Di Marco (ed.) International Trade and Development, Essays in Honor of Raúl Prebisch, New York, Academic Press.

Chipman, J.S. (1978) 'A Reconsideration of the "Elasticity Approach" to Balance-of-Payments Adjustment Problems', in J.S. Dreyer (ed.) Breadth and Depth in Economics, Fritz Machlup - The Man and his Ideas, Lexington, Lexington Books.

Corden, W.M. (1971) 'The Effects of Trade on the Rate of Growth', in J. Bhagwati et al. (eds.) Trade, Balance of Payments and Welfare, Essays in Honor of C.P. Kindleberger, Amsterdam, North-Holland.

Daly, H.E. (1977) Steady-State Economics; The Economics of Biophysical Equilibrium and Moral Growth, San Francisco, Freeman.

Deardorff, A.V. (1973) 'The Gains from Trade in and out of Steady State', Oxford Economic Papers, N.S., 25, 173-191.

Deardorff, A.V. (1974a) 'Trade Reversals and Growth Stability', Journal of International Economics, 4, 83-90.

Deardorff, A.V. (1974b) 'A Geometry of Growth and Trade', Canadian Journal of Economics, 7, 295-306.

Deardorff, A.V. (1974c) 'Factor Proportions and Comparative Advantage in the Long Run: Comment', Journal of Political Economy, 82, 829-833.

Deardorff, A.V. and J.A. Hanson (1978) 'Accumulation and a Long Run Heckscher-Ohlin Theorem', Economic Inquiry, 16, 288-292.

Dei, F. (1979) 'Dynamic Gains from International Capital Movements', Journal of International Economics, 9, 417-421.

Denison, E.F. (1979) Accounting for Slower Economic Growth: The United States in the 1970's, Washington, The Brookings Institution.

Der, W. (1979) 'Multi-Intermediate-Goods Trade: the Gains and a Heckscher-Ohlin Analysis', American Economic Review, 69, 575-586.

Diaz-Alejandro, C.F. (1975) 'Trade Policies and Economic Development', in P.B. Kenen (ed.) International Trade and Finance, Cambridge, Cambridge University Press.

Diaz-Alejandro, C.F. (1980) 'Changes in Trade Shares and Economic Growth, Discussion', American Economic Review, 70, 299-300.

Dixit, A. (1978) 'On Rybczinski's Theorem in a Setting of Growth', Journal of International Economics, 8, 127-129.

Dixit, A. (1981) 'The Export of Capital Theory', Journal of International Economics, 11, 279-294.

Dornbusch, R. (1975) 'Exchange Rates and Fiscal Policy in a Popular Model of International Trade', American Economic Review, 65, 859-871.

Drandakis, M. (1963) 'Factor Substitution in the Two-Sector Growth Model', Review of Economic Studies, 30, 217-228.

Edgeworth, F.Y. (1894) 'The Theory of International Values, 1, 2 and 3', Economic Journal, 4, 35-50, 424-443, 606-638.

Elkan, P.G. (1970) 'A Model of Industrialization and Trade with external and Internal Scale Effects', Oxford Economic Papers, N.S., 22, 194-219.

Emmanuel, A. (1969) L'exchange Inégal, Paris, Librairie François Masparo.

Emmanuel, A. (1978) 'A Note on Trade Pattern Reversals', Journal of International Economics, 8, 143-145.

Ethier, W. (1979a) 'The Theorems of International Trade in Time-Phased Economies', Journal of International Economics, 9, 225-238.

Ethier, W. (1979b) 'Internationally Decreasing Costs and World Trade', Journal of International Economics, 9, 1-24.

Ethier, W. (1981) 'A Reply to Professors Metcalfe and Steedman', Journal of International Economics, 11, 273-277.

Findlay, R. (1970) 'Factor Proportions and Comparative Advantage in the Long Run', Journal of Political Economy, 78, 27-34.

Findlay, R. (1978) 'An "Austrian" Model of International Trade and Interest Rate Equalization', Journal of Political Economy, 86, 989-1007.

Findlay, R. (1980) 'The Terms of Trade and Equilibrium Growth in the World Economy', American Economic Review, 70, 291-299.

Finger, J.M. and D.A. De Rosa (1979) 'Trade Overlap, Comparative Advantage and Protection', in H. Giersch (ed.) On the Economics of Intra-Industry Trade, Tübingen, J.C.B. Mohr (Paul Siebeck).

Fischer, S. and J.A. Frenkel (1972) 'Investment, the Two-Sector Model, and Trade in Debt and Capital Goods', Journal of International Economics, 2, 211-233.

Fischer, S. and J.A. Frenkel (1974a) 'Interest Rate Equalization and Patterns of Production, Trade and Consumption in a Two-Country Growth Model', Economic Record, 50, 555-580.

Fischer, S. and J.A. Frenkel (1974b) 'Economic Growth and Stages in the Balance of Payments, a Theoretical Model', in G. Horwich and P.A. Samuelson (eds.) Trade, Stability and Macro-Economics, Essays in Honor of L.A. Metzler, New York, Academic Press.

Fisher, F.M. (1969) 'The Existence of Aggregate Production Functions', Econometrica, 37, 553-577.

Fisher, F.M. (1971) 'Aggregate Production Functions and the Explanation of Wages: a Simulation Experiment', Review of Economics and Statistics, 53, 305-326.

Fisher, F.M., R.M. Solow and J.M. Kearl (1977) 'Aggregate Production Functions: Some CES Experiments', Review of Economic Studies, 44, 305-320.

Fleming, W.H. and R.W. Rishel (1975) Deterministic and Stochastic Optimal Control, Berlin, Springer.

Frenkel, J.A. (1971) 'A Theory of Money, Trade and the Balance of Payments in a Model of Accumulation', Journal of International Economics, 1, 159-187.

Gabisch, G. (1975) 'A Vintage Capital Model of International Trade, the Case of Trade with Second Hand Machines', Journal of International Economics, 5, 365-383.

Gabisch, G. (1977) 'Ein Dynamisches Aussenhandelsmodell vom Harrod-Domar Typ', in H. Albach et al. (eds.) Quantitative Wirtschaftsforschung, Wilhelm Krelle zum 60. Geburtstag, Tübingen, J.C.B. Mohr (Paul

Siebeck).

Gale, D. (1971) 'General Equilibrium with Imbalance of Trade', Journal of International Economics, 1, 141-158.

Gale, D. (1974) 'The Trade Imbalance Story', Journal of International Economics, 4, 119-137.

Giarini, O. (1980) Dialogue on Wealth and Welfare; an Alternative View of World Capital Formation, Oxford, Pergamom Press.

Gilbert, C.L. (1980) 'Statistical Methodology and the Use of Economic and Social Indicators in the Estimation of Per Capita GDP Levels for Developing Countries', Oxford Bulletin of Economics and Statistics, 42, 281-303.

Haberler, G. (1949) 'The Market for Foreign Exchange and the Stability of the Balance of Payments, a Theoretical Analysis', Kyklos, 3, 193-218

Hahn, F.H. and R.C.O. Matthews (1964) 'The Theory of Economic Growth: a Survey', Economic Journal, 74, 779-902.

Hahn, W. (1967) Stability of Motion, Berlin, Springer.

Hanson, J.A. (1971) Growth in Open Economics, Berlin, Springer.

Harrod, R.F. (1936) The Trade Cycle, Oxford, Oxford University Press.

Hasselman, B.H., J.J. Post and C.A. van den Beld (1977) 'The Fix-Point Estimation Method and a Revision of the 69-C Annual Model', in C.A. van Bochove et al. (eds.), Modeling for Government and Business, Essays in Honor of Prof.Dr.P.J. Verdoorn, Leiden, Martinus Nijhoff.

Hicks, J.R. (1932) The Theory of Wages, London, Macmillan.

Hilgerdt, F. (1945) Industrialisation et Commerce Extérieur, Geneve, Sociètè des Nations.

Hill, C.T. and J.M. Utterback (1979) Technological Innovation for a Dynamic Economy, New York, Pergamom.

Hirsch, S. (1975) 'The Product Cycle Model of International Trade - A Multi-Country Cross-Section Analysis', Oxford Bulletin of Economics and Statistics, 37, 305-317.

Hirschman, A.O. (1949) 'Devaluation and the Trade Balance: a Note', Revie of Economcis and Statistics, 31, 50-53.

Hoffman, L. and B. Weber (1976) 'Economies of Scale, Factor Intensities and Substitution: Micro Estimates for Malaysia's Manufacturing Industries', Weltwirtschaftliches Archiv, 112, 111-135.

Hori, H. and J.L. Stein (1977) 'International Growth with Free Trade in Equities and Goods', International Economic Review, 18, 83-100.

Houthakker, H.S. (1955/6) 'The Pareto Distribution and the Cobb-Douglas Production Function in Activity Analysis', Review of Economic Studies, 23, 27-31.

Humphries, J. (1976) 'Causes of Growth', Economic Development and Cultural Change, 25, 339-353.

Inada, K.I. (1962/3) 'On a Two-Sector Model of Economic Growth: Comments and a Generalization', Review of Economic Studies, 30, 119-127.

Inada, K.I. (1968) 'Free Trade, Capital Accumulation and Factor Price Equalization', Economic Record, 44, 322-341.

Inada, K.I. (1971) 'Development in Monocultural Economics', International Economic Review, 12 161-185.

Itsumi, Y and C. Morigushi (1978) 'Terms of Trade and Full Capacity Growth in a Resource Importing Economy', Journal of International Economics, 8, 117-126.

Johnson, H.G. (1953) 'Equilibrium Growth in an International Economy', Canadian Journal of Economics and Political Science, 19, 478-500.

Johnson, H.G. (1953/4) 'Optimum Tariffs and Retaliation', Review of Economic Studies, 21, 142-153.

Johnson, H.G. (1958) International Trade and Economic Growth, Studies in Pure Theory, London, Allen and Unwin.

Johnson, H.G. (1971a) 'The Theory of Trade and Growth: a Diagrammetic Analysis', in J. Bhagwati et al. (eds.) Trade, Balance of Payments and Welfare, Essays in Honor of C.P. Kindleberger, Amsterdam, North Holland.

Johnson, H.G. (1971b) 'Trade and Growth: a Geometrical Exposition', Journal of International Economics, 1, 83-101.

Johnson, H.G. (1972) 'Trade and Growth, a Correction', Journal of International Economics, 2, 87-88.

Jones, R.W. (1970) 'The Transfer Problem Reconsidered', Economica, N.S., 37, 178-184.

Jones, R.W. (1975) 'Presumption and the Transfer Problem', Journal of International Economics, 5, 263-274.

Jones, R.W. (1976) 'Terms of Trade and Transfer: the Relevance of the Literature', in D. Leipziger (ed.) The International Monetary System and the Developing Nations, Washington, AID.

Jones, R.W. (1979) International Trade: Essays in Theory, Amsterdam, North Holland.

Jorgenson, D.W. and Z. Griliches (1967) 'The Explanation of Productivity Change', Review of Economic Studies, 34, 249-283.

Kapur, B.K. (1981) 'Traded Goods, Nontraded Goods, and the Balance of Payments: a Steady-State Analysis', International Economic Review, 22, 167-178.

Kemp, M.C. (1964) The Pure Theory of International Trade, Englewood Cliffs, Prentice Hall.

Kemp, M.C. (1968) 'International Trade and Investment in a Context of Growth', Economic Record, 44, 211-223.

Kemp, M.C. (1969) The Pure Theory of International Trade and Investment, Englewood Cliffs, Prentice Hall.

Kemp, M.C. (1970) 'International Trade between Countries with Different Natural Rates of Growth', Economic Record, 46, 467-481.

Kemp, M.C. (1973) 'Heterogeneous Capital Goods and Long Run Stolper Samuelson Theorems', Australian Economic Papers, 12, 253-260.

Kemp, M.C. and C. Khang (1977) 'On the Relationship between Commodity Prices and Gross Outputs in a General Neo-Classical Technology', International Economic Review, 18, 241-245.

Kemp, M.C. and N.V. Long (1979) 'International Trade with an Exhaustible Resource: a Theorem of Rybczinsky Type', International Economic Review, 20, 671-677.

Kemp, M.C. and N.V. Long (1980) Exhaustible Resources, Optimality, and Trade, Amsterdam, North Holland.

Kennedy, C. and A.P. Thirlwall (1973) 'Technical Progress', in The Royal Economic Society, The Social Science Research Council, Surveys of Applied Economics, London, Macmillan.

Keynes, J.M. (1929) 'The German Transfer Problem', Economic Journal, 39, 1-7; 'The Reparations Problem: a Discussion, II, a Rejoinder', ibid, 179-182; 'Mr. Keynes' Views on the Transfer Problem III, a Reply', ibid, 404-408.

Khang, C. (1968) 'A Neoclassical Growth Model of a Resource-Poor Open Economy', International Economic Review, 9, 329-338.

Khang, C. (1969) 'A Dynamic Model of Trade between the Final and the Intermediate Products', Journal of Economic Theory, 1, 416-437.

Khang, C. (1971) 'Equilibrium Growth in the International Economy: the Case of Unequal Natural Rates of Growth', International Economic Review, 12, 239-249.

Kohli, U.R. (1978) 'A Gross National Product Function and the Derived Demand for Imports and the Supply of Exports', Canadian Journal of Economics, 11, 167-182.

Kravis, I.B. (1970) 'Trade as a Handmaiden of Growth: Similarities between the Nineteenth and the Twentieth Centuries', Economic Journal, 80, 850-872.

Krelle, W. (1969) Produktionsthorie, Teil 1; Preistheorie, 2. Auflage, Tübingen, J.C.B. Mohr (Paul Siebeck).

Kreyger, R.G. (1980) 'Imports as a Factor of Production: the Substitution Characteristics of Labour, Capital and Material Imports in the Dutch Enterprise Sector', Report AE 7180, Faculty of Actuarial Science and Econometrics, University of Amsterdam.

Krueger, A.O. (1980) 'Trade Policy as an Input to Development', American Economic Review, 70, 288-292.

Krugman, P. (1981) 'Trade, Accumulation and Uneven Development', Journal of Development Economics, 8, 149-161.

Kuga, K. (1973) 'Tariff Retaliation and Policy Equilibrium', Journal of International Economics, 3, 351-366.

Kuo, C.Y. (1977) 'Intermediate Products and the Two-Sector Growth Model in an Open Economy', Economic Record, 53, 96-109.

Kuznets, S. (1967) 'Quantitative Aspects of the Economic Growth of Nations: X, Level and Structure of Foreign Trade: Long Term Trends', Economic Development and Cultural Change, 15, 1-40.

Kuznets, S. (1972) 'Problems in Comparing Recent Growth Rates for Developed and Less Developed Countries', Economic Development and Cultural Change, 20, 185-209.

Landes, D.S. (1980) 'The "Great Drain" and Industrialization: Commodity Flows from Periphery to Center in Historical Perspective', in R.C.O. Matthews (ed.) Economic Growth and Resources, Volume 2, Trends and Factors, London, Macmillan.

Leakey, E. and R. Lewin (1979) People of the Lake, Mankind and its Beginnings, New York, Avon.

Leontief, W. (1936) 'Note on the Pure Theory of Capital Transfer', in Exploration in Economics, Notes and Essays Contributed in Honor of F.W. Taussig, New York, Mc.Graw Hill.

Leontief, W. (1941) The Structure of American Economy, 1919-1929, Cambridge, Harvard University Press.

Leontief, W. (1947a) 'A Note on the Interrelation of Subsets of Independent Variables of a Continuous Function with Continuous First Derivatives', Bulletin of the Am.Math.Soc., 53, 343-350.

Leontief, W. (1947b) 'Introduction to a Theory of the Internal Structure of Functional Relationships', Econometrica, 15, 361-373.

Lerner, A.P. (1936) 'The Symmetry between Import and Export Taxes', Economica, N.S., 3, 306-313.

Lerner, A.P. (1944) The Economics of Control, Principles of Welfare Economics, New York, Macmillan.

Levhari, D. (1968) 'A Note on Houthakker's Aggregate Production Function in a Multifirm Industry', Econometrica, 36, 151-154.

Lewis, W.A. (1952) 'World Production, Prices and Trade, 1870-1960', Manchester School of Economic and Social Studies, 20, 105-138.

Lewis, W.A. (1980) 'The Slowing Down of the Engine of Growth', American Economic Review, 70, 555-564.

Machlup, F. (1943) International Trade and the National Income Multiplier Philadelphia, Blakeston.

Maddison, A. (1980) 'Phases of Capitalist Development', in R.C.O. Matthews (ed.) Economic Growth and Resources, Volume 2, Trends and Factors, London, Macmillan.

Malinvaud, E. (1980) 'Costs of Economic Growth', in E. Malinvaud (ed.) Economic Growth and Resources, Volume 1, The Major Issues, London, Macmillan.

Manning, R. (1981) 'Specialization and Dynamics in a Trade Model', Economic Record, 57, 251-260.

Marshall, A. (circa 1873) 'Essay on Absenteism', in J.K. Whitaker (ed.) The Early Economic Writings of Alfred Marshall, 1867-1890, Part I, London, Macmillan, 1975.

Marshall, A. (circa 1874) 'Essay on International Trade', in J.K. Whitaker (ed.) The Early Economic Writings of Alfred Marshall, 1867-1890, Part I, London, Macmillan, 1975.

Marshall, A. (1879) The Pure Theory of Foreign Trade. The Pure Theory of Domestic Values, Privately Printed. Reprinted (1930, 1935, 1949) by The London School of Economics, and in J.K. Whitaker The Early Economic Writings of Alfred Marshall, Volume 2, London, Macmillan, 1975.

Marshall, A. (1923) Money, Credit and Commerce, London, Macmillan.

Marx, K. (1885) Das Kapital, Kritik der Politischen Oekonomie, 2, Der Zirkulationsprozess des Kapitals, Hamburg, Otto Meissner. Page references to Karl Marx - Friedrich Engels, Werk, 24, Berlin, Dutz Verlag, 1963.

McDougall, I.A. (1965) 'Non-Traded Goods and the Transfer Problem', Review of Economic Studies, 32, 67-84.

Meade, J. (1948, 1949) 'National Income, National Expenditure and the Balance of Payments', Part 1, Economic Journal, 58, 483-505, Continued, ibid, 59, 17-39.

Meade, J. (1951) The Theory of International Economic Policy, Volume one, The Balance of Payments, Mathematical Supplement, Oxford, Oxford University Press.

Melvin, J.R. (1968) 'Production and Trade with Two Factors and Three Goods', American Economic Review, 58, 1249-1268.

Metcalfe, J.S. and I. Steedman (1981) 'On the Transformation of Theorems', Journal of International Economics, 11, 267-271.

Metzler, L.A. (1942) 'Unemployment Equilibrium in International Trade', Econometrica, 10, 97-112.

Mill, J.S. (1844) 'Of the Laws of Interchange between Nations', in Essays on Some Unsettled Questions of Political Economy, London, Parker. Page references to Collected Works of John Stuart Mill, vol. IV, London, University of Toronto Press, 1967.

Morishima, M. (1969) The Theory of Economic Growth, Oxford, Oxford University Press.

Mosley, P. (1980) 'Aid, Savings and Growth Revisited', Oxford Bulletin of Economics and Statistics, 42, 79-95.

Mulhall, M.G. (1909) The Dictionary of Statistics, Fourth Edition, Reimpression, London, Routhledge and Sons.

Mundell, R.A. (1960) 'The Pure Theory of International Trade', American Economic Review, 50, 67-110.

Mundell, R.A. (1968) International Economics, New York, Macmillan.

Negishi, T. (1968) 'Approaches to the Analysis of Devaluation', International Economic Review, 9, 218-227.

Negishi, T. (1972) General Equilibrium Theory and International Trade, Amsterdam, North Holland.

Nurkse, R. (1959) 'Patterns of Trade and Development' (1959 Wicksell Lectures), in G. Haberler and R.M. Stern (eds.) Equilibrium and

Growth in the World Economy, Economic Essays by Ragnar Nurkse, Cambridge, Harvard University Press, 1961.

Ohlin, B. (1929) 'The Reparations Problem: a Discussion I, Transfer Problems, Real and Imagined', Economic Journal, 39, 172-178; 'Mr. Keynes' Views on the Transfer Problem, II, a Rejoinder', ibid, 400-404.

Oniki, H. and H. Uzawa (1965) 'Patterns of Trade and Investment in a Dynamic Model of International Trade', Review of Economic Studies, 32, 15-38.

Orme, M. (1979) Micros: a Pervasive Force. A Study of the Impact of Micro-Electronics on Business and Society 1946-90, London, Associated Business Press.

Papanek, G. (1972) 'The Effect of Aid and Other Resource Transfers on Savings and Growth in Less Developed Countries', Economic Journal, 82, 934-980.

Parrinello, S. (1970) 'Introduzione ad una Teoria Nericardiana del Commercio Internazionale' Studi Economici, 267-321.

Pawson, E. (1979) The Early Industrial Revolution. Britain in the Eighteenth Century, London, Batsford Academic.

Petith, H.C. (1972) 'Vintage Capital, Joint Production and the Theory of International Trade', International Economic Review, 13, 148-159.

Petith, H.C. (1974) 'The Pattern of Trade in a Neoclassical Growth Model with a General Saving Function', Journal of International Economics, 4, 387-393.

Petith, H.C. (1976) 'The Stolper Samuelson Theorem, the Rybczinski Theorem, and the Pattern of Trade in Neoclassical and Vintage Capita Trade and Growth Models', International Economic Review, 17, 57-75.

Pontryagin, L.S., V.E. Boltyanskii, R.V. Gamkrelidze, and E.F. Mischenko (1962) The Mathematical Theory of Optimal Processes, translated by K.N. Trirogoff (edited by L.W. Neustadt), New York, John Wiley; also translated by D.E. Brown, New York, Pergamom Press, 1964; original edition: Moscow, Fizmatgiz, 1961.

Powers, R.M. (1980) Planetary Encounters, the Future of Unmanned Spaceflight, revised edition, New York, Warner Books.

Ramanathan, R. (1975) 'Monetary Expansion, Balance of Trade and Economic Growth', Economic Record, 51, 31-39.

Ricardo, D. (1817) On the Principles of Political Economy and Taxation,

London, John Murray. Modern edition: P. Sraffa (ed.) The Works and Correspondence of David Ricardo, vol. 1, Cambridge, Cambridge University Press, 1951.

Roberts, W.W. (1978) 'Monetary Expansion in an Open Economy of Intermediate Size', Economic Record, 54, 380-386.

Robinson, J. (1937a) 'Beggar-my-Neighbour Remedies for Unemployment', in Essays in the Theory of Employment, London, Macmillan.

Robinson, J. (1937b) 'The Foreign Exchanges' in Essays in the Theory of Employment, London, Macmillan.

Rostow, W.W. (1977) 'Economic Growth: Past and Future', in C.L. Cooper (ed.) Growth in America, Westport, London, Greenwood Press.

Rostow, W.W. (1978) The World Economy, History and Prospect, London, Macmillan.

Rostow, W.W. (1980) Why the Poor Get Richer and the Rich Slow Down; Essays in the Marshallian Long Period, London, Macmillan.

Ruffin, R.J. (1979) 'Growth and the Long-Run Theory of International Capital Movements', American Economic Review, 69, 832-842.

Ryder, H.E. (1967) 'Optimal Accumulation and Trade in an Open Economy of Moderate Size', in K. Shell (ed.) Essays in the Theory of Optimal Economic Growth, Cambridge, MIT Press.

Samuelson, P.A. (1942) 'The Stability of Equilibrium: Linear and Non-Linear Systems', Econometrica, 10, 1-25.

Samuelson, P.A. (1947) Foundations of Economic Analysis, Cambridge, Harvard University Press.

Samuelson, P.A. (1951) 'Abstract of a Theorem Concerning Substitutability in Open Leontief Models', in T.C. Koopmans (ed.) Activity Analysis of Production and Allocation, New York, John Wiley.

Samuelson, P.A. (1952) 'The Transfer Problem and Transport Costs: the Terms of Trade when Impediments are Absent', Economic Journal, 62, 278-304.

Samuelson, P.A. (1954) 'The Transfer Problem and Transfer Costs II: Analysis of Effects of Trade Impediments', Economic Journal, 62, 278-304.

Samuelson, P.A. (1965) 'Equalization by Trade of the Interest Rate along with the Real Wage', in R.E. Baldwin et al. (eds.) Trade, Growth and the Balance of Payments, Chicago, Rand Mc.Nally and Company.

Samuelson, P.A. (1968) 'The Transfer Problem and Transfer Costs (condensed version of 1952 and 1954 papers), R.E. Caves and H.G. Johnson (eds.) Readings in International Economics, Homewood, Illinois.

Samuelson, P.A. (1971) 'On the Trail of Conventional Beliefs about the Transfer Problem', in J. Bhagwati et al. (eds.) Trade, Balance of Payments and Growth: Papers in Honor of Charles Kindleberger, Amsterdam, North Holland.

Samuelson, P.A. (1973) 'Deadweight Loss in International Trade from the Profit Motive', in L.F. Bergsten and W.G. Tyler (eds.) Leading Issues in International Economic Policy: Essays in Honor of George N. Halm, Lexington, Lexington Books.

Samuelson, P.A. (1974) 'Marx as a Mathematical Economist, Steady State and Exponential Growth Equilibrium', in G. Horwich and P.A. Samuelson (eds.) Trade, Stability and Macro-Economics, Essays in Honor of L.A. Metzler, New York, Academic Press.

Samuelson, P.A. (1975) 'Trade Pattern Reversals in Time-Phased Ricardian Systems and Intertemporal Efficiency', Journal of International Economics, 5, 309-363.

Samuelson, P.A. (1976) 'Illogic of Neo-Marxian Doctrine of Unequal Exchange', in D.A. Belsley et al. (eds.) Inflation, Trade and Taxes, Essays in Honor of Alice Bourneuf, Columbus, Ohio State University Press.

Samuelson, P.A. (1978a) 'The Canonical Classical Model of Political Economy', Journal of Economic Literature, 16, 1415-34.

Samuelson, P.A. (1978b) 'Interest Rate Equalization and Non-Equalization by Trade in Leontief-Sraffa Models', Journal of International Economics, 8, 21-27.

Samuelson, P.A. (1978c) 'Free Trade's Intertemporal Pareto Optimality', Journal of International Economics, 8, 147-149.

Samuelson, P.A. (1978d) 'Pseudo Maximization to the Rescue of Derived Factor Demand of a Competitive Industry', in J.S. Dreyer (ed.) Breadth and Depth in Economics, Fritz Machlup - the Man and his Ideas, Lexington, Lexington Books.

Sato, K. (1966) 'On the Adjustment Time in Neo-Classical Growth Models', Review of Economic Studies, 33, 263-268.

Sato, K. (1967) 'A Two-Level Constant Elasticity of Substitution Production Function', Review of Economic Studies, 34, 201-218.

Sato, K. (1975) Production Functions and Aggregation, Amsterdam, North

Holland.

Sato, R. (1963) 'Fiscal Policy in a Neo-Classical Growth Model: An Analysis of Time Required for Equilibrating Adjustment', Review of Economic Studies, 30, 16-23.

Sato, R. (1969) 'Stability Conditions in Two-Sector Models of Economic Growth', Journal of Economic Theory, 1, 107-117.

Sawyer, T.A. (1979) (ed.) Modelling the International Transmission Mechanism, Applications and Extensions of the LINK System, North Holland, Amsterdam.

Scitovsky, T. (1941/2) 'A Reconsideration of the Theory of Tariffs', Review of Economic Studies, 23, 101-108.

Schmid, M. (1976) 'A Model of Trade in Money, Goods and Factors', Journal of International Economics, 6, 347-361.

Seers, D. (1962) 'A Model of Comparative Rates of Growth in the World Economy', Economic Journal, 72, 45-78.

Shieh, Y.N. and A. Takayama (1980) 'Monetary Expansion, Balance of Trade and Economic Growth: Comments and Clarifications', Economic Record, 56, 94-98.

Smallwood, C. (1975) 'Economic Growth and the Pure Theory of International Trade', Scottish Journal of Political Economy, 22, 135-159.

Smith, M.A.M. (1974) 'International Trade in Second Hand Machines', Journal of Development Economics, 1, 261-278.

Smith, M.A.M. (1976a) 'International Trade Theory in Vintage Models', Review of Economic Studies, 43, 99-113.

Smith, M.A.M. (1976b) 'Trade, Growth and Consumption in Alternative Models of Capital Accumulation', Journal of International Economics, 6, 371-384.

Smith, M.A.M. (1976c) 'Trade in Second Hand Machines, a Comment', Journal of International Economics, 6, 389.

Smith, M.A.M. (1977) 'Capital Accumulation in the Open Two-Sector Economy', Economic Journal, 87, 273-282.

Smith, M.A.M. (1979) 'Intertemporal Gains from Trade', Journal of International Economics, 9, 239-248.

Solow, J. (1979) 'A General Equilibrium Approach to Capital-Energy Complementarity', Economics Letters, 2, 91-94.

Solow, R.M. (1965/6) 'The Production Function and the Theory of Capital', Review of Economic Studies, 23, 101-108.

Solow, R.M. (1958) 'A Skeptical Note on the Constancy of Relative Shares', American Economic Review, 48, 618-631.

Solow, R.M. (1964) 'Capital, Labour, and Income in Manufacturing', in The Behavior of Income Shares, Studies in Income and Wealth, Vol. 27, Princeton, Princeton University Press.

Sono, M. (1945) 'The Effect of Price Changes on the Demand and Supply of Separable Goods', Japanese, Kokumin Keisai Zasshi, 74, 1-51. English translation (1961) International Economic Review, 2, 239-271.

Sraffa, P. (1960) Production of Commodities by means of Commodities, Prelude to a Critique of Economic Theory, Cambridge, Cambridge University Press.

Steedman, I. (1979a) (ed.) Fundamental Issues in Trade Theory, London, Macmillan.

Steedman, I. (1979b) Trade amongst Growing Economies, Cambridge, Cambridge University Press.

Stein, L. (1981) 'The Growth and Implications of LDC Manufactured Exports to Advanced Countries', Kyklos, 34, 36-59.

Stiglitz, J.E. (1970) 'Factor Price Equalization in a Dynamic Economy', Journal of Political Economy, 77, 456-488.

Takayama, A. (1972) International Trade. An Approach to the Theory, New York, Holt, Rinehart and Winston.

Takayama, A. (1974) Mathematical Economics, New York, Holt, Rinehart and Winston.

Taussig, F.W. (1906) 'Wages and Prices in Relation to International Trade', Quarterly Journal of Economics, 20, 497-522.

Taussig, F.W. (1912) Principles of Economics, Part I, New York, Macmillan.

Taussig, F.W. (1915) Some Aspects of the Tariff Question, Cambridge, Harvard University Press.

Taylor, L. (1981) 'South-North Trade and Southern Growth, Bleak Prospects from the Structuralist Point of View', Journal of International Economics, 11, 589-602.

Tinbergen, J. (1941) 'Unstable and Indifferent Equilibria in Economic Systems', Revue de l'Institut International de Statistique, 9, 36-50.

Tinbergen, J. and H.C. Bos (1962) Mathematical Models of Economic Growth, New York, McGraw Hill.

Togan, S. (1975) 'The Gains from International Trade in the Context of a Growing Economy', Journal of International Economics, 5, 229-238.

Toynbee, A. (1976) Mankind and Mother Earth. A Narrative History of the World, New York, Oxford University Press.

Tsuru, S. (1980) Economic Growth and Resources, Volume 5, Problems Relating to Japan, London, Macmillan.

UNIDO (1979) World Industry since 1960: Progress and Prospects, special issue of the Industrial Development Survey for the third general conference of UNIDO, New York, United Nations.

Uzawa, H. (1961/2, 1962/3) 'On a Two-Sector Model of Economic Growth', Review of Economic Studies, 29, 40-47; II, 30, 105-118.

Van Bochove, C.A. and A.S.W. De Vries (1977) 'Two-Way Trade in a Verdoorn Type Model', in C.A. Van Bochove et al. (eds.) Modeling for Government and Business, Essays in Honor of Prof.dr. P.J. Verdoorn, Leiden, Martinus Nijhoff.

Van Bochove, C.A. (1981) 'Stability of International Trade Equilibrium with Import Adjustment', De Economist, 129, 262-265.

Van der Zwan, A. et al. (1980) 'Plaats en Toekomst van de Nederlandse Industrie', Rapporten aan de Regering, Wetenschappelijke Raad voor het Regeringsbeleid, 18, Den Haag, Staatsuitgeverij.

Vanek, J. (1971) 'Economic Growth and International Trade in Pure Theory', Quarterly Journal of Economics, 85, 377-390.

Verdoorn, P.J. (1952) 'Welke zijn de Achtergronden en Vooruitzichten van de Economische Integratie in Europa en welke Gevolgen zou deze Integratie hebben, met name voor de Welvaart in Nederland?', Praeadviezen, Vereniging voor de Staathuishoudkunde, 47-135.

Verdoorn, P.J. (1956) ' Complementarity and Long-Range Projections', Econometrica, 24, 429-450.

Verdoorn, P.J. (1959) 'The Role of Capital in Long Term Projection Models', Cahiers Economiques de Bruxelles, 5, 49-69.

Verdoorn, P.J. (1960) 'The Intra-Bloc Trade of BENELUX', in E.A.G. Robinson (ed.) Economic Consequences of the Size of Nations, London, Macmillan.

Verdoorn, P.J. and F.J.M. Meyer zu Schlochtern (1964) 'Trade Creation and Trade Diversion in the Common Market', in Collège d'Europe, Intégration Européenne et Realité Economique, Brugge, De Tempel.

Verdoorn, P.J. and A.N.R. Schwartz (1972) 'Two Alternative Estimates of the Effects of EEC and EFTA on the Pattern of Trade', European Economic Review, 3, 291-335.

Verdoorn, P.J. and C.A. Van Bochove (1972) 'Measuring Integration Effects: a Survey', European Economic Review, 3, 337-349.

Verdoorn, P.J. (1973) 'Some Long Run Dynamic Elements of Factor Price Inflation', in H.C. Bos et al. (eds.) Economic Structure and Development, Essays in Honour of Jan Tinbergen, North Holland, Amsterdam.

Viner, T. (1924) Canada's Balance of International Indebtedness, 1900-1913, Cambridge, Harvard University Press.

Voivodas, C. (1973) 'Exports, Foreign Capital Inflow and Economic Growth', Journal of International Economics, 3, 337-349.

Von Neumann, J. (1938) 'Ueber ein Oekonomisches Gleichungssystem und eine Verallgemeinerung des Brouwerschen Fixpunktsatzes', (Paper read at 1932 Princeton University Mathematical Seminar), in K. Menger (ed.) Ergebnisse eines Mathematischen Seminars, Vienna. English translation: 'A Model of General Economic Equilibrium', Review of Economic Studies, 13 (1945-6).

Waelbroeck, J. (1976) (ed.) The Models of Project Link, North Holland, Amsterdam.

Wan, H.Y. jr. and M. Majundar (1980) 'Trade under Temporary Equilibrium, Evolution in a Loglinear World', Journal of International Economics, 10, 37-62.

Wasow, B. (1978) 'Dependent Growth in a Capital Importing Economy: the Case of Puerto Rico', Oxford Economic Papers, N.S., 30, 117-129.

Wasow, B. (1979) 'Saving and Dependence with Externally Financed Growth', Review of Economics and Statistics, 61, 150-156.

Woodland, A.D. (1977) 'Joint Outputs, Intermediate Inputs and International Trade Theory', International Economic Review, 18, 517-533.

Yates, P.L. (1959) Forty Years of Foreign Trade, a Statistical Handbook with Special Reference to Primary Products and Under-Development Countries, London, Allen and Unwin.

Zarembka, P. (1972) 'A Long Run Economic Growth Model for Developing Countries', in L.E. Di Marco (ed.) International Economics and Development, Essays in Honor of Raúl Prebisch, New York, Academic Press.

LIST OF MAIN SYMBOLS

As a rule, greek characters refer to constants, latin ones to variables; lower-case latin characters usually indicate original variables, upper-case transformations and functions of the latter.

Occasionally a symbol is used with different meanings in two chapters; in that case the list indicates to which chapter the meaning given applies.

Dots refer to time derivates; bars to foreign-country variables and parameters or to the south; hats indicate relative total differentials.

Lower-case latin characters

b	non-price growth rate of the south's demand for the north's exports; $b = -\bar{e}\bar{\nu} - \{\bar{e}(\bar{\rho}-1) - 1\}\{\bar{q}_{\bar{\ell}}\bar{\lambda} + (1 - \bar{q}_{\bar{\ell}})\bar{g}\}$; Chapter 6
c	volume of consumption
e	terms of trade elasticity of import demand; $e = v_m/mv_{mm}$
g	rate of growth of capital off the steady-growth path; $g = \dot{k}/k$
k	volume of physical capital
ℓ	volume of labour
m	volume of imports
$\bar{m}$	volume of exports; in two-region models the south's imports
n	transfer from north to south, in units of the north's output
p	price of output and exports
$\bar{p}$	price of imports; in two-region models the south's price of output and exports
p_k	auxiliary variable; Section 7.3
$\bar{p}_{\bar{k}}$	auxiliary variable; Section 7.3
q_ℓ	labour's value share in domestic factors; $q_\ell = \ell z_\ell/z$
q'_ℓ	labour's value share in total factor inputs; $q'_\ell = \ell v_\ell/v$
q_m	imports' value share in total factor input; $q_m = mv_m/v$
s	volume of savings
t	time
t_0	initial time
v	volume of output
v_x	v's (partial) derivative to x

v_{xr} v_x's (partial) derivative to r

y volume of national income

z linear homogeneous function of domestic factors capital and labour; $z(1,1) = 1$

z_x z's (partial) derivative to x

z_{xr} z_x's (partial) derivative to r

Upper-case latin characters

A Chapter 7: ratio of total exports to exports without transfer; $A = \bar{m}/(\bar{m} - n)$

Other chapters: function of the capital-labour ratio; $A(K) = z(1, k/\ell)$

A_K A's derivative to K

A_{KK} A_K's derivative to K

B $1 + E + \bar{\varepsilon}$

C $\lambda(\rho-1) + \nu + (\rho q - \rho + 1)(\lambda - g)$

D $\beta - \lambda - (1+\bar{\varepsilon})\{\lambda(\rho-1) + \nu\} + \gamma(1-q_\ell)(\lambda-g)$

E direct Hicks elasticity of substitution imports-domestic factors;

$$E = \frac{d \ln z}{d \ln v_z/v_m} \text{ (v constant)}$$

H Section 7.3: Hamiltonian, cf. (7.45)

Elsewhere: direct Hicks elasticity of substitution capital-labour;

$$H = \frac{d \ln K}{d \ln v_k/v_\ell} \text{ (m, v constant)}$$

K capital-labour ratio; $K = k/\ell$

L $\rho q_\ell - \rho + 1 + (1-q_\ell)\gamma M$

M $$\frac{q_m\{e(\rho-1) - 1\}}{(1-q_m)(1+e+\bar{\varepsilon})} = \frac{q_m\{E(\rho-1) - 1\}}{(1-q_m)B+q_m E\gamma}$$

N $M\beta + \{1 - (1+\bar{\varepsilon})M\}\nu + (\rho - \gamma M)q_\ell\lambda$; Chapter 4

P terms of trade; in two-region models the north's terms of trade; $P = p/\bar{p}$

S Chapter 2: per capita saving; $S = s/\ell$

Chapter 7: rate of saving of the north; $S = s/(v - \bar{m})$

T final point of planning horizon; Chapter 7.

V function of Z; $V = v(1, z/m)$

V_Z V's derivative to Z
V_{ZZ} V_Z's derivative to Z
Z ratio of domestic factors to imports; Z = z/m

Greek characters

α maximum of the ratio of total exports to exports without transfer; $\alpha = (1 + \varepsilon - \alpha_0)/(1+\varepsilon)$; Section 7.3
α_0 maximum of aid to income ratio
β rate of growth of foreign demand at constant terms of trade
γ $\bar{\varepsilon}(\rho-1) + \rho$; chapters 4, 5, 6
Δ small positive constant
E_i lim $E(Z \to i)$ $(i = 0, \infty)$
$\bar{\varepsilon}$ terms of trade elasticity of foreign demand, in two-region models the south's terms of trade elasticity of import demand (when constant a priori)
ε_i lim $e(z \to i)$ $(i = 0, \infty)$
H_i lim $H(K \to i)$ $(i = 0, \infty)$
θ_i $\rho\xi_{\ell\infty} - \rho + 1 + (1 - \xi_{\ell\infty})\gamma\mu_i$ $(i = 0, \infty)$
θ_{au} $\rho\xi_{\ell\infty} - \rho + 1$
λ natural rate (rate of growth of labour)
μ_i lim $M(z \to i)$ $(i = 0, \infty)$
ν rate of Hicks-neutral technical progress
ξ_ℓ labour's value share in domestic factors (when constant a priori)
$\xi_{\ell i}$ lim $q_\ell(K \to i)$ $(i = 0, \infty)$
ξ_m imports value share in total factor input (when constant a priori)
ξ_{mi} lim $q_m(Z \to i)$ $(i = 0, \infty)$
ρ rate of returns to scale
σ rate of saving (when constant)
σ_1 the north's minimum rate of saving
σ_2 the north's maximum rate of saving
τ ad valorem import duty
$\bar{\tau}$ foreign ad valorem import duty
τ_{opt} optimum import duty without retaliation
τ'_{opt} optimum import duty with retaliation
ϕ $\{1 - \rho(1-\xi_m)(1-\xi_\ell)\}\{1 - \bar{\rho}(1-\bar{\xi}_{\underline{m}})(1-\bar{\xi}_{\underline{\ell}})\} - \rho\bar{\rho}\xi_m\bar{\xi}_{\underline{m}}$; Chapter 6

χ rate of growth of capital, income and exports on the steady-growth path; $\chi = \lim g \ (t \to \infty)$

χ_{au} 'autarkic' growth rate of capital and income on the steady-growth path

ω $1 + 2\varepsilon$

AUTHOR INDEX

SUBJECT INDEX

Printed in the United States
54510LVS00001B/235

9 789024 730520